# THE CAMBRIDGE EDITION OF THE WORKS OF
# F. SCOTT FITZGERALD

# The High Cost of Macaroni

by

F. Scott Fitzgerald

Like most other Americans we are in Europe. We came over here a year and a half ago to try and save money. We are going to try it for another year and a half and then if we haven't succeeded any better we're coming home and get something to eat.

If you like such travel articles as "A Merry Two Years' Ramble in Europe" you have opened at the wrong page. Turn on. This is an unpleasant story with all sorts of sinister characters in it whose business is to take money away from noble and good-hearted Americans. Whenever we hear of another couple who have come over here to lay something by we bend our heads and weep into whatever is at hand - usually macaroni.

When we first came over we went down to Southern France where we worried along for six months trying to support a large and constantly increasing French family who jokingly referred to themselves as our "servants." By the end of that time we had salted down in the bank and in various stocks and bonds and development schemes a little over one hundred dollars. This was the all too

Page 1 of the surviving typescript of "The High Cost of Macaroni."
The cancelled title is "What Price Macaroni?"
Princeton University Libraries.

# LAST KISS

*  *  *

## F. SCOTT FITZGERALD

Edited by
JAMES L. W. WEST III

CAMBRIDGE
UNIVERSITY PRESS

# CAMBRIDGE
## UNIVERSITY PRESS

University Printing House, Cambridge CB2 8BS, United Kingdom

One Liberty Plaza, 20th Floor, New York, NY 10006, USA

477 Williamstown Road, Port Melbourne, VIC 3207, Australia

4843/24, 2nd Floor, Ansari Road, Daryaganj, Delhi - 110002, India

79 Anson Road, #06-04/06, Singapore 079906

Cambridge University Press is part of the University of Cambridge.

It furthers the University's mission by disseminating knowledge in the pursuit of education, learning and research at the highest international levels of excellence.

www.cambridge.org
Information on this title: www.cambridge.org/9780521766135

© 2017 Eleanor Lanahan, Eleanor Blake Hazard, and Charles Byrne, Trustees under agreement dated 3 July 1975, created by Frances Scott Fitzgerald Smith.

Thoughtbook © 2013 University of Minnesota Press

Introduction and notes © 2017 James L. W. West III

This edition © 2017 Cambridge University Press

This publication is in copyright. Subject to statutory exception and to the provisions of relevant collective licensing agreements, no reproduction of any part may take place without the written permission of Cambridge University Press.

First published 2017

Printed and bound in the United Kingdom by TJ International Ltd. Padstow Cornwall

*A catalogue record for this publication is available from the British Library*

ISBN 978-0-521-76613-5 Hardback

Cambridge University Press has no responsibility for the persistence or accuracy of URLs for external or third-party internet websites referred to in this publication, and does not guarantee that any content on such websites is, or will remain, accurate or appropriate.

# CONTENTS

| | |
|---|---|
| Acknowledgments | *page* xi |
| Illustrations | xiii |
| Abbreviations | xiv |
| Introduction | xv |

| | |
|---|---|
| THOUGHTBOOK OF FRANCIS SCOTT KEY FITZGERALD | 1 |
| Text, annotations, and commentary by Dave Page | 3 |
| THE VEGETABLE | 35 |
| POEMS | 125 |
| A Dirge (Apologies to Wordsworth) | 127 |
| Sleep of a University | 128 |
| Lamp in a Window | 129 |
| Obit on Parnassus | 130 |
| To a Beloved Infidel | 132 |
| BOOK REVIEWS | 135 |
| The Baltimore Anti-Christ | 137 |
| Three Soldiers | 140 |

vi · Contents

| Poor Old Marriage | 143 |
| Aldous Huxley's "Crome Yellow" | 145 |
| Tarkington's "Gentle Julia" | 148 |
| "Margey Wins the Game" | 150 |
| Homage to the Victorians | 152 |
| A Rugged Novel | 154 |
| The Defeat of Art | 156 |
| Sherwood Anderson on the Marriage Question | 159 |
| Minnesota's Capital in the Rôle of Main Street | 162 |
| Under Fire | 165 |

## SHORT FICTION 167

| On Your Own | 169 |
| Lo, the Poor Peacock! | 187 |
| The End of Hate | 207 |
| A Full Life | 221 |
| Discard | 227 |
| Last Kiss | 242 |
| News of Paris—Fifteen Years Ago | 261 |

Contents

## PUBLIC LETTERS  267

The Claims of the *LIT*.  269

The Credo of F. Scott Fitzgerald  271

Confessions  273

Letter to A. Philip Randolph  275

In Literary New York  276

Who's Who in This Issue  278

Letter to Class Secretary  279

F. Scott Fitzgerald Is Bored by Efforts at Realism in 'Lit'  280

Unfortunate "Tradition"  282

Fitzgerald Sets Things Right about His College  283

False and Extremely Unwise Tradition  284

Letter to H. N. Swanson  285

Confused Romanticism  286

An Open Letter to Fritz Crisler  288

Anonymous '17  290

Letter to Harvey H. Smith (1938)  291

Letter to Harvey H. Smith (1939)  292

## JOURNALISM — 293

| | |
|---|---|
| The Cruise of the Rolling Junk | 295 |
| The High Cost of Macaroni | 343 |
| "Why Blame It on the Poor Kiss…" | 356 |
| Does a Moment of Revolt… | 362 |
| What Kind of Husbands Do "Jimmies" Make? | 364 |
| Our Young Rich Boys | 371 |

## MISCELLANEOUS — 377

| | |
|---|---|
| The Author's Apology | 379 |
| Contributions to *The American Credo* | 380 |
| An Interview with Mr. Fitzgerald | 382 |
| On the Girl Scouts | 385 |
| This Is a Magazine | 386 |
| Three Cities | 391 |
| Reminiscenses of Donald Stewart | 394 |
| What I Was Advised to Do—and Didn't | 397 |
| How I Would Sell My Book If I Were a Bookseller | 398 |
| Some Stories They Like to Tell Again | 400 |

## Contents

| | |
|---|---|
| 10 Best Books I Have Read | 401 |
| Censorship or Not | 402 |
| The Most Disgraceful Thing I Ever Did | 403 |
| The Most Pampered Men in the World | 405 |
| My Old New England Homestead on the Erie | 410 |
| From *Three Years* (Testimonial) | 413 |
| Ten Years in the Advertising Business | 414 |
| Salesmanship in the Champs-Élysées | 416 |
| The Death of My Father | 418 |
| On "Family in the Wind" | 421 |
| Fitzgerald's List of Neglected Books | 422 |
| The True Story of Appomattox | 423 |
| 'My Ten Favorite Plays' No. 152.— | 425 |
| The Broadcast We Almost Heard Last September | 426 |
| From *These Stories Went to Market* | 428 |
| Huckleberry Finn | 429 |
| A Book of One's Own | 430 |
| Foreword to *Colonial and Historic Homes of Maryland* | 432 |

## Contents

| | |
|---|---|
| Record of Variants | 435 |
| Explanatory Notes | 439 |
| Illustrations | 461 |

# ACKNOWLEDGMENTS

I am grateful to Eleanor Lanahan, Eleanor Blake Hazard, and Chris Byrne, the Trustees of the F. Scott Fitzgerald Estate, for their support and cooperation, and to Phyllis Westberg and Craig Tenney of Harold Ober Associates, Inc., for their assistance with permissions and copyrights.

The evidence employed to establish many of the texts in this volume is housed in the F. Scott Fitzgerald Papers, Manuscript Division, Department of Rare Books and Special Collections, Princeton University. I thank Don Skemer, Curator of Manuscripts at Princeton, for many courtesies during my visits there. Permission to publish facsimiles and other reproductions has been granted by Princeton University Libraries and Harold Ober Associates, Inc., on behalf of the Fitzgerald Trust.

For permission to include the *Thoughtbook* in this volume, I thank the University of Minnesota Press, publishers of a 2013 edition of the document, edited by Dave Page. The original *Thoughtbook* is part of the Matthew J. and Arlyn Bruccoli Collection of F. Scott Fitzgerald, Irvin Department of Rare Books and Special Collections, University of South Carolina. I am indebted to the director, Elizabeth Sudduth, and to her staff for access.

At Penn State I acknowledge the long-term support of the College of the Liberal Arts and the Department of English. Susan Welch, my dean; Mark Morrisson, my department head; and Bob Burkholder, my acting head during the preparation of this volume—all provided valuable support. Stephen Wheeler of the Department of Classics and Ancient Mediterranean Studies gave assistance with Latin; Willa Z. Silverman, Department of French and Francophone Studies, has again helped with the French language.

Assistance with transcriptions, annotations, and proofreading was supplied by my Penn State editorial and research assistants, Chris Weinmann, LaVerne Maginnis, Jeanne Alexander, Bethany Mannon, Ethan Mannon, and Robert Birdwell.

J. L. W. W. III

# ILLUSTRATIONS
*(Beginning on p. 461)*

*Frontispiece.* Page 1, typescript of "The High Cost of Macaroni."

1. Page 12, typescript of "The High Cost of Macaroni."
2. "The End of the World," addenda to *The Vegetable*.
3. Title page, Fitzgerald's copy of *The American Credo*.
4. *College Humor* text of "My Old New England Homestead."

# ABBREVIATIONS

| | |
|---|---|
| *Crack-Up* | F. Scott Fitzgerald, *The Crack-Up*, ed. Edmund Wilson. New York: New Directions, 1945. |
| *Price* | *The Price Was High: The Last Uncollected Stories of F. Scott Fitzgerald*, ed. Matthew J. Bruccoli. New York: Harcourt Brace Jovanovich, 1979. |
| *Fortune* | Bryant Mangum, *A Fortune Yet: Money in the Art of F. Scott Fitzgerald's Short Stories*. New York: Garland, 1991. |
| *Stories* | *The Short Stories of F. Scott Fitzgerald: A New Collection*, ed. Matthew J. Bruccoli. New York: Scribners, 1989. |
| *Scott/Max* | *Dear Scott/Dear Max: The Fitzgerald-Perkins Correspondence*, ed. John Kuehl and Jackson R. Bryer. New York: Scribners, 1971. |
| *As Ever* | *As Ever, Scott Fitz— Letters between F. Scott Fitzgerald and His Literary Agent Harold Ober, 1919–1940*, ed. Matthew J. Bruccoli and Jennifer McCabe Atkinson. Philadelphia and New York: Lippincott, 1972. |
| *Poems* | F. Scott Fitzgerald, *Poems, 1911–1940*, ed. Matthew J. Bruccoli. Bloomfield Hills, Michigan: Bruccoli Clark, 1981. |
| *Own Time* | *F. Scott Fitzgerald in His Own Time: A Miscellany*, ed. Matthew J. Bruccoli and Jackson R. Bryer. Kent, Ohio: Kent State University Press, 1971. |
| *Egoists* | *The Romantic Egoists*, ed. Matthew J. Bruccoli, Scottie Fitzgerald Smith, and Joan P. Kerr. New York: Scribners, 1974. |
| *Ledger* | *F. Scott Fitzgerald's Ledger: A Facsimile*, ed. Matthew J. Bruccoli. Washington, DC: NCR/Microcard, 1972. |

# INTRODUCTION

*Last Kiss* is a miscellany, a gallimaufry, a florilegium. It brings together items that have not found a place in any of the earlier volumes in the Cambridge Fitzgerald Edition. This volume presents writings in a range of genres: Fitzgerald's *Thoughtbook*, an adolescent diary of sorts; *The Vegetable*, his only published play; the five poems that he published after he became a full-time author; twelve book reviews, all published between 1921 and 1923; seven short stories from the last decade of his career; seventeen public letters, ten of which appeared in Princeton University publications; six items of journalism, in four of which Fitzgerald attempts to explain the "flapper" phenomenon; and twenty-eight miscellaneous pieces, including a self-interview, several short autobiographical exercises, an essay on the movie business, and an unfinished reminiscence about his father.

The most important writings in *Last Kiss* are the *Thoughtbook* and *The Vegetable*. The *Thoughtbook*, set down by Fitzgerald at the ages of thirteen and fourteen, is a private document in which he recorded the romantic crushes and competitions for popularity among a group of boys and girls from his dancing classes. The *Thoughtbook* is a remarkable piece of writing; it reveals young Scott Fitzgerald's urge, already strong in his adolescent years, to observe and put down on paper the inner workings of a social group—the impermanent affections and shifts in status that would interest him as an adult, and would appear repeatedly in his fiction.

*The Vegetable* is an anomaly in Fitzgerald's career. It is his only published play—indeed, his only effort to write professionally for the stage—and his greatest failure. Fitzgerald should have been able to produce a Broadway hit. Much of his apprentice work was in the dramatic line: four plays written as a teenager for a local theatrical group in his home town of St. Paul, three musical comedies at Princeton for which he supplied book and/or lyrics, and a handful of one-act playlets that he published early in his career as a magazinist. Fitzgerald knew that a successful play could be profitable. ("I am concieving a play which is to make my fortune," he wrote to Harold Ober, his literary agent, late in 1921.[1]) The box office returns from a long run on Broadway followed by the receipts from a road production could provide steady income, money that would free him from the toils of magazine work and make it possible for him to write his novels.

Fitzgerald produced a preliminary script of his play, first entitled "Gabriel's Trombone," in the early months of 1922. He revised the text in the summer of that year and revised it further in the fall. Early in 1923 he decided to publish the play, now called *The Vegetable*, in book form, hoping to interest a producer in taking it on. In a January 1923 letter to Maxwell Perkins, his editor at Charles Scribner's Sons, Fitzgerald called this published version "a book of humor" that was "written to be read."[2] The Broadway producer Sam H. Harris signed a contract with Fitzgerald to mount a stage production. Harris gave Fitzgerald a $500 advance and agreed to pay him 5 percent of the first $5000, 7.5 percent of the next $2500, and 10 percent thereafter—all payments to be calculated on gross receipts. Fitzgerald retained the book, serial, magazine, newspaper, and musical rights. If the play ran for fifty performances, Harris and Fitzgerald would divide stock, amateur, and repertoire receipts fifty–fifty.[3]

None of this came to pass. Fitzgerald labored further on the play in the summer and fall of 1923 and participated in the rehearsals for a one-week tryout in Atlantic City. The play opened on 19 November at Nixon's Apollo Theatre. In Zelda Fitzgerald's words,

---

[1] *As Ever*, p. 32.
[2] *Scott/Max*, p. 66.
[3] James L. W. West III, *American Authors and the Literary Marketplace since 1900* (Philadelphia: University of Pennsylvania Press, 1988): 135–36. The original contract between Harris and Fitzgerald for *The Vegetable* is preserved in the files of the American Play Company, Berg Collection, New York Public Library.

it "flopped as flat as one of Aunt Jemimas famous pancakes."[4] Fitzgerald attempted repairs, but the play never reached Broadway.

The text of *The Vegetable* in *Last Kiss* is that of the published version, issued by Scribners in a single printing of 7,650 copies on 27 April 1923. This is the text that was "written to be read." In 1976 Charles Scribner III produced an expanded edition of the play, also published by Scribners, comprising an offset reproduction of the 1923 text, an introduction, and unpublished scenes and corrections taken from Fitzgerald's marked copy of *The Vegetable* and from other addenda among his papers at Princeton. These materials anticipated a possible second production of the play, a production that never materialized.[5]

Two other genres that Fitzgerald abandoned—poetry and book reviews—are represented in *Last Kiss*.[6] In the early part of his career he thought of himself as a man of letters who might excel in several kinds of writing, but as the years passed he learned to concentrate his efforts on fiction and autobiography. His book reviews are lively and combative, but book reviews (for which he was usually paid a pittance) absorbed time better spent on short stories and novels. The book reviews reprinted in *Last Kiss* provide a glimpse of Fitzgerald as literary critic. They record his reactions to the writings of several important authors of his time, including H. L. Mencken, John Dos Passos, Aldous Huxley, Booth Tarkington, Shane Leslie, Sherwood Anderson, and Thomas Boyd.

The following stories have been omitted from the Cambridge Edition: "Shaggy's Morning," *Esquire* 3 (May 1935); "The Passionate

---

[4] Zelda Fitzerald to Xandra Kalman, n.d., Zelda Fitzgerald Papers, Princeton University Library.

[5] Additional material from *The Vegetable*, including scenes cut from Act 2 before book publication, has been reproduced in facsimile in *F. Scott Fitzgerald Manuscripts*, vol. VI, part 1, ed. Matthew J. Bruccoli (New York and London: Garland Publishing, Inc., 1991): 3–57.

[6] Fitzgerald's undergraduate poems and book reviews are included in a previous volume of the Cambridge Edition, *Spires and Gargoyles*, published in 2010. For a full gathering of his poetry, see *F. Scott Fitzgerald: Poems, 1911–1940*, ed. Matthew J. Bruccoli (Bloomfield Hills, Michigan, and Columbia, South Carolina: Bruccoli Clark, Inc., 1981).

Eskimo," *Liberty* 12 (8 June 1935); "'Send Me in, Coach,'" *Esquire* 6 (November 1936); "The Honor of the Goon," *Esquire* 7 (June 1937); "Strange Sanctuary," *Liberty* 16 (9 December 1939); and the four Count of Darkness stories: "In the Darkest Hour," *Redbook* 63 (October 1934); "The Count of Darkness," *Redbook* 65 (June 1935); "The Kingdom in the Dark," *Redbook* 65 (August 1935); and "Gods of Darkness," *Redbook* 78 (November 1941). Scottie Fitzgerald, the author's daughter, judged these stories to be so far below the level of writing that her father was capable of that they should not be reprinted. These stories are available online or through interlibrary loan. Also omitted are the four plays that Fitzgerald wrote for the Elizabethan Dramatic Club, a teenage theatrical group in St. Paul. A scholarly edition of these plays is available: Alan Margolies, ed., *F. Scott Fitzgerald's St. Paul Plays, 1911–1914* (Princeton: Princeton University Library, 1978). The four blurbs produced by Fitzgerald during his career have been reprinted in Matthew J. Bruccoli and Jackson Bryer, eds., *F. Scott Fitzgerald in His Own Time: A Miscellany* (Kent, Ohio: Kent State University Press, 1971). The collaborations with Zelda Fitzgerald are available in Matthew J. Bruccoli, ed., *Zelda Fitzgerald: The Collected Writings* (New York: Scribners, 1991). *The St. Paul Daily Dirge*, a spoof newspaper produced by Fitzgerald and distributed to friends on Friday, 13 January 1922, has been facsimiled in *F. Scott Fitzgerald in His Own Time* (p. 233), and in Matthew J. Bruccoli, *F. Scott Fitzgerald: A Descriptive Bibliography*, rev. ed. (Pittsburgh: University of Pittsburgh Press, 1987), p. 36. Fitzgerald's screenwriting survives in manuscripts and typescripts housed at the Ernest F. Hollings Special Collections Library, University of South Carolina. His final unpublished stories have recently been published in Anne Margaret Daniel, ed., *I'd Die for You* (New York: Scribners, 2017).

The several editorial strategies employed in this volume have been selected to suit the materials presented. The *Thoughtbook* is rendered in a line-by-line type facsimile, in diplomatic text, without substantive emendation and with all misspellings and other irregularities preserved. This approach captures, as nearly as possible, the flavor of the original handwritten pages.[7] *The Vegetable* has been edited in documentary style with only two substantive emendations, both recorded in the apparatus. The spelling and punctuation of the published text has not been altered. Obvious typographical errors have been silently corrected in the poems, book reviews, public letters, journalism, and miscellaneous writings. No attempt has been made to restyle the punctuation, orthography, or word division of these items. Two passages have been restored to "The High Cost of Macaroni"; both are identified in the Record of Variants.

The seven short stories in *Last Kiss* have been edited according to the principles and practices employed in previous volumes of this series. All extant prepublication versions of the texts have been examined; these versions have been compared (or collated when appropriate) with the first-published texts. Surviving typescripts are described in the apparatus for each story. No evidence of bowdlerization has emerged. Emendations are listed in the apparatus.

Within each section, items are arranged chronologically by date of first publication or, in the case of the short stories, by date of composition. Citations to first appearances in print, together with explanatory information about the composition of certain items, will be found in headnotes or in other annotations. The history of subsequent publication is recorded in the revised edition of *F. Scott Fitzgerald: A Descriptive Bibliography*.

---

[7] The *Thoughtbook* was originally published as a facsimile, with commentary by John Kuehl, in the *Princeton University Library Chronicle* 26 (Winter 1965): 102–08 and unpaginated plates. A separately bound edition of this facsimile was issued by Princeton University Library in April 1965. A new edition of the *Thoughtbook*, with the text typeset, and with an introduction and afterword by Dave Page, was published by the University of Minnesota Press in 2013.

# THOUGHTBOOK
OF
FRANCIS SCOTT KEY FITZGERALD
OF
ST PAUL MINN. U.S.A.

# VIII

My girls                    August, 1910

My recollections of Nancy are rather dim but one day stands out above the rest. The Gardeners had their home three miles out of town and one day James Inham[1], Inky for short, my best friend, and I were invited out to spend the day. I was about nine years old Nancy about eight and we were quite infatuated with each other. It was in the middle of the winter so as soon as we got there we began playing on the toboggan. Nancy and I and Inky were on one toboggan and Ham (Nancies big brother came along and wanted to get on. He made a leap for the toboggan but I pushed off just in time and sent him on his head. He was awful mad. He said he'd kick me off and that it wasn't my toboggan and that I couldn't play. However Nancy smoothed it over and we went into lunch.

---

[1] Fitzgerald, writing in the third person, notes in his *Ledger* entry for September 1906: "He made up shows in Ingham's attic, all based on the American Revolution." Many of the entries for 1908–1911 in the *Ledger* mention events that are recorded in the *Thoughtbook*. It is likely that Fitzgerald had the *Thoughtbook* at his elbow as he inscribed the *Ledger*. Some of the girls' names in the *Thoughtbook* appear on a dance card reproduced in *Romantic Egoists*, p. 11.

## IX

Kitty Williams is much plainer to my
memory. I met her first at dancing
school and as Mr. Van Arnumn[2] (our
dancing teacher) chose me to lead the
march I asked her to be my pardner. The
next day she told Marie Lautz and Marie
repeated it to Dorothy Knox who in turn
passed it on to Earl, that I was third
in her affections. I dont remember who
was first but I know that Earl was
second and as I was already quite
over come by her charms I then and there
resolved that I would gain first place
As in the case of Nancy there was one day which was
preeminent in my memory. I went in Honey Chilenton's
yard one morning where the kids usually congregated and beheld
Kitty. We talked and talked and finally she asked
me if I was going to Robin's[3] party and it was
there that my eventful day was. We played
postoffice, pillow, clappin and clapp
out and other foolish but interesting

---

[2] Charles H. Van Arnam appears in Lee F. Heacock, ed., *The Buffalo Artists' Register*, Vol. *1—1926* (copy at Buffalo Public Library). His studio was located at the Hotel Statler in Buffalo; he gave "carnivals" at the Twentieth Century Club with his pupils.

[3] Robin's identity remains a mystery, although in his *Ledger* Fitzgerald wrote that Robin was a cousin of the Penfields (p. 162). Katherine Penfield, born in October 1895, and her siblings lived at 87 Highland, a short distance from the Fitzgeralds. Katherine's father was a magnesia manufacturer; the family had two live-in servants. New York State Archives; Albany, New York; *State Population Census Schedules*, *1905*; Election District: E.D. *03*; City: *Buffalo Ward* 24; County: *Erie*; Page: 96.

## X

games.[4] It was impossible to count the
number of times I kissed Kitty that
afternoon. At any rate when we
went home I had secured the coveted 1st
place. I held this until dancing school
stopped in the spring and then relinquished
it to Johnny Gowns[5] a rival. On valentines day that
year Kitty recieved no less than eighty four valentines.
She sent me one which I have now as also one
which Nancy gave me. Along in a box with them
is a lock of hair—but wait I'll come to that. That
Christmas I bought a five pound box of candy and
took it around to her house. What was my surprise
when Kitty opend the door. I nearly fell down with
embarresment but I finally stammered "Give this
to Kitty," and ran home.

---

[4] In the children's game "Clap In and Clap Out," a player who has been sent from the room returns and attempts to guess which other player has chosen him or her for a partner. If the guess is wrong, the other players clap their hands loudly.

[5] Johnny Gowans was a local amateur athletic star.

## XI

### Indians and Violet  Sept 1910

Violet Stockton was a neice of Mrs. Finch
and she spent a summer in Saint Paul.
She was very pretty with dark brown hair and
eyes big and soft. She spoke with a soft southern
accent leaving out the r's. She was a year older
than I but together with most of the other boys
liked her very much. I met her through Jack
Mitchell who lived next door to her. He himself
was very attached as was Art. Foley and together
they sneaked up behind her and cut off her hair
that is a snip of it. We had a game we played
called Indians which I made up. One side were
the Indians and went off and hid somewhere.
The cowboys then started off to find them
and when the indians saw their chance
they would jump out and take them by surpris
We were all armed with croquet mallets.
There were about fifteen of us. Kitty Shultz, Betty
Mudge, Betty Foster, Elenor Mitchell, Marie
Hersey, Dorothy Green, Violet Stockton and Harrit
Foster. The boys were Adolph Sholly, Wharton

## XII

Smith, Jack Mitchell, Arthur Foley, Archie
Mudge and Roger Foster. Every day for a month
we played this and then we turned
into truth. At that time I was more popular
with girls than I ever have been befor. In truth
Kitty Shultz, Dorothy, Violet, Marie and Catherine
Tie[6] all liked me best. At the present moment
it is the reverse with probably most
of these; with at least two, Kitty Shultz
and Katherine tie. However I am wandering
from the subject. Finally Violet had a
party which was very nice and it was the day after this
that we had the quarrel. She had some
sort of a book called flirting by sighns
and Jack and I got it away from
Violet and showed it too all the boys.
Violet got very mad and went into
the house. I got very mad and therefor I
went home. Imediatly Violet repented
and called me up on the phone to see
if I was mad. However I did not

---

[6] Probably Katherine Tighe, who would later offer Fitzgerald editorial advice for *This Side of Paradise*.

## XIII

want to make up just then
and so I slammed down the receiver.
The next morning I went down to
Jacks to find that Violet had said
she was not coming out that
day. It was now my turn
to repent and I did so and
she came out that evening befor how
ever I had heard several
things and, as I found
afterwards so had Violet and
I wanted to have justified. Violet
and I sat down on the hill back
of Shultze's a little away from
the others.
      "Violet," I began, "Did you call me a brat."
      "No".
      "Did you say that you wanted your ring and your picture and your hair back."[7]

---

[7] Rings, photographs, and locks of hair were among the items traded by the romantically inclined. A small photograph, presumably of Violet, was at some point glued to this page within a pencilled frame. Only the glue marks now remain.

## XIV

"No"
"Did you say that you hated me"
"Of course not, is that what you went home for",
"No, but Archie Mudge told me those things yesterday evening."
"He's a little scamp" said Violet Indignantly.
At this juncture Elenor Michell almost went into histerics because Jack was teasing her, and Violet had to go home with her. That afternoon I spanked Archie Mudge and finished making up with Violet.

<u>Extract from my diary the next day</u>
Wednesday. Aug. 20
Didnt do much today but learned a few valuble things to wit
1) that I was a fool to make up with Violet,—From Harriet Foster
2) that Violet wished she had my teeth from Elenor Mitchell

## XV

   3) that Violet had said that she wanted her
      ring as soon as she could get it—From
      Betty Mudge
      Thursday Aug. 21
      I learned two things from Betty Mudge
   1) that Violet thought I was a flirt
   2) that Violet did not like me half
      as well as she used to

      Friday Aug. 22
      I learned in truth[8]
1st) that Betty Mudges fellows were
      Bob Harrington, Tom Daniels
      and Bob Driscoll
2nd) that I had a new rival in Wharton
      Smith
3d) that Dorothy's fellows were me
      and Aurther Foley
4th) I also learned that as Harriet Foster
      said Violet said some things
      that wern't honest

---

[8] That is, the children's game of Truth—in which prevarication is not allowed.

## XVI

Mon. Aug 25th

I heard that Violet got mad at me
because I got mad so easily from Wharton.
That Kitty Shultzes bows [beaus] were me
and T. Daniels, from her
Dorothy Green said that when I was
dippy she liked Wharton Smith better
but that usually she liked me
better.
Harriet Foster said some sarcastic
things as usual

Saturday Aug. 30
    <u>I just hate Violet</u>
Jack Mitchell said that Violets opinion
of my character was that I was
polite and had a nice disposition and
that I thought I was the whole
push[9] and that I got mad too
easily.

---

[9] "The whole push" is slang for "the entire crowd."

## XVII

Sept 29th

Not much has happened since Violet went away. The day she went away was my birthday and she gave me a box of candy. Her latest fancy is Arther Foley. He has her ring She wrote him a letter to ask him for his picture.

\*\*\*\*\*\*\*\*\*\*\*\*\*\*\*\*\*\*\*\*\*\*\*\*\*\*

And that is the story of Violet Stockton.

## XX

November 1910

One day Marie Hersey wrote me a note
which began either "Dear Scott I
love you very much, or I like you very
much," and ever since then she has
been rather shy when she meets me.
Dorothy Green and Caroline Clark are tomboys
Bob Clark is interesting to talk to because
he lets me do a lot of talking (which
I like) and not like some people I
know of never letting you get in a
word edgewise.
I had a midnight conversation one night
with Jim and Cecil and afterwards
found that Susana Rice[10] had heard
evry word of it from her front window.
Alida Bigelow is the most popular
girl I know of. I know five boys who
like her <u>best</u>.

---

[10] Fitzgerald's friend spelled her name "Susanne Rice" in the Frontenac Hotel register in July 1909, the same month in which Scott visited the resort.

## XXI

These are the boys and girls I like best in order
First three boys are tie.

| | | |
|---|---|---|
| Art | This list | ⎧ Alida Bigelow |
| Bob | changes | ⎪ Margaret Armstrong |
| Cecil | continually | ⎪ Kitty Schulze |
| Shumier | Only | ⎨ Elizabeth Dean |
| Boardmen | authentic | ⎪ Marie Hersey |
| Biglow | at | ⎪ Dorothy Green |
| <u>Sturgis</u> | date | ⎪ Caroline Clark |
| <u>Jim</u> | of | ⎩ Julia Door |
| D. Driscoll | Chapter | |
| R. Washington | | |
| Paul | | |
| Speply | When I first came to St. Paul | |
| Rube | these were my favorite | |
| Mitchell | <u>boys</u> | <u>girls</u> |
| Smith | Wharton Smith | Violet Stockton |
| | Arthur Foley | Dorothy Green |
| | Adolph Sholly | Harriet Foster |

## XXII

This is an extract from something I wrote after dancing school in Buffalo one night.

                            Fri Jan 19, 1908

(11 years old)

I just love Kitty Williams. Today in dancing school I told her she was my best girl. I dared Earl Knox to say "I love you Kitty," to her and he did it. Then I did too She asket me if I liked dancing school and I said I liked it if she went. Then she said she liked it if I went.

O Fudge

The looks of the girls

|  | (1911) |  | (1912) |  |
|---|---|---|---|---|
| 1st | | Kitty Schultze | | Elenor Alair |
| 2nd | | Alida Bigelow | | Kitty Schultz |
| 3rd | | Elenor Alair | | Marie Hersey |
| 4th | | Marie Hersey | | |
| 5th | | Julia Dorr | | |

## XXIII

Paul and Art.    Chap. VI    Feb. 12, 1911

    I devote a whole chapter to these two because for a long time they were my ideals but lately one has fallen in my estimation. For a long time I was Pauls ardent admirer Cecil and I went with him all the time and we thought him a hero. Physically he is the strongest boy I have ever seen and he is a fine foot ball, baseball and tennis player and a fair Hockey player and swimer. All last winter we three went together and skeed a lot but since I have gone with Bob Clark however I have not liked Paul half so well. In the first place we thought Paul a hero and be both considered him our best friend. He was awfully funny strong as an ox, cool in the face of danger polite and at times very interesting. Now I dont dislike him. I have simply out grown him.

*Last Kiss*

## XXIX

Chap. VII  Dancing school in 1911  Feb. 12, 1911

Since dancing school opened this
last time I have deserted Alida. I have
two new Crushes, to wit—Margaret Armstrong
and Marie Hersey. I have not quite
decided yet which I like the best.
The 2$^{nd}$ is the prettiest. The 1$^{st}$ the best
talker. The 2$^{nd}$ the most popular with
T. Ames, J. Porterfield, B. Griggs,[11] C. Read,
R Warner, ect. and I am crazy about
her. I think it is charming to hear her
say, "Give it to me as a comp-pliment"
when I tell her I have a trade last[12] for her.
I think Una Bachus[13] is the most unpop
ular girl in dancing schools Last
year in dancing school I got
11 valentines and this year 15.
Dorothy Green sent a valentine to
every girl and one to every boy.
There are 3 new girls and one new boy in
dancing school this year. The girls are

---

[11] Theodore "Ted" Ames and Ben Griggs.
[12] "A trade last" can be defined as "a compliment that I heard about you that I'll trade for a compliment that you heard about me."
[13] Una Backus was the daughter of Clinton and Carrie Backus, who operated Backus' School for Girls. Several of Fitzgerald's female friends attended the school.

## XXX

Constance James, Elenor Elair, and Margaret
Winchester. The new boy is William Lindig.[14]
I have a season engagement for every dance
up to the ninth. We boys got up a petition
to get E. Elair into dancing school and
gave it to Mrs. Townsend.[15] We are
going to get up another petition to
be taught the Boston. One day about
a week ago some of the boys including
Arthur Foley, Cecil Reade, Donald
Bigelow, and Laurence Boardman refused
to do the Grand March. They went out in
the hall and began to put on their
shoes. Mr. Baker almost had a fit
but his efforts to make them march
were unavailing. Those of us that were
in the march messed it up
evry which way so now the
grand march is abolished and we
have three other dances in its
place.

---

[14] Probably William Lindeke. The Lindekes were a prominent St. Paul family.

[15] How Mrs. Townsend fits into the picture is unclear. Jean McLaren Ingersoll, the mother of Jean Ingersoll, one of Fitzgerald's friends, organized the class at Ramaley School of Dance. (Jean Ingersoll Summersby, letter to John Koblas dated 12 November 1976.)

## XXXI

Chap VIII    The gooserah and other clubs.    Feb 24—11

The first club I remember really
belonging to was "the white handkerchief,"
Arthur and I were the originators
of this and later we admitted Adolf
Sholly and George Gardner.[16] Then came
Cecil Reade and Phil Foley[17] making
six members. Our first meeting
was held in the yellow house next
to Michell's[18] old house. Adolph Sholly
was elected president and I secretary
dues were fixed at 5 cents per
fortnight 5 cents a week being
considered too exravagent. Ours was
a secret society and we were bound
to tell none of the secrets tho I doubt
muchly if there were any to tell. This
club died a natural death unlike
the next one I was in which came to a
sudden and dramatic ending. The
members were H. Green,[19] P. Ballion
Cecil Reade and me and we entitled

---

[16] Truman Gardner, George's younger brother, was in Fitzgerald's dancing class.
[17] Philip was Arthur's younger brother, born ca. 1900.
[18] Jack Mitchell.
[19] Harold Green was not a member of Dorothy Greene's family (although it is a possibility, given Fitzgerald's tendency to misspell proper names).

## XXXII

ourselves the "boy's secret service
of St. Paul." I was chief scout, Cecil
chief spy; Paul President, and
Harold Green Cheif detective. The
'finis' of this club is narrated
in the chapter on Paul and Art.
Once I belong to a cruelty to animals
society and Betty Mudge told them that
I cut off rats tails and so I received
a note signed by ten girls telling
me politly but firmly that I was fired
from the organization.
    The best club I ever belonged
to was the Gooserah club gotten up by
myself. The club originated with
the name. There was a boy in our
sunday school[20] class named Alfred Geisan[21] and
they call him Goosan. One day quite
by accident Paul said Rah for Goose
Gooserah.[22] The absurdity of the name

---

[20] In an April *1910 Ledger* entry, Fitzgerald wrote: "I used to go to St. Mary's Sunday School.... Became desperately Holy." The original Gothic church, dedicated in 1866, was demolished around 1920. A baptismal font donated in 1883 by Fitzgerald's aunt, Annabel McQuillan, is still used in the church that replaced it. Annabel was reportedly the first person to be baptized in the church. See Dave Page and Jack Koblas, *F. Scott Fitzgerald in Minnesota: Toward the Summit* (St. Cloud, Minn.: North Star Press, 1996): 3.

[21] Probably Alfred Giesen, born ca. 1897. Year: *1910*; Census Place: *St Paul Ward 7, Ramsey, Minnesota*; Roll: *T624_720*; Page: *10B*; Enumeration District: *0090*; FHL microfilm: *1374733*.

[22] Cecil Read would later name his boat at the White Bear Yacht Club *The Gooserah* (Page and Koblas: 60).

## XXXIII

struck us and I sugested that we get
up a club named thus. The first
member was Cecil and Paul and I
subjected him to a most horrible initiation
which consisted of having him eat
raw eggs and of operating on him with
saw, cold ice, and needle accomanied
by a basin. Then we initiated Sam Sturgis
Jim Porterfield, Bob Clark, and Bobby Shurmier.
There was a rival organization gotten up by
Art, Don, and Laurie intitled the buliphants[23]
and from the first we were sworn enemies
We cleared out Cecil's 3d floor for a
club room and part of the basement for
a gymnasium which last was quite creditable.
It consisted of 4 pairs dumbells, 2 pairs indian
clubs, 2 pairs (8 gloves) boxing gloves, 1 pair
[w]rist exercisers 1 punching bag 1 wall
excerciser, 1 trapeze, 1 pair swinging
rings. Paul was the boxing master

---

[23] Carol Irish, a teacher at St. Paul Academy, later wrote: "Alida Bigelow Butler remembers Fitzgerald as one who instigated projects for the crowd, projects usually designed to reveal the social structure for the group. At one point he founded two rival clubs, the Elephants and the Bull Elephants. He seems to have thought little about the purposes of the clubs; he centered his interest in the selection of members. Once complex election and initiation rites were worked out, Fitzgerald lost his enthusiasm and the project was abandoned." See "The Myth of Success in Fitzgerald's Boyhood" in the Autumn 1973 issue of *Studies in American Fiction*, p. 179.

## XXXIV

and Bob Shurmier and I were the fencing teachers. There were 3 degrees in the club: 1st, 2nd + 3d The first degree is anyone who has been initiated, 2nd anyone who has been or is an officer and the 3d anyone who renders an especial service to the club. That summer the club disbanded and so far this winter we have had 2 meetings in one of which were voted in 3 members and the second in which we initiated them. The new members are D. Biglow, L. Shepley, M. Seymour[24] respectivly.

---

[24] McNeil Seymour. His name is misspelled in the program for one of Fitzgerald's juvenile plays, *Assorted Spirits*, as McNeil Seymore.

## XXXV

Chap IX    Alida + Margaret                Feb. 24

This chapter should be named Margaret
+ Alida but when I wrote this name in
the index I liked Alida best so it is excusable
I am just crazy about Margaret
Armstrong and I have the most awful
crush on her that ever was. This has been
the case ever since Bob's party. She is
not pretty but I think she is very
attractive looking. She is extremely
gracful and a very good dancer and
the most interesting talker I have ever
seen or rather heard. One Saturday night
I was surprised by a visit from Margaret
asking me to the Bachus school dance[25]
Of course I accepted with pleasure and
that night took her to it. I had a
fine time including four dances
from Margaret. The next day Julia
invited a large crowd of boys and girls
to make a visit to a house on Pleasant
Ave that was said to be haunted.[26]

---

[25] Mrs. Backus' School for Girls was also known as Oak Hall. A short walk from the Fitzgeralds' home on Holly, it provided the performance venue for one of Fitzgerald's juvenile plays, *The Captured Shadow*, on 23 August 1912.

[26] Two months earlier, Mrs. Emma Sebastian and her five children claimed to have seen a "man with a black mustache, furry coat and wearing moccasins" in their home at 486 Pleasant. Unnerved, Mrs. Sebastian moved from the house, where some bones, a crucifix and rosary were later found, buried in the basement. The bones turned out to be from a pig. See Oliver Towne, *St. Paul is My Beat* (St. Paul, Minn.: North Central Pub. Co., 1958): 117.

## XXXVI

Of course we went and the bad part of
it was that Jim walked all the
way out with Margaret and I
was left in the lurch. Jim did
not have such a walkover going
back because I was on the other
side of Margaret but just the
same I felt pretty glum that night for I
knew that up to that time I had
been almost first with Margaret for
a week and now Jim had to step
in and cheat me. Wednesday an
eventful day dawned clear and
warm. Jim Porterfeild and I were invited
to call on Elizabeth Dean by Elizabeth and when
we got there we found her too and we
started out for a walk. Margaret and Jim
walked ahead and Elizabeth and I behind
This made me mad and this was furthur inflamed
when they got a block ahead of us. Then

## XXXVII

Elizabeth told me some things. She said that Margaret had given her a note the day befor in school which said "I know I am fickle but I like Jim just as much as I do Scott." When I learned this I was jealous of Jim as I had never been of anyone before. I said some ridiculous things about how I was going to get even with him in Margarets estimation when we reached the country club.* Elizabeth went ahead and asked Margaret which of us she liked the best. Margaret said she liked me best. All the way home I was in the seventh heaven of delight. The next time I saw Margaret was Friday. I met Elizabeth and she on the corner near Cecil's house and we talked about 5 minutes.

---

* A note here in Fitzgerald's hand reads "Margaret's Hair." Perhaps a lock of hair was originally pasted on this page.

## XXXVIII

Then I took Margaret home and
I told her I was invited to the sophmore
assembly by C. James[27] and she said that she
would have invited
me if she had
thought of it. I had
three invites
because when I got
home I found that
Alida Biglow had
invited me also.*
As Margaret and
I walked
along we had
quite an interesting conversation.
    <u>Said I</u>. "Jim was so confident the
other night that you had a crush on
him."
    "Well Jim gets another think."
    "Shall I let him know you
don't like him."

---

[27] Constance James.
  * A photograph once pasted here has been removed.

## XXXIX

"No but you can let him know that he isn't first."

"I'll do that"

"Now if you had thought that it might be different."

"Good" said I

"Good" repeated she and then the convestion lagged. She asked me to call for her at eight and go to the play with her and I said yes. Then we said good bye + I went home. Then, sad to say, Margaret called me up + said that she couldn't go. The play was very good but Margaret was not there boo hoo.

One Saturday night about two weeks later my finish came We were over at Ben Grigg's four boys, Reub, Ben, Ted + I, and four girls Margaret, Marie, Elizabeth + Dorothy + that evening Margaret

## XXXX

got an awful crush on Reuben which
at the time I write this is still active[28]
More about Margaret later on
      Alida is considered by some the
prettiest girl in dancing school.
Bob Clark, E. Driscoll,[29] D. Driscoll, A. Foley, and
I all had a crush on her last winter
and this fall. Evry night Bob + I would
go over to see Don[30] + incidently see
Alida. She liked Art 1st, Egbert 2nd
I third & Bob 4th. Bob is south now
+ writes her a letter 3 times a week.

---

[28] Fitzgerald later produced a fictionalized account of this episode for the Basil Duke Lee series. The story, entitled "The Scandal Detectives," appeared in the *Saturday Evening Post* on 28 April 1928. According to the obituary for Marie Hersey Hamm in the *Minneapolis Star and Tribune* (25 Nov. 1982, p. 6b), she was "a lumber baron's daughter, the wife of William Hamm Jr. and the childhood sweetheart of F. Scott Fitzgerald." Marie is often cited as the original for Margaret Torrence in "The Scandal Detectives." The hero of the story, Basil Duke Lee, is based on Fitzgerald; Bill Kempf is modeled after Paul Baillon, Hubert Blair after Reuben Warner.

[29] Egbert Driscoll.

[30] Donald Bigelow, Alida's brother.

## COMMENTARY

DAVE PAGE

F. Scott Fitzgerald's *Thoughtbook* comprises a title page followed by thirteen leaves—all inscribed, recto and verso, in his youthful hand.[1] Fitzgerald began penciling his observations in the *Thoughtbook* during the late summer of 1910, just before his fourteenth birthday. He continued to set down his thoughts, in a haphazardly organized series of vignettes, until February of the following year. He was living with his father, mother, sister, and one servant in modest quarters: a rented duplex at 514 Holly Avenue in St. Paul, Minnesota, a few blocks from the show street of the city, Summit Avenue, where many of his friends lived. Summit Avenue was lined with spacious Victorian-style residences, all with accommodations for servants and many with separate stables and garages.

Although St. Paul provides the setting for much of the *Thoughtbook*, some of the episodes occur in Buffalo, New York, to which the Fitzgeralds had moved in April 1898 after the failure of a wicker-furniture business for which Edward Fitzgerald, the author's father, had served as President. In Buffalo and later in Syracuse, to which the family moved in 1901, Edward labored as a salesman for the dry-goods firm of Procter & Gamble. In March 1908 Edward lost this job; in July the family returned to St. Paul. Thereafter Edward sold groceries wholesale, working from a desk in the real-estate office of his wife's brother. The Fitzgeralds lived in a succession of apartments and row houses, supported primarily by Mrs. Fitzgerald's inheritance from her father, Philip McQuillan, an Irish immigrant

---

[1] The original of the *Thoughtbook* is housed in the Bruccoli Collection at the Irvin F. Hollings Special Collections Library, University of South Carolina. The pages are numbered in Roman numerals. The pagination begins with numeral VIII, suggesting that there were originally seven other pages, now lost. These pages were already missing when Arthur Mizener, Fitzgerald's first biographer, examined the *Thoughtbook* in the late 1940s. See Mizener, *The Far Side of Paradise* (Boston: Houghton Mifflin, 1951): 17. The pagination (VIII–XVII, XX–XXIII, XXIX–XXXX) indicates that additional pages might have gone missing.

who had built a successful business in wholesale groceries before dying prematurely in 1877, at the age of forty-three.

***

At the top of page VIII of the *Thoughtbook*, young Scott Fitzgerald wrote "My girls August, 1910." What follows is a succession of tales about young romance, perhaps motivated by Violet Stockton's diary of gossip which, according to Scott, was entitled "flirting by sighns." (The misspelling, like many others in the *Thoughtbook*, is his.) Scott seems to have thought that Violet was a Southern girl—he writes that she "spoke with a soft southern accent leaving out the r's"—but in fact she was from New Jersey. She was a member of a prominent family there: her father, Richard Stockton, was the United States Consul to Rotterdam. He had married her mother, Clemence Finch, in St. Paul on 19 January 1887. Clemence's father, George R. Finch, was a partner in a successful St. Paul wholesale grocery business. Among the 600 wedding guests was Richard's father, former U.S. Senator John Potter Stockton.[2] One of Violet's great-grandfathers also served as a U.S. Senator from New Jersey, as did a great-great-grandfather. One of her great-great-great-grandfathers had signed the Declaration of Independence. (Scott, for his part, could have mentioned to Violet that he was named for a distant relative, Francis Scott Key, who had written the words to "The Star-Spangled Banner.") Scott courted Violet with some success but eventually lost her to a rival, Arthur Foley, who lived with his mother, Mrs. Thomas (Jessie) A. Foley, three sisters, four brothers, a housekeeper, cook, chauffeur, seamstress, and housemaid in a four-story dwelling at 236 Summit Avenue,[3] next door to the massive stone residence of the great Midwestern empire builder James J. Hill.

Violet celebrated her fourteenth birthday the summer she met Scott. Certainly she made a deep impression on him; her story takes

---

[2] *New York Times*, 20 January 1887, p. 1.
[3] Year: *1910*; Census Place: *St Paul Ward 7, Ramsey, Minnesota*; Roll: T624_720; Page: *5B*; Enumeration District: *0092*; FHL microfilm: *1374733*. The house is no longer standing.

up seven of the twenty-six pages in the *Thoughtbook*. He remembered her later in his life: it is probable that she stood in part as the model for one of his most memorable characters—Ermine Gilberte Labouisse (Minnie) Bibble in the Basil Duke Lee stories, a series of tales that Fitzgerald published in the *Saturday Evening Post* in 1928 and 1929. Minnie appears for the first time in "He Thinks He's Wonderful," published in the *Post* for 29 September 1928. Fitzgerald writes in the story (offering a possible clue) that Minnie's head "had reminded otherwise not illiterate young men of damp blue violets." Basil encounters Minnie again in "Forging Ahead," which appeared in the *Post* on 30 March 1929, and yet again in "Basil and Cleopatra," the last story in the series, published in the *Post* on 27 April 1929. By this time Minnie has taken on many of the characteristics of Ginevra King, a beautiful fifteen-year-old society girl from Lake Forest, Illinois, whom Fitzgerald met in St. Paul in January 1915, and with whom he carried on an intense epistolary romance over the following year and a half.[4]

The first of "My Girls" to appear in the pages of the *Thoughtbook* is Nancy Gardener. Born in December 1898, she lived with her father, mother, older brother, and two Irish servants in Buffalo at 42 Ashland Avenue, roughly seven blocks southwest of 71 Highland Avenue, where the Fitzgeralds were living in October 1905. When Scott and his parents first relocated to Buffalo from St. Paul, they resided at the Lenox, an apartment house with "breakfast nooks and servants' quarters."[5] After a stint in Syracuse, where Scott's sister, Annabel, was born, the family returned to 29 Irving Place in Buffalo, which the Fitzgeralds occupied along with a servant and a nurse.[6] In October 1905, they moved to 71 Highland, a somewhat more impressive address. The family was residing there when the Buffalo episodes in the *Thoughtbook* took place.

---

[4] James L. W. West III, *The Perfect Hour: The Romance of F. Scott Fitzgerald and Ginevra King* (New York: Random House, 2005).
[5] Chuck LaChiusa, "F. Scott Fitzgerald in Buffalo, NY," *Buffalo as an Architectural Museum*, 2002. See http://www.buffaloah.com/a/fitzbflo/fitzbflo.html
[6] New York State Archives; Albany, New York; *State Population Census Schedules, 1905*; Election District: *E.D. 02*; City: *Buffalo Ward 21*; County: *Erie*; Page: 12.

Two girls named Kitty play prominent roles in the *Thoughtbook*: Kitty Williams in Buffalo and Kitty Schulze in St. Paul. The Schulzes are one of three St. Paul families listed by name near the end of *The Great Gatsby*, in the memorable passage about returning to the Midwest at Christmas.[7] The Schulzes lived in a castle-like dwelling at 226 Summit Avenue,[8] two houses down from the Hill mansion and next door to the Foleys. Kitty's father, Theodore Schulze, Sr., had achieved success as a wholesale dealer in shoes. The household consisted of himself, his wife, three daughters, a son, two housemaids, a cook, and two chauffeurs.[9]

Another of the *Thoughtbook* girls (her family is also mentioned near the end of *Gatsby*) is Marie Hersey. She was one of Scott's best friends and was Ginevra King's roommate at Westover School in Middlebury, Connecticut. According to the 1910 U.S. Census, the Hersey household was large. It was made up of the widowed mother, Mary Hersey, plus Marie, Marie's two older sisters and four younger brothers, seven servants, and Mary's brother and sister-in-law and their five children.[10] There was money in the family. Marie's grandfather, Samuel F. Hersey, was a congressman from Maine who invested successfully in Wisconsin and Minnesota lumber. (One of his main competitors in banking and logging was Frederick Weyerhaeuser, who came to St. Paul in 1891, moved into a turreted mansion on the other side of James J. Hill's property from the Foleys, and made enough money to become the eighth richest American of all time.) Marie Hersey's second husband was William Hamm, Jr., a scion of the Hamm brewing family.

This world of money and mansions and servants, recovered from census records and other documents, provides a partial backdrop for the dancing lessons and fleeting crushes recorded in the *Thoughtbook*. Young Scott Fitzgerald, who would later make his mark as

---

[7] In the passage, which appears on pp. 211–12 of the Scribners 1925 first edition, the family name is given as "Schultze."
[8] The house is no longer standing, but several photographs survive.
[9] Year: *1910*; Census Place: *St Paul Ward 7, Ramsey, Minnesota*; Roll: T624_720; Page: *5B*; Enumeration District: *0092*; FHL microfilm: *1374733*.
[10] Year: *1910*; Census Place: *St Paul Ward 7, Ramsey, Minnesota*; Roll: T624_720; Page: *17B*; Enumeration District: *0093*; FHL microfilm: *1374733*.

a novelist of manners, observed this small society with interest. He watched, listened, and recorded; already his instinct was to set down his observations on paper. He was not, strictly speaking, a poor boy keeping company with the rich. Class distinctions in St. Paul were fluid, and he could mix easily enough with the daughters and sons of the wealthy. Still, he must have been aware of his marginal position in this group: he was *of* it but not quite *in* it. He knew what created popularity—good looks, charm, and a clever line. Later he would learn that true status was another matter. The trump cards in this game were wealth and possessions, and knowledge of how to display and deploy them. Such lessons, present everywhere in his fiction, are adumbrated strongly in the *Thoughtbook*.

# NAMES

Many of the names in the *Thoughtbook* are given incompletely; many are misspelled. Below from page XXI are the names of most of the players in these youthful dramas, recorded in full and spelled correctly. Corrections are also to be found in the footnotes to the *Thoughtbook* text.

| *Boys* | *Girls* |
|---|---|
| Arthur Foley | Alida Bigelow |
| Robert Clark | Margaret Armstrong |
| Cecil Read | Kitty Schulze |
| Gus Schurmeier | Elisabeth Dean |
| Larry (Lawrence) Boardman | Marie Hersey |
| Donald Bigelow | Dorothy Greene |
| Sam Sturgis | Caroline Clark |
| Jim Porterfield | Julia Dorr |
| Donald Driscoll | |
| Richard "Tubby" Washington | |
| Paul Baillon | |
| Leonard Shepley | |
| Reuben Warner III | |
| Jack Mitchell | |

\*\*\*

| Wharton Smith | Violet Stockton |
| Arthur Foley | Dorothy Greene |
| Adolph Scholle | Harriet Foster |

# THE VEGETABLE
(1923)

# THE VEGETABLE
## or
## from President to postman

By

F. SCOTT FITZGERALD

*"Any man who doesn't want to get on in the world, to make a million dollars, and maybe even park his toothbrush in the White House, hasn't got as much to him as a good dog has—he's nothing more or less than a vegetable."*
—*From a Current Magazine.*

TO
KATHERINE TIGHE AND EDMUND WILSON, JR.
WHO DELETED MANY ABSURDITIES
FROM MY FIRST TWO NOVELS I RECOMMEND
THE ABSURDITIES SET DOWN HERE

# THE VEGETABLE

## Act I

*This is the "living" room of Jerry Frost's house. It is evening. The room (and, by implication, the house) is small and stuffy—it's an awful bother to raise these old-fashioned windows; some of them stick, and besides it's extravagant to let in much cold air, here in the middle of March. I can't say much for the furniture, either. Some of it's instalment stuff, imitation leather with the grain painted on as an after-effect, and some of it's dingily, depressingly old. That bookcase held "Ben Hur" when it was a best-seller, and it's now trying to digest "A Library of the World's Best Literature" and the "Wit and Humor of the United States in Six Volumes." That couch would be dangerous to sit upon without a map showing the location of all craters, hillocks, and thistle-patches. And three dead but shamefully unburied clocks stare eyelessly before them from their perches around the walls.*

*Those walls—God! The history of American photography hangs upon them. Photographs of children with puffed dresses and depressing leers, taken in the Fauntleroy nineties, of babies with toothless mouths and idiotic eyes, of young men with the hair cuts of '85 and '90 and '02, and with neckties that loop, twist, snag, or flare in conformity to some esoteric, antiquated standard of middle-class dandyism. And the girls! You'd have to laugh at the girls! Imitation Gibson girls, mostly; you can trace their histories around the room, as each of them withered and staled. Here's one in the look-at-her-little-toes-aren't-they-darling period, and here she is later when she was a little bother of ten. Look! This is the way she was when she was after a husband. She might be worse. There's a certain young charm or something, but in the next picture you can see what five years of general housework have done to her. You wouldn't turn your eyes half a degree to watch her in the street. And that was taken six years ago—now she's thirty and already an old woman.*

*You've guessed it. That last one, allowing for the photographer's kind erasure of a few lines, is Mrs. Jerry Frost. If you listen for a minute, you'll hear her, too.*

*But wait. Against my will, I'll have to tell you a few sordid details about the room. There's got to be a door in plain sight that leads directly outdoors, and then there are two other doors, one to the dining-room and one to the second floor—you can see the beginning of the stairs. Then there's a window somewhere that's used in the last act. I hate to mention these things, but they're part of the plot.*

*Now you see when the curtain went up, Jerry Frost had left the little Victrola playing and wandered off to the cellar or somewhere, and Mrs. Jerry (you can call her Charlotte) hears it from where she is up-stairs. Listen!*

"Some little bug is going to find you, so-o-ome day!"

*That's her. She hasn't got much of a voice, has she? And she will sing one key higher than the Victrola. And now the darn Victrola's running down and giving off a ghastly minor discord like the death agony of a human being.*

CHARLOTTE. [*She's up-stairs, remember.*] Jerry, wind up the graphophone.

> *There's no answer.*

Jer-ry!

> *Still no answer.*

Jerry, wind up the graphophone. It isn't good for it.

> *Yet again no answer.*

All right—[*smugly*]—if you want to ruin it, *I* don't care.

> *The phonograph whines, groans, gags, and dies, and almost simultaneously with its last feeble gesture a man comes into the room, saying: "What?" He receives no answer. It is Jerry Frost, in whose home we are.*

> *Jerry Frost is thirty-five. He is a clerk for the railroad at $3,000 a year. He possesses no eyebrows, but nevertheless he constantly tries to knit them. His lips are faintly pursed at all times, as though about to emit an enormous opinion upon some matter of great importance.*

*On the wall there is a photograph of him at twenty-seven—just before he married. Those were the days of his high yellow pompadour. That is gone now, faded like the rest of him into a docile pattern without grace or humor.*

*After his mysterious and unanswered "What?" Jerry stares at the carpet, surely not in esthetic approval, and becomes engrossed in his lack of thoughts. Suddenly he gives a twitch and tries to reach with his hand some delicious sector of his back. He can almost reach it, but not quite—poor man!—so he goes to the mantelpiece and rubs his back gently, pleasingly, against it, meanwhile keeping his glance focussed darkly upon the carpet.*

*He is finished. He is at physical ease again. He leans over the table—did I say there was a table?—and turns the pages of a magazine, yawning meanwhile and tentatively beginning a slow clog step with his feet. Presently this distracts him from the magazine, and he looks apathetically at his feet. Then suddenly he sits in a chair and begins to sing, unmusically, and with faint interest, a piece which is possibly his own composition. The tune varies considerably, but the words have an indisputable consistency, as they are composed wholly of the phrase: "Everybody is there, everybody is there!"*

*He is a motion-picture of tremendous, unconscious boredom.*

*Suddenly he gives out a harsh, bark-like sound and raises his hand swiftly, as though he were addressing an audience. This fails to amuse him; the arm falters, strays lower——*

JERRY. Char-*lit!* Have you got the Saturday Evening Post?

*There is no reply.*

Char-*lit!*

*Still no reply.*

Char-*lit!*

CHARLOTTE [*with syrupy recrimination*]. You didn't bother to answer me, so I don't think I should bother to answer you.

JERRY [*indignant, incredulous*]. Answer you what?

CHARLOTTE. You know what I mean.

JERRY. I mos' certainly do not.

CHARLOTTE. I asked you to wind up the graphophone.

JERRY [*glancing at it indignantly*]. The phonograph?

CHARLOTTE. Yes, the graphophone!

JERRY. It's the first time I knew it. [*He is utterly disgusted. He starts to speak several times, but each time he hesitates. Disgust settles upon his face, in a heavy pall. Then he remembers his original question.*] Have you got the Saturday Evening Post?

CHARLOTTE. Yes, I told you!

JERRY. You did not tell me!

CHARLOTTE. I can't help it if you're deaf!

JERRY. Deaf? Who's deaf? [*After a pause.*] No more deaf than you are. [*After another pause.*] Not half as much.

CHARLOTTE. Don't talk so loud—you'll wake the people next door.

JERRY [*incredulously*]. The people next door!

CHARLOTTE. You heard me!

> *Jerry is beaten, and taking it very badly. He is beginning to brood when the telephone rings. He answers it.*

JERRY. Hello!... [*With recognition and rising interest.*] Oh, hello.... Did you get the stuff.... Just one gallon is all I want.... No, I can't use more than one gallon.... [*He looks around thoughtfully.*] Yes, I suppose so, but I'd rather have you mix it before you bring it.... Well, about nine o'clock, then. [*He rings off, gleeful now, smiling. Then sudden worry, and the hairless eyebrows knit together. He takes a note-book out of his pocket, lays it open before him, and picks up the receiver.*] Midway 9191.... Yes.... Hello, is this Mr.—Mr. S-n-o-o-k-s's residence?... Hello, is this Mr. S-n-o-o-k-s's residence?... [*Very distinctly.*] Mr. Snukes or Snooks.... Mr. S-n-, the boo—the fella that gets *stuff*, hooch... h-o-o-c-h.... No, Snukes or Snooks is the man I want.... Oh. Why, a fella down-town gave me your husband's name and he called me up—at least, I called him up first, and then he called me up just now—see?... You see? Hello—is this—am I talking to the wife of the—of the—of the fella that gets *stuff* for you? The b-o-o-t-l-e-g-g-e-r? Oh, you know, the bootlegger. [*He breathes hard after this word.* Do you suppose Central will tell on *him?*] . . . Oh. Well, you see, I wanted to tell him when he comes tonight to come to the back door. . . . No, Hooch is not my name. My name is Frost. 2127 Osceola Avenue. . . . Oh, he's left already? Oh, all right. Thanks. . . . Well, good-by. . . . Well, good-by . . . good-by. [*He rings off. Again his hairless brows are knit with worry.*] Charlit!

CHARLOTTE [*abstractedly*]. Yes?

JERRY. Charlit, if you want to read a good story, read the one about the fella who gets shipwrecked on the Buzzard Islands and meets the Chinese girl, only she isn't a Chinese girl at all.

CHARLOTTE [*she's still up-stairs, remember*]. What?

JERRY. There's one story in there—are you reading the Saturday Evening Post?

CHARLOTTE. I would be if you didn't interrupt me every minute.

JERRY. I'm not. I just wanted to tell you there's one story in there about a Chinese girl who gets wrecked on the Buzzard Islands that isn't a Chinese—

CHARLOTTE. Oh, let up, for heaven's sakes! Don't *nag* me.

*Clin-n-ng! That's the door-bell.*

There's the door-bell.

JERRY [*with fine sarcasm*]. Oh, really? Why, I thought it was a cow-bell.

CHARLOTTE [*witheringly*]. Ha-ha!

*Well, he's gone to the door. He opens it, mumbles something, closes it. Now he's back.*

JERRY. It wasn't anybody.

CHARLOTTE. It must have been.

JERRY. What?

CHARLOTTE. It couldn't have rung itself.

JERRY [*in disgust*]. Oh, gosh, you think that's funny. [*After a pause.*] It was a man who wanted 2145. I told him this was 2127, so he went away.

*Charlotte is now audibly descending a crickety flight of stairs, and here she is! She's thirty, and old for her age, just like I told you, shapeless, slack-cheeked, but still defiant. She would fiercely resent the statement that her* attractions have declined ninety per cent since her marriage, and in the same breath she would assume that there was a responsibility and shoulder it on her husband. She talks in a pessimistic whine and, with a sort of dowdy egotism, considers herself generally in the right. Frankly, I don't like her, though she can't help being what she is.

CHARLOTTE. I thought you were going to the Republican Convention down at the Auditorium.

JERRY. Well, I am. [*But he remembers the b-o-o—*.] No, I can't.

CHARLOTTE. Well, then, for heaven's sakes don't spend the evening sitting here and nagging me. I'm nervous enough as it is.

*They both sit. She produces a basket of sewing, selects a man's nightshirt and begins, apparently, to rip it to pieces. Meanwhile Jerry, who has picked up a magazine, regards her out of the corner of his eye. During the first rip he starts to speak, and again during the second rip, but each time he restrains himself with a perceptible effort.*

JERRY. What are you tearing that up for?

CHARLOTTE [*sarcastically*]. Just for fun.

JERRY. Why don't you tear up one of your own?

CHARLOTTE [*exasperated*]. Oh, I know what I'm doing. For heaven's sakes, don't *n-a-a-ag* me!

JERRY [*feebly*]. Well, I just asked you. [*A long pause.*] Well, I got analyzed to-day.

CHARLOTTE. What?

JERRY. I got analyzed.

CHARLOTTE. What's that?

JERRY. I got analyzed by an expert analyzer. Everybody down at the Railroad Company got analyzed. [*Rather importantly.*] They got a chart about me that long. [*He expresses two feet with his hands.*] Say— [*He rises suddenly and goes up close to her.*] What color my eyes?

CHARLOTTE. Don't ask me. Sort of brown, I guess.

JERRY. Brown? That's what I told 'em. But they got me down for blue.

CHARLOTTE. What was it all about? Did they pay you anything for it?

JERRY. Pay me anything? Of course not. It was for my benefit. It'll do me a lot of good. I was *analyzed*, can't you understand? They found out a lot of stuff about me.

CHARLOTTE [*dropping her work in horror*]. Do you think you'll lose your job?

JERRY [*in disgust*]. A lot you know about business methods. Don't you ever read "Efficiency" or the "Systematic Weekly"? It's a sort of examination.

CHARLOTTE. Oh, I know. When they feel all the bumps on your head.

JERRY. No, not like that at all. They ask you questions, see?

CHARLOTTE. Well, you needn't be so cross about it.

*He hasn't been cross.*

I hope you had the spunk to tell them you thought you deserved a better position than you've got.

JERRY. They didn't ask me things like that. It was up-stairs in one of the private offices. First the character analyzer looked at me sort of hard and said "Sit down!"

CHARLOTTE. Did you sit down?

JERRY. Sure; the thing is to do what they tell you. Well, then the character analyzer asked me my name and whether I was married.

CHARLOTTE [*suspiciously*]. What did you tell her?

JERRY. Oh, it was a man. I told him yes, of course. What do you think I am?

CHARLOTTE. Well, did he ask you anything else about me?

JERRY. No. He asked me what it was my ambition to be, and I said I didn't have any ambition left, and then I said, "Do you mean when I was a kid?" And he said, "All right, what did you want to do then?" And I said "Postman," and he said, "What sort of a job would you like to get now?" and I said, "Well, what have you got to offer?"

CHARLOTTE. Did he offer you a job?

JERRY. No, he was just kidding, I guess. Well, then, he asked me if I'd ever done any studying at home to fit me for a higher position, and I said, "Sure," and he said, "What?" and I couldn't think of anything off-hand, so I told him I took music lessons. He said no, he meant about railroads, and I said they worked me so hard that when I got home at night I never want to hear about railroads again.

CHARLOTTE. Was that all?

JERRY. Oh, there were some more questions. He asked me if I'd ever been in jail.

CHARLOTTE. What did you tell him?

JERRY. I told him "no," of course.

CHARLOTTE. He probably didn't believe you.

JERRY. Well, he asked me a few more things, and then he let me go. I think I got away with it all right. At least he didn't give me any black marks on my chart—just a lot of little circles.

CHARLOTTE. Oh, you got away with it "all right." That's all you care. You got away with it. Satisfied with nothing. Why didn't you talk right up to him: "See here, I don't see why I shouldn't get more money." That's what you'd have ought to said. He'd of respected you more in the end.

JERRY [*gloomily*]. I did have ambitions once.

CHARLOTTE. Ambition to do what? To be a postman. That was a fine ambition for a fella twenty-two years old. And you'd have been one if I'd let you. The only other ambition you ever had was to marry me. And that didn't last long.

JERRY. I know it didn't. It lasted one month too long, though.

*A mutual glare here—let's not look.*

And I've had other ambitions since then—don't you worry.

CHARLOTTE [*scornfully*]. What?

JERRY. Oh, that's all right.

CHARLOTTE. What, though? I'd like to know what. To win five dollars playing dice in a cigar store?

JERRY. Never you mind. Don't you worry. Don't you fret. It's all right, see?

CHARLOTTE. You're afraid to tell me.

JERRY. No, I'm not. Don't you worry.

CHARLOTTE. Yes, you are.

JERRY. All right then. If you want to know, I had an ambition to be President of the United States.

CHARLOTTE [*laughing*]. Ho—*ho*—ho—*ho!*
> *Jerry is pretending to be interested only in sucking his teeth—but you can see that he is both sorry he made his admission and increasingly aware that his wife is being unpleasant.*

CHARLOTTE. But you decided to give that up, eh?

JERRY. Sure. I gave up everything when I got married.

CHARLOTTE. Even gave up being a postman, eh? That's right. Blame it all on me! Why, if it hadn't been for me you wouldn't even be what you are—a fifty-dollar-a-week clerk.

JERRY. That's right. I'm only a fifty-dollar-a-week clerk. But you're only a thirty-dollar-a-week wife.

CHARLOTTE. Oh, I am, am I?

JERRY. I made a big mistake when I married you.

CHARLOTTE. Stop talking like that! I wish you were dead—dead and buried—cremated! Then I could have some fun.

JERRY. Where—in the poorhouse?

CHARLOTTE. That's where I'd be, I know.
> *Charlotte is not really very angry. She is merely smug and self-satisfied, you see, and is only mildly annoyed at this unexpected resistance to her brow-beating. She knows that Jerry will always stay and slave for her. She has begun this row as a sort of vaudeville to assuage her nightly boredom.*

CHARLOTTE. Why didn't you think of these things before we got married?

JERRY. I did, a couple of times, but you had me all signed up then.
> *The sound of uncertain steps creaking down from the second floor. Into the room at a wavering gait comes Jerry's father, Horatio—"Dada."*
>
> *Dada was born in 1834, and will never see eighty-eight again—in fact, his gathering blindness prevented him from seeing it very clearly in the first place. Originally he was probably Jerry's superior in initiative, but he did not prosper, and during the past twenty years his mind has been steadily failing. A Civil War pension has*

*kept him quasi-independent, and he looks down as from a great dim height upon Jerry (whom he thinks of as an adolescent) and Charlotte (whom he rather dislikes). Never given to reading in his youth, he has lately become absorbed in the Old Testament and in all Old Testament literature, over which he burrows every day in the Public Library.*

*In person he is a small, shrivelled man with a great amount of hair on his face, which gives him an unmistakable resemblance to a French poodle. The fact that he is almost blind and even more nearly deaf contributes to his aloof, judicial pose, and to the prevailing impression that something grave and thoughtful and important is going on back of those faded, vacant eyes. This conception is entirely erroneous. Half the time his mind is a vacuum, in which confused clots of information and misinformation drift and stir—the rest of the time he broods upon the minute details of his daily existence. He is too old, even, for the petty spites which represent to the aged the single gesture of vitality they can make against the ever-increasing pressure of life and youth.*

*When he enters the room he looks neither to left nor right, but with his head shaking faintly and his mouth moving in a shorter vibration, makes directly for the bookcase.*

JERRY. Hello, Dada.

*Dada does not hear.*

JERRY [*louder*]. Looking for the Bible, Dada?

DADA. [*He has reached the bookcase, and he turns around stiffly.*] I'm not deaf, sir.

JERRY. [*Let's draw the old man out.*] Who do you think will be nominated for President, Dada?

DADA [*trying to pretend he has just missed one word*]. The—

JERRY [*louder*]. Who do you think'll be nominated for President, to-night?

DADA. I should say that Lincoln was our greatest President. [*He turns back to the bookcase with an air of having settled a trivial question for all time.*]

JERRY. I mean to-night. They're getting a new one. Don't you read the papers?

DADA [*who has heard only a faint murmur*]. Hm.

CHARLOTTE. You *know* he never reads anything but the Bible. Why do you nag him?

JERRY. He reads the encyclopædia at the Public Library. [*With a rush of public spirit.*] If he'd just read the newspapers he'd know what was going on and have something to talk about. He just sits around and never says anything.

CHARLOTTE. At least he doesn't gabble his head off all day. He's got sense enough not to do that *any*way, haven't you, Dada?

*Dada does not answer.*

JERRY. Lookit here, Charlit. I don't call it gabbling if I meet a man in the street and he says, "Well, I see somebody was nominated for President," and I say, "Yes, I see saw—see so." Suppose I said, "Yes, Lincoln was our greatest President." He'd say, "Why, if that fella isn't a piece of cheese I never saw a piece of cheese."

DADA [*turning about plaintively*]. Some one has taken my Bible.

JERRY. No, there it is on the second shelf, Dada.

DADA. [*He doesn't hear.*] I don't like people moving it around.

CHARLOTTE. Nobody moved it.

DADA. My old mother used to say to me, "Horatio—" [*He brings this word out with an impressive roundness, but as his eye, at that moment, catches sight of the Bible, he loses track of his thought. He pounces upon the Holy Book and drags it out, pulling with it two or three other books, which crash to the floor. The sound of their fall is very faint on his ears—and under the delusion that his error is unnoticed, he slyly kicks the books under the bookcase. Jerry and Charlotte exchange a glance. With his Bible under his arm Dada starts stealthily toward the staircase. He sees something bright shining on the first step, and, not without difficulty, stoops to pick it up. His efforts are unsuccessful.*] Hello, here's a nail that looks just like a ten-cent piece. [*He starts up-stairs.*]

JERRY. He thought he found a ten-cent piece.

CHARLOTTE [*significantly*]. Nobody has yet in *this* house.

*In the ensuing silence Dada can be heard ascending the stairs. About half-way up there is a noise as if he had slipped down a notch. Then a moment of utter silence.*

JERRY. You all right, Dada?

*No answer. Dada is heard to resume his climb.*

He was just resting. [*He goes over and starts picking up the books. Cli-n-ng! There's the front door-bell again. It occurs to him that it's the b-o-o.*] I'll answer it.

CHARLOTTE [*who has risen*]. I'll answer it. It's my own sister Doris, I *know*. You answered the last one.

JERRY. That was a mistake. It's my turn this time by rights.

*Answering the door-bell is evidently a pleasant diversion over which they have squabbled before.*

CHARLOTTE. I'll answer it.

JERRY. You needn't bother.

*Cli-n-ng! An impatient ring that.*

CHARLOTTE AND JERRY [*together*]. Now, listen here—

*They both start for the door. Jerry turns, only trying to argue with her some more, and what does the woman do but slap his face! Then, quick as a flash, she is by him and has opened the door.*

*What do you think of that? Jerry stands there with an expressionless face. In comes Charlotte's sister Doris.*

*Well, now, I'll tell you about Doris. She's nineteen, I guess, and pretty. She's nice and slender and dressed in an astonishingly close burlesque of the current fashions. She's a member of that portion of the middle-class whose girls are just a little bit too proud to work and just a little bit too needy not to. In this city of perhaps a quarter of a million people she knows a few girls who know a few girls who are "social leaders," and through this connection considers herself a member of the local aristocracy. In her mind, morals, and manners she is a fairly capable imitation of the current moving-picture girl, with overtones of some of the year's débutantes whom she sees down-town. Doris knows each débutante's* first name and reputation, and she follows the various affairs of the season as they appear in the society column.

*She walks—walks, not runs—haughtily into the room, her head inclined faintly forward, her hips motionless. She speaks always in a bored voice, raising her eyebrows at the important words of each sentence.*

DORIS. Hello, people.

JERRY [*a little stiffly—he's mad*]. Why, hello, Doris.

*Doris sits down with a faint glance at her chair, as though suspecting its chastity.*

DORIS. Well, I'm engaged again.

*She says this as though realizing that she is the one contact this couple have with the wider and outer world. She assumes with almost audible condescension that their only objective interest is the fascinating spectacle of her career. And so there is nothing personal in her confidences; it is as though she were reporting dispassionately an affair of great national, or, rather, passional importance. And, indeed, Jerry and Charlotte respond magnificently to her initial remark by saying "Honestly?" in incredulous unison and staring at her with almost bated breath.*

DORIS [*laconically*]. Last night.

CHARLOTTE [*reproachfully*]. Oh, Doris! [*Flattering her, you see, by accusing her of being utterly incorrigible.*]

DORIS. I simply couldn't help it. I couldn't stand him any longer, and this new fella I'm engaged to now simply had to know—because he was keeping some girl waiting. I just couldn't stand it. The strain was awful.

CHARLOTTE. Why couldn't you stand it? What was the trouble?

DORIS [*coolly*]. He drank.

*Charlotte, of course, shakes her head in sympathy.*

He'd drink anything. Anything he could get his hands on. He used to drink all these mixtures and then come round to see me.

*A close observer might notice that at this statement Jerry, thinking of his nefarious bargain with the b-o-o, perceptibly winces.*

CHARLOTTE. Oh, that's too bad. He was such a clean-cut fella.

DORIS. Yes, Charlotte, he was clean-cut, but that was all. I couldn't stand it, honestly I couldn't. I never saw such a man, Charlotte. He took the platinum sardine. When they go up in your room and steal your six-dollar-an-ounce perfume, a girl's got to let a man go.

CHARLOTTE. I should say she has. What did he say when you broke it off?

DORIS. He couldn't say anything. He was too pie-eyed. I tied his ring on a string, hung it around his neck and pushed him out the door.

JERRY. Who's the new one?

DORIS. Well, to tell you the truth, I don't know much about him, but I'll tell you what I *do* know from what information I could gather from mutual friends, and so forth. He's not quite so clean-cut as the first one, but he's got lots of other good qualities. He comes from the State of Idaho, from a town named Fish.

JERRY. Fish? F-i-s-h?

DORIS. I think so. It was named after his uncle . . . a Mr. Fish.

JERRY [*wittily*]. They're a lot of Fish out there.

DORIS [*not comprehending*]. Well, these Fishes are very nice. They've been mayor a couple of times and all that sort of thing, if you know what I mean. His father's in business up there now.

JERRY. What business?

DORIS. He's in the funereal-parlor business.

JERRY [*indelicately*]. Oh, undertaker.

DORIS. [*She's sensitive to the word.*] Well, not exactly, but something like that. A funeral parlor is a sort of—oh, a sort of a *good* undertaking place, if you know what I mean. [*And now confidentially.*] As a matter of fact, that's the part of the thing I don't like. You see, we may have to live out in Fish, right over his father's place of business.

JERRY. Why, that's all right. Think how handy it'll be if—
CHARLOTTE. Keep still, Jerry!
JERRY. Is he in the same business as his father?
DORIS. No. At least not now. He was for a while, but the business wasn't very good and now he says he's through with it. His father's bought him an interest in one of the stores.
JERRY. A Fish store, eh?
*The two women look at him harshly.*
CHARLOTTE [*wriggling her shoulders with enjoyment*]. Tell us more about him.
DORIS. Well, he's wonderful looking. And he dresses, well, not loud, you know, but just *well*. And when anybody speaks to him he goes sort of—[*To express what Mr. Fish does when any one speaks to him, Doris turns her profile sharply to the audience, her chin up, her eyes half-closed in an expression of melancholy scorn.*]
CHARLOTTE. I know—like Rudolph Valentine.
DORIS [*witheringly—do you blame her?*]. Valentino.
JERRY. What does it mean when he does that?
DORIS. I don't know, just sort of—sort of passion.
JERRY. Passion!
DORIS. Emotion sort of. He's very emotional. That's one reason I didn't like the last fella I was engaged to. He wasn't very emotional. He was sort of an old cow most of the time. I've got to have somebody emotional. You remember that place in the Sheik where the fella says: "Must I play valet as well as lover?" That's the sort of thing I like.
CHARLOTTE [*darting a look at Jerry*]. I know *just* what you mean.
DORIS. He's not really as tall as I'd like him to be, but he's got a wonderful build and a good complexion. I can't stand anybody without a good complexion—can you? He calls me adorable egg.
JERRY. What does he mean by that?
DORIS [*airily*]. Oh, "egg" is just a name people use nowadays. It's considered sort of the thing.
JERRY [*awed*]. Egg?
CHARLOTTE. When do you expect to get married?

Doris. You never can tell!

*A pause, during which they all sigh as if pondering. Then Doris, with a tremendous effort at justice, switches the conversation away from herself.*

Doris [*patronizingly, condescendingly*]. How's everything going with you two? [*To Jerry.*] Does your father still read the Bible?

Jerry. Well, a lot of the time he just thinks.

Doris. He hasn't had anything to do for the last twenty years but just think, has he?

Jerry [*impressed*]. Just think of the things he's probably thought out.

Doris [*blasphemously*]. That old dumb-bell?

*Charlotte and Jerry are a little shocked.*

How's everything else been going around here?

Jerry. I got analyzed to-day at——

Charlotte [*interrupting*]. The same as ever.

Jerry. I got anal——

Charlotte [*to Jerry*]. I wish you'd be polite enough not to interrupt me.

Jerry [*pathetically*]. I thought you were through.

Charlotte. Well, you've driven what I had to say right out of my head. [*To Doris.*] What do you think he said to-night? He said if he hadn't married me he'd be President of the United States.

*At this Jerry drops his newspaper precipitately, walks in anger to the door, and goes out without speaking.*

You see? Just a display of temper. But it doesn't worry *me*. [*She sighs—the shrew.*] I'm used to it.

*Doris tactfully makes no reply. After a momentary silence she changes the subject.*

Doris. Well, I find I just made an awful mistake.

Charlotte [*eagerly*]. Not keeping both those men for a while? That's what I think.

Doris. No. I mean—do you remember those three dresses I had lengthened?

Charlotte [*breathlessly*]. Yes.

Doris [*tragically*]. I'll never be able to wear them.

CHARLOTTE. Why?

DORIS. There's a picture of Mae Murray in the new Motion Picture Magazine... my dear, half her calf!

CHARLOTTE. Really?

> At this point the door leading to the dining-room opens and Jerry comes in. Looking neither to left nor to right, he marches to his lately vacated place, snatches up half his newspaper, and goes out without speaking. The two women bestow on him a careless glance and continue their discussion.

DORIS. It was just my luck. I wish I'd hemmed them like I thought of doing, instead of cutting them off. That's the way it always is. As soon as I get my hair bobbed, Marilyn Miller begins to let hers grow. And look at mine—[*She removes her hat.*] I can't do a thing with it. [*She replaces her hat.*] Been to the Bijou Theatre?

CHARLOTTE. No, what's there?

> Again Jerry comes in, almost unbearably self-conscious now. The poor man has taken the wrong part of the paper. Silently, with a strained look, he makes the exchange under the intense supervision of four eyes, and starts back to his haven in the dining-room. Then he jumps as Doris speaks to him.

DORIS. Say!

JERRY [*morosely dignified*]. What?

DORIS [*with real interest*]. What makes you think you could be President?

JERRY [*to Charlotte*]. That's right. Make a fool of me in front of all your relations! [*In his excitement he bangs down his paper upon a chair.*]

CHARLOTTE. I haven't said one word—not one single solitary word—have I, Doris?

> Jerry goes out hastily—without his paper!

Did I say one word, Doris? I'll leave it to you. Did I say one single word to bring down all that uproar on my head? To have him *swear* at me?

> Jerry, crimson in the face, comes in, snatches up his forgotten paper, and rushes wildly out again.

He's been nagging at me all evening. He said I kept him from doing everything he wanted to. And you know very well, Doris, he'd have been a postman if it hadn't been for me. He said he wished I was dead.

> *It seems to me it was Charlotte who wished Jerry was dead!*

He said he could get a better wife than me for thirty dollars a week.

DORIS [*fascinated*]. Did he really? Where did he say he could get her?

CHARLOTTE. That's the sort of man *he* is.

DORIS. He'd never be rich if you *gave* him the money. He hasn't got any *push*. I think a man's got to have *push*, don't you? I mean sort of *uh*! [*She gives a little grunt to express indomitable energy, and makes a sharp gesture with her hand.*] I saw in the paper about a fella that didn't have any legs or arms forty years old that was a millionaire.

CHARLOTTE. Maybe if Jerry didn't have any legs or arms he'd do better. How did this fella make it?

DORIS. I forget. Some scheme. He just thought of a scheme. That's the thing, you know—to think of some scheme. Some kind of cold cream or hair—say, I wish somebody'd invent some kind of henna that nobody could tell. Maybe Jerry could.

CHARLOTTE. He hasn't brains enough.

DORIS. Say, I saw a wonderful dog to-day.

CHARLOTTE. What kind of a dog?

DORIS. It was out walking with Mrs. Richard Barton Hammond on Crest Avenue. It was pink.

CHARLOTTE. Pink! I never saw a pink dog.

DORIS. Neither did I before. Gosh, it was cunning.... Well, I got to go. My fiancé is coming over at quarter to nine and we're going down to the theatre.

CHARLOTTE. Why don't you bring him over some time?

DORIS. All right. I'll bring him over after the movies if you'll be up.

> *They walk together to the door. Doris goes out and Charlotte has scarcely shut the door behind her when the bell*

*rings again. Charlotte opens the door and then retreats half-way across the room, with an alarmed expression on her face. A man has come in, with a great gunny-sack slung over his shoulder. It is none other than Mr. Snooks or Snukes, the bootlegger.*

*I wish I could introduce you to the original from whom I have taken Mr. Snooks. He is as villainous-looking a man as could be found in a year's search. He has a weak chin, a broken nose, a squint eye, and a three days' growth of beard. If you can imagine a race-track sport who has fallen in a pool of mud you can get an idea of his attire. His face and hands are incrusted with dirt. He lacks one prominent tooth, lacks it with a vulgar and somehow awful conspicuousness. His most ingratiating smile is a criminal leer, his eyes shift here and there upon the carpet, as he speaks in a villainous whine.*

CHARLOTTE [*uneasily*]. What do you want?

*Mr. Snooks leers and winks broadly, whereat Charlotte bumps back against the bookcase.*

SNOOKS [*hoarsely*]. Tell your husband Sandy Claus is here.

CHARLOTTE [*calling nervously*]. Jerry, here's somebody wants to see you. He says he's—he's Santa Claus.

*In comes Jerry. He sees the situation, but the appearance of the b-o-o evidently shocks him, and a wave of uneasiness passes over him. Nevertheless, he covers up these feelings with a magnificent nonchalance.*

JERRY. Oh, yes. How de do? How are you? Glad to see you.

SNOOKS [*wiggling the bag, which gives out a loud, glassy clank*]. Hear it talking to you, eh?

*Charlotte looks from one to the other of them darkly.*

JERRY. It's all right, Charlit. I'll tend to it. You go up-stairs. You go up-stairs and read that—there's a story in the Saturday Evening Post about a Chinese girl on the Buzzard Islands that—

CHARLOTTE. I know. Who isn't a Chinese girl. Never mind that. I'll stay right here.

*Jerry turns from her with the air of one who has done his best—but now—well, she must take the consequences.*

JERRY [*to Snooks*]. Is this Mr. Snukes? Or Snooks?

SNOOKS. Snooks. Funny name, ain't it? I made it up. I got it off a can of tomatoes. I'm an Irish-Pole by rights. [*Meanwhile he has been emptying the sack of its contents and setting them on the table. First come two one-gallon jars, one full, the other empty. Then a square, unopened one-gallon can. Finally three small bottles and a medicine dropper.*]

CHARLOTTE [*in dawning horror*]. What's that? A still?

SNOOKS [*with a wink at Jerry*]. No, lady, this here's a wine-press.

JERRY. [*He's attempting to conciliate her.*] No, no, Charlit. Listen. This gentleman here is going to make me some gin—very, very cheap.

CHARLOTTE. Some gin!

JERRY. Yes, for cocktails.

CHARLOTTE. For whose cocktails?

JERRY. For you and me.

CHARLOTTE. Do you think *I'd* take one of the poison things?

JERRY [*to Snooks*]. They're not poison, are they?

SNOOKS. Poison! Say, lady, I'd be croaked off long ago if they was. I'd be up wid de angels! This ain't *wood* alcohol. This is *grain* alcohol. [*He holds up the gallon can, on which is the following label*]:

WOOD ALCOHOL!
POISON!

CHARLOTTE [*indignantly*]. Why, it says wood alcohol right on the can!

SNOOKS. Yes, but it ain't. I just use a wood-alcohol can, so in case I get caught. You're allowed to sell wood alcohol, see?

JERRY [*explaining to Charlotte*]. Just in case he gets caught—see?

CHARLOTTE. I think the whole performance is perfectly terrible.

JERRY. No, it isn't. Mr. Snooks has sold this to some of the swellest families in the city—haven't you, Mr. Snooks?

SNOOKS. Sure. You know old man Alec Martin?

JERRY [*glancing at Charlotte, who is stony-eyed*]. Sure. Everybody knows who *they* are.

SNOOKS. I sole 'em a gallon. And John B. Standish? I sole him five gallons and he said it was the best stuff he ever tasted.

JERRY [*to Charlotte*]. See—? The swellest people in town.

SNOOKS. I'd a got here sooner, only I got double crossed to-day.

JERRY. How?

SNOOKS. A fella down-town sold me out to the rev'nue officers. I got stuck for two thousand dollars and four cases Haig and Haig.

JERRY. Gee, that's too bad!

SNOOKS. Aw, you never know who's straight in this game. They'll double cross you in a minute.

JERRY. Who sold you out?

SNOOKS. A fella. What do you suppose he got for it?

JERRY. What?

SNOOKS. Ten dollars. What do you know about a fella that'd sell a guy out for ten dollars? I just went right up to him and said: "Why, you Ga—"

JERRY [*nervously*]. Say, don't tell us!

SNOOKS. Well, I told him where he got off at, anyways. And then I plastered him one. An' the rev'nue officers jus' stood there and laughed. My brother 'n I are goin' 'round an' beat him up again tomorra.

JERRY [*righteously*]. He certainly deserved it.

*A pause.*

SNOOKS [*after a moment's brooding*]. Well, I'll fix this up for you now.

CHARLOTTE [*stiffly*]. How much is it?

SNOOKS. This? Sixteen a gallon.

JERRY [*eagerly*]. See, that makes two gallons of the stuff, Charlotte, and that's eight quarts, and eight quarts of the stuff makes sixteen quarts of cocktails. That's enough to last us—oh, three years anyhow. Just think how nice it'll be if anybody comes in. Just say: "Like a little cocktail?" "Sure." "All right." [*He makes a noise to express orange squeezing.*] Oranges! [*A noise to express the cracking of ice.*] Ice! [*A noise to express the sound of a shaker.*] Shaker! [*He pours the imaginary compound into three imaginary glasses. Then he drinks off one of the imaginary glasses and pats his stomach.*]

CHARLOTTE [*contemptuously*]. Well, I think you're a little crazy, if you ask me.

SNOOKS [*taking off his hat and coat*]. You got a big bowl?

CHARLOTTE. No. Why didn't you bring your own bowl?

JERRY [*uncertainly*]. There's a nice big bowl in the kitchen.

CHARLOTTE. All right. Go on and spoil all the kitchen things.

JERRY. I'll wash it afterward.

CHARLOTTE. Wash it? [*She laughs contemptuously, implying that washing will do it no good then. Jerry, nevertheless, goes for the bowl. He feels pretty guilty by this time, but he's going through with it now, even though he may never hear the last of it.*]

SNOOKS [*hollering after him*]. Get a corkscrew, too. [*He holds up the tin can to Charlotte.*] Grain alcohol. [*Charlotte's lips curl in answer. He holds up a small bottle.*] Spirits of Jupiter. One drop of this will smell up a whole house for a week. [*He holds up a second bottle.*] Oila Aniseed. Give it a flavor. Take the arsenic out. [*He holds up a third bottle.*] Oila Coreander.

CHARLOTTE [*sardonically*]. Wouldn't you like me to look in the medicine-chest and see if there's something there you could use? Maybe you need some iodine. Or some of Dada's ankle-strengthener.

*Jerry comes in, laden.*

JERRY. Here's the bowl and the corkscrew.

CHARLOTTE. You forgot the salt and pepper.
> *Amid great pounding the bootlegger breaks the corkscrew on the tin can. His exertions send him into a fit of coughing.*

You'll have to stop coughing. You'll wake the people next door.

SNOOKS. You got a hairpin, lady?

CHARLOTTE. No.

SNOOKS. Or a scissors?

CHARLOTTE. No.

SNOOKS. Say, what kind of a house is this? [*He finally manages to open the can.*]

SNOOKS. [*With some pride.*] Grain alcohol. Costs me $6.00 a gallon. [*To Charlotte.*] Smell it.

> *She retreats from it hastily.*

CHARLOTTE. I can smell *some*thing horrible.

SNOOKS. That's the spirits of Jupiter. I haven't opened it yet. It rots a cork in ten days. [*He fills the bowl with water from one jar.*]

JERRY [*anxiously*]. Hadn't you better measure it?

SNOOKS. I got my eye trained.

CHARLOTTE. What's that—arsenic?

SNOOKS. Distilled water, lady. If you use regular water it gets cloudy. You want it clear. [*He pours in alcohol from the can.*] Got a spoon? . . . Well, never mind. [*He rolls up his sleeve and undoubtedly intends to plunge his whole arm into the mixture.*]

JERRY [*hastily*]. Here! Wait a minute. No use—no use getting your hand wet. I'll get you a spoon. [*He goes after it.*]

CHARLOTTE [*sarcastically*]. Get one of the best silver ones.

SNOOKS. Naw. Any kind'll do.

> *Jerry returns with one of the best silver spoons, which he hands to Mr. Snooks.*

CHARLOTTE. I might have known you would—you fool!

> *Mr. Snooks stirs the mixture—the spoon turns rust-colored—Charlotte gives a little cry.*

SNOOKS. It won't hurt it, lady. Just leave it out in the sun for an hour. Now the spirits of Jupiter. [*He fills the medicine dropper from a small bottle and lets a slow, interminable procession of drops fall into the bowl. Jerry watches intently and with gathering anxiety. At about the fourteenth drop he starts every time one falls. Finally Mr. Snooks ceases.]*

JERRY. How many did you count?

SNOOKS. Sixteen.

JERRY. I counted eighteen.

SNOOKS. Well, a drop or so won't make no difference. Now you got a funnel?

JERRY. I'll get one. [*He goes for it.*]

SNOOKS. Good stuff, lady. This is as good as what you used to buy for the real thing.

*Charlotte does not deign to answer.*

You needn't worry about that spoon. If that spoon had a been the real thing it w'na done like that. You can try out all your stuff that way. A lot of stuff is sold for silver nowadays that ain't at all.

*Jerry returns with the funnel, and Mr. Snooks pours the contents of the bowl into the two glass jars.*

SNOOKS [*holding up one jar admiringly*]. The real thing.

CHARLOTTE. It's cloudy.

SNOOKS [*reproachfully*]. Cloudy? You call that cloudy? That isn't cloudy. Why, it's just as clear—

*He holds it up and pretends to look through it. This is unquestionably a mere gesture, for the mixture is heavily opaque and not to be pierced by the human eye.*

CHARLOTTE [*disregarding him and turning scornfully to Jerry*]. I wouldn't drink it if it was the last liquor in the world.

SNOOKS. Lady, if this was the last liquor in the world it wouldn't be for sale.

JERRY [*doubtfully*]. It does look a little—cloudy.

SNOOKS. No-o-o—! Why you can see right through it. [*He fills a glass and drinks it off.*] Why, it just needs to be filtered. That's just nervous matter.

CHARLOTTE AND JERRY [*together*]. Nervous matter?

JERRY. When did we put that in?

SNOOKS. We didn't put it in. It's just a deposit. Sure, that's just nervous matter. Any chemis' will tell you.

CHARLOTTE [*sardonically*]. Ha-ha! "Nervous matter." There's no such thing.

SNOOKS. Sure! That's just nervous matter. [*He fills the glass and hands it to her.*] Try it!

CHARLOTTE. Ugh!

> *As he comes near she leans away from him in horror. Snooks offers the glass to Jerry.*

If you drink any of that stuff they'll have to analyze you all over again.

> *But Jerry drinks it.*

CHARLOTTE. I can't stand this. When your—when *he's* gone I'll thank you to open the windows. [*She goes out and upstairs.*]

SNOOKS [*with a cynical laugh*]. Your old lady's a little sore on you, eh?

JERRY [*bravely*]. No. She doesn't care what I do.

SNOOKS. You ought to give her a bat in the eye now and then. That'd fix her.

JERRY [*shocked*]. Oh, no; you oughtn't to talk that way.

SNOOKS. Well, if you like 'em to step around.... Sixteen bucks, please.

> *Jerry searches his pockets.*

JERRY [*counting*]. —thirteen—fourteen—let's see. I can borrow the ice-man's money if I can find where—Just wait a minute, Mr. Snooks.

> *He goes out to the pantry. Almost immediately there are steps upon the stairs, and in a moment Dada, resplendent in a flowing white nightshirt, trembles into Mr. Snooks's vision. For a moment Mr. Snooks is startled.*

DADA [*blinking*]. I thought I smelled something burning.

SNOOKS. I ain't smelled nothin', pop.

DADA. How do you do, sir. You'll excuse my costume. I was awake and it occurred to me that the house was on fire. I am Mr. Frost's father.

SNOOKS. I'm his bootlegger.

DADA. The—?

SNOOKS. His bootlegger.

DADA [*enthusiastically*]. You're my son's employer?
*They shake hands.*

DADA. Excuse my costume. I was awake, and I thought I smelled something burning.

SNOOKS [*decisively*]. You're kiddin' yourself.

DADA. Perhaps I was wrong. My sense of smell is not as exact as it was. My son Jerry is a fine boy. He's my only son by my second wife, Mr.—? The—? [*He is evidently under the impression that Snooks has supplied the name and that he has missed it.*] I'm glad to meet his employer. I always say I'm a descendant of Jack Frost. We used to have a joke when I was young. We used to say that the first Frosts came to this state in the beginning of winter. Ha-ha-ha! [*He is convinced that he is giving Jerry a boost with his employer.*]

SNOOKS [*bored*]. Ain't it past your bedtime, pop?

DADA. Do you see? "Frosts" and "frosts." We used to laugh at that joke a great deal.

SNOOKS. Anybody would.

DADA. "Frosts," you see. We're not rich, but I always say that it's easier for a camel to get through a needle's eye than for a rich man to get to heaven.

SNOOKS. That's the way I always felt.

DADA. Well, I think I'll turn in. My sense of smell deceived me. No harm done. [*He laughs.*] Good night, Mr.—?

SNOOKS [*humorously*]. Good night, pop. Sleep tight. Don't let the bedbugs bite.

DADA [*starting away*]. I hope you'll excuse my costume. [*He goes upstairs. Jerry returns from the pantry just in time to hear his voice.*]

JERRY. Who was that? Dada?

SNOOKS. He thought he was on fire.

JERRY [*unaware of the nightshirt*]. That's my father. He's a great authority on—oh, on the Bible and a whole lot of other things. He's been doing nothing for twenty years but thinking out a lot of things—here's the money. [*Jerry gives him sixteen bucks.*]

SNOOKS. Thanks. Well, I guess you're all fixed. Drink a couple of these and then you'll know what to say to your wife when she gets fresh.

CHARLOTTE [*from upstairs*]. Shut the door! I can smell that way up here!

*Jerry hastily shuts the door leading upstairs.*

SNOOKS. Like any whiskey?

JERRY. I don't believe so.

SNOOKS. Or some cream de menthy?

JERRY. No, I don't believe so.

SNOOKS. How about some French vermuth?

JERRY. I don't think I'll take anything else now.

SNOOKS. Just try a drink of this.

JERRY. I did.

SNOOKS. Try another.

*Jerry tries another.*

JERRY. Not bad. Strong.

SNOOKS. Sure it's strong. Knock you over. Hard to get now. They gyp you every time. The country's goin' to the dogs. Most of these bootleggers, you can't trust 'em two feet away. It's awful. They don't seem to have no conscience.

JERRY [*warming*]. Have you ever been analyzed, Mr. Snooks?

SNOOKS. Me? No, I never been arrested by the regular police.

JERRY. I mean when they ask you questions.

SNOOKS. Sure, I know. Thumb-prints—all that stuff.

*Jerry takes another drink.*

JERRY. You ought to want to rise in the world.

SNOOKS. How do you know I oughta.

JERRY. Why—why, everybody ought to. It says so.

SNOOKS. What says so.

JERRY [*with a burst of inspiration*]. The Bible. It's one of the commandments.

SNOOKS. I never could get through that book.

JERRY. Won't you sit down?

SNOOKS. No, I got to hustle along in a minute.

JERRY. Say, do you mind if I ask you a personal question?

SNOOKS. Not at all. Shoot!

JERRY. Did you ever—did you ever have any ambition to be President?
SNOOKS. Sure. Once.
JERRY [*ponderously*]. You did, eh?
SNOOKS. Once. I guess bootleggin's just as good, though. More money in it.
JERRY [*weightily*]. Yes, that's true.
SNOOKS. Well, I got to hustle along now. I got to take my old woman to church.
JERRY. Oh. Yes.
SNOOKS. Well, so long. You got my address in case you go dry.
*They both smile genially at this pleasantry.*
JERRY [*opening the door*]. All right. I'll remember.
*Snooks goes out. Jerry hesitates—then he opens the door to the upstairs.*
JERRY. Oh, Char-lit!
CHARLOTTE [*crossly*]. Please keep that door shut. That smell comes right up here. It'll start my hay-fever.
JERRY [*genially*]. Well, I just wanted to ask you if you'll take one little cocktail with me.
CHARLOTTE. *No!* How many times do I have to tell you?
JERRY [*crestfallen*]. Well, you don't need to be so disagreeable about it.

*He receives no answer. He would like to talk some more, but he shuts the door and returns to the table. Picking up one of the jars, he regards its opaqueness with a quizzical eye. But it is his and quite evidently it seems to him good. He looks curiously at the three little bottles, smells one of them curiously and hastily replaces the cork. He hesitates. Then he repairs to the dining-room, singing: "Everybody is there!"—and returns immediately with an orange, a knife, and another glass. He cuts the orange, squeezes half of it into a glass, wipes his hands on the fringe of the tablecloth, and adds some of his liquor. He drinks it slowly—he waits. He prepares another potation with the other half of the orange.*

*No! He does not choke, make horrible faces, nor feel his throat as it goes down. Nor does he stagger. His elation is evinced only by the vague confusion with which he mislays knife, oranges, and glasses.*

*Impelled by the gregarious instinct of mankind, he again repairs to the door that leads upstairs, and opens it.*

JERRY [*calling*]. Say, Char-*lit!* The convention must be over. I wonder who was nominated.

CHARLOTTE. I asked you to shut that door.

*But the impulse to express himself, to fuse his new elation into the common good, is irresistible. He goes to the telephone and picks up the receiver.*

JERRY. Hello. . . . Hello, hello. Say! I wonder'f you could tell me who was nominated for President. . . . All right, give me Information. . . . Information, I wonder if you could tell me who was nominated for President. . . . Why not? . . . Well, that's information, isn't it? . . . It doesn't matter what *kind* of information it is. It's information, isn't it? Isn't it? It's information, isn't it? . . . Say, what's your hurry? [*He bobs the receiver up and down.*] Hello, give me Long Distance again. . . . Hello, is this Information? . . . This is *mis*information, eh? Ha-ha! Did you hear that? *Mis*information. . . . I asked for Information. . . . Well, you'll do, Long Distance. . . . Long Distance—how far away are you? A long distance! Ha-ha! . . . Hello . . . Hello!

*She has evidently rung off. Jerry does likewise.*

JERRY [*sarcastically*]. Wonderful telephone service! [*He goes quickly back to the 'phone and picks up the receiver.*] Rottenest telephone service I ever saw! [*He slams up and returns to his drink.*]

*There is a call outside, "Yoo-hoo!" and immediately afterward Doris opens the front door and comes in, followed by Joseph Fish, a red-headed, insipid young man of about twenty-four. Fish is dressed in a ready-made suit with a high belt at the back, and his pockets slant at a rakish angle. He is the product of a small-town high-school and a one-year business course at a state university.*

*Doris has him firmly by the arm. She leads him up to Jerry, who sets down his glass and blinks at them.*

Doris. Gosh! This room smells like a brewery. [*She notices the jars and the other débris of Jerry's domestic orgy.*] What on earth have you been doing? Brewing whiskey?

Jerry [*attempting a dignified nonchalance*]. Making cocktails.

Doris [*with a long whistle*]. What does Charlotte say?

Jerry [*with dignity*]. Charlit is up-stairs.

Doris. Well, I want you to meet my fiancé, Mr. Fish. Mr. Fish, this is my brother-in-law, Mr. Frost.

Jerry. Pleased to meet you, Mr. Fish.

Fish. How de do. [*He laughs politely.*]

Jerry [*horribly*]. Is this the undertaker?

Doris [*tartly*]. You must be tight.

Jerry [*to Fish*]. Have a little drink?

Doris. He doesn't use it.

Fish. Thanks. I don't use it. [*Again he laughs politely.*]

Jerry [*with a very roguish expression*]. Do you know Ida?

Fish. Ida who?

Jerry. Idaho. [*He laughs uproariously at his own wit.*] That's a joke I heard to-day. I thought I'd tell it to you because you're from Idaho.

Fish [*resentfully*]. Gosh, that's a rotten joke.

Jerry [*high-hatting him*]. Well, Idaho's a rotten state. I wouldn't come from that state.

Doris [*icily*]. Maybe they'd feel the same way about you. I'm going up and see Charlotte. I wish you'd entertain Mr. Fish politely for a minute.

> *Doris goes upstairs. The two men sit down. Fish is somewhat embarrassed.*

Jerry [*with a wink*]. Now she's gone, better have a little drink.

Fish. No, thanks. I don't use it anymore. I used to use it a good deal out in Idaho, and then I quit.

> *A faint, almost imperceptible noise, as of a crowd far away, begins outside. Neither of the men seems to notice it, however.*

Jerry. Get good liquor up there?

Fish. Well, around the shop we used to drink embalming fluid, but it got so it didn't agree with me.

JERRY [*focussing his eyes upon Fish, with some difficulty*]. I shouldn't think it would.

FISH. It's all right for some fellas, but it doesn't agree with me at all.

JERRY [*suddenly*]. How old are you?

FISH. Me? Twenty-five.

JERRY. Did you ever—did you ever have any ambition to be President?

FISH. President?

JERRY. Yes.

FISH. Of a company?

JERRY. No. Of the United States.

FISH [*scornfully*]. No-o-o-o!

JERRY [*almost pleadingly*]. Never did, eh?

FISH. Never.

JERRY. Tha's funny. Did you ever want to be a postman?

FISH [*scornfully*]. No-o-o-o! ... The thing to be is to be a Senator.

JERRY. Is that so?

FISH. Sure. I'm goin' to be one. Say! There's where you get the *real* graft.

> *Jerry's eyes close sleepily and then start open.*

JERRY [*attentively*]. Do you hear a noise?

FISH [*after listening for a moment*]. I don't hear a sound.

JERRY [*puzzled*]. That's funny. I hear a noise.

FISH [*scornfully*]. I guess you're seeing things.

> *Another pause.*

JERRY. And you say you never wanted to be President?

FISH. Na-ah!

> *The noise outside has now increased, come nearer, swollen to the dimensions of a roar. Presently it is almost under the windows. Fish apparently does not hear it, but Jerry knits his hairless brows and rises to his feet. He goes to the window and throws it open. A mighty cheer goes up and there is the beating of a bass drum.*

JERRY. Good gosh!

> *Cli-in-ng! Cli-in-ng! Cli-in-ng! The door-bell! Then the door swings open, and a dozen men rush into the room. In the lead is Mr. Jones, a politician.*

MR. JONES [*approaching Jerry*]. Is this Mr. Jeremiah Frost?

JERRY [*with signs of fright*]. Yes.

MR. JONES. I'm Mr. Jones, the well-known politician. I am delegated to inform you that on the first ballot you were unanimously given the Republican nomination for President.

> *Wild cheers from inside and out, and renewed beating of the bass drum. Jerry shakes Mr. Jones's hand, but Fish, sitting in silence, takes no heed of the proceeding—apparently does not see or hear what is going on.*

JERRY [*to Mr. Jones*]. My golly! I thought you were a revenue officer.

> *Amid a still louder burst of cheering Jerry is elevated to the shoulders of the crowd, and borne enthusiastically out the door as*

THE CURTAIN FALLS

## Act II

*Any one who felt that the First Act was perhaps a little vulgar, will be glad to learn that we're now on the lawn of the White House. Indeed, a corner of the Executive Mansion projects magnificently into sight, and steps lead up to the imposing swinging doors of a "Family Entrance." From the window of the President's office a flag flutters, and the awning displays this legend:*

THE WHITE HOUSE
JERRY FROST, PRES.

*And if you look hard enough at the office window you can see the President himself sitting at his desk inside.*

*The lawn, bounded by a white brick wall, is no less attractive. Not only are there white vines and flowers, a beautiful white tree, and a white table and chairs, but, also, a large sign over the gate, which bears the President's name pricked out in electric bulbs.*

*Two white kittens are strolling along the wall, enjoying the ten-o'clock sunshine. A blond parrot swings in a cage over the table, and one of the chairs is at present occupied by a white fox-terrier puppy about the size of your hand.*

*That's right. "Isn't it darling!" We'll let you watch it for a moment before we move into the Whirl of Public Affairs.*

*Look! Here comes somebody out. It's Mr. Jones, the well-known politician, now secretary to President Frost. He has a white broom in his hands, and, after delighting the puppy with an absolutely white bone, he begins to sweep off the White House steps. At this point the gate swings open and Charlotte Frost comes in. As befits the First Lady of the Land, she is elaborately dressed—in the height of many fashions. She's evidently been shopping—her arms are full of packages—but she has nevertheless seen fit to array herself in a gorgeous evening dress, with an interminable train. From her wide picture hat a plume dangles almost to the ground.*

*Mr. Jones politely relieves her of her bundles.*

CHARLOTTE [*abruptly*]. Good morning, Mr. Jones. Has everything gone to pieces?

*Mr. Jones looks her over in some surprise.*

JONES [*apologetically*]. Well, perhaps the petticoat—

CHARLOTTE [*a little stiffly*]. I didn't mention myself, I don't think, Mr. Jones. I meant all my husband's public affairs.

JONES. He's been in his office all morning, Mrs. Frost. There are a lot of people waiting to see him.

CHARLOTTE. [*She's relieved.*] I heard them calling an extra, and I thought maybe everything had gone to pieces.

JONES. No, Mrs. Frost, the President hasn't made any bad mistake for some time now. Of course, a lot of people objected when he appointed his father Secretary of the Treasury; his father's being so old—

CHARLOTTE. Well, I've had to stand for his family all my life—so I guess the country can. [*Confidentially.*]

JONES [*a little embarrassed*]. I see you've been shopping.

CHARLOTTE. I've been buying some things for my sister's wedding reception this afternoon.

> *The window of President Frost's office opens abruptly. A white cigar emerges—followed by Jerry's hairless eyebrows—passionately knit.*

JERRY. All right. Go on and yell—and then when I make some awful mistake and the country goes to pieces, blame it on me!

CHARLOTTE [*very patiently*]. Nagging me again. Picking on me. Pick—pick—pick! All day!

JERRY. Gosh, you can be disagreeable, Charlit!

CHARLOTTE. Pick—pick—pick!

JERRY [*confused*]. Pick?

CHARLOTTE [*sharply*]. Pick!

> *Jerry jams down his window.*
>
> *Meanwhile from the window above has emerged a hand holding a mirror. The hand is presently followed by a head with the hair slicked back damply. Doris, sister-in-law to the President, is seeking more light for her afternoon toilet.*

DORIS [*disapprovingly*]. I can hear you two washing your clothes in public all over the lawn.

CHARLOTTE. He keeps nagging at me.

*Doris begins to apply a white lotion to her face. She daubs it at a freckle on her nose, and gazes passionately at the resultant white splotch.*

DORIS [*abstractedly*]. I should think you'd get so you could stand him in public, anyways.

CHARLOTTE. He makes me madder in public than anywhere else.

*She gathers her bundles and goes angrily into the White House. Doris glances down at Mr. Jones, and, deciding hastily that she is too publicly placid, withdraws her person from sight.*

*Jones picks up his broom and is about to go inside when a uniformed chauffeur opens the gate and announces:* "The Honorable Joseph Fish, Senator from Idaho."

*And now here's Joseph Fish, in an enormous frock-coat and a tall silk hat, radiating an air of appalling prosperity.*

FISH. Good morning, Mr. Jones. Is my fiancée around?

JONES. I believe she's in her boudoir, Senator Fish. How is everything down at the capital?

FISH [*gloomily*]. Awful! I'm in a terrible position, Mr. Jones—and this was to have been my wedding reception day. Listen to this. [*He takes a telegram from his pocket.*] "Senator Joseph Fish, Washington, D.C. Present the State of Idaho's compliments to President Frost and tell him that the people of Idaho demand his immediate resignation."

JONES. This is terrible!

FISH. It's because he made his father Secretary of the Treasury.

JONES. This will be depressing news to the President.

FISH. But think of *me!* This was to have been my wedding reception day. What will Doris say when she hears about this. I've got to ask her own brother-in-law to—to move out of his home?

JONES. Have a cocktail.

*He takes a shaker and glasses from behind a porch pillar and pours out two drinks.*

JONES. I saw this coming. But I'll tell you now, Senator Fish, the President won't resign.

FISH. Then it'll be my duty to have him impeached.

JONES. Shall I call the President now?

FISH. Let's wait until eleven o'clock. Give me one more hour of happiness. [*He raises his eyes pathetically to the upper window.*] Doris—oh Doris!

> *Doris, now fully dressed and under the influence of cosmetics, comes out onto the lawn. Mr. Jones, picking up the broom and the puppy, goes into the White House.*

FISH [*jealously*]. Where were you all day yesterday?

DORIS [*languidly*]. An old beau of mine came to see me and kept hanging around.

FISH [*in wild alarm*]. Good God! What'd he say?

DORIS. He said I was stuck up because my brother-in-law was President, and I said: "Well, what if I am? I'd hate to say what your brother-in-law is."

FISH [*fascinated*]. What is he?

DORIS. He owns a garbage disposal service.

FISH [*even more fascinated*]. Is that right? Can you notice it on his brother-in-law?

DORIS. Something awful. I wouldn't of let him come in the house. Imagine if somebody came in to see you and said: "Sniff. Sniff. Who's been sitting on these chairs?" And you said: "Oh, just my brother-in-law, the garbage disposal man."

FISH. Doris—Doris, an awful thing has occurred—

DORIS [*looking out the gate*]. Here comes Dada. Say, he must be going on to between eighty and ninety years old, if not older.

FISH [*gloomily*]. Why did your brother-in-law have to go and make him Secretary of the Treasury? He might as well have gone to an old men's home and said: "See here, I want to get eight old dumb-bells for my cabinet."

DORIS. Oh, Jerry does everything all wrong. You see, he thought his father had read a lot of books—the Bible and the Encyclopædia and the Dictionary and all.

> *In totters Dada. Prosperity has spruced him up, but not to any alarming extent. The hair on his face is not under cultivation. His small, watery eyes gleam dully in their ragged ovals. His mouth laps faintly at all times, like a lake with tides mildly agitated by the moon.*

FISH. Good morning, Mr. Frost.
DADA [*dimly*]. Hm.
> *He is under the impression that he has made an adequate response.*

DORIS [*tolerantly*]. Dada, kindly meet my fiancé—Senator Fish from Idaho.
DADA [*expansively*]. Young man, how do you do? I feel very well. You wouldn't think I was eighty-eight years old, would you?
FISH [*politely*]. I should say not.
DORIS. You'd think he was two hundred.
DADA [*who missed this*]. Yeah. [*A long pause.*] We used to have a joke when I was young—we used to say the first Frosts came to this country in the beginning of winter.
DORIS. Funny as a crutch.
DADA [*to Fish*]. Do you ever read the Scriptures?
FISH. Sometimes.
DADA. I'm the Secretary of the Treasury, you know. My son made me the Secretary of the Treasury. He's the President. He was my only boy by my second wife.
DORIS. The old dumb-bell!
DADA. I was born in 1834, under the presidency of Andrew Jackson. I was twenty-seven years old when the war broke out.
DORIS [*sarcastically*]. Do you mean the Revolutionary War?
DADA [*witheringly*]. The Revolutionary War was in 1776.
DORIS. Tell me something I don't know.
DADA. When you grow older you'll find there are a lot of things you don't know. [*To Fish.*] Do you know my son Jerry?
DORIS [*utterly disgusted*]. Oh, gosh!
FISH. I met your son before he was elected President and I've seen him a lot of times since then, on account of being Senator from Idaho and all, and on account of Doris. You see, we're going to have our wedding reception this afternoon—
> *In the middle of this speech Dada's mind has begun to wander. He utters a vague "Hm!" and moves off, paying no further attention, and passing through the swinging doors into the White House.*

FISH [*impressed in spite of himself by Dada's great age*]. He's probably had a lot of experience, that old bird. He was alive before you were born.

DORIS. So were a lot of other old nuts. Come on—let's go hire the music for our wedding reception.

FISH [*remembering something with a start*]. Doris—Doris, would you have a wedding reception with me if you knew—if you knew the disagreeable duty—

DORIS. Knew what?

FISH. Nothing. I'm going to be happy, anyways [*he looks at his watch*]—for almost an hour.

*They go out through the garden gate.*

*And now President Jerry Frost himself is seen to leave his window and in a minute he emerges from the Executive Mansion. He wears a loose-fitting white flannel frock coat, and a tall white stovepipe hat. His heavy gold watch-chain would anchor a small yacht, and he carries a white stick, ringed with a gold band.*

*After rubbing his back sensuously against a porch pillar, he walks with caution across the lawn and his hand is on the gate-latch when he is hailed from the porch by Mr. Jones.*

JONES. Mr. President, where are you going?

JERRY [*uneasily*]. I thought I'd go down and get a cigar.

JONES [*cynically*]. It doesn't look well for you to play dice for cigars, sir.

*Jerry sits down wearily and puts his hat on the table.*

JONES. I'm sorry to say there's trouble in the air, Mr. President. It's what we might refer to as the Idaho matter.

JERRY. The Idaho matter?

JONES. Senator Fish has received orders from Idaho to demand your resignation at eleven o'clock this morning.

JERRY. I never liked that bunch of people they got out there in Idaho.

JONES. Well, I just thought I'd tell you—so you could think about it.

JERRY [*hopefully*]. Maybe I'll get some idea how to fix it up. I'm a very resourceful man. I always think of something.

JONES. Mr. President, would you—would you mind telling me how you got your start?

JERRY [*carelessly*]. Oh, I got analyzed one day, and they just found I was sort of a good man and would just be wasting my time as a railroad clerk.

JONES. So you forged ahead?

JERRY. Sure. I just made up my mind to be President, and then I went ahead and did it. I've always been a very ambitious sort of—sort of domineerer.

*Jones sighs and takes several letters from his pocket.*

JONES. The morning mail.

JERRY [*looking at the first letter*]. This one's an ad, I'll bet. [*He opens it.*] "Expert mechanics, chauffeurs, plumbers earn big money. We fit you in twelve lessons." [*He looks up.*] I wonder if there's anything personal in that. If there is it's a low sort of joke.

JONES [*soothingly*]. Oh, I don't think there is.

JERRY [*offended*]. Anybody that'd play a joke like that on a person that has all the responsibility of being President, and then to have somebody play a low, mean joke on him like that!

JONES. I'll write them a disagreeable letter.

JERRY. All right. But make it sort of careless, as if it didn't matter to me.

JONES. I can begin the letter "Damn Sirs" instead of "Dear Sirs."

JERRY. Sure, that's the idea. And put something like that in the ending, too.

JONES. "Yours insincerely," or something like that... Now there's a few people waiting in here to see you, sir. [*He takes out a list.*] First, there's somebody that's been ordered to be hung.

JERRY. What about him?

JONES. I think he wants to arrange it some way so he won't be hung. Then there's a man that's got a scheme for changing everybody in the United States green.

JERRY [*puzzled*]. Green?

JONES. That's what he says.

JERRY. Why green?

JONES. He didn't say. I told him not to wait. And there's the Ambassador from Abyssinia. He says that one of our sailors on leave in Abyssinia threw the king's cousin down a flight of thirty-nine steps.

JERRY [*after a pause*]. What do you think I ought to do about that?

JONES. Well, I think you ought to—well, send flowers or something, to sort of recognize that the thing had happened.

JERRY [*somewhat awed*]. Is the king's cousin sore?

JONES. Well, naturally he—

JERRY. I don't mean sore that way. I mean did he—did he take it hard? Did he think there was any ill feeling from the United States Government in the sailor's—action?

JONES. Why, I suppose you might say yes.

JERRY. Well, you tell him that the sailor had no instructions to do any such thing. Demand the sailor's resignation.

JONES. And Major-General Pushing has been waiting to see you for some time. Shall I tell him to come out here?

JERRY. All right.

> *Jones goes into the White House and returns, announcing: "Major-General Pushing, U. S. A."*
>
> *Out marches General Pushing. He is accompanied at three paces by a fifer and drummer, who play a spirited march. When the General reaches the President's table the trio halt, the fife and drum cease playing, and the General salutes.*
>
> *The General is a small fat man with a fierce gray mustache. His chest and back are fairly obliterated with medals, and he is wearing one of those great shakos peculiar to drum-majors.*

JERRY. Good morning, General Pushing. Did they keep you waiting?

GENERAL PUSHING [*fiercely*]. That's all right. We've been marking time—it's good for some of the muscles.

JERRY. How's the army?

GENERAL PUSHING. Very well, Mr. President. Several of the privates have complained of headaches. [*He clears his throat portentously.*] I've called on you to say I'm afraid we've got to have war. I held a conference last night with two others of our best generals. We discussed the matter thoroughly, and then we took a vote. Three to nothing in favor of war.

JERRY [*alarmed*]. Look at here, General Pushing, I've got a lot of things on my hands now, and the last thing I want to have is a war.

GENERAL PUSHING. I knew things weren't going very well with you, Mr. President. In fact, I've always thought that what this country needs is a military man at the head of it. The people are restless and excited. The best thing to keep their minds occupied is a good war. It will leave the country weak and shaken—but docile, Mr. President, docile. Besides—we voted on it, and there you are.

JERRY. Who is it against?

GENERAL PUSHING. That we have not decided. We're going to take up the details to-night. It depends on—just how much money there is in the Treasury. Would you mind calling up your—*father*—[*the General gives this word an ironic accentuation*]—and finding out?

> *Jerry takes up the white telephone from the table. Jones meanwhile has produced the shaker and glasses. He pours a cocktail for every one—even for the fifer and drummer.*

JERRY [*at the 'phone*]. Connect me with the Treasury Department, please.... Is this the Treasury?... This is President Frost.... Oh, I'm very well, thanks. No, it's better. Much better. The dentist says he doesn't think I'll have to have it out now.... Say, what I called you up about is to find how much money there is in the Treasury.... Oh, I see.... Oh, I see. Thanks. [*He hangs up the receiver.*]

JERRY [*worried*]. General Pushing, things seem to be a little confused over at the Treasury. Dada—the Secretary of the Treasury isn't there right now—and they say nobody else knows much about it.

GENERAL PUSHING [*disapprovingly*]. Hm! I could put you on a nice war pretty cheap. I could manage a battle or so for almost nothing. [*With rising impatience.*] But a good President ought to be able to tell just how much we could afford.

JERRY [*chastened*]. I'll find out from Dada.

GENERAL PUSHING [*meaningly*]. Being President is a sacred trust, you know, Mr. Frost.

JERRY. Well, I know it's a sacred trust, don't I?

GENERAL PUSHING [*sternly*]. Are you proud of it?

JERRY [*utterly crestfallen*]. Of course, I'm proud of it. Don't I look proud? I'm proud as a pecan. [*Resentfully.*] What do you know about it, anyways? You're nothing but a common soldier—I mean a common general.

GENERAL PUSHING [*pityingly*]. I came here to help you, Mr. Frost. [*With warning emphasis.*] Perhaps you are aware that the sovereign State of Idaho is about to ask your resignation.

JERRY [*now thoroughly resentful*]. Look at here, suppose you be the President for a while, if you know so much about it.

GENERAL PUSHING [*complacently*]. I've often thought that what this country needs is a military man at the head of it.

JERRY. All right, then, you just take off that hat and coat!

> *Jerry takes of his own coat. Jones rushes forward in alarm.*

JONES. If there's going to be a fight hadn't we all better go into the billiard-room?

JERRY [*insistently to General Pushing*]. Take off that hat and coat!

GENERAL PUSHING [*aghast*]. But, Mr. President—

JERRY. Listen here—if I'm the President you do what I say.

> *General Pushing obediently removes his sword and takes off his hat and coat. He assumes a crouching posture and, putting up his fists, begins to dance menacingly around Jerry.*
>
> *But, instead of squaring off, Jerry gets quickly into the General's hat and coat and buckles on the sword.*

JERRY. All right, since you know so much about being President, you put on my hat and coat and try it for a while.

*The General, greatly taken aback, looks from Jerry to Jerry's coat, with startled eyes. Jerry swaggers up and down the lawn, brandishing the sword. Then his eyes fall with distaste upon the General's shirtsleeves.*

JERRY. Well, what are you moping around for?

GENERAL PUSHING [*plaintively*]. Come on, Mr. President, be reasonable. Give me that coat and hat. Nobody appreciates a good joke any more than I do, but—

JERRY [*emphatically*]. No, I *won't* give them to you. I'm a general, and I'm going to war. You can stay around here. [*Sarcastically, to Mr. Jones.*] He'll straighten everything out, Mr. Jones.

GENERAL PUSHING [*pleadingly*]. Mr. President, I've waited for this war for forty years. You wouldn't take away my coat and hat like that, just as we've got it almost ready.

JERRY [*pointing to the shirtsleeves*]. That's a nice costume to be hanging around the White House in.

GENERAL PUSHING [*brokenly*]. I can't help it, can I? Who took my coat and hat, anyhow?

JERRY. If you don't like it you can get out.

GENERAL PUSHING [*sarcastically*]. Yes. Nice lot of talk it'd cause if I went back to the War Department looking like this. "Where's your hat and coat, General?" "Oh, I just thought I'd come down in my suspenders this morning."

JERRY. You can have my coat—and my troubles.

*Charlotte comes suddenly out of the White House, and they turn startled eyes upon her, like two guilty schoolboys.*

CHARLOTTE [*staring*]. What's the matter? Has everything gone to pieces?

GENERAL PUSHING [*on the verge of tears*]. He took my coat and hat.

CHARLOTTE [*pointing to the General*]. Who is that man?

GENERAL PUSHING [*in a dismal whine*]. I'm Major-General Pushing, I am.

CHARLOTTE. I don't believe it.

JERRY [*uneasily*]. Yes, he is, Charlit. I was just kidding him.

CHARLOTTE [*understanding immediately*]. Oh, you've been *nag*ging people again.

JERRY [*beginning to unbutton the coat*]. The General was nagging me, Charlit. I've just been teaching him a lesson—haven't I, General?

> *He struggles out of the General's coat and into his own. The General, grunting his relief and disgust, re-attires himself in the military garment.*

JERRY [*losing confidence under Charlotte's stare*]. Honest, everything's getting on my nerves. First it's some correspondence school getting funny, and then *he* [*indicating the General*] comes around, and then all the people out in Idaho—

CHARLOTTE [*with brows high*]. Well, if you want to know what *I* think, *I* think everything's going to pieces.

JERRY. No, it isn't, Charlit. I'm going to fix everything. I've got a firm grip on everything. Haven't I, Mr. Jones? I'm just nervous, that's all.

GENERAL PUSHING [*now completely buttoned up, physically and mentally*]. In my opinion, sir, you're a very dangerous man. I have served under eight Presidents, but I have never before lost my coat and hat. I bid you good morning, Mr. President. You'll hear from me later.

> *At his salute the fife and drum commence to play. The trio execute about face, and the escort, at three paces, follows the General out the gate.*
>
> *Jerry stares uneasily after them.*

JERRY. Everybody's always saying that I'm going to hear from 'em later. They want to kick me out of this job—that's what they want. They think I don't know.

JONES. The people elected you, Mr. President. And the people want you—all except the ones out in Idaho.

CHARLOTTE [*anxiously*]. Couldn't you be on the safe side and have yourself reduced to Vice-President, or something?

A NEWSBOY [*outside*]. Extra! Extra! Idaho says: "Resign or be Impeached."

JERRY. Was that newsboy yelling something about me?

CHARLOTTE [*witheringly*]. He never so much as mentioned you.

*In response to Mr. Jones's whistle a full-grown newsboy comes in at the gate. He hands Jerry a paper and is given a bill.*

JERRY [*carelessly*]. Keep the change. It's all right. I've got a big salary.

THE NEWSBOY [*pointing to Jerry's frock coat*]. I almost had one of them dress suits once.

JERRY [*not without satisfaction*]. I got six of them.

THE NEWSBOY. I hadda get one so I could take a high degree in the Ku Klux. But I didn't get one.

JERRY [*absorbed in the paper*]. I got six of 'em.

THE NEWSBOY. I ain't got none. Well, much obliged. So long.

*The newsboy goes out.*

JONES [*reading over Jerry's shoulder*]. It says: "Idaho flays Treasury choice."

CHARLOTTE [*wide-eyed*]. Does that mean they're going to flay Dada?

JONES [*looking at his watch*]. Senator Fish will be here at any moment now.

CHARLOTTE. Well, all I know is that I'd show some spunk and not let them kick *me* out, even if I *was* the worst President they ever had.

JERRY. Listen, Charlit, you needn't remind me of it every minute.

CHARLOTTE. I didn't remind you of it. I just mentioned it in an ordinary tone of voice.

*She goes into the White House. Senator Joseph Fish comes in hesitantly through the gate.*

JERRY [*to Jones*]. Here comes the State of Idaho.

FISH [*timorously*]. Good morning, Mr. President. How are you?

JERRY. Oh, I'm all right.

FISH [*hurriedly producing the telegram and mumbling his words*]. Got a little matter here, disagreeable duty. Want to get through as quickly as possible. "Senator Joseph Fish, Washington, D. C. Present the State of Idaho's compliments to President Frost, and tell him that the people of Idaho demand his immediate resignation." [*He folds up the telegram and puts it in his pocket.*] Well,

Mr. President, I guess I got to be going. [*He moves toward the gate and then hesitates.*] This was to have been my wedding-reception day. Of course, Doris will never marry me now. It's a very depressing thing to me, President Frost. [*With his hand on the gate latch.*] I suppose you want me to tell 'em you won't resign, don't you?

JONES. We won't resign.

FISH. Well, then it's only right to tell you that Judge Fossile of the Supreme Court will bring a motion of impeachment at three o'clock this afternoon.

*He turns melancholy eyes on Doris's window. He kisses his hand toward it in a tragic gesture of farewell. Then he goes out.*

*Jerry looks at Mr. Jones as though demanding encouragement.*

JERRY. They don't know the man they're up against, do they, Mr. Jones?

JONES. They certainly do not.

JERRY [*lying desperately and not even convincing himself*]. I've got resources they don't know about.

JONES. If you'll pardon a suggestion, I think the best move you could make, Mr. President, would be to demand your father's resignation immediately.

JERRY [*incredulously*]. Put Dada out? Why, he used to work in a bank when he was young, and he knows all about the different amounts of money.

*A pause.*

JERRY [*uncertainly*]. Do you think I'm the worst President they ever had?

JONES [*considering*]. Well, no, there was that one they impeached.

JERRY [*consoling himself*]. And then there was that other fellow—I forget his name. He was *terrible*. [*Another disconsolate pause*] I suppose I might as well go down and get a cigar.

JONES. There's just one more man out here to see you and he says he came to do you a favor. His name is—the Honorable Snooks, or Snukes, Ambassador from Irish Poland.

JERRY. What country's that?

JONES. Irish Poland's one of the new European countries. They took a sort of job lot of territories that nobody could use and made a country out of them. It's got three or four acres of Russia and a couple of mines in Austria and a few lots in Bulgaria and Turkey.

JERRY. Show them all out here.

JONES. There's only one. [*He goes into the White House, returning immediately.*]

JONES. The Honorable Snooks, or Snukes, Ambassador to the United States from Irish Poland.

> *The Honorable Snooks comes out through the swinging doors. His resemblance to Mr. Snooks, the bootlegger, is, to say the least, astounding. But his clothes—they are the clothes of the Corps Diplomatique. Red stockings enclose his calves, fading at the knee into black satin breeches. His coat, I regret to say, is faintly reminiscent of the Order of Mystic Shriners, but a broad red ribbon slanting diagonally across his diaphragm gives the upper part of his body a svelte, cosmopolitan air. At his side is slung an unusually long and cumbersome sword.*
>
> *He comes in slowly, I might even say cynically, and after a brief nod at Jerry, surveys his surroundings with an appraising eye.*
>
> *Jones goes to the table and begins writing.*

SNOOKS. Got a nice house, ain't you?

JERRY [*still depressed from recent reverses*]. Yeah.

SNOOKS. Wite, hey?

JERRY [*as if he had just noticed it*]. Yeah, white.

SNOOKS [*after a pause*]. Get dirty quick.

JERRY [*adopting an equally laconic manner*]. Have it washed.

SNOOKS. How's your old woman?

JERRY [*uneasily*]. She's all right. Have a cigar?

SNOOKS [*taking the proffered cigar*]. Thanks.

JERRY. That's all right. I got a lot of them.

SNOOKS. That's some cigar.

JERRY. I got a lot of them. I don't smoke that kind myself, but I got a lot of them.

SNOOKS. That's swell.

JERRY [*becoming boastful*]. See that tree? [*The white tree.*] Look, that's a special tree. You never saw a tree like that before. Nobody's got one but me. That tree was given to me by some natives.

SNOOKS. That's swell.

JERRY. See this cane? The band around it's solid gold.

SNOOKS. Is that right? I thought maybe it was to keep the squirrels from crawling up. [*Abruptly.*] Need any liquor? I get a lot, you know, on account of bein' an ambassador. Gin, vermuth, bitters, absinthe?

JERRY. No, I don't.... See that sign? I bet you never saw one like that before. I had it invented.

SNOOKS [*bored*]. Class. [*Switching the subject.*] I hear you made your old man Secretary of the Treasury.

JERRY. My father used to work in a—

SNOOKS. You'd ought to made him official Sandy Claus.... How you gettin' away with your job?

JERRY [*lying*]. Oh, fine—fine! You ought to see the military review they had for me last week. Thousands and thousands of soldiers, and everybody cheered when they saw me. [*Heartily.*] It was sort of inspiring.

SNOOKS. I seen you plantin' trees in the movies.

JERRY [*excitedly*]. Sure. I do that almost every day. That's nothing to some of the things I have to do. But the thing is, I'm not a bit stuck up about any of it. See that gate?

SNOOKS. Yeah.

JERRY [*now completely and childishly happy*]. I had it made that way so that anybody passing by along the street can look in. Cheer them up, see? Sometimes I come out here and sit around just so if anybody passes by—well, there I am.

SNOOKS [*sarcastically*]. You ought to have yourself covered with radium so they can see you in the dark. [*He changes his tone now and comes down to business.*] Say, you're lucky I found you in this morning. Got the time with you?

> *Jerry pulls out his watch. Snooks takes it as though to inspect it more closely.*

Look here now, Mr. President. I got a swell scheme for you.

JERRY [*trying to look keen*]. Let's hear it.

SNOOKS. You needn't got to think now, just 'cause I'm a hunerd per cent Irish Pole, that I ain't goin' to do the other guy a favor once in a while. An' I got somep'm smooth for you. [*He puts Jerry's watch in his own pocket—the nerve of the man!*]

JERRY. What is it?

SNOOKS [*confidentially*]. Islands.

JERRY. What islands?

SNOOKS. The Buzzard Islands.

*Jerry looks blank.*

Ain't you neva hearda the Buzzard Islands?

JERRY [*apologetically*]. I never was any good at geography. I used to be pretty good in penmanship.

SNOOKS [*in horror*]. You ain't neva hearda the Buzzard Islands?

JERRY. It's sort of a disagreeable name.

SNOOKS. The Buzzard Islands. Property of the country of Irish Poland. Garden spots. Flowery paradises ina middle of the Atlantic. Rainbow Islandsa milk an' honey, palms an' pines, smellin' with good-smellin' woods and high-priced spices. Fulla animals with million buck skins and with birds that's got feathers that the hat dives on Fifth Avenue would go nuts about. The folks in ee islands—swell-lookin', husky, square, rich, one hunerd per cent Buzzardites.

JERRY [*startled*]. You mean Buzzards?

SNOOKS. One hunerd per cent Buzzardites, crazy about their island, butter, milk, live stock, wives, and industries.

JERRY [*fascinated*]. Sounds sort of pretty, don't it?

SNOOKS. Pretty? Say, it's smooth! Now here's my proposition, an' take it from me, it's the real stuff. [*Impressively.*] The country of Irish Poland wants to sell you the Buzzard Islands—cheap.

JERRY [*impressed*]. You're willing to sell 'em, eh?

SNOOKS. Listen. I'll be fair with you. [*I regret to say that at this point he leans close to Jerry, removes the latter's stick pin and places it in his own tie*] I've handed you the swellest proposition ever laid before a President since Andrew Jackson bought the population of Ireland from Great Britain.

JERRY. Yeah?

SNOOKS [*intently*]. Take it from me, Pres, and snap it up—dead cheap.

JERRY. You're sure it's a good—

SNOOKS [*indignantly*]. Say, do you think an ambassador would tell you something that ain't true?

JERRY ["*man to man*"]. That's right, Mr. Snooks. I beg your pardon for that remark.

SNOOKS [*touching his handkerchief to his eyes*]. You hurt me, Pres, you hurt me, but I forgive you.

> They shake hands warmly.
>
> And now Jerry has an idea—a gorgeous idea. Why didn't he think of it before? His voice literally trembles as he lays his plan before Snooks.

JERRY. Honorable Snooks, listen. I'll tell you what I'll do. I'll—I'll take those Islands and pay—oh, say a round million dollars for them, on one condition.

SNOOKS [*quickly*]. Done. Name your condition.

JERRY [*breathlessly*]. That you'll let me throw in one of the States on the trade.

SNOOKS. What State?

JERRY. The State of Idaho.

SNOOKS. How much do you want for it?

JERRY [*hastily*]. Oh, I'll just throw that in free.

> Snooks indicates Mr. Jones with his thumb.

SNOOKS. Get him to take it down.

> Jones takes pen in hand. During the ensuing conversation he writes busily.

JERRY [*anxiously*]. The State of Idaho is just a gift, see? But you *got* to take it.

> Suddenly the Honorable Snooks realizes how the land lies. He looks narrowly at Jerry, marvelling at an opportunity so ready to his hand.

JERRY [*to Jones*]. Here, get this down. We agree to buy the Buzzard Islands from the nation of Irish Poland for one million—

SNOOKS [*interrupting*]. Two million.

JERRY. Two million dollars, on condition that Irish Poland will also incorporate into their nation the State of Idaho, with all its people. Be sure and get that, Jones. With all its people.

JONES. I have it. The State of Idaho and four hundred and thirty-one thousand, eight hundred and sixty-six people. Including colored?

JERRY. Yes, including colored.

SNOOKS [*craftily*]. Just a minute, Pres. This here State of Idaho is mostly mountains, ain't it?

JERRY [*anxiously*]. I don't know. Is it, Mr. Jones?

JONES. It has quite a few mountains.

SNOOKS [*hesitating*]. Well, now, I don't know if we better do it after all—

JERRY [*quickly*]. Three millions.

SNOOKS. I'll tell you, I'd like to pull it off for you, Pres, but you see a State like that has gotta have upkeep. You take one of them mountains, for instance. You can't just let a mountain alone like you would a—a ocean. You got to—to groom it. You got to—to chop it down. You got to explore it. Now take that alone—you got to explore it.

JERRY [*swallowing*]. Four millions.

SNOOKS. That's more like it. Now these Buzzard Islands don't require no attention. You just have to let 'em alone. But you take the up-keep on a thing like the State of Idaho.

JERRY [*wiping his brow*]. Five millions.

SNOOKS. Sold! You get the Buzzard Islands and we get five million bucks and the State of Idaho.

JERRY. Got that down, Jones?

SNOOKS. On second thoughts—

JERRY [*in a panic*]. No, no, you can't get out of it. It's all down in black and white.

SNOOKS [*resignedly*]. Awright. I must say, Mr. President, you turned out to be a real man. When I first met you I wouldn't have thought it, but I been pleasantly surprised.

> *He slaps Jerry heartily on the back. Jerry is so tickled at the solution of the Idaho problem that he feverishly seizes Snooks's hand.*

SNOOKS. And even if Irish Poland gets stung on the deal, we'll put it through. Say, you and me ain't politicians, fella, we're statesmen, real statesmen. You ain't got a cigarette about you, have you?

*Jerry hands him his cigarette case. Snooks, after taking one, returns the case to his own pocket.*

JERRY [*enthusiastically*]. Send me a post-card, Ambassador Snooks. The White House, City, will reach me.

SNOOKS. Post-card! Say, lay off. You and me are pals. I'd do anything for a pal. Come on down to the corner and I'll buy you a cigar.

JERRY [*to Mr. Jones*]. I guess I can go out now for a while.

JONES. Oh, yes.

JERRY. Hang on to that treaty. And, say, when the Secretary of the Treasury wakes up tell him I've got to have five million dollars right away.

JONES. If you'll just come into the office for a moment you can put your signatures on it right away.

*Jerry and the Honorable Snooks go into the White House arm in arm, followed by Mr. Jones. Presently Jerry can be seen in the window of the President's office.*

*A moment later the doors swing open again, this time for the tottering egress of Dada.*

*Dada, not without difficulty, arranges himself a place in the sun. He is preparing for his morning siesta, and, indeed, has almost managed to spread a handkerchief over his face when in through the gate comes Doris. Her eye falls on him and a stern purpose is born. Dada, seeing her approach, groans in anticipation.*

DORIS. Dada, I want to speak to you.

*Dada blinks up at her, wearily.*

Dada, I want to tell you something for your own good and for Jerry's good. You want Jerry to keep his position, don't you?

DADA. Jerry's a fine boy. He was born to my second wife in eighteen hundred and—

DORIS [*interrupting impatiently*]. Yes, I know he was. But I mean now.

DADA. No, I'll never have any more children. Children are hard to raise properly.

*This is aimed at her.*

DORIS. Look at here, Dada. What I think is the best thing to do is to resign your position.

DADA. The—?

DORIS. You're too old, you see, if you know what I mean. You're sort of—oh, not crazy, but just sort of feeble-minded.

DADA [*who has caught one word*]. Yes, I'm a little feeble. [*He dozes off.*]

DORIS [*absorbed in her thesis*]. I don't mean you're crazy. Don't get mad. I don't mean you go around thinking you're like Napoleon or a poached egg or anything like that, but you're sort of feeble-minded. Don't you understand, yourself? Sort of simple.

DADA [*waking up suddenly*]. How's that?

DORIS [*infuriated*]. That's *just* the sort of thing I was talking about! Going to sleep like that when a person's trying to tell you something for your own son's good. That's just *exactly* what I mean!

DADA [*puzzled but resentful*]. I don't like you. You're a very forward young girl. Your parents brought you up very unsuccessfully indeed.

DORIS [*smugly*]. All right. You're just making me think so more than ever. Go right ahead. Don't mind me. Go right ahead. Then when you begin to really *rave* I'll send for the lunatic-asylum wagon.

DADA [*with an air of cold formality*]. I'll ask you to excuse me. [*He wants to get to sleep.*]

DORIS. First thing you know you'll take all the money in the Treasury and hide it and forget where you put it.

DADA [*succinctly*]. There isn't any money in the Treasury.

DORIS [*after a stunned pause*]. Just what do you mean by that statement?

DADA [*drowsily*]. There isn't any money in the Treasury. There was seven thousand dollars left yesterday, but I worked from morning till night and now there isn't one red penny in there.

Doris. You must be crazy.

Dada. [*He can scarcely keep awake.*] Hm.

Doris. Look at here! What do you mean—have you been spending that money—that doesn't belong to you, you know—on some fast woman?

Dada [*as usual, he doesn't quite hear*]. Yes, it's all gone. I went down yesterday morning and I said to myself: "Horatio, you got only seven thousand dollars left, and you got to work from morning till night and get rid of it." And I did.

Doris [*furious, but impressed at the magnitude of the crime*]. How much was there altogether?

Dada. Altogether? I haven't the figures with me.

Doris. Why, you old dumb-bell, you. Imagine an old man your age that hasn't had anything to do for twenty years but just sit around and *think*, going crazy about a woman at your age! [*With scornful pity.*] Don't you know she just made a fool of you?

Dada [*shaking his finger at her*]. You must not talk like that. Be courteous and—

Doris. Yes, and pretty soon some woman comes along and you get "courteous" with her to the extent of all the money in the Treasury.

Dada. Yes, that's one thing that stood me in good stead. My mother used to say to me: "Horatio—"

Doris [*paying no attention to him*]. What was her name?

Dada. Her name was Roxanna.

Doris. Where did she get hold of you?

Dada. My mother?

Doris. Your paramour.

Dada. She used to say to me: "Horatio—"

Doris. She probably used to say a lot more than that! Oh, I know how they handle old men like you. I've seen a lot of that. Slush is what appeals to old men like you.

Dada. No—I said courtesy.

Doris. You mean slush. What did she call you?—her old toodledums? And all that sort of thing? How perfectly disgusting!

> *Out comes Jerry now, just in time to catch Dada's next remark, and to realize that there's persecution in the air.*

DADA [*to Doris*]. It's been a hot day and I'll ask you to excuse me. I never liked you, you know.

JERRY. Say, Doris, why can't you leave Dada alone? He's got more important things to think about than your new dresses and your silk stockings.

DORIS. Got something more important than silk stockings, has he? Ask him!

JERRY. Dada's got a lot more to him than anybody ever gives him credit for, haven't you, Dada?

DORIS [*excitedly*]. Yeah, yeah. All right. Wait till you hear what he's done now. Wait till you hear. [*To Dada.*] Tell him what you did at your age. Some woman came up to him and said "Horatio—" [*She gives an awe-inspiring imitation of a passionate woman.*] and he said: "Here—"

JERRY [*interrupting*]. What woman did?

DORIS. Her name was Roxanna. Ask him where all the money in the Treasury is. At his age.

JERRY [*in growing alarm*]. Look at here, Doris—

DORIS. The—old—dumb-bell! I take back what I said about your not being really crazy. [*To Jerry.*] Look out, he'll begin to rave. [*She pretends to be alarmed.*] Yes, Dada, you're a poached egg. It's all right. I'll send for the lunatic-asylum wagon.

DADA. I've been working in the dark. I thought it best.

DORIS. You needn't tell us all the disgusting details. Please respect my engagement. You must have bought her about everything in the world. No wonder I can't get any good shoes in Washington. Jerry should have got you analyzed.

*Jerry now begins to realize that something appalling has indeed happened. He sits down weakly.*

DADA. I was working in the dark.

DORIS. Well, Jerry should of had you analyzed in the dark.

JERRY [*suddenly*]. Char-lit!

CHARLOTTE [*at the upper window*]. Stop screaming at me!

JERRY. Charlit, come on out here!

DORIS. Dada's done something awful. At his age!

JERRY. Hurry up out, Charlit!

CHARLOTTE. You wouldn't want me to come out in my chemise, would you?

DORIS. It wouldn't matter. We'll be kicked out, anyways.

CHARLOTTE. Has Dada been drinking?

DORIS. Worse than that. Some woman's got ahold of him.

CHARLOTTE. Don't let him go till I come down. I can handle him.

*Mr. Jones comes out.*

DADA [*impressively*]. I think the world is coming to an end at three o'clock.

DORIS [*wildly*]. We've got a maniac here. Go get some rope.

MR. JONES [*in horror*]. Are you going to hang him?

*Out rushes Charlotte.*

DADA. The United States was the wealthiest country in all the world. It's easier for a camel to pass through a needle's eye than for a wealthy man to enter heaven.

*They all listen in expectant horror.*

So all the money in the Treasury I have had destroyed by fire, or dumped into the deep sea. We are all saved.

JERRY. Do you mean to say that you haven't even got five million dollars?

DADA. I finished it all up yesterday. It was not easy. It took a lot of resourcefulness, but I did it.

JERRY [*in horror*]. But I've got to have five million dollars this afternoon or I can't get rid of Idaho, and I'll be impeached!

DADA [*complacently*]. We're all saved.

JERRY [*wildly*]. You mean we're all lost!

*He sinks disconsolately into a chair and buries his face in his hands. Charlotte, who knew everything would go to pieces, stands over him with an "I told you so" air. Doris shakes her finger at Dada, who shakes his finger vigorously back at her. Mr. Jones, with great presence of mind, produces the cocktail shaker and passes around the consoling glasses to the violently agitated household.*

. . . . . . . . .
. . . . . . . . .
. . . . . . . . .

*At two-thirty the horizontal sunlight is bright upon the White House lawn. Through the office window the President can be seen, bent over his desk in an attitude of great dejection. And here comes the Honorable Snooks through the gate, looking as if he'd been sent for. Mr. Jones hurries forth from the White House to greet him.*

SNOOKS. Did you send for me, fella?

JONES [*excitedly*]. I should say we did, Honorable Snooks. Sit down and I'll get the President.

*As Mr. Jones goes in search of the President, Dada comes in through the gate at a triumphant tottering strut. He includes the Honorable Snooks in the splendor of his elation.*

DADA [*jubilantly*]. Hooray! Hooray! I worked in the dark, but I won out!

SNOOKS [*with profound disgust*]. Well, if it ain't Sandy Claus!

DADA. This is a great day for me, Mr.— You see the world is coming to an end.

SNOOKS. Well, Sandy Claus, everybody's got a right to enjoy themselves their own way.

DADA. That's in strict confidence, you understand.

SNOOKS. I wouldn't spoil the surprise for nothin'.

*Out rushes Jerry.*

JERRY [*in great excitement*]. Honorable Snooks—Honorable Snooks—

DADA [*suddenly*]. Hooray! In at the finish.

*He tries to slap the Honorable Snooks on the back, but the Honorable Snooks steps out of the way, and Dada loses his balance. Snooks and Jerry pick him up.*

JERRY [*suspiciously*]. Dada, have you been drinking?

DADA. Just a little bit. Just enough to fortify me. I never touched a drop before to-day.

SNOOKS. You're a naughty boy.

DADA. Yes, I think I'll go in and rest up for the big event.

*He wanders happily into the White House.*

JERRY [*in a hushed voice*]. Honorable Snooks, Dada has done something awful.

SNOOKS [*pointing after Dada*]. Him?

JERRY. He took all the money in the Treasury and destroyed it.

SNOOKS. What type of talk is that? You tryin' to kid me?

JERRY. You see, he's a very religious man, Honorable Snooks—

SNOOKS. You mean you ain't got five million for me. [*Jerry shakes his head.*] Good *night!* This is a swell country. A bunch of Indian givers!

JERRY. There's no use cursing at me, Honorable Snooks. I'm a broken man myself.

SNOOKS. Say, can the sob stuff an' call up the Treasury. Get 'em to strike off a couple billion dollars more. You're the President, ain't you?

*Cheering up a little, Jerry goes to the telephone.*

JERRY. Give me the Treasury Department.... Say, this is President Frost speaking. I just wanted to ask you if you couldn't strike off a little currency, see? About—about five million dollars, see? And if you didn't know whose picture to put on 'em you could put my picture on 'em, see? I got a good picture I just had taken.... You can't strike any off?... Well, I just asked you.... Well, I just thought I'd ask you.... Well, no harm done—I just *asked* you—it didn't hurt to *ask*, did it? [*He rings off despondently.*] It didn't hurt 'em to *ask*.

SNOOKS. Nothin' doin', eh?

*In comes Mr. Jones.*

JONES. It's all over, Mr. President. I've just received word that Chief Justice Fossile of the Supreme Court, accompanied by the Senate Committee on Inefficiency, is on his way to the White House.

*Jerry sits down, completely overcome. Jones retires.*

SNOOKS. They goin' to throw you out on your ear, eh?

JERRY [*brooding*]. It's that low, mean bunch of people out in Idaho.

*Snooks, who has been ruminating on the situation, comes to a decision.*

SNOOKS. Look at here, Mr. President, I'm goin' to help you out. I'll pass up that five million bucks and we'll make a straight swap of the Buzzard Islands for the State of Idaho.

JERRY [*in amazement*]. You'll give me the Buzzard Islands for the State of Idaho?

*Snooks nods. Jerry wrings his hand in great emotion.*
*At this point Charlotte comes out of the White House. At the sight of the Honorable Snooks a somewhat disapproving expression passes over her face.*

JERRY [*excitedly*]. Charlit—Charlit. This gentleman has saved me.

CHARLOTTE [*suspiciously*]. Who is he?

JERRY. His name is The Honorable Snooks, Charlit.

SNOOKS [*under Charlotte's stern eye*]. Well, I guess I got to be goin'.

CHARLOTTE. Won't you stay for my husband's impeachment? We're having a few people in.

*Out comes Doris, accompanied by Dada. Dada is in such a state of exultation that much to Doris's annoyance he is attempting a gavotte with her.*

DORIS [*repulsing him*]. Say, haven't I got enough troubles having to throw over my fiancé, without having you try to do your indecent old dances with me?

*Dada sits down and regards the heavens with a long telescope.*

*Jerry has now recovered his confidence and is marching up and down waving his arms and rehearsing speeches under his breath. Snooks taps Dada's head and winks lewdly at Charlotte and Doris.*

DORIS. Honestly, everybody seems to be going a little crazy around here. Is Jerry going to be fired or isn't he?

CHARLOTTE. He says he isn't, but I don't believe him for a minute.

*Jones comes out, followed by an excitable Italian gentleman with long, musical hair.*

JONES. This gentleman said he had an appointment with Miss Doris.

JERRY. Who are you?

THE GENTLEMAN. I am Stutz-Mozart's Orang-Outang Band. I am ordered to come here with my band at three o'clock to play high-class jazz at young lady's wedding reception.

DORIS. I remember now. I *did* order him. It's supposed to be the best jazz band in the country.

JERRY [*to Stutz-Mozart*]. Don't you know there's going to be a big political crisis here at three o'clock?

DORIS. We can't use you now, Mr. Stutz-Mozart. Anyways, I had to throw over my fiancé on account of political reasons.

STUTZ-MOZART [*indignantly*]. But I have my orang-outang band outside.

CHARLOTTE [*her eyes staring*]. Real orang-outangs?

DORIS. Of course not. They just call it that because they look kind of like orang-outangs. And they play kind of like orang-outangs, sort of. I mean the way orang-outangs would play if they knew how to play at all.

JERRY [*to Stutz-Mozart*]. Well, you'll have to get them away from here. I can't have a lot of senators and judges coming in and finding me with a bunch of men that look like orang-outangs.

STUTZ-MOZART. But I have been hired to play.

JERRY. Yes, but what do you think people would say? They'd say: Yes, here's a fine sort of President we've got. All his friends look sort of like orang-outangs.

STUTZ-MOZART. You waste my time. You pay me or else we play.

JERRY. Look at here. If you're one of these radical agitators my advice to you is to go right back where you came from.

STUTZ-MOZART. I came from Hoboken.

*He goes threateningly out the gate.*

JONES [*announcing from the steps*]. Chief Justice Fossile of the Supreme Court, accompanied by a committee from the Senate!

CHARLOTTE [*to Jerry*]. Speak right up to them. Show them you're not just a vegetable.

*Here they come! Chief Justice Fossile, in a portentous white wig, is walking ponderously at the head of the procession. Five of the six Senators who follow him are large, grave gentlemen whose cutaway coats press in their swollen stomachs. Beside them Senator Fish seems frail and ineffectual.*

*The delegation comes to a halt before Jerry, who regards it defiantly, but with some uneasiness.*

JUDGE FOSSILE. To the President of the United States—greetings.

JERRY [*nervously*]. Greetings yourself.

> Mr. Jones has provided chairs, and the Senators seat themselves in a row, with Judge Fossile in front. Fish looks miserably at Doris. The Honorable Snooks lurks in the shadow of the Special Tree.

JUDGE FOSSILE. Mr. President, on the motion of the gentleman from Idaho—[*He points to Fish, who tries unsuccessfully to shrink out of sight*] we have come to analyze you, with a view to impeachment.

JERRY [*sarcastically*]. Oh, is that so? [*He looks for encouragment at Charlotte. Charlotte grunts.*]

JUDGE FOSSILE. I believe that is the case, Senator Fish?

FISH [*nervously*]. Yes, but personally I like him.

CHARLOTTE. Oh, you do, do you? [*She nudges Jerry.*] Speak right up to them like that.

JERRY. Oh, you do, do you?

JUDGE FOSSILE. Remove that woman!

> *No one pays any attention to his request.*

JUDGE FOSSILE. Now, Mr. President, do you absolutely refuse to resign on the request of the Senator from Idaho?

JERRY. You're darn right I refuse!

JUDGE FOSSILE. Well, then, I—

> At this point Mr. Stutz-Mozart's Orang-Outang Band outside of the wall launches into a jovial jazz rendition of "Way Down upon the Suwanee River." Suspecting it to be the national anthem, the Senators glance at each other uneasily, and then, removing their silk hats, get to their feet, one by one. Even Judge Fossile stands at respectful attention until the number dies away.

JERRY. Ha-ha! That wasn't "The Star-Spangled Banner."

> *The Senators look confused.*

DORIS [*tragically*]. This was to have been my wedding reception day.

> *Senator Fish begins to weep softly to himself.*

JUDGE FOSSILE [*angrily to Jerry*]. This is preposterous, sir! You're a dangerous man! You're a menace to the nation! We will proceed no further. Have you anything to say before we vote on the motion made by the State of Idaho?

CHARLOTTE. Yes, he has. He's got a whole mouthful!

DORIS. This is the feature moment of my life. Cecil B. DeMille would shoot it with ten cameras.

JUDGE FOSSILE. Remove these women.

*The women are not removed.*

JERRY [*nervously*]. Gentlemen, before you take this step into your hands I want to put my best foot forward. Let us consider a few aspects. For instance, for the first aspect let us take, for example, the War of the Revolution. There was ancient Rome, for example. Let us not only live so that our children who live after us, but also that our ancestors who preceded us and fought to make this country what it is!

*General applause.*

And now, gentlemen, a boy to-day is a man to-morrow—or, rather, in a few years. Consider the winning of the West—Daniel Boone and Kit Carson, and in our own time Buffalo Bill and—and Jesse James!

*Prolonged applause.*

Finally, in closing, I want to tell you about a vision of mine that I seem to see. I seem to see Columbia—Columbia—ah—blindfolded—ah—covered with scales—driving the ship of state over the battle-fields of the republic into the heart of the golden West and the cotton-fields of the sunny South.

*Great applause. Mr. Jones, with his customary thoughtfulness, serves a round of cocktails.*

JUDGE FOSSILE [*sternly*]. Gentlemen, you must not let yourselves be moved by this man's impassioned rhetoric. The State of Idaho has moved his impeachment. We shall put it to a vote—

JERRY [*interrupting*]. Listen here, Judge Fossile, a state has got to be part of a country in order to impeach anybody, don't they?

JUDGE FOSSILE. Yes.

JERRY. Well, the State of Idaho doesn't belong to the United States any more.

*A general sensation. Senator Fish stands up and sits down.*

JUDGE FOSSILE. Then who does it belong to?
SNOOKS [*pushing his way to the front*]. It belongs to the nation of Irish Poland.
> *An even greater sensation.*

JERRY. The State of Idaho is nothing but a bunch of mountains. I've traded it to the nation of Irish Poland for the Buzzard Islands.
> *Mr. Jones hands the treaty to Judge Fossile.*

FISH [*on his feet*]. Judge Fossile, the people of Idaho—
SNOOKS. Treason! Treason! Set down, fella! You're a subject of the nation of Irish Poland.
JERRY [*pointing to Fish*]. Those foreigners think they can run this country.
> *The other Senators shrink away from Fish.*

JUDGE FOSSILE [*to Fish*]. If you want to speak as a citizen of the United States, you'll have to take out naturalization papers.
SNOOKS. I won't let him. I'm goin' to take him with me. He's part of our property.
> *He seizes the indignant Fish firmly by the arm and pins a large "Sold" badge to the lapel of his coat.*

DORIS [*heartily*]. Well, I'm certainly glad I didn't marry a foreigner.
> *Just at this point, when Jerry seems to have triumphed all around, there is the noise of a fife and drum outside, and General Pushing marches in, followed by his musical escort. The General is in a state of great excitement.*

GENERAL PUSHING. Mr. President, I am here on the nation's business!
THE SENATORS. Hurrah!
GENERAL PUSHING. War must be declared!
THE SENATORS. Hurrah!
JERRY. Who is the enemy?
GENERAL PUSHING. The enemy is the nation of Irish Poland!
> *All eyes are now turned upon Snooks, who looks considerably alarmed.*

GENERAL PUSHING [*raising his voice*]. On to the Buzzard Islands!
THE SENATORS. Hurrah! Hurrah! Down with Irish Poland!

JUDGE FOSSILE. Now, Mr. President, all treaties are off!

GENERAL PUSHING [*looking scornfully at Jerry*]. He tried to trade the State of Idaho for some islands full of Buzzards. Bah!

THE SENATORS. Bah!

SNOOKS [*indignantly*]. What's ee idea? Is this a frame-up to beat the nation of Irish Poland outa their rights? We want the State of Idaho. You want the Buzzard Islands, don't you?

GENERAL PUSHING. We can take them by force. We're at war. [*To the Senators.*] We've ordered all stuffed Buzzards to be removed from the natural history museums. [*Cheers.*] And domestic Buzzards are now fair game, both in and out of season. [*More cheers.*] Buzzard domination would be unthinkable.

JUDGE FOSSILE [*pointing to Jerry*]. And now, Senators. How many of you vote for the impeachment of this enemy of the commonwealth?

*The five Senators stand up.*

JUDGE FOSSILE [*to Jerry*]. The verdict of a just nation. Is there any one here to say why this verdict should not stand?

*Dada, who all this time has been absorbed in the contemplation of the heavens, suddenly throws down his telescope with a crash.*

DADA [*in a tragic voice*]. It's too late!

ALL. Too late?

DADA. Too late for the world to end this afternoon. I must have missed the date by two thousand years. [*Wringing his hands.*] I shall destroy myself!

*Dada tries to destroy himself. He produces a pistol, aims at himself, and fires. He flounders down—but he has missed.*

DORIS [*standing over him and shaking her finger*]. You miss *ev*erything! I'm going to send for the lunatic-asylum wagon—if it'll come!

DADA [*shaking his finger back at her*]. Your parents brought you up very unsuccessfully—

JUDGE FOSSILE. Silence! I will pronounce sentence of impeachment on this enemy of mankind. Look upon him!

*They all look dourly at Jerry.*

Now, gentlemen, the astronomers tell us that in the far heavens, near the southern cross, there is a vast space called the hole in the sky, where the most powerful telescope can discover no comet nor planet nor star nor sun.

> *They all look very cold and depressed. Jerry shivers. Fish picks up Dada's abandoned telescope and begins an eager examination of the firmament.*

In that dreary, cold, dark region of space the Great Author of Celestial Mechanism has left the chaos which was in the beginning. If the earth beneath my feet were capable of expressing its emotions it would, with the energy of nature's elemental forces, heave, throw, and project this enemy of mankind into that vast region, there forever to exist in a solitude as eternal as—as eternity.

> *When he finishes a funereal silence falls.*

JERRY [*his voice shaken with grief*]. Well, Judge, all I've got to say is that no matter what you'd done I wouldn't want to do all those things to you.

JUDGE FOSSILE [*thunderously*]. Have you anything more to say?

JERRY [*rising through his defeat to a sort of eloquent defiance*]. Yes. I want to tell you all something. I don't want to be President. [*A murmur of surprise.*] I never asked to be President. Why—why, I don't even know how in hell I ever *got* to be President!

GENERAL PUSHING [*in horror*]. Do you mean to say that there's one American citizen who does not desire the sacred duty of being President? Sir, may I ask, then, just what you do want?

JERRY [*wildly*]. Yes! I want to be left alone.

> *Outside the wall Mr. Stutz-Mozart's Orang-Outang Band strikes up "The Bee's Knees." The Senators arise respectfully and remove their hats, and General Pushing, drawing his sword, stands at the salute.*

> *Four husky baggage smashers stagger out of the White House with the trunks of the Frost family, and hurry with them through the gate. Half a dozen assorted suitcases are flung after the trunks.*

*The music continues to play, the Senators continue to stand. The Frost family gaze at their departing luggage, each under the spell of a different emotion.*
*Charlotte is the first to pick up her grip. As she turns to the Senators, the music sinks to pianissimo, so her words are distinctly audible.*

CHARLOTTE. If it's any satisfaction to you, I'm going to be a different wife to him from now on. From now on I'm going to make his life perfectly miserable.

*Charlotte goes out to a great burst of jazz. Dada, with some difficulty, locates his battered carpet-bag.*

DADA. I find I missed the date by two thousand years. Eventually I will destroy myself.

*Dada is gone now, hurried out between two porters, and Doris is next. With dignity she selects her small but arrogant hand-bag.*

DORIS. All I want to say is if Cecil B. DeMille ever saw the White House he'd say: "All right, that may do for the gardener's cottage. Now I'll start building a *real* house."

*As she leaves she tries desperately to walk out of step with the music and avoid the suggestion of marching. The attempt is not altogether successful.*
*President Jerry Frost now picks up his bag.*

JERRY [*defiantly*]. Well, anyways I showed you you couldn't put anything over on me. [*Glancing around, his eye falls on the "Special Tree." He goes over and pulls it up by the roots.*] This was given to me by some natives. That sign's mine, too. I had it invented. [*He pauses.*] I guess you think I wasn't much good as a President, don't you? Well, just try electing me again.

GENERAL PUSHING [*sternly*]. We won't! As a President you'd make a good postman.

*At this sally there is a chorus of laughter.*
*Then Charlotte's voice again. Does it come from outside the gate, or, mysteriously enough, from somewhere above?*

CHARLOTTE [*very distinctly*]. Shut the door! I can smell that stuff up here!

*A bewildered look comes into Jerry's eyes. He says*

"What?" in a loud voice. Then with the tree in one hand and his grip in the other, he is hurried, between two porters, briskly toward the gate, while the Orang-Outang Band crashes into louder and louder jazz and

THE CURTAIN FALLS

## Act III

*Now we're back at the Frosts' house, and it's a week after the events narrated in Act I. It is about nine o'clock in the morning, and through the open windows the sun is shining in great, brave squares upon the carpet. The jars, the glasses, the phials of a certain memorable night have been removed, but there is an air about the house quite inconsistent with the happy day outside, an air of catastrophe, a profound gloom that seems to have settled even upon the "Library of Wit and Humor" in the dingy bookcase.*

*There is brooding going on upon the premises.*

*A quick tat-tat-tat from outdoors—the clatter of someone running up the porch steps. The door opens and Doris comes in, Doris in a yellowish skirt with a knit jersey to match, Doris chewing, faintly and delicately, what can surely be no more than a sheer wisp of gum.*

DORIS [*calling*]. Char-lotte.

A VOICE [*broken and dismal, from upstairs*]. Is that you, Doris?

DORIS. Yeah. Can I come up?

THE VOICE. [*It's Charlotte's. You'd scarcely have recognized it.*] I'll come down.

DORIS. Heard any thing from Jerry?

CHARLOTTE. Not a word.

> *Doris regards herself silently, but with interest, in a small mirror on the wall. In comes Charlotte—and oh, how changed from herself of last week. Her nose and eyes are red from weeping. She's chastened and depressed.*

DORIS [*with cheerful pessimism*]. Haven't heard a word, eh?

CHARLOTTE [*lugubriously*]. No. Not one.

DORIS [*impressed in spite of herself*]. Son of a gun! And he sneaked away a week ago to-night.

CHARLOTTE. It was that awful liquor, I *know*. He sat up all night and in the morning he was gone.

Doris. It's the funniest thing I ever heard of, his sneaking off this way.... Say, Charlotte, I've been meaning to say something to you for a couple of days, but I didn't want to get you depressed.

Charlotte. How could I possibly be any more depressed than I am?

Doris. Well, I just wanted to ask you if you'd tried the morgue yet. [*Charlotte gives a little scream.*] Wait a minute. Get control of yourself. I simply think you ought to *try* it. If he's anywhere you ought to locate him.

Charlotte [*wildly*]. Oh, he's not dead! He's not dead!

Doris. I didn't say he was, did I? I didn't say he was. But when a fella wanders out tight after drinking some of this stuff, you can't tell *where* you'll find him. Let me tell you, Charlotte, I've had more experience with this sort of thing than you have.

Charlotte. The detective is coming to report this morning.

Doris. Has he been combing the dives? You ought to have him comb the dives, Charlotte. I saw a picture last week that ought to be a lesson to any woman that loses her husband in a funny way like this. The woman in this picture lost her husband and she just combed the dives and—there he was.

Charlotte [*suspiciously*]. What was he doing?

Doris. Some vampire was sitting on his lap in a café. [*Charlotte moans.*] But it does show that if you do have the dives combed, you can find 'em. That's what this woman did.... There's where most men go when they wander out like that.

Charlotte. Oh, no, Jerry wouldn't go to the dives, or the—the morgue, either. He's never drank or done anything like that till that night. He's always been so mild and patient.

*This is a new note from Charlotte.*

Doris [*after a thoughtful pause*]. Maybe he's gone to Hollywood to go in the movies. They say a lot of lost men turn up there.

Charlotte [*brokenly*]. I don't know what to do. Maybe I'm re-responsible. He said that night he might have been P-President if it hadn't been for me. He'd just been analyzed, and they found he was per-perfect.

DORIS. Well, with no reflections on the dead or anything like that, Charlotte, he wasn't so wonderful as you make out. You can take it from me, he never would have been anything more than a postman if you hadn't made him be a railroad clerk.... I'd have the dives combed.

CHARLOTTE [*eulogistically*]. He was a good husband.

DORIS. You'll get over it.

CHARLOTTE. What?

DORIS. Cheer up. In a year or so you'll never know you ever had a husband.

CHARLOTTE [*bursting into tears at this*]. But I want him back.

DORIS [*reminiscently*]. Do you know the song? Do you know the song? [*She sings:*]

"A good man is hard to find
You always get the other kind
And when you think that he is your friend
You look around and find him scratching
'Round some other hen—"

*She has forgotten her ethical connection and begins to enjoy the song for itself, when Charlotte interrupts.*

CHARLOTTE [*in torture*]. Oh, don't! Don't!

DORIS. Oh, excuse me. I didn't think you'd take it personally.... It's just about colored people.

CHARLOTTE. Oh, do you suppose he's with some colored women?

DORIS [*scornfully*]. No-o-o! What you need is to get your mind off it for a while. Just say to yourself if he's in a dive, he's in a dive, and if he's in Hollywood, he's in Hollywood, and if he's in the morgue—

CHARLOTTE [*frantically*]. If you say that word again, I'll go crazy!

DORIS. —well, in that *place*, then, just say: "I can't do anything about it, so I'm going to forget it." That's what you want to say to yourself.

CHARLOTTE. It's easy enough to *say*, but I can't get my mind—

DORIS. Yes, you can. [*Magnanimously.*] I'll tell you about what I've been doing. I've had sort of a scrap with Joseph.

CHARLOTTE. Joseph who?

DORIS. Joseph Fish. He's that fella I brought around here, only you didn't meet him. I told you about him. The one I got engaged to about ten days ago. His parents were in the mortuary business.

CHARLOTTE. Oh.

DORIS. Well, I been trying to make him stop chewing gum. I offered to give it up if he would. I think it's sort of common when two people that go together are always whacking away at a piece of gum, don't you?

*There's a ring at the door-bell.*

CHARLOTTE. That's the detective.

DORIS [*prudently*]. Have you got that liquor hidden?

CHARLOTTE. I threw that horrible stuff away. Go let him in.

*Charlotte goes to the door and ushers in the detective. The detective wears an expression of profound sagacity upon his countenance.*

Have you found him?

THE DETECTIVE [*impressively*]. Mrs. Frost, I think so.

CHARLOTTE. Alive?

THE DETECTIVE. Alive.

CHARLOTTE. Where is he?

THE DETECTIVE. Wait. Be calm. I've had several clews, and I've been following them up one at a time. And I've located a man, who answers to the first name of Jerry, that I think is your husband.

CHARLOTTE. Where did you find him?

THE DETECTIVE. He was picked up trying to jimmy his way into a house on Crest Avenue.

CHARLOTTE. Good heavens!

THE DETECTIVE. Yep—and his name is Jerry. He had it tattooed on his arm.

CHARLOTTE. Good God!

THE DETECTIVE. But there's one thing that's different from your description. What color is your husband's hair?

CHARLOTTE. Brown.

THE DETECTIVE. Brown? Are you sure?

CHARLOTTE. Am I sure? Of course I'm sure.

THE DETECTIVE [*to Doris*]. Do you collaborate that?
DORIS. When he left here it was brown.
THE DETECTIVE. Well, this fella's hair was red.
CHARLOTTE. Oh, it's not Jerry then—it's not Jerry.
DORIS [*to Charlotte*]. Well, now, how do you know? Maybe— [*She turns to the detective.*] You see, this fella had been drinking some of this funny liquor you get around here sometimes and it may just have turned his hair red.
CHARLOTTE [*to the detective*]. Oh, do you think so?
THE DETECTIVE. I never heard of a case like that. I knew a fella whose hair was turned white by it.
DORIS. I knew one, too. What was the name of the fella you knew?
CHARLOTTE. Did this man claim to be my husband?
THE DETECTIVE. No, madam, he didn't. He said he had two wives out in Montana, but none that he knew of in these parts. But of course he may have been bluffing.
DORIS. It doesn't sound like Jerry to me.
THE DETECTIVE. But you can identify him by that tattoo mark.
CHARLOTTE [*hastily*]. Oh, he never had one.
THE DETECTIVE. Are you sure?
CHARLOTTE. Oh, yes.
THE DETECTIVE [*his face falling*]. Well, then, he's not our man, because this fella's tattoo marks are three years old. Well, that's a disappointment. That's a great disappointment for me. I've wasted some time over this man. I'd been hoping he'd—ah—do.
CHARLOTTE [*hastily*]. Oh, no, he wouldn't do at all. I'll have to have the right man or I won't pay you.
THE DETECTIVE. Well, now then, I've been following up another clew. Did your husband ever have aphasia?
CHARLOTTE. Oh, no, he's always been very healthy. He had some skin trouble about—
DORIS. He doesn't mean that, Charlotte. Aphasia's where a man runs off and commits murder and falls in love with a young girl under another name.
CHARLOTTE. Oh, no, he's never done anything like this ever before.

THE DETECTIVE. Suppose you tell me exactly what did happen.

CHARLOTTE. Well, I told you he'd been drinking something that had spirits of nitrogen in it.

THE DETECTIVE. Spirits of nitrogen!

CHARLOTTE. That's what the man said. It was sympathetic gin that this man had persuaded Jerry into buying.

THE DETECTIVE. Yes.

CHARLOTTE. And he'd been talking all evening about all the things he could have done if I hadn't stood in his way. He had some examination he'd just taken.

DORIS [*explaining*]. A psychical examination.

THE DETECTIVE [*wisely*]. I see.

CHARLOTTE. And my sister came over with the man she's going to marry, and she came up to see me, and when she came down Jerry was asleep in his chair. Well, I didn't go down. I wish I had now. And my sister here and her fellow went away. Then I went to bed, and it seems to me I could hear Jerry talking to himself in his sleep all night. I woke up about twelve, and he was saying something loud, and I told him to shut the door, because I could smell that awful sympathetic gin way up-stairs.

THE DETECTIVE. Yes.

CHARLOTTE. And that's all. When I came down next morning at seven, he was gone.

THE DETECTIVE [*rising*]. Well, Mrs. Frost, if your man can be located, I'm going to locate him.

DORIS. Have you thought of combing the dives?

THE DETECTIVE. What?

DORIS. Have you combed the dives? It seems to me that I'd make the rounds of all the dives, and I wouldn't be a bit surprised if you'd see this man with somebody sitting on his knee.

THE DETECTIVE [*to Charlotte*]. Does he run to that?

CHARLOTTE [*hurriedly*]. Oh, no. Oh, no.

DORIS [*to Charlotte*]. How do you know?

> *A brisk knock at the door. Doris opens it eagerly, admitting a small, fat, gray-haired man in a state of great indignation.*

THE DETECTIVE [*to Charlotte*]. Is this the pursued?

THE MAN [*sternly*]. You are speaking to Mr. Pushing. I employ or did employ the man who lives in this house.

CHARLOTTE [*wildly*]. Oh, where is he?

MR. PUSHING. That's what I came here to find out. He hasn't been at work for a week. I'm going to let him go.

DORIS. You ought to be ashamed of yourself. He may be dead.

MR. PUSHING. Dead or alive, he's fired. I had him analyzed. He didn't have any ambition, and my analyzer gave him nothing but a row of goose-eggs. Bah!

CHARLOTTE. I don't care. He's mine.

DORIS [*correcting her*]. "Was" mine.

THE DETECTIVE. Maybe you could tell me something about his habits in business hours.

MR. PUSHING. If you'll come along with me I'll show you his analyzed record. We're having it framed. [*Contemptuously.*] Good morning.

> *He goes out. The Detective, after a nod at Charlotte and Doris, follows him.*

DORIS. Well, I should think you'd be encouraged.

CHARLOTTE. Why?

DORIS. Well, that detective found a fella that's something like him. The same first name, anyway. That shows they're getting warm.

CHARLOTTE. Somehow it doesn't encourage me.

> *Uncertain steps on the stairs. Dada appears wearing a battered hat and carrying a book under his arm.*

DORIS. Hello, Dada. Where you going?

DADA [*hearing vague words*]. Hm.

CHARLOTTE. He's going down to the library.

DADA [*in spirited disagreement*]. No. You were wrong that time. I'm not going to the park. I'm going to the library.

DORIS [*sternly*]. Where do you think your son is?

DADA. The—?

DORIS [*louder*]. Where do you think Jerry is, by this time?

DADA [*to Charlotte*]. Didn't you tell me he was away?

> *Charlotte nods drearily.*

DADA [*placidly*]. Hasn't come back yet?

DORIS. No. We're having the dives combed.

DADA. Well, don't worry. I remember I ran away from home once. It was in 1846. I wanted to go to Philadelphia and see the Zoo. I tried to get home, but they took me and locked me up.

DORIS [*to Charlotte*]. In the monkey house, I bet.

DADA. [*He missed this, thank God!*] Yes, that's the only time I ever ran away.

DORIS. But this is a more serious thing, Dada.

DADA. Boys will be boys.... Well, it looks like a nice day.

CHARLOTTE [*to Doris*]. He doesn't care. He doesn't even understand what it's all about. When the detective searched his bedroom he thought it was the plumber.

DORIS. He understands. Sure you do, don't you, Dada? You understand what it's all about, don't you, Dada?

DADA [*aggravatingly*]. The—?

CHARLOTTE. Oh, let him go. He makes me nervous.

DORIS. Maybe he could think out some place where Jerry's gone. He's supposed to *think* so much.

DADA. Well, good afternoon. I think I'll go down to the library. [*Dada goes out by the front door.*]

DORIS. Listen, Charlotte. I was going to tell you about Joseph—to get your mind off yourself, don't you remember?

CHARLOTTE. Yes.

DORIS. I've gotten sort of tired of him. Honestly, I ought to get myself psychoanalyzed.

CHARLOTTE. Why don't you throw him over then? You ought to know how by this time.

DORIS. Of course, having been unlucky in your own marriageable experience, you aren't in a position to judge what I should do.

CHARLOTTE. Do you love him?

DORIS. Well, not—not especially.

CHARLOTTE. Then throw him over.

DORIS. I would—except for one thing. You see, it'd be sort of hard.

CHARLOTTE. No, it wouldn't.

DORIS. Yes, it would. It wouldn't be any cinch.

CHARLOTTE. Why?
DORIS. Well, you see I've been married to him for three days.
CHARLOTTE [*astounded*]. What!
DORIS. That isn't very long, but you see in marriage every day counts.
CHARLOTTE. Well, then, you can't throw him over.
DORIS. It's next to impossible, I guess.
CHARLOTTE. Was it a secret marriage?
DORIS. Yes, there was nobody there but I and Joseph and the fella that did it. And I'm still living at home. You see, this girl that Joe was keeping waiting to see whether he was going to marry me or not, got impatient, and said she couldn't be kept waiting any longer. It made her sort of nervous. She couldn't eat her meals.
CHARLOTTE. So you got married. And now you're tired of him.
DORIS. No, not exactly that, but it just sort of makes me uncomfortable, Charlotte, to know that you can't throw over the man you've got without causing a lot of talk. Suppose he took to drink or something. You know everybody can't get rid of their husbands as easy as you did.
CHARLOTTE. One husband was always enough for me.
DORIS. One may be all right for you, Charlotte, because you're a monographist, but supposing Rodolph Valentino, or the Prince of Wales, or John D. Rockefeller was to walk in here and say: "Doris, I've worshipped you from a distance on account of the picture that you sent to the fame and fortune contest of the movie magazine, that got left out by accident or lost or something. Will you marry me?" What would you say, Charlotte?
CHARLOTTE. I'd say no. I'd say, give me back Jerry.
DORIS. Would you let having a husband stand in the way of your life's happiness? I tell you I wouldn't. I'd say to Joe: "You run up to the store and buy a bag of peanuts and come back in about twenty years." I would, Charlotte. If I could marry Douglas Fairbanks I'd get rid of Joseph in some peaceful way if I *could*—but if I couldn't I'd give him some glass cough-drops without a minute's hesitation.
CHARLOTTE [*horrified*]. Doris!

DORIS. And I told Joseph so, too. This marriage business is all right for narrow-minded people, but I like to be where I can throw over a fella when it gets to be necessary.

CHARLOTTE. If you had Jerry you wouldn't feel that way.

DORIS. Why, can't you see, Charlotte, that's the way Jerry must have felt?

*Charlotte, overcome, rises to go.*

And, Charlotte, I don't want to depress you, but if he *is*—if it turns out that he is in the mor—in that place—I know where you can get some simply *stunning* mourning for—

*Charlotte begins to weep.*

Why, what's the matter? I just thought it'd cheer you up to know you could get it cheap. You'll have to watch your money, you know.

*Charlotte hurries from the room.*

DORIS. I wonder what's the matter with her.

JOSEPH FISH [*outside*]. Oh, Doris!

*Doris goes to the window.*

DORIS. How did you know I was here?

FISH [*outside*]. They told me at your house. Can I come in?

DORIS. Yes, but don't holler around so. Haven't you got any respect for the missing?

*Fish comes in.*

FISH. Doris, I'm awfully sorry about—

DORIS. Oh, Joseph, haven't you got any sense? Sitting there last night everything was perfect, and just when I was feeling sentimental you began talking about embalming—in the *twi*light. And I was just about to take out my removable bridge....

FISH. I'm sorry.... Have they found your sister's husband yet?

DORIS. No.

FISH. Has he gone away permanently? Or for good?

DORIS. We don't know. We're having the dives combed. Listen, has any one in your family ever had aphasia?

FISH. What's that?

DORIS. Where you go off and fall in love with girls and don't know what you're doing.

FISH. I think my uncle had that.

DORIS. Sort of dazed?

FISH. Well, sort of. When there was any women around he got sort of dazed.

DORIS [*thoughtfully*]. I wonder if you could inherit a thing from your uncle. [*She removes her gum secretly.*] What are you chewing, Joe?

FISH. Oh, just an old piece of something I found in my mouth.

DORIS. It's gum. I thought I asked you not to chew gum. It doesn't look clean-cut for a man to be chewing gum. You haven't got any sense of what's nice, Joseph. See here, suppose I was at a reception and went up to Mrs. Astor or Mrs. Vanderbilt or somebody, like this: [*She replaces her own gum in her mouth—she needs it for her imitation.*] How do you do, Mrs. Vanderbilt? [*Chew, chew.*] What do you think she'd say? Do you think she'd stand it? Not for a minute.

FISH. Well, when I start going with Mrs. Vanderbilt will be plenty of time to stop.

> *From outside is heard the sound of a metallic whistle, a melodious call in C major.*

What's that?

DORIS. Don't ask me.

FISH. It's pretty. It must be some kind of bird.

> *The whistle is repeated. It is nearer.*

There it is again.

> *Doris goes to the window.*

DORIS. It's only the postman.

FISH. I never heard a postman with a whistle like that.

DORIS. He must be a new one on this beat. That's too bad. The old one used to give me my mail wherever I met him, even if he was four or five blocks from my house.

> *The sound again—just outside the door now.*

I'll let him in.

> *She goes to the door and opens it. The figure of the new postman is outlined in the doorway against the morning sky. It is Jerry Frost.*
>
> *But for a particular reason neither Doris nor Joseph Fish recognize him. He is utterly changed. In the gray*

uniform his once flabby figure appears firm, erect—even defiant. His chin is up—the office stoop has gone. When he speaks his voice is full of confidence, with perhaps a touch of scorn at the conglomerate weaknesses of humanity.*

JERRY. Good morning. Would you like some mail?

DORIS [*taken somewhat aback*]. Why, sure. I guess so.

JERRY. It's a nice morning out. You two ought to be out walking.

FISH [*blankly*]. Huh?

JERRY. Is this number 2127? If it is, I've got a good-looking lot of mail for you.

DORIS [*with growing interest*]. What do you mean, a good-looking lot of mail?

JERRY. What do I *mean*? Why, I mean it's got variety, of course. [*Rummaging in his bag.*] I got eight letters for you.

DORIS. Say, you're new on this beat, aren't you?

JERRY. Yes, I'm new but I'm good. [*He produces a handful of letters.*] I'm the best one they ever had.

FISH. How do you know? Did they tell you?

JERRY. No, I just feel it. I know my job. I can give any other mailman stamps and post-cards and beat him with bundles. I'm just naturally *good*. I don't know why.

DORIS. I never heard of a mailman being *good*.

JERRY. They're mostly all good. Some professions anybody can get into them, like business or politics for instance, but you take postmen—they're like angels, they sort of pick 'em out. [*Witheringly.*] They not only pick 'em out—they select 'em.

FISH [*fascinated*]. And you're the best one.

JERRY [*modestly*]. Yes, I'm the best one they ever had. [*He looks over the letters.*] Now here's what I call a clever ad. Delivered a lot of these this morning. Children like 'em, you know. They're from the carpet company.

FISH. Let's see it. [*He takes the ad eagerly.*]

JERRY. Isn't that a nice little thing? And I got two bills for you here. I'll hide those, though. Still, maybe you want to clear up all your accounts. Some people like to get bills. The old lady next door wanted to get hers. I gave her three and you'd think they were checks. Anyways, these two don't look very big, from the outside, anyhow. But of course you can't tell from the outside.

DORIS. Let me see them.

FISH. Let me see them too.

*They squabble mildly over the bills.*

JERRY. The thing is for everybody in the house to write what they guess is the amount of the bill on the outside of the envelope, and then when you open the envelope the one who guessed the closest has to pay the bill.

FISH. Or he could get a prize.

JERRY. Something like that. [*He winks at Doris.*] And here's a couple of post-cards. They're sort of pretty ones. This one's—the Union Station at Buffalo.

FISH. Let me see it.

JERRY. And this one says Xmas greetings. It's four months late. [*To Doris.*] I guess these are for you.

DORIS. No, they're for my sister.

JERRY. Well, I haven't read what's written on the back. I never do. I hope it's good news.

DORIS [*inspecting the backs*]. No, they're from an aunt or something. Anything else?

JERRY. Yes, here's one more. I think it's one of the neatest letters I've had this morning. Now, isn't that a cute letter? I call that a cute letter. [*He weighs it in his hand and smells it.*] Smell it.

DORIS. It does smell good. It's a perfume ad.

FISH. Say, that sure does smell good.

JERRY. Well, I've done pretty well by *you* this morning. Maybe you got a letter for me.

DORIS. No, there's none to-day.

JERRY. Funny thing: I came near leaving that pink letter with a little girl down the street who looked as if she needed one pretty bad. I thought that maybe it was really meant for her, and just had the wrong name and address on by mistake. It would of tickled her. I get tempted to leave mail where it really ought to go instead of where it's addressed to. Mail ought to go to people who appreciate it. It's hard on a postman, especially when he's the best one they ever had.

DORIS. I guess it must be.
FISH. Yeah, it must be tough.
*They are both obviously fascinated.*
DORIS. Well, there's somebody in this house who needs the right letter something *aw*ful. If you get one that looks as if it might do for her you could leave it by here.
JERRY. Is that so? Well, that's too bad. I'll certainly keep that in mind. The next one I think'll do, I'll leave it by here.
DORIS. Thanks.
JERRY. I've got one of these special delivery love-letters for a girl around the corner, and I want to hurry up and give it to her, so as to see her grin when she gets it. It's for Miss Doris—
DORIS [*interrupting*]. That's me. Give it to me now.
JERRY. Sure. Say, this is lucky. [*He starts to hand it to her.*] Say, listen—why are you like a stenographer?
DORIS. Me?
JERRY. Yes.
DORIS. I don't know. Why?
JERRY. Because I say to you, "Take a letter."
FISH [*wildly amused*]. Ha-ha! Ha-ha-ha!
JERRY [*with some satisfaction*]. That's a good one, isn't it? I made that one up this morning.
FISH. Ha-ha! Ho-ho!
DORIS. Joseph, I asked you to have some respect for the missing. [*To Jerry.*] You see there's a fella missing here and it's his wife that needs the letter.
FISH [*jealously*]. Who's *your* letter from?
DORIS [*reading it*]. It's from my last fiancé. It says he didn't mean to drink the perfume, but the label was off the bottle and he thought it was bay rum.
FISH. My God! Will you forgive him?
JERRY. Don't worry, my boy. Bay rum or perfume, he killed her love with the first swallow. [*He goes toward the door.*] Good-by. I'll try to find that letter for the lady here that needs it so bad.
DORIS. Good-by—and thanks.
FISH. Let me open the door.

*He opens the door. Jerry goes out. Doris and Fish stare at each other.*

DORIS. Isn't he wonderful?

FISH. He's a peach of a fella, but—

DORIS. I know what you're going to say; that you've seen him somewhere before.

FISH. I'm trying to think where. Maybe he's been in the movies.

DORIS. I think it's that he looks like some fella I was engaged to once.

FISH. He's *some* mailman.

DORIS. The nicest one I ever saw. Isn't he for you?

FISH. By far. Say, Charlie Chaplin's down at the Bijou.

DORIS. I don't like him. I think he's vulgar. Let's go and see if there's anything artistic.

*Fish makes an indistinguishable frightened noise.*

DORIS. What's the matter?

FISH. I've swallowed my gum.

DORIS. It ought to teach you a moral.

*They go out. Charlotte comes in drearily. She glances first eagerly, then listlessly at the letters and throws them aside.*

*Clin-ng! The door-bell. She starts violently, runs to open it. It is that astounding product of our constitution, Mr. Snooks.*

CHARLOTTE [*in horror*]. Oh, what do you want?

SNOOKS [*affably*]. Good morning, lady. Is your husband around?

CHARLOTTE. No. What have you done with him, you beast!

SNOOKS [*surprised*]. Say, what's biting you, lady?

CHARLOTTE. My husband was all right until you came here with that poison! What have you done with him? Where is he? What did you give him to drink? Tell me, or I'll scream for the police! Tell me! Tell me!

SNOOKS. Lady, I ain't seen your husband.

CHARLOTTE. You lie! You know my husband has run away.

SNOOKS [*interested*]. Say now, has he? I had a hunch he would, sooner or later.

CHARLOTTE. You made him. You told him to, that night, after I went out of the room! You suggested it to him. He'd never have thought of it.

SNOOKS. Lady, you got me wrong.

CHARLOTTE. Then where is he? If I'm wrong, find him.

SNOOKS [*after a short consideration*]. Have you tried the morgue?

CHARLOTTE. Oh-h-h! Don't say that word!

SNOOKS. Oh, he ain't in the morgue. Probably some Jane's got hold of him. She'll send him home when she gets all his dough.

CHARLOTTE. He isn't a brute like you. He's been kidnapped.

SNOOKS. Maybe he's joined the Marine Corpse.... Howsoever, if he ain't here I guess I'll be movin' on.

CHARLOTTE. What do you want of him now? Do you want to sell him some more wood alcohol?

SNOOKS. Lady, I don't handle no wood alcohol. But I found a way of getting the grain alcohol out of iodine an' practically eliminatin' the poison. Just leaves a faint brownish tinge.

CHARLOTTE. Go away.

SNOOKS. All right. I'll beat it.

*So he beats it.*

*Charlotte's getting desperate from such encounters. With gathering nervousness she wanders about the room, almost collapsing when she comes upon one of Jerry's coats hanging behind a door. Scarcely aware of what she's doing, she puts on the coat and buttons it close, as if imagining that Jerry is holding her to him in the brief and half-forgotten season of their honeymoon.*

*Outside a storm is come up. It has grown dark suddenly, and a faint drum of thunder lengthens into a cataract of doom. A louder rolling now and a great snake of lightning in the sky. Charlotte, lonesome and frightened, hurriedly closes the windows.*

*Then, in sudden panic, she runs to the 'phone.*

CHARLOTTE. Summit 3253.... Hello, this is me. This is Charlotte.... Is Doris there? Do you know where she is?... Well, if she comes in tell her to run over. Everything's getting dark and I'm frightened.... Yes, *may*be somebody'll come in, but *no*body goes out in a storm like this. Even the policeman on the corner has gotten under a tree.... Well, I'll be all right. I'm just lonesome, I guess, and scared.... Good-by.

> *She rings off and stands silently by the table. The storm reaches its height. Simultaneously with a terrific burst of thunder that sets the windows rattling the front door blows open suddenly, letting in a heavy gust of rain.*
> *Charlotte is on the verge of hysterics.*
> *Then there is a whistle outside—the bright, mellow whistle of the postman. She springs up, clasping her hands together. Jerry comes in, covered with a rain cape dripping water. The hood of the cape partially conceals his face.*

JERRY [*cheerfully*]. Well, it certainly is a rotten day.

CHARLOTTE [*starting at the voice*]. It's awful.

JERRY. But I heard there was a lady here that was expecting a letter, and I had one that I thought'd do, so no rain or anything could keep me from delivering it.

CHARLOTTE [*greedily*]. A letter for me? Let me have it.

> *He hands it to her and she tears it open.*

It's from Jerry!

> *She reads it quickly.*

JERRY. Is it what you wanted?

CHARLOTTE [*aloud, but to herself*]. It doesn't say where he is. It just says that he's well and comfortable. And that he's doing what he wants to do and what he's got to do. And he says that doing his work makes him happy. [*With suspicion.*] I wonder if he's in some dive.... If I wrote him a letter do you think you could find him with it, Mr. Postman?

JERRY. Yes, I can find him.

CHARLOTTE. I want to tell him that if he'll come home I won't nag him any more, that I won't try to change him, and that I won't fuss at him for being poor.

JERRY. I'll tell him that.

CHARLOTTE [*again talking to herself*]. I was trying to nag him *into* something, I guess. Before we were married I always thought there must be some sort of mysterious brave things he did when he wasn't with me. I thought that maybe sometimes he'd sneak away to hunt bears. But when he'd sneak away it was just to roll dice for cigars down at the corner. It wasn't forests—it was just—toothpicks.

JERRY. Suppose that he was nothing but a postman now—like me.

CHARLOTTE. I'll be proud of him if he's a postman, because I know he always wanted to be one. He'd be the best postman in the world and there's something kind of exciting about being the best. It wasn't so much that I wanted him to be rich, I guess, but I wanted him to do something he wouldn't always be beat at. I was sort of glad he got drunk that night. It was about the first exciting thing he ever did.

JERRY. You never would of told him that.

CHARLOTTE [*stiffening*]. I should say I wouldn't of.

*Jerry rises.*

JERRY. I'll try to get him here at six o'clock.

CHARLOTTE. I'll be waiting. [*Quickly.*] Tell him to stop by a store and get some rubbers.

JERRY. I'll tell him. Good-by.

CHARLOTTE. Good-by.

> *Jerry goes out into the rain, Charlotte sits down and bows her head upon the table.*
>
> *Again there are steps on the porch. This time it is Dada, who comes in, closing a dripping umbrella.*

DADA [*as one who has passed through a great crisis*]. I borrowed an umbrella from a man at the library.

CHARLOTTE [*in a muffled voice*]. Jerry's coming back.

DADA. Is he? A man at the library was kind enough to lend me his umbrella. [*He goes over to the bookcase and begins an unsuccessful search for the Scriptures. Plaintively*]. Some one has hidden my Bible.

CHARLOTTE. In the second shelf.

> *He finds it. As he pulls it from its place, several other books come with it and tumble to the floor. After a glance at Charlotte, he kicks them under the bookcase. Then, with his Bible under his arm, he starts for the stairs, but*

*is attracted by something bright on the first stair, and attempts, unsuccessfully, to pick it up.*

DADA. Hello, here's a nail that looks like a ten-cent piece.

*He goes upstairs. When he is half-way up, there is a sound as if he had slipped back a notch, then silence.*

CHARLOTTE [*raising her head*]. Are you all right, Dada?

*No answer. Dada is heard to resume his climb.*

Oh, if I could only sleep till six o'clock!

*The storm has blown away, and the sun is out and streaming in the window, washing the ragged carpet with light. From the street there comes once again, faint now and far away, the mellow note of the postman's whistle.*

CHARLOTTE [*lifting her arms rapturously*]. The best postman in the world!

CURTAIN

# POEMS

## A DIRGE

*(Apologies to Wordsworth)*

It lay among the untrodden ways,
   'Twas very small in size;
A bar whom there were none to praise,
   And few to patronize.

But when the drought had well begun
   One winked a wicked eye!
—'Twas like a star when only one
   Is shining in the sky!

It served unknown and few could know
   The wink that fixed the tea;
But now it too is closed, and, oh,
   The difference to me!

---

*Judge* 77 (20 December 1919): 30. This poem is done in imitation of Wordsworth's "She Dwelt among the Untrodden Ways" (1800). *Judge* was a weekly magazine of satire. After the coming of Prohibition on 16 January 1919, many bars continued to serve liquor—but in teacups. Eventually this ruse was detected by the authorities, and most of these establishments were closed.

## SLEEP OF A UNIVERSITY

Watching through the long, dim hours
Like statued Mithras, stand ironic towers;
Their haughty lines severe by light
Are softened and gain tragedy at night.
Self-conscious, cynics of their charge,
Proudly they challenge the dreamless world at large.

From pseudo-ancient Nassau Hall, the bell
Crashes the hour, as if to pretend "All's well!"
Over the campus then the listless breeze
Floats along drowsily, filtering through the trees,
Whose twisted branches seem to lie
Like *point d'Alençon* lace against a sky
Of soft gray-black—a gorgeous robe
Buttoned with stars, hung over a tiny globe.

With life far off, peace sits supreme:
The college slumbers in a fatuous dream,
While, watching through the moonless hours
Like statued Mithras, stand the ironic towers.

---

*Nassau Literary Magazine* 76 (November 1920): 161. Fitzgerald's poem is a "paraphrase" of "Princeton Asleep," a poem by a student named Aiken Reichner published on p. 158 of this same issue of the *Nassau Lit*.

## LAMP IN A WINDOW

Do you remember, before keys turned in the locks,
    When life was a closeup, and not an occasional letter,
That I hated to swim naked from the rocks
    While you liked absolutely nothing better?

Do you remember many hotel bureaus that had
    Only three drawers? But the only bother
Was that each of us got holy, then got mad
    Trying to give the third one to the other.

East, west, the little car turned, often wrong
    Up an erroneous Alp, an unmapped Savoy river.
We blamed each other, wild were our words and strong,
    And, in an hour, laughed and called it liver.

And, though the end was desolate and unkind:
    To turn the calendar at June and find December
On the next leaf; still, stupid-got with grief, I find
    These are the only quarrels that I can remember.

---

*New Yorker* 11 (23 March 1935): 18. The text presented here is Fitzgerald's final revision of the poem; this version first appeared in *Crack-Up*, p. 163.

## OBIT ON PARNASSUS

Death before forty's no bar. Lo!
   These had accomplished their feats:
Chatterton, Burns, and Kit Marlowe,
   Byron and Shelley and Keats.

Death, the eventual censor,
   Lays for the forties, and so
Took off Jane Austen and Spenser,
   Stevenson, Hood, and poor Poe.

You'll leave a better-lined wallet
   By reaching the end of your rope
After fifty, like Shakespeare and Smollett,
   Thackeray, Dickens, and Pope.

Try for the sixties—but say, boy,
   That's when the tombstones were built on
Butler and Sheridan, the play boy,
   Arnold and Coleridge and Milton.

Three score and ten—the tides rippling
   Over the bar; slip the hawser.
Godspeed to Clemens and Kipling,
   Swinburne and Browning and Chaucer.

Some staved the debt off but paid it
   At eighty—that's after the law.
Wordsworth and Tennyson made it,
   And Meredith, Hardy, and Shaw.

---

*New Yorker* 13 (5 June 1937): 27. The approximate ages at which the various authors died are not invariably accurate; Walter Savage Landor, for example, expired a few months short of his ninetieth birthday. For a letter from the *New Yorker* concerning this matter, see *As Ever, Scott Fitz—*, p. 305. "Hood," in line 8, is the English poet and humorist Thomas Hood (1799-1845).

But, Death, while you make up your quota,
  Please note this confession of candor—
That I wouldn't give an iota
  To linger till ninety, like Landor.

## TO A BELOVED INFIDEL

That sudden smile across a room
  Was certainly not learned from me,
That first faint quiver of the bloom,
  The eyes' initial ecstacy.
Whoever taught you how to page
  Your loves so sweetly—now as then
I thank him for my heritage
  That glance made bright by other men.

No slumberous pearl is valued less
  For years spent in a Rajah's crown
And I should rather rise and bless
  Your earliest love than cry him down.
Whoever tuned your heart up knew
  His job. How can I hate him when
He did his share to fashion you,
  A heart made warm by other men?

Some kisses nature doesn't plan—
  She works in such a sketchy way—
The child, though father to the man,
  Must be instructed how to play.
What traffic your lips had with mine
  Don't lie in any virgin's ken—
I found the oldest, richest wine
  On lips once soft for other men.

---

Fitzgerald submitted this poem to *Esquire* on 23 February 1940, together with the short story "Dearly Beloved." Arnold Gingrich, the editor of the magazine, rejected both pieces. The poem, written for Sheilah Graham, was first published in facsimile (a fair copy inscribed in Fitzgerald's hand) on the endpapers of Graham's memoir *Beloved Infidel: The Education of a Woman* (1958). The text published here is that of the final typescript, preserved among Fitzgerald's papers at Princeton.

## Last Kiss

I'm even glad someone and you
    Found it was joyous to rehearse,
Made it an art to fade into
    The passion of the universe.
The world all crowded in an hour
    Wrapped up in moonbeams—that has been
Your life, your wealth, your curious dower
    The things you learned from other men.

The lies you tell are lyric things
    No amateur would ever try
Soft little parables with wings—
    I know not even God would cry.
Let every lover be the last
    And whisper: "This is *now* not *then*."
That sweet denial of the past
    The tale you told to other men.

This little time you opened up
    A window let me look inside
Gave me the plate, the spoon, the cup,
    The very coat of love that died
Or seemed to die—for as your hand
    Touched mine it was alive again
And we were in a lovely land
    The world you had from other men.

And when I join the other ghosts
    Who lay beside your flashing fire
I must be proud and join their toasts
    To one who was a sweet desire
And sweet fulfillment—all they found
    Was worth remembering—and then
He'll hear us as the glass goes round
    This Godspeed from us other men.

# BOOK REVIEWS

## THE BALTIMORE ANTI-CHRIST

The incomparable Mencken will, I fear, meet the fate of Aristides. He will be exiled because one is tired of hearing his praises sung. In at least three contemporary novels he is mentioned as though he were dead as Voltaire and as secure as Shaw with what he would term "a polite bow". His style is imitated by four-fifths of the younger critics—moreover he has demolished his enemies and set up his own gods in the literary supplements.

Of the essays in the new book the best is the autopsy on the still damp bones of Roosevelt. In the hands of Mencken Roosevelt becomes almost a figure of Greek tragedy; more, he becomes alive and loses some of that stuffiness that of late has become attached to all 100% Americans. Not only is the essay most illuminating but its style is a return to Mencken's best manner, the style of "Prefaces", with the soft pedal on his amazing chord of adjectives and a tendency to invent new similes instead of refurbishing his amusing but somewhat overworked old ones.

Except for the section on American aristocracy there is little new in the first essay "The National Letters": an abundance of wit and a dozen ideas that within the past year and under his own deft hand have become bromides. The Knights of Pythias, Right Thinkers, On Building Universities, Methodists, as well as the corps of journeyman critics and popular novelists come in for their usual bumping, this varied with unexpected tolerance toward "The Saturday Evening Post" and even a half grudging mention of Booth Tarkington. Better than any of this comment, valid and vastly entertaining as it is, would be a second Book of Prefaces say on Edith Wharton, Cabell, Woodrow Wilson—and Mencken himself. But the section of the essay devoted to the Cultural Background rises to brilliant analysis. Here again he is thinking slowly, he is on comparatively fresh ground, he brings the force of his clarity and invention to bear

---

*Bookman* 53 (March 1921): 79–81. A review of H. L. Mencken, *Prejudices, Second Series*.

on the subject—passes beyond his function as a critic of the arts and becomes a reversed Cato of a civilization.

In "The Sahara of Bozart" the dam breaks, devastating Georgia, Carolina, Mississippi, and Company. The first trickle of this overflow appeared in the preface to "The American Credo"; here it reaches such a state of invective that one pictures all the region south of Mason-Dixon to be peopled by moron Catilines. The ending is gentle—too gentle, the gentleness of ennui.

To continue in the grand manner of a catalogue: "The Divine Afflatus" deals with the question of inspiration and the lack of it, an old and sad problem to the man who has done creative work. "Examination of a Popular Virtue" runs to eight pages of whimsical excellence—a consideration of ingratitude decided at length with absurd but mellow justice. "Exeunt Omnes", which concerns the menace of death, I choose to compare with a previous "Discussion" of the same subject in "A Book of Burlesques". The comparison is only in that the former piece, which I am told Mencken fatuously considers one of his best, is a hacked out, glued together bit of foolery, as good, say, as an early essay of Mark Twain's, while this "Exeunt Omnes", which follows it by several years, is smooth, brilliant, apparently jointless. To my best recollection it is the most microscopical examination of this particular mote on the sun that I have ever come across.

Follows a four paragraph exposition of the platitude that much music loving is an affectation and further paragraphs depreciating opera as a form. As to the "Music of Tomorrow" the present reviewer's ignorance must keep him silent, but in "Tempo di Valse" Mencken, the modern, becomes Victorian by insisting that what people are tired of is more exciting than what they have just learned to do. If his idea of modern dancing is derived from watching men who learned it circa thirty-five, toiling interminably around the jostled four square feet of a cabaret, he is justified; but I see no reason why the "Bouncing Shimmee" efficiently performed is not as amusing and as graceful and certainly as difficult as any waltz ever attempted. The section continues with the condemnation of a musician named Hadley, an ingenious attempt to preserve a portrait of Dreiser, and a satisfactory devastation of the acting profession.

In "The Cult of Hope" he defends his and "Dr. Nathan's" attitude toward constructive criticism—most entertainingly—but the next section "The Dry Millennium", patchworked from the Ripetizione Generale, consists of general repetitions of theses in his previous books. "An Appendix on a Tender Theme" contains his more recent speculations on women, eked out with passages from "The Smart Set".

An excellent book! Like Max Beerbohm, Mencken's work is inevitably distinguished. But now and then one wonders—granted that, solidly, book by book, he has built up a literary reputation most to be envied of any American, granted also that he has done more for the national letters than any man alive, one is yet inclined to regret a success so complete. What will he do now? The very writers to the press about the blue Sabbath hurl the bricks of the buildings he has demolished into the still smoking ruins. He is, say, forty; how of the next twenty years? Will he find new gods to dethrone, some eternal "yokelry" still callous enough to pose as intelligenzia before the Menckenian pen fingers? Or will he strut among the ruins, a man beaten by his own success, as futile, in the end, as one of those Conrad characters that so tremendously enthrall him?

## THREE SOLDIERS

With the exception of a couple of tracts by Upton Sinclair, carefully disguised as novels but none the less ignored by the righteous booksellers of America, "Three Soldiers" by a young Harvard man named John Dos Passos is the first war book by an American which is worthy of serious notice. Even "The Red Badge of Courage" is pale beside it. Laying "Three Soldiers" down I am filled with that nameless emotion that only a piece of work created in supreme detachment can arouse. This book will not be read in the West. "Main Street" was too much of a strain—I doubt if the "cultured" public of the Middle Border will ever again risk a serious American novel, unless it is heavily baited with romantic love.

No—"Three Soldiers" will never compete with "The Sheik" or with those salacious sermons whereby Dr. Crafts gives biological thrills to the wives of prominent butchers and undertakers,—nor will it ever do aught but frighten the caravanserie of one hundred and twenty-proof Americans, dollar a year men and slaughter crazy old maids who waited in line at the book stores to buy and read the war masterpiece of the Spanish Zane Grey, the one that is now being played in the movies by a pretty young man with machine oil on his hair.

To a dozen or so hereabouts who require more seemly recreation I heartily recommend "Three Soldiers." The whole gorgeous farce of 1917–1918 will be laid before him. He will hear the Y.M.C.A. men with their high-pitched voices and their set condescending smiles, saying "That's great, boys. I would like to be with you only my eyes are weak. \*\*\* Remember that your women folk are praying for you this minute. \*\*\* I've heard the great heart of America beat. \*\*\* O boys! Never forget that you are in a great Christian cause."

He will hear such stuff as that and he will see these same obnoxious prigs charging twenty cents for a cup of chocolate and making shrill, preposterous speeches full of pompous ministers' slang. He

---

*St. Paul Daily News*, 25 September 1921, Feature Section, p. 6. A review of John Dos Passos, *Three Soldiers*.

will see the Military Police (the M.P.'s) ferociously "beating up" privates for failure to salute an officer.

He will see filth and pain, cruelty and hysteria and panic, in one long three-year nightmare and he will know that the war brought the use of these things not to some other man or to some other man's son, but to himself and to his OWN son, that same healthy young animal who came home two years ago bragging robustly of the things he did in France.

Dan Fuselli, from California, petty, stupid and ambitious, is the first soldier. His miserable disappointments, his intrigues, his amiable and esurient humanities are traced from the camp where he gets his "training" to postwar Paris where, considerably weakened in his original cheap but sufficing fibre, he has become a mess-cook.

The second soldier, Chrisfield, a half-savage, southern-moralled boy from Indiana, murders his fancied oppressor—not because of any considerable wrong, but simply as the reaction of his temperament to military discipline—and is A.W.O.L. in Paris at the end.

These two inarticulate persons are woven in the pattern with a third, a musician, who is in love with the mellifluous rythms of Flaubert.

It is with this John Andrews, the principal protagonist of the story, that John Dos Passos allows himself to break his almost Flaubertian detachment and begin to Britling-ize the war. This is immediately perceptible in his style, which becomes falsely significant and strewn with tell-tale dots. But the author recovers his balance in a page or two and flies on to the end in full control of the machine.

This is all very careful work. There is none of that uncorrelated detail, that clumsy juggling with huge masses of material which shows in all but one or two pieces of American realism. The author is not oppressed by the panic-stricken necessity of using all his data at once lest some other prophet of the new revelation uses it before him. He is an artist—John Dos Passos. His book could wait five years or ten or twenty. I am inclined to think that he is the best of all the younger men on this side.

The deficiency in his conception of John Andrews is this: John Andrews is a little too much the ultimate ineffectual, the

Henry-Adams-in-his-youth sort of character. This sort of young man has been previously sketched many times—usually when an author finds need of a mouthpiece and yet does not wish to write about an author.

With almost painstaking precaution the character is inevitably made a painter or a musician, as though intelligence did not exist outside the arts. Not that Andrews' puppet-ness is frequent. Nor is it ever clothed in aught but sophistication and vitality and grace—nevertheless the gray ghosts of Wells' heroes and those of Wells' imitators seem to file by along the margin, reminding one that such a profound and gifted man as John Dos Passos should never enlist in Wells' faithful but anemic platoon along with Walpole, Floyd Dell and Mencken's late victim, Ernest Poole. The only successful Wellsian is Wells. Let us slay Wells, James Joyce and Anatole France that the creation of literature may continue.

In closing I will make an invidious comparison: Several weeks ago a publisher sent me a book by a well-known popular writer, who has evidently decided that there is better pay of late in becoming a deep thinker, or to quote the incomparable Mencken "a spouter of great causes." The publishers informed me that the book was to be issued in October, that in their opinion it was the best manuscript novel that had ever come to them, and ended by asking me to let them know what I thought of it. I read it. It was a desperate attempt to do what John Dos Passos has done. It abounded with Fergus Falls mysticism and undigested Haeckel and its typical scene was the heroic dying Poilu crying "Jesu!" to the self-sacrificing Red Cross worker! It reached some sort of decision—that Life was an Earnest Matter or something! When it was not absurd it was so obvious as to be painful. On every page the sawdust leaked out of the characters. If anyone wishes to cultivate the rudiments of literary taste let him read "The Wasted Generation" by Owen Johnson and "Three Soldiers" by John Dos Passos side by side. If he can realize the difference he is among the saved. He will walk with the angels in Paradise.

## POOR OLD MARRIAGE

Although not one of the first I was certainly one of the most enthusiastic readers of Charles Norris's "Salt"—I sat up until five in the morning to finish it, stung into alertness by the booming repetition of his title phrase at the beginning of each section. In the dawn I wrote him an excited letter of praise. To me it was utterly new. I had never read Zola or Frank Norris or Dreiser—in fact the realism which now walks Fifth Avenue was then hiding dismally in Tenth Street basements. No one of my English professors in college ever suggested to his class that books were being written in America. Poor souls, they were as ignorant as I—possibly more so. But since then Brigadier General Mencken has marshaled the critics in an acquiescent column of squads for the campaign against Philistia.

In the glow of this crusade I read "Brass" and suffered a distinct disappointment. Although it is a more difficult form than "Salt" and is just as well, perhaps more gracefully, constructed, the parallel marriages are by no means so deftly handled as the ones in Arnold Bennett's "Whom God Hath Joined". It is a cold book throughout and it left me unmoved. Mr. Norris has an inexhaustible theme and he elaborates on it intelligently and painstakingly—but, it seems to me, without passion and without pain. There is not a line in it that compares with Griffith Adams's broken cry of emotion, "Why, I love you my girl, better than any other God damned person in the world!"

There was a fine delicacy in Frank Norris's work which does not exist in his brother's. Frank Norris had his realistic tricks—in "McTeague" for instance where the pictures are almost invariably given authenticity by an appeal to the sense of smell or of hearing rather than by the commoner form of word painting—but he seldom strengthens his dose from smelling salts to emetics. "Brass" on the contrary becomes at times merely the shocker—the harrowing

---

*Bookman* 54 (November 1921): 253–54. A review of Charles G. Norris, *Brass: A Novel of Marriage*. Griffith Adams, in the second paragraph, is a character in Norris's novel, *Salt* (1919).

description of Leila's feet could only be redeemed by a little humor, of which none is forthcoming. Early in the book one finds the following sentence:

> He inflated his chest... pounding with shut fists the hard surface of his breast, alternately digging his finger-tips into the firm flesh about the nipples.

Here he has missed his mark entirely. I gather from the context that he has intended to express the tremendous virility of his hero in the early morning. Not questioning the accuracy of the details in themselves it is none the less obvious that he has chosen entirely the *wrong* details. He has given a glimpse not into Philip's virility but into the Bronx zoo.

Save for the pseudo-Shavian discussion on marriage near the end Mr. Norris manages to avoid propaganda and panacea. Some of the scenes are excellent—Philip's first courtship, his reunion with Marjorie after their first separation, his final meeting with her. Marjorie and Philip's mothers are the best characters in the book, despite the care wasted on Mrs. Grotenberg. Leila is too much a series of tricks—she is not in a class with Rissie in "Salt".

Had this novel appeared three years ago it would have seemed more important than it does at present. It is a decent, competent, serious piece of work—but excite me it simply doesn't. A novel interests me on one of two counts: either it is something entirely new and fresh and profoundly felt, as, for instance, "The Red Badge of Courage" or "Salt", or else it is a tour de force by a man of exceptional talent, a Mark Twain or a Tarkington. A great book is both these things—"Brass", I regret to say, is neither.

## ALDOUS HUXLEY'S "CROME YELLOW"

Now this man is a wit. He is the grandson of the famous Huxley who, besides being one of the two great scientists of his time, wrote clear and beautiful prose—better prose than Stevenson could ever muster.

This is young Huxley's third book—his first one, "Limbo," was a collection of sketches—his second, "Leda," which I have never read, contained one long poem and, I believe, a few lyrics.

To begin with, Huxley, though he is more like Max Beerbohm than any other living writer (an ambiguity which I shall let stand, as it works either way), belongs as distinctly to the present day as does Beerbohm to the '90's. He has an utterly ruthless habit of building up an elaborate and sometimes almost romantic structure and then blowing it down with something too ironic to be called satire and too scornful to be called irony. And yet he is quite willing to withhold this withering breath from certain fabulous enormities of his own fancy—and thus we have in "Crome Yellow" the really exquisite fable of the two little dwarfs which is almost, if not quite, as well done as the milkmaid incident in Beerbohm's "Zuleika Dobson."

In fact I have wanted a book such as "Crome Yellow" for some time. It is what I thought I was getting when I began Norman Douglas' "South Wind." It is something less serious, less humorous and yet infinitely wittier than either "Jurgen" or "The Revolt of the Angels." It is—but by telling you all the books it resembles I will get you no nearer to knowing whether or not you will want to buy it.

"Crome Yellow" is a loosely knit (but not loosely written) satirical novel concerning the gay doings of a house party at an English country place known as Crome. The book is yellow within and without—and I do not mean yellow in the slangy sense. A sort of yellow haze of mellow laughter plays over it. The people are now like great awkward canaries trying to swim in saffron pools, now

---

*St. Paul Daily News*, 26 February 1922, Feature Section, p. 6. A review of Aldous Huxley, *Crome Yellow*.

like bright yellow leaves blown along a rusty path under a yellow sky. Placid, impoignant, Nordic, the satire scorns to burn deeper than a pale yellow sun, but only glints with a desperate golden mockery upon the fair hair of the strollers on the lawn; upon those caught by dawn in the towers; upon those climbing into the hearse at the last—beaten by the spirit of yellow mockery.

This is the sort of book that will infuriate those who take anything seriously, even themselves. This is a book that mocks at mockery. This is the highest point so far attained by Anglo-Saxon sophistication. It is written by a man who has responded, I imagine, much more to the lyric loves of lovers' long dust than to the contemporary seductions of contemporary British flappers. His protagonist—what a word for Denis, the mocked-at mocker—is lifted from his own book, "Limbo." So is Mr. Scoogan, but I don't care. Neither do I care that it "fails to mirror life;" that it is "not a novel"—these things will be said of it, never fear. I find Huxley, after Beerbohm, the wittiest man now writing in English.

The scene where Denis was unable to carry Anne amused me beyond measure.

And listen to this, when Huxley confesses to a but second-hand knowledge of the human heart:

In living people one is dealing with unknown and unknowable qualities. One can only hope to find out anything about them by a long series of the most disagreeable and boring human contacts, involving a terrible expense of time. It is the same with current events; how can I find out anything about them except by devoting years of the most exhausting first-hand studies, involving once more an endless number of the most unpleasant contacts? No, give me the past. It does not change; it is all there in black and white, and you can get to know about it comfortably and decorously, and, above all, privately—by reading.

Huxley is just 30, I believe. He is said to know more about French, German, Latin and medieval Italian literature than any man alive. I refuse to make the fatuous remark that he should know less about books and more about people. I wish to heaven that Christopher Morley would read him and find that the kittenish need not transgress upon the whimsical.

I expect the following addenda to appear on the green jacket of "Crome Yellow" at any moment:

"Drop everything and read "Crome Yellow."
—H.-yw-d Br-n.

---

"Places Huxley definitely in the first rank of American (sic!) novelists."
—General Chorus.

(The "sic" is mine. It is not harsh as in "sic 'im!" but silent as in "sick room.")

---

"It may be I'm old—it may be I'm mellow,
But I cannot fall for Huxley's "Crome Yellow."
—F. P. A.

---

"Exquisite. Places Huxley among the few snobs of English literature."
—G-tr-de Ath-r-t-n.[1]

---

[1] The invented blurbs are by a reviewer, a newspaper columnist, and a popular author of the period: Heywood Broun, Franklin P. Adams, and Gertrude Atherton.

## TARKINGTON'S "GENTLE JULIA"

Tarkington's latest consists of half a dozen excellent short stories sandwiched in between half a dozen mediocre short stories and made into an almost structureless novel on the order of "Seventeen." But it has not "Seventeen's" unity of theme nor has it a dominant character to hold it together like the Penrod books. In fact, the book could be called after little Florence as well as after her popular older cousin, Julia. Nevertheless, in parts it is enormously amusing.

The stories which make up the narrative were written over a period of ten years. They concern Herbert, age 14; his cousin Florence, age 13, and their cousin Julia, age 19—and Julia's beaux, in particular one unbelievably calfish one named Noble Dill. From much interior evidence I doubt whether they were originally intended to form a continuous story at all. For instance, the Julia who is cross and peremptory with Florence in the early chapters, is scarcely the gentle Julia who cannot bear to hurt a simple suitor's feelings in the last—and in addition the book jumps around from character to character in a way that is occasionally annoying, as it proceeds from the lack of any unity of design. Add to this that Tarkington seems a bit tired. He has used material throughout the book practically identical with material he has used before. The dance is the dance of "Seventeen," though not so fresh and amusing. The little girl, Jane, grown up, is legitimately new but the little boy repeats the experiences of Hedrick in "The Flirt"—it is held over his head by a shrewd female that he has made love to a little girl, he lives in torture for awhile and finally when the secret is exposed he becomes the victim of his public school.

All the above sounds somewhat discouraging, as if Tarkington, our best humorist since Mark Twain, had turned stale in mid-career. This is not the case. Parts of the book—the whole scene of the walk, for example, and the astounding abuse of Florence's poem by the amateur printers—are as funny as anything he has ever done. Even

---

*St. Paul Daily News*, 7 May 1922, Feature Section, p. 6. A review of Booth Tarkington, *Gentle Julia*.

the inferior parts of the book are swiftly moving and easily readable. When Noble Dill flicked his cigaret into the cellar I howled with glee. When Florence waved her hand at her mother and assured her that it was "all right," I found that I was walking with the party in a state of almost delirious merriment. In fact, the only part of the book which actively bored me was the incident of the bugs—which had the flavor of Katzenjammer humor.[1] I expected this incident to be bad because Edward J. O'Brien, the world's greatest admirer of mediocre short stories, once gave it a star when it appeared in story form under the title of "The Three Foological Wishes."

The book is prefaced by a short paragraph in which Mr. Tarkington defends, for some curious Freudian reasons, his right to make cheerful books in the face of the recent realism. But no one questions it and the greatest whoopers for "Three Soldiers" and "Main Street" and "My Antonia" have admitted and admired the sheer magic of "Seventeen." We simply reserve the right to believe that when Mr. Tarkington becomes mock-sociological and symbolical about smoke as in "The Turmoil," he is navigating out of his depth and invading the field of such old-maids' favorites as Winston Churchill.[2] His ideas, such as they are, are always expressed best in terms of his characters as in the case of "Alice Adams" and parts of "The Flirt." Mr. Tarkington is not a thoughtful man nor one profoundly interested in life as a whole and when his ideas cannot be so expressed they are seldom worth expressing. "Ramsey Milholland," one of the most wretched and absurd novels ever written, showed this. So did the spiritualistic climax of "The Magnificent Ambersons."

It is a pity that the man who writes better prose than any other living American was brought up in a generation that considered it a crime to tell the truth.

But read "Gentle Julia,"—it will give you a merry evening. With all its faults it is the best piece of light amusement from an American this past year.

---

[1] *The Katzenjammer Kids* was the title of a popular comic strip that began appearing in American newspapers in 1912.

[2] Fitzgerald means Winston Churchill (1871–1947), a popular American novelist of the early twentieth century.

## "MARGEY WINS THE GAME"

This here story's about a Jane named Margey that used to rub the 3-in-1 off the tall part of straight chairs whenever she tried to step out on the polished pine, until none of her dresses never had no backs to them. She shook a mean Conrad, but she thought Chicago was a city instead of a patent shimmee.

All she wanted was to light the candles and vamp teachers with them jazz proverbs they call epa grams. She was no Gloria Swanson, but she wouldn't gag you in a close-up. The trouble was her duds looked like she was trying to say it with towels, and she had no more line than a cow has cuticle.

Well, her brother was a mean guy, and he told her that as a flapper she was the bunk. That made this Souse Baker sore, and as he was sort of a simple duke that had been a school inspector all his life he said lay off. And that starts the signal for the jazz to begin.

Well, this guy Souse Baker he dressed this Margey up like she was a super in a Cecil B. de Mille Civil War feature and then he blind-folded her and shoved her in front of a lot of pink-blooded he-men at a cake-eaters' ball. From her shoes up to the roll of her stockings she was Ziegfeld stuff, so they fell for Souse's bunk and began chasing her around like she would give them a job or something.

By the time they got the blinders off her she had a lot of them bound and gagged, and they stuck around just from habit because everybody was there and they didn't want that they should be lonesome. But this Souse guy was getting stuck on her hisself, so he had a tough time whenever she went to some swell dive with one of the other cake-eaters. But the Jane thought it was all the bunk anyways.

She wanted to light up the tallows and swap highbrow jokes with a book-weasel from the big school. She didn't let on though for a while because she was sorry for the guy Souse, so she kept shaking the weight off her shoulders until she got a bid to the gas-fitters'

---

*New York Tribune*, 7 May 1922, Section 4, p. 7. A review of John V. A. Weaver, *Margey Wins the Game*.

ball, which was considered swell—and which was what she wanted so everybody would think she was a big cheese and then she could sneak back to the bulge-brain that she was really nuts about....

***

I give up. I can't do it. It requires a Rabelasian imagination and a patent Roth memory. Let me introduce you to John V. A. Weaver, who can.

After the immediate and deserved success of "In American" he has bubbled over into semi-dialect prose. The new book—it runs, I imagine, into less than 20,000 words—is called "Margey Wins the Game," a bright, ebullient story, shot through with sentiment and dedicated to the proposition that personal magnetism can be captured in the set snare of self-confidence.

Marge (she becomes Marge once she's past the title) is a wealthy wall flower—something rare in New York, but easily to be found in a thousand mid-Western country clubs. She lives in Chicago, thinly veiled under the name of Dearborn, amid those mysterious complexities of North Side and South Side and in that smoky, damp and essentially romantic atmosphere which over-hangs our second metropolis and makes it so incomprehensible to all but the initiated inhabitant.

We meet the "Nebraska Glee Club," a touch of exceptional humor, and attend a raid on an Italian café. The cross-section of gay Chicago is well done. The people, hastily sketched, are types, but convincing as such. The story is admirably constructed, and it seems to me that the author should do others of the same type and go a little more thoroughly into the matter, for the field is large and unexplored and he is well equipped to deal with it.

At present he has merely touched the surface with a highly amusing, swiftly moving tale of the jazz-nourished generation. But why only one story? My appetite is whetted for more.

## HOMAGE TO THE VICTORIANS

Now, Shane Leslie is the son of an Anglo-Irish baronet. He is an old Etonian and he is chamberlain to the Pope. He is half a mystic, and he is entirely a cousin of the utilitarian Winston Churchill.[1] In him there is a stronger sense of old England, I mean a sense not of its worth or blame, but of its *being*, than is possessed by any one living, possibly excepting Lytton Strachey.

It is almost impossible to review a book of his and resist the temptation to tell anecdotes of him—how a hair-pin fell from heaven, for instance, and plumped into the King of Spain's tea, of a certain sentimental haircut, of the fact that he has been the hero of two successful modern novels—but with such precious material I can be no more than tantalizing, for it belongs to his biographer, not to me.

He first came into my life as the most romantic figure I had ever known. He had sat at the feet of Tolstoy, he had gone swimming with Rupert Brooke, he had been a young Englishman of the governing classes when the sense of being one must have been, as Compton Mackenzie says, like the sense of being a Roman citizen.

Also, he was a convert to the church of my youth, and he and another, since dead, made of that church a dazzling, golden thing, dispelling its oppressive mugginess and giving the succession of days upon gray days, passing under its plaintive ritual, the romantic glamour of an adolescent dream.

He had written a book then. It had a sale—not the sale it deserved. "The End of the Chapter," it was; and bought by the snap-eyed ladies who follow with Freudian tenseness the missteps of the great. They missed its quality of low, haunting melancholy, of great age, of a faith and of a social tradition that with the years could not but have taken on a certain mellow despair—apparent perhaps

---

[1] Leslie was a first cousin of the eventual British Prime Minister, not of the novelist of the same name.

---

*New York Tribune*, 14 May 1922, Section 4, p. 6. A review of Shane Leslie, *The Oppidan*.

only to the most sensitive but by them realized with a sensuous poignancy.

Well, he has written another book—with a wretched, puzzling title, "The Oppidan," which to an American means nothing, but to Leslie an intriguing distinction, that has endured since Henry VIII. An Oppidan is an Etonian who either lives in college or doesn't—I am not quite sure which—and what does it matter, for the book is all of Eton. Once, years ago I picked up a novel called "Grey Youth," and I stared fascinated at that perfect title. I have never read it nor heard tell of it—I'm sure it was worthless—but what two words!

And that is what Leslie's new book should be named—a tale of that gray, gray cocoon, where the English-butterfly sheds its cocoon. It should have been called "Grey Youth." Once in it and you are carried back to the time of Shelley, of day-long fights with occasionally tragic, nay, fatal culminations, of Wellington's playing fields, of intolerable bullyings and abominable raggings. And even more intimately we are shown Eton of the late 90s, and the last magnificence of the Victorian age is spread in front of us, a play done before shadowed tapestries of the past.

The book interested me enormously. Mr. Leslie has a sharp eye for the manners of his age. If he does not plumb the motives of his people or his creations with the keen analysis of Strachey it is because he refers finer judgments to the court of the Celtic deity which he has accepted for his own—and where the inscrutability of men is relinquished beyond analysis, to fade into that more immense inscrutability in which all final answers and judgments lie.

Those who are interested in the great patchwork quilt picture of Victorian England, which is being gradually pieced together from the memories of survivors and the satire of their commentators, will enjoy "The Oppidan."

## A RUGGED NOVEL

This is a rugged, uneven, and sometimes beautiful novel which concerns four girls, sisters, of Chicago's middle class. These girls believed in—— Listen:

Ward Harris, at twenty, wore a virginal look like golden rain infiltrated through the stuff of a morning meadow; a look that came from her trust in the love legend, in which she had put all the capital of her youthful hopes, since her mother's whispered story of the prince who was to come and change the world with a magic kiss.

That sentence, a lovely, ill-constructed sentence, opens the book. Ward was the Mary of the family—her three sisters were Marthas. Ward believed in the love legend which "like hope, is deathless." One sister, Sari, who wanted a career on the stage, became absorbed in the business of life, the business of poverty, the business of children. Another sister wanted to be a writer. She had a story accepted by a "Mr. Hopkins," whom I suspect of being a composite Mencken and Nathan. In one of the few artificial scenes in the novel she discovers she cannot marry a fool. She goes on writing. Nita, less intelligent than the others but more shrewd, marries well in the Far West, and, because of this, incurs the faint hostility of the author.

And Ward goes on believing in the love legend, which, like hope, is deathless.

This novel is enormously amusing. The incidental portraits, the Jewish family into which Sari marries, for example, and the environment of the man "Oz," whom Ward loves, are excellent. They're convincing and they're intensely of Chicago—couldn't have existed anywhere else. Easily the best picture of Chicago since "Sister Carrie." All done in little circles and eddies and glimpses with no mooning about the heart or voice or "clangor" or smell of the city. Suddenly you're there. Suddenly you realize that all these

---

*Literary Review of the New York Evening Post*, 28 October 1922, pp. 143–44. A review of Woodward Boyd, *The Love Legend*.

people you are reading about—possibly excepting Ward—talk with slightly raised voices and are enormously self-confident.

\*\*

The book is obviously by a woman, but her methods of achieving an effect are entirely masculine—even the defects in the book are masculine defects—intellectual curiosity in what amounts to a riot, solid blocks of strong words fitted into consecutive pages like bricks, a lack of selective delicacy, and, sometimes, a deliberately blunted perception. Read the scene where Cecil goes to work in the machine shop and try to think what other women writers could have written it.

This is not a perfect first novel—but it is honest, well written, if raggedy, and thoroughly alive: Compare it, for instance, with "Dancers in the Dark" as a portrait of young people and the modern young mind. Of course, this is hardly fair because "Dancers in the Dark" is merely a jazzed-up version of the juvenile sweetbooks—and the characters are merely puppets who have read flapper editorials. The characters in the "Love Legend" are real in conception, and where the author fails to get her effects it is because of inexpertness and uncertainty rather than because of dishonesty or "faking."

The book is formless. In first novels this is permissible, perhaps even to be encouraged, as the lack of a pattern gives the young novelist more of a chance to assert his or her individuality, which is the principal thing. The title is excellent and covers the novel adequately as it jumps from character to character. The only one of the girls I liked was Ward—the other three I detested. A good book—put it upon the shelf with "Babbitt" and "The Bright Shawl" and watch and pray for more such entertainment this autumn.

## THE DEFEAT OF ART

By no less an authority than that of our leading humorist, Heywood Broun has been pronounced the best all-around newspaper man in America. And he is. He can report a football game, a play, a literary dinner, a prizefight, scandal, murder, his own domestic interests, his moods, the konduct of the klan and the greatness of Charlie Chaplin with the same skill and the same unfailing personality.

"Now," says Heywood Broun, "every scribbler in Christendom is writing an immortal novel while I continue my ephemeral output. I shall crystallize some of this so-called personality of mine into a novel and preserve it against the short memory of man."

The result is called "The Boy Grew Older."

Before I talk of this novel I want to list Heywood Broun's most obvious insufficiencies. His literary taste, when it is not playing safe, is pretty likely to be ill-considered, faintly Philistine and often downright absurd. He seems to have no background whatsoever except a fairly close reading of fashionable, contemporary novels by British and American novelists. He seems unacquainted with anything that was written before 1900, possibly excepting the English units required for entering Harvard.

This lack is, in an American novelist, a positive advantage insofar as it puts no limit on the width of his appeal. There is nothing in "The Boy Grew Older" to puzzle a movie director or a scenario writer. It is a book free from either the mark or the pretense of erudition.

Once upon a time, in the early days of the American literary revival, Mr. Broun mistook the fact that "Moon Calf," by Floyd Dell, was a seriously attempted novel for the fact that it was a successful piece of work. "Drop everything and read 'Moon Calf,'" said Mr. Broun to the public. "Drop everything and read Henry James," said the Dial to Mr. Dell. But the public trusts Heywood

---

*St. Paul Daily News*, 21 January 1923, Section 2, p. 6. A review of Heywood Broun, *The Boy Grew Older*.

Broun and because of his shove "Moon Calf" dragged in the wake of "Main Street" to a sale of 30,000 copies or more.

So when I began to read "The Boy Grew Older" I feared that, in the "Moon Calf" tradition, it would be thick with dots and bestrewn with quotations from Tennyson, Eddie Guest and the early poetic efforts of Mr. Broun.[1] On the contrary it is a competently written, highly interesting and somewhat sketchy story which concerns the soul of a newspaper man named Peter Neale. And the book is about Peter chiefly—about a simple and rather fine man who has somewhat the same devotion to his profession that Mark Twain had to his piloting or Joseph Conrad to the sea. What does it matter if Peter Neale's gorgeously ethical newspaper world is imaginary? By such books and such men as the author of "The Boy Grew Older" such an idealized concept is made a reality. After Kipling, every private in the British army tried to be like "Soldiers Three."

With a boyish hatred of emotional sloppiness Mr. Broun has utterly failed to visualize for us the affair with Maria. When she leaves Peter I was sorry. But not sorry that she was gone—not with the feeling that something young and beautiful had ceased to be—I was only sorry Peter was wounded.

Peter gets drunk. In the best "cafe fight" I have ever read about, Peter is slugged with a bottle. He meets another woman. Mr. Broun hesitates for a moment whether to be correctly the Harvard man and public "good egg" or whether to make Peter's second affair human and vital and earthy and alive. Somewhere on a dark staircase the question disappears and never emerges from its obscurity.

The boy grows older. The reality he possessed as a portrait of Heywood III fades out when he grows older than his model. At Harvard he plays in 1915 in a football game that took place in 1921. He comes to New York and works for a while under an excellent pen portrait of a famous liberal editor. He has a voice,

---

[1] Edgar "Eddie" Guest, known as "The People's Poet," wrote sentimental verse for the newspapers; he was best known for his dialect poem "Home." "Mr. Broun" is a dig at the author of the book under review, a newspaperman with whom Fitzgerald sometimes sparred in print.

so his mother takes him away and leaves Peter to his work and to his rather fine concept of honor and to his memories—which, if the incidents had been just a little more emotionally visualized when they occurred—would have made the book more moving at the close.

But Heywood Broun can write. If he will forget himself and let go, his personality will color almost every line he chooses to set down. It is a real talent that even the daily grind of newspaper work cannot dull. His second book is decidedly worth waiting for.

## SHERWOOD ANDERSON ON THE MARRIAGE QUESTION

In the last century literary reputations took some time to solidify. Not Tennyson's or Dickens's—despite their superficial radicalism such men flowed with the current of popular thought. Not Wilde's or De Musset's, whose personal scandals made them almost legendary figures in their own lifetimes. But the reputations of Hardy, Butler, Flaubert and Conrad were slow growths. These men swam up stream and were destined to have an almost intolerable influence upon succeeding generations.

First they were esoteric with a group of personal claqueurs. Later they came into a dim rippling vogue. Their contemporaries "tried to read *one* of their books" and were puzzled and suspicious. Finally some academic critic would learn from his betters that they were "the thing," and shout the news aloud with a profound air of discovery, arguing from interior evidence that the author in question was really in full accord with Florence Nightingale and Gen. Booth. And the author, old and battered and with a dozen imitators among the younger men was finally granted a period of wide recognition.

The cultural world is closer knit now. In the last five years we have seen solidify the reputations of two first class men—James Joyce and Sherwood Anderson.

"Many Marriages" seems to me the fullblown flower of Anderson's personality. It is good enough for Lee Wilson Dodd to write a kittenish parody for the Conning Tower. On the strength of "Many Marriages" you can decide whether Anderson is a neurotic or whether you are one and Anderson a man singularly free of all inhibitions. The noble fool who has dominated tragedy from Don Quixote to Lord Jim is not a character in "Many Marriages." If there is nobility in the book it is a nobility Anderson has created as surely as Rousseau created his own natural man. The genius conceives a cosmos with such transcendental force that it supersedes, in certain sensitive minds, the cosmos of which they have been

---

*New York Herald*, 4 March 1923, Section 9, p. 5. A review of Sherwood Anderson, *Many Marriages*.

previously aware. The new cosmos instantly approximates ultimate reality as closely as did the last. It is a bromide to say that the critic can only describe the force of his reaction to any specific work of art.

I read in the paper every day that, without the slightest warning, some apparently solid and settled business man has eloped with his stenographer. This is the central event of "Many Marriages." But in the glow of an unexhaustible ecstasy and wonder what is known as a "vulgar intrigue" becomes a transaction of profound and mystical importance.

The book is the story of two moments—two marriages. Between midnight and dawn a naked man walks up and down before a statue of the Virgin and speaks of his first marriage to his daughter. It was a marriage made in a moment of half mystical, half physical union and later destroyed in the moment of its consummation.

When the man has finished talking he goes away to his second marriage and the woman of his first marriage kills herself out of a little brown bottle.

The method is Anderson's accustomed transcendental naturalism. The writing is often tortuous. But then just as you begin to rail at the short steps of the truncated sentences (his prose walks with a rope around the ankle and a mischievous boy at the end of the rope) you reach an amazingly beautiful vista seen through a crack in the wall that long steps would have carried you hurriedly by. Again—Anderson feels too profoundly to have read widely or even well. What he takes to be only an empty tomato can whose beauty he has himself discovered may turn out to be a Greek vase wrought on the Ægean twenty centuries before. Again the significance of the little stone eludes me. I believe it to have no significance at all. In the book he has perhaps endowed lesser things with significance. In the case of the stone his power is not in evidence and the episode is marred.

There is a recent piece of trash entitled "Simon Called Peter,"[1] which seems to me utterly immoral, because the characters move in a

---

[1] *Simon Called Peter* was a semi-scandalous novel by the British writer Robert Keable, published in the U.S. in 1921. In *The Great Gatsby*, Nick finds a copy on a table in the apartment that Tom keeps for his rendezvous with Myrtle (p. 34 of the Scribners 1925 first edition). Fitzgerald was apprehensive about mentioning the novel in his text. See his letter to Maxwell Perkins, ca. 1 December 1924, *Scott/Max*, p. 85.

continual labyrinth of mild sexual stimulation. Over this stimulation play the colored lights of romantic Christianity.

Now anything is immoral that consoles, stimulates or confirms a distortion. Anything that acts in place of the natural will to live is immoral. All cheap amusement becomes, at maturity, immoral—the heroin of the soul.

"Many Marriages" is not immoral—it is violently anti-social. But if its protagonist rested at a defiance of the fallible human institution of monogamy the book would be no more than propaganda. On the contrary, "Many Marriages" begins where "The New Machiavelli" left off. It does not so much justify the position of its protagonist as it casts a curious and startling light on the entire relation between man and woman. It is the reaction of a sensitive, highly civilized man to the phenomenon of lust—but it is distinguished from the work of Dreiser, Joyce and Wells (for example) by utter lack both of a concept of society as a whole and of the necessity of defying or denying such a concept. For the purpose of the book no such background as Dublin Catholicism, middle Western morality or London Fabianism could ever have existed. For all his washing machine factory the hero of "Many Marriages" comes closer than any character, not excepting Odysseus, Lucifer, Attila, Tarzan and, least of all, Conrad's Michaelis, to existing in an absolute vacuum. It seems to me a rather stupendous achievement.

I do not like the man in the book. The world in which I trust, on which I seem to set my feet, appears to me to exist through a series of illusions. These illusions need and occasionally get a thorough going over ten times or so during a century.

The man whose power of compression is great enough to review this book in a thousand words does not exist. If he does he is probably writing subtitles for the movies or working for a car card company.

## MINNESOTA'S CAPITAL IN THE RÔLE OF MAIN STREET

Along comes another of those annoying novels of American manners, one of those ponderous steel scaffoldings upon which the palaces of literature may presently arise. It is something native and universal, clumsy in its handling of an enormous quantity of material; something which can be called a document, but can in no sense be dismissed as such.

Grace Flandrau's "Being Respectable", the book of the winter and in all probability of the spring, too—is superior to Sinclair Lewis's "Babbitt" in many ways, but inferior in that it deals with too many characters. The characters are complete and excellently motivated in themselves, but there is no one Babbitt or Nostromo to draw together the entire novel. It is a satirical arraignment of the upper class of a Middle Western city—in this case St. Paul, Minnesota, as "Babbitt," speaking generally, was concerned with the upper middle-class of Minneapolis. Poor Minnesota! Sauk Centre, Minneapolis and St. Paul have been flayed in turn by the State's own sons and daughters. I feel that I ought to take up the matter of Duluth and make the thing complete.

Now St. Paul, altho a bloodbrother of Indianapolis, Minneapolis, Kansas City, Milwaukee and Co., feels itself a little superior to the others. It is a "three generation" town, while the others boast but two. In the fifties the climate of St. Paul was reputed exceptionally healthy. Consequently there arrived an element from the East who had both money and fashionable education. These Easterners mingled with the rising German and Irish stock, whose second generation left the cobbler's last, forgot the steerage, and became passionately "swell" on its own account. But the pace was set by the tubercular Easterners. Hence the particular social complacency of St. Paul.

---

*Literary Digest International Book Review* 1 (March 1923): 35–36. A review of Grace Flandrau, *Being Respectable*. Carol Kennicott, in the fourth paragraph, is the heroine of Sinclair Lewis's novel *Main Street* (1920).

"Being Respectable" starts with a typical family of to-day—the sort of family that Tarkington sketched brilliantly but superficially in the first part of "The Magnificent Ambersons." There is the retired father, a product of the gilded eighties, with his business morality and his utter lack of any ideas except the shop-worn and conventional illusions current in his youth. His son, Charles, is the typical healthy vegetable which Yale University turns out by the hundred every year. The younger daughter, Deborah, is a character frequently met with in recent fiction—and also in life—ever since Shaw shocked the English-speaking world with his emancipated woman of 1900. In her very Carol-Kennicotting against the surrounding conventions Deborah is the most conventional character of all. Her conversations (which, of course, consist of the author's own favorite ideas) are the least important part of the book. The unforgetable part is the great gallery of dumb-bells of which the elder sister, Louisa, is Number One.

Louisa is a woman completely engrossed in St. Paul's passionate imitation of Chicago imitating New York imitating London. Every once in a while some woman's imitation becomes ineffective. The woman "gets in wrong and drops out." The society itself, however, goes on in its distorted and not a little ridiculous fashion. It is a society from which there is no escape. On one side there is nothing but the "common fast set" and just below are the thousand Babbitts, who from time to time furnish recruits to society itself.

Louisa is the real protagonist of the book—Louisa and her young married crowd. They are portraits to the life, differing by less than a hair from each other and from the women on whom they are modeled. They are set down here in all their energy, their dulness, their fear, their boredom—forty well-drest automatons moving with deft, unpleasant gestures through their own private anemic and exclusive Vanity Fair. It is a fine accomplishment to have captured them so—with sophistication, satire, occasional bitterness, and a pervading irony.

A thoroughly interesting and capable novel. The writing is solid throughout, and sometimes beautiful. Like Sinclair Lewis and Woodward Boyd, the author has little sense of selection—seems to have poured the whole story out in a flood. The book lacks the careful balance of "Three Soldiers," and it is not nearly so successful in handling its three or four protagonists. It skips from character to character in a way that is often annoying. But there it is, the newest and in some ways the best of those amazing documents which are (as Mencken might say) by H. G. Wells out of Theodore Dreiser, and which yet are utterly national and of to-day. And, when our Conrad or Joyce or Anatole France comes, such books as this will have cleared his way. Out of these enormous and often muddy lakes of sincere and sophisticated observation will flow the clear stream—if there is to be a clear stream at all.

Incidentally, the remarkable portrait of Valeria is the best single instance of artistic power in the book. The entire personality and charm of the woman is conveyed at second-hand. We have scarcely a glimpse of her, and she says only one line throughout. Yet the portrait is vivid and complete.

## UNDER FIRE

I did not know how good a man I was till then.... I remember my youth and the feeling that will never come back any more—the feeling that I could last forever, outlast the sea, the earth, and all men... the triumphant conviction of strength, the heat of life in the handful of dust, the glow in the heart that with every year grows dim, grows cold, grows small, and expires, and expires too soon—before life itself.

So, in part, runs one of the most remarkable passages of English prose written these thirty years—a passage from Conrad's "Youth"—and since that story I have found in nothing else even the echo of that lift and ring until I read Thomas Boyd's "Through the Wheat." It is the story of certain privates in a marine regiment, which the jacket says, was rushed into action under a bright June sunlight five years ago to stop the last thrust of the German Army towards Paris. These men were sustained by no democratic idealism, no patriotic desperation, and by no romance, except the romance of unknown adventure. But they were sustained by something else at once more material and more magical, for in the only possible sense of the word they were picked men—they were exceptionally solid specimens of a healthy stock. No one has a greater contempt than I have for the recent hysteria about the Nordic theory, but I suppose that the United States marines were the best body of troops that fought in the war.

Now, young Hicks, Mr. Boyd's protagonist, is taken as an average individual in a marine regiment, put through a short period of training in France, a trench raid, a long wait under shell fire (a wait during which, if C. E. Montague is to be believed, the average English regiment of the last year would have been utterly demoralized), and finally ordered forward in the face of machine gun fire through an endless field of yellow wheat. The action is utterly real. At first the very exactitude of the detail makes one expect no more than another piece of expert reporting, but gradually the thing

---

*Literary Review of the New York Evening Post*, 26 May 1923, p. 715. Review of Thomas Boyd, *Through the Wheat*.

begins to take on significance and assume a definite and arresting artistic contour. The advance goes on—one by one the soldiers we have come to know, know fragmentarily and by sudden flashes and illuminations, go down and die, but young Hicks and the rest go on, heavy footed and blind with sweat, through the yellow wheat. Finally, without one single recourse to sentiment, to hysteria, or to trickery, the author strikes one clear and unmistakable note of heroism, of tenuous and tough-minded exaltation, and with this note vibrating sharply in the reader's consciousness the book ends.

There is a fine unity about it all which only becomes fully apparent when this note is struck. The effect is cumulative in the sheerest sense; there are no skies and stars and dawns pointed out to give significance to the insignificant or to imply a connection where there is no connection. There are no treasured-up reactions to æsthetic phenomena poured along the pages, either for sweetening purposes or to endow the innately terrible with a higher relief. The whole book is written in the light of one sharp emotion and hence it is as a work of art rather than as a textbook for patrioteer or pacifist that the book is arresting.

Already I have seen reviews which take it as propaganda for one side or the other—in both cases this is unfair. The fact that both sides claim it tends to prove the author's political disinterestedness. As Thomas Boyd has been one of the loudest in praise of "Three Soldiers" and "The Enormous Room," it is to his credit that he has not allowed any intellectualism, however justified, to corrupt the at once less thoughtful and more profound emotion of his attitude. Still less has he been influenced by the Continental reaction to the last year of war. This, too, is as it should be, for that poignant despair, neatly as our novelists have adapted it to their ends, could not have been part of the mental make-up of the Fifth and Sixth Marines. Dos Passos and Elliot Paul filtered the war through an artistic intellectualism and in so doing attributed the emotions of exhausted nations to men who for the most part were neither exhausted nor emotional.

To my mind, this is not only the best combatant story of the great war, but also the best war book since "The Red Badge of Courage."

# SHORT FICTION

# ON YOUR OWN

*This story, originally called "Home to Maryland," draws upon Fitzgerald's experiences at his father's funeral in January 1931. Fitzgerald sent a reworked version, entitled "On Your Own," to Harold Ober in mid-May 1931 (As Ever, 176). Over a period of five years, Ober offered the story to* College Humor, Collier's, Good Housekeeping, Pictorial Review, Redbook, *the* Saturday Evening Post, *and* Woman's Home Companion—*but without success. "On Your Own" first appeared in* Esquire *91 (30 January 1979): 56–67.*

The third time he walked around the deck Evelyn stared at him. She stood leaning against the bulwark and when she heard his footsteps again she turned frankly and held his eyes for a moment until his turned away, as a woman can when she has the protection of other men's company. Barlotto, playing ping-pong with Eddie O'Sullivan, noticed the encounter. "Aha!" he said, before the stroller was out of hearing, and when the rally was finished: "Then you're still interested even if it's not the German Prince."

"How do you know it's not the German Prince?" Evelyn demanded.

"Because the German Prince is the horse-faced man with white eyes. This one—" He took a passenger list from his pocket, "—is either Mr. George Ives, Mr. Jubal Early Robbins and valet, or Mr. Joseph Widdle with Mrs. Widdle and six children."

It was a medium-sized German boat, five days westbound from Cherbourg. The month was February and the sea was dingy grey and swept with rain. Canvas sheltered all the open portions of the promenade deck, even the ping-pong table was wet.

*K'tap K'tap K'tap K'tap.* Barlotto looked like Valentino—since he got fresh in the rumba number she had disliked playing opposite him. But Eddie O'Sullivan had been one of her best friends in the company.

Subconsciously she was waiting for the solitary promenader to round the deck again but he didn't. She faced about and looked at the sea through the glass windows; instantly her throat closed and she held herself close to the wooden rail to keep her shoulders from shaking. Her thoughts rang aloud in her ears: My father is dead—when I was little we would walk to town on Sunday morning, I in my starched dress, and he would buy the Washington paper and a cigar and he was so proud of his pretty little girl. He was always so proud of me—he came to New York to see me when I opened with the Marx Brothers and he told everybody in the hotel he was my father, even the elevator boys. I'm glad he did, it was so much pleasure for him, perhaps the best time he ever had since he was young. He would like it if he knew I was coming all the way from London.

"Game and set," said Eddie.

She turned around.

"We'll go down and wake up the Barneys and have some bridge, eh?" suggested Barlotto.

Evelyn led the way, pirouetting once and again on the moist deck, then breaking into an "Off to Buffalo" against a sudden breath of wet wind. At the door she slipped and fell inward down the stair, saved herself by a perilous one-arm swing—and was brought up against the solitary promenader. Her mouth fell open comically—she balanced for a moment. Then the man said "I beg your pardon," in an unmistakably southern voice. She met his eyes again as the three of them passed on.

The man picked up Eddie O'Sullivan in the smoking room the next afternoon.

"Aren't you the London cast of 'Chronic Affection'?"

"We were until three days ago. We were going to run another two weeks but Miss Lovejoy was called to America so we closed."

"The whole cast on board?" The man's curiosity was inoffensive, it was a really friendly interest combined with a polite deference to the romance of the theatre. Eddie O'Sullivan liked him.

"Sure, sit down. No, there's only Barlotto, the juvenile, and Miss Lovejoy and Charles Barney, the producer, and his wife. We left in twenty-four hours—the others are coming on the *Homeric*."

"I certainly did enjoy seeing your show. I've been on a trip around the world and I turned up in London two weeks ago just ready for something American—and you had it."

An hour later Evelyn poked her head around the corner of the smoking room door and found them there.

"Why are you hiding out on us?" she demanded. "Who's going to laugh at my stuff? That bunch of card sharps down there?"

Eddie introduced Mr. George Ives. Evelyn saw a handsome, well-built man of thirty with a firm and restless face. At the corners of his eyes two pairs of fine wrinkles indicated an effort to meet the world on some other basis than its own. On his part George Ives saw a rather small dark-haired girl of twenty-six, burning with a vitality that could only be described as "professional." Which is to say it was not amateur—it could never use itself up upon any one person or group. At moments it possessed her so entirely, turning every shade of expression, every casual gesture, into a thing of such moment that she seemed to have no real self of her own. Her mouth was made of two small intersecting cherries pointing off into a bright smile; she had enormous, dark brown eyes. She was not beautiful but it took her only about ten seconds to persuade people that she was. Her body was lovely with little concealed muscles of iron. She was in black now and overdressed—she was always very *chic* and a little overdressed.

"I've been admiring you ever since you hurled yourself at me yesterday afternoon," he said.

"I had to make you some way or other, didn't I? What's a girl going to do with herself on a boat—fish?"

They sat down.

"Have you been in England long?" George asked.

"About five years—I go bigger over there." In its serious moments her voice had the ghost of a British accent. "I'm not really very good at anything—I sing a little, dance a little, clown a little, so the English think they're getting a bargain. In New York they want specialists."

It was apparent that she would have preferred an equivalent popularity in New York.

Barney, Mrs. Barney and Barlotto came into the bar.

"Aha!" Barlotto cried when George Ives was introduced. "She won't believe he's not the Prince." He put his hand on George's knee. "Miss Lovejoy was looking for the Prince the first day when she heard he was on board. We told her it was you."

Evelyn was weary of Barlotto, weary of all of them, except Eddie O'Sullivan, though she was too tactful to have shown it when they were working together. She looked around. Save for two Russian priests playing chess their party was alone in the smoking room—there were only thirty first-class passengers, with accommodations for two hundred. Again she wondered what sort of an America she was going back to. Suddenly the room depressed her—it was too big, too empty to fill and she felt the necessity of creating some responsive joy and gaiety around her.

"Let's go down to my salon," she suggested, pouring all her enthusiasm into her voice, making them a free and thrilling promise. "We'll play the phonograph and send for the handsome doctor and the chief engineer and get them in a game of stud. I'll be the decoy."

As they went downstairs she knew she was doing this for the new man. She wanted to play to him, show him what a good time she could give people. With the phonograph wailing "You're driving me crazy" she began building up a legend. She was a "gun moll" and the whole trip had been a frame to get Mr. Ives into the hands of the mob. Her throaty mimicry flicked here and there from one to the other; two ship's officers coming in were caught up in it and without knowing much English still understood the verve and magic of the impromptu performance. She was Ann Pennington, Helen Morgan, the effeminate waiter who came in for an order, she was everyone there in turn, and all in pace with the ceaseless music.

Later George Ives invited them all to dine with him in the upstairs restaurant that night. And as the party broke up and Evelyn's eyes sought his approval he asked her to walk with him before dinner.

The deck was still damp, still canvassed in against the persistent spray of rain. The lights were a dim and murky yellow and blankets tumbled awry on empty deck chairs.

"You were a treat," he said. "You're like—Mickey Mouse."

She took his arm and bent double over it with laughter.

"I like being Mickey Mouse. Look—there's where I stood and stared at you every time you walked around. Why didn't you come around the fourth time?"

"I was embarrassed so I went up to the boat deck."

As they turned at the bow there was a great opening of doors and a flooding out of people who rushed to the rail.

"They must have had a poor supper," Evelyn said. "No—look!"

It was the *Europa*—a moving island of light. It grew larger minute by minute, swelled into a harmonious fairyland with music from its deck and searchlights playing on its own length. Through field-glasses they could discern figures lining the rail and Evelyn spun out the personal history of a man who was pressing his own pants in a cabin. Charmed, they watched its sure matchless speed.

"Oh, Daddy, buy me that!" Evelyn cried, and then something suddenly broke inside her—the sight of beauty, the reaction to her late excitement choked her up and she thought vividly of her father. Without a word she went inside.

Two days later she stood with George Ives on the deck while the gaunt scaffolding of Coney Island slid by.

"What was Barlotto saying to you just now?" she demanded.

George laughed.

"He was saying just about what Barney said this afternoon, only he was more excited about it."

She groaned.

"He said that you played with everybody—and that I was foolish if I thought this little boat flirtation meant anything—everybody had been through being in love with you and nothing ever came of it."

"He wasn't in love with me," she protested. "He got fresh in a dance we had together and I called him for it."

"Barney was wrought up too—said he felt like a father to you."

"They make me tired," she exclaimed. "Now they think they're in love with me just because—"

"Because they see I am."

"Because they think I'm interested in you. None of them were so eager until two days ago. So long as I make them laugh it's all right but the minute I have any impulse of my own they all bustle up and think they're being so protective. I suppose Eddie O'Sullivan will be next."

"It was my fault telling them we found we lived only a few miles from each other in Maryland."

"No, it's just that I'm the only decent-looking girl on an eight-day boat, and the boys are beginning to squabble among themselves. Once they're in New York they'll forget I'm alive."

Still later they were together when the city burst thunderously upon them in the early dusk—the high white range of lower New York swooping down like a strand of a bridge, rising again into uptown New York, hallowed with diadems of foamy light, suspended from the stars.

"I don't know what's the matter with me," Evelyn sobbed. "I cry so much lately. Maybe I've been handling a parrot."

The German band started to play on deck but the sweeping majesty of the city made the march trivial and tinkling; after a moment it died away.

"Oh, God! It's so beautiful," she whispered brokenly.

If he had not been going south with her the affair would probably have ended an hour later in the customs shed. And as they rode south to Washington next day he receded for the moment and her father came nearer. He was just a nice American who attracted her physically—a little necking behind a life-boat in the darkness. At the iron grating in the Washington station where their ways divided she kissed him goodbye and for the time forgot him altogether as her train shambled down into the low-forested clayland of southern Maryland. Screening her eyes with her hands Evelyn looked out upon the dark infrequent villages and the scattered farm lights. Rocktown was a shrunken little station and there was her brother with a neighbor's Ford—she was ashamed that her luggage was so good against the exploded upholstery. She saw a star she knew and heard Negro laughter from out of the night; the breeze was cool but in it there was some smell she recognized—she was home.

At the service next day in the Rocktown churchyard, the sense that she was on a stage, that she was being watched, froze Evelyn's grief—then it was over and the country doctor lay among a hundred Lovejoys and Dorseys and Crawshaws. It was very friendly leaving him there with all his relations around him. Then as they turned from the grave-side her eyes fell on George Ives who stood a little apart with his hat in his hand. Outside the gate he spoke to her.

"You'll excuse my coming. I had to see that you were all right."

"Can't you take me away somewhere now?" she asked impulsively. "I can't stand much of this. I want to go to New York tonight."

His face fell. "So soon?"

"I've got to be learning a lot of new dance routines and freshening up my stuff. You get sort of stale abroad."

He called for her that afternoon, crisp and shining as his coupe. As they started off she noticed that the men in the gasoline stations seemed to know him with liking and respect. He fitted into the quickening spring landscape, into a legendary Maryland of graciousness and gallantry. He had not the range of a European; he gave her little of that constant reassurance as to her attractiveness—there were whole half hours when he seemed scarcely aware of her at all.

They stopped once more at the churchyard—she brought a great armful of flowers to leave as a last offering on her father's grave. Leaving him at the gate she went in.

The flowers scattered on the brown unsettled earth. She had no more ties here now and she did not know whether she would come back any more. She knelt down. All these dead, she knew them all, their weather-beaten faces with hard blue flashing eyes, their spare violent bodies, their souls made of new earth in the long forest-heavy darkness of the seventeenth century. Minute by minute the spell grew on her until it was hard to struggle back to the old world where she had dined with kings and princes, where her name in letters two feet high challenged the curiosity of the night. A line of William McFee's surged through her:

> *O staunch old heart that toiled so long for me*
> *I waste my years sailing along the sea.*

The words released her—she broke suddenly and sat back on her heels, crying.

How long she was staying she didn't know; the flowers had grown invisible when a voice called her name from the churchyard and she got up and wiped her eyes.

"I'm coming." And then, "Goodbye then Father, all my fathers."

George helped her into the car and wrapped a robe around her. Then he took a long drink of country rye from his flask.

"Kiss me before we start," he said suddenly.

She put up her face toward him.

"No, really kiss me."

"Not now."

"Don't you like me?"

"I don't feel like it, and my face is dirty."

"As if that mattered."

His persistence annoyed her.

"Let's go on," she said.

He put the car into gear.

"Sing me a song."

"Not now, I don't feel like it."

He drove fast for half an hour—then he stopped under thick sheltering trees.

"Time for another drink. Don't you think you better have one—it's getting cold."

"You know I don't drink. You have one."

"If you don't mind."

When he had swallowed he turned toward her again.

"I think you might kiss me now."

Again she kissed him obediently but he was not satisfied.

"I mean really," he repeated. "Don't hold away like that. You know I'm in love with you and you say you like me."

"Of course I do," she said impatiently, "but there are times and times. This isn't one of them. Let's go on."

"But I thought you liked me."

"I won't if you act this way."

"You don't like me then."

"Oh don't be absurd," she broke out, "of course I like you, but I want to get to Washington."

"We've got lots of time." And then as she didn't answer, "Kiss me once before we start."

She grew angry. If she had liked him less she could have laughed him out of this mood. But there was no laughter in her—only an increasing distaste for the situation.

"Well," he said with a sigh, "this car is very stubborn. It refuses to start until you kiss me." He put his hand on hers but she drew hers away.

"Now look here." Her temper mounted into her cheeks, her forehead. "If there was anything you could do to spoil everything it was just this. I thought people only acted like this in cartoons. It's so utterly crude and—" she searched for a word, "—and *American*. You only forgot to call me 'baby.'"

"Oh." After a minute he started the engine and then the car. The lights of Washington were a red blur against the sky.

"Evelyn," he said presently. "I can't think of anything more natural than wanting to kiss you, I—"

"Oh, it was so clumsy," she interrupted. "Half a pint of corn whiskey and then telling me you wouldn't start the car unless I kissed you. I'm not used to that sort of thing. I've always had men treat me with the greatest delicacy. Men have been challenged to duels for staring at me in a casino—and then you, that I liked so much, try a thing like that. I can't stand it—" And again she repeated, bitterly, "It's so American."

"Well, I haven't any sense of guilt about it but I'm sorry I upset you."

"Don't you *see*?" she demanded. "If I'd wanted to kiss you I'd have managed to let you know."

"I'm terribly sorry," he repeated.

They had dinner in the station buffet. He left her at the door of her pullman car.

"Goodbye," she said, but coolly now. "Thank you for an awfully interesting trip. And call me up when you come to New York."

"Isn't this silly," he protested. "You're not even going to kiss me goodbye."

She didn't want to at all now and she hesitated before leaning forward lightly from the step. But this time he drew back.

"Never mind," he said. "I understand how you feel. I'll see you when I come to New York."

He took off his hat, bowed politely and walked away. Feeling very alone and lost Evelyn went on into the car. That was for meeting people on boats, she thought, but she kept on feeling strangely alone.

II

She climbed a network of steel, concrete and glass, walked under a high echoing dome and came out into New York. She was part of it even before she reached her hotel. When she saw mail waiting for her and flowers around her suite, she was sure she wanted to live and work here with this great current of excitement flowing through her from dawn to dusk.

Within two days she was putting in several hours a morning limbering up neglected muscles, an hour of new soft-shoe stuff with Joe Crusoe, and making a tour of the city to look at every entertainer who had something new.

Also she was weighing the prospects for her next engagement. In the background was the chance of going to London as a co-featured player in a Gershwin show then playing New York. Yet there was an air of repetition about it. New York excited her and she wanted to get something here. This was difficult—she had little following in America, show business was in a bad way—after a while her agent brought her several offers for shows that were going into rehearsal this fall. Meanwhile she was getting a little in debt and it was convenient that there were almost always men to take her to dinner and the theatre.

March blew past. Evelyn learned new steps and performed in half a dozen benefits; the season was waning. She dickered with the usual young impressarios who wanted to "build something around her," but who seemed never to have the money, the theatre and the material at one and the same time. A week before she must decide about the English offer she heard from George Ives.

She heard directly, in the form of a telegram announcing his arrival, and indirectly in the form of a comment from her lawyer when she mentioned the fact. He whistled.

"Woman, have you snared George Ives? You don't need any more jobs. A lot of girls have worn out their shoes chasing him."

"Why, what's his claim to fame?"

"He's rich as Croesus—he's the smartest young lawyer in the South, and they're trying to run him now for governor of his state. In his spare time he's one of the best polo players in America."

Evelyn whistled.

"This is news," she said.

She was startled. Her feelings about him suddenly changed—everything he had done began to assume significance. It impressed her that while she had told him all about her public self he had hinted nothing of this. Now she remembered him talking aside with some ship reporters at the dock.

He came on a soft poignant day, gentle and spirited. She was engaged for lunch but he picked her up at the Ritz afterwards and they drove in Central Park. When she saw in a new revelation his pleasant eyes and his mouth that told how hard he was on himself, her heart swung toward him—she told him she was sorry about that night.

"I didn't object to what you did but to the way you did it," she said. "It's all forgotten. Let's be happy."

"It all happened so suddenly," he said. "It was disconcerting to look up suddenly on a boat and see the girl you've always wanted."

"It was nice, wasn't it?"

"I thought that anything so like a casual flower needn't be respected. But that was all the more reason for treating it gently."

"What nice words," she teased him. "If you keep on I'm going to throw myself under the wheels of the cab."

Oh, she liked him. They dined together and went to a play and in the taxi going back to her hotel she looked up at him and waited.

"Would you consider marrying me?"

"Yes, I'd consider marrying you."

"Of course if you married me we'd live in New York."

"Call me Mickey Mouse," she said suddenly.

"Why?"

"I don't know—it was fun when you called me Mickey Mouse."

The taxi stopped at her hotel.

"Won't you come in and talk for a while?" she asked. Her bodice was stretched tight across her heart.

"Mother's here in New York with me and I promised I'd go and see her for a while."

"Oh."

"Will you dine with us tomorrow night?"

"All right."

She hurried in and up to her room and put on the phonograph.

"Oh, gosh, he's going to respect me," she thought. "He doesn't know anything about me, he doesn't know anything about women. He wants to make a goddess out of me and I want to be Mickey Mouse." She went to the mirror swaying softly before it.

*Lady play your mandolin*
*Lady let that tune begin.*

At her agent's next morning she ran into Eddie O'Sullivan.

"Are you married yet?" he demanded. "Or did you ever see him again?"

"Eddie, I don't know what to do. I think I'm in love with him but we're always out of step with each other."

"Take him in hand."

"That's just what I don't want to do. I want to be taken in hand myself."

"Well, you're twenty-six—you're in love with him. Why don't you marry him? It's a bad season."

"He's so American," she answered.

"You've lived abroad so long that you don't know what you want."

"It's a man's place to make me certain."

It was in a mood of revolt against what she felt was to be an inspection that she made a midnight rendezvous for afterwards to go to Chaplin's film with two other men, "—because I frightened him in Maryland and he'll only leave me politely at my door." She pulled all her dresses out of her wardrobe and defiantly chose a startling gown from Vionnet; when George called for her at seven she summoned him up to her suite and displayed it, half hoping he would protest.

"Wouldn't you rather I'd go as a convent girl?"

"Don't change anything. I worship you."

But she didn't want to be worshipped.

It was still light outside and she liked being next to him in the car. She felt fresh and young under the fresh young silk—she would be glad to ride with him forever, if only she were sure they were going somewhere.

... The suite at the Plaza closed around them; lamps were lighted in the salon.

"We're really almost neighbors in Maryland," said Mrs. Ives. "Your name's familiar in St. Charles county and there's a fine old house called Lovejoy Hall. Why don't you buy it and restore it?"

"There's no money in the family," said Evelyn bluntly. "I'm the only hope, and actresses never save."

When the other guest arrived Evelyn started. Of all shades of her past—Colonel Cary. She wanted to laugh, or else hide—for an instant she wondered if this had been calculated. But she saw in his surprise that it was impossible.

"Delighted to see you again," he said simply.

As they sat down at table Mrs. Ives remarked:

"Miss Lovejoy is from our part of Maryland."

"I see," Colonel Cary looked at Evelyn with the equivalent of a wink. His expression annoyed her and she flushed. Evidently he knew nothing about her success on the stage, remembered only an episode of six years ago. When champagne was served she let a waiter fill her glass lest Colonel Cary think that she was playing an unsophisticated role.

"I thought you were a teetotaller," George observed.

"I am. This is about the third drink I ever had in my life."

The wine seemed to clarify matters; it made her see the necessity of anticipating whatever the Colonel might afterwards tell the Ives. Her glass was filled again. A little later Colonel Cary gave an opportunity when he asked:

"What have you been doing all these years?"

"I'm on the stage." She turned to Mrs. Ives. "Colonel Cary and I met in my most difficult days."

"Yes?"

The Colonel's face reddened but Evelyn continued steadily.

"For two months I was what used to be called a 'party girl.'"

"A party girl?" repeated Mrs. Ives puzzled.

"It's a New York phenomenon," said George.

Evelyn smiled at the Colonel. "It used to amuse me."

"Yes, very amusing," he said.

"Another girl and I had just left school and decided to go on the stage. We waited around agencies and offices for months and there were literally days when we didn't have enough to eat."

"How terrible," said Mrs. Ives.

"Then somebody told us about 'party girls.' Business men with clients from out of town sometimes wanted to give them a big time—singing and dancing and champagne, all that sort of thing, make them feel like regular fellows seeing New York. So they'd hire a room in a restaurant and invite a dozen party girls. All it required was to have a good evening dress and to sit next to some middle-aged man for two hours and laugh at his jokes and maybe kiss him good night. Sometimes you'd find a fifty-dollar bill in your napkin when you sat down at table. It sounds terrible, doesn't it—but it was salvation to us in that awful three months."

A silence had fallen, short as far as seconds go but so heavy that Evelyn felt it on her shoulders. She knew that the silence was coming from some deep place in Mrs. Ives's heart, that Mrs. Ives was ashamed for her and felt that what she had done in the struggle for survival was unworthy of the dignity of woman. In those same seconds she sensed the Colonel chuckling maliciously behind his bland moustache, felt the wrinkles beside George's eyes straining.

"It must be terribly hard to get started on the stage," said Mrs. Ives. "Tell me—have you acted mostly in England?"

"Yes."

What had she said? Only the truth and the whole truth in spite of the old man leering there. She drank off her glass of champagne.

George spoke quickly, under the Colonel's roar of conversation: "Isn't that a lot of champagne if you're not used to it?"

She saw him suddenly as a man dominated by his mother; her frank little reminiscence had shocked him. Things were different for a girl on her own and at least he should see that it was wiser than that Colonel Cary might launch dark implications thereafter. But she refused further champagne.

After dinner she sat with George at the piano.

"I suppose I shouldn't have said that at dinner," she whispered.

"Nonsense! Mother knows everything's changed nowadays."

"She didn't like it," Evelyn insisted. "And as for that old boy that looks like a Peter Arno cartoon!"

Try as she might Evelyn couldn't shake off the impression that some slight had been put upon her. She was accustomed only to having approval and admiration around her.

"If you had to choose again would you choose the stage?" Mrs. Ives asked.

"It's a nice life," Evelyn said emphatically. "If I had daughters with talent I'd choose it for them. I certainly wouldn't want them to be society girls."

"But we can't all have talent," said Colonel Cary.

"Of course most people have the craziest prejudices about the stage," pursued Evelyn.

"Not so much nowadays," said Mrs. Ives. "So many nice girls go on the stage."

"Girls of position," added Colonel Cary.

"They don't usually last very long," said Evelyn. "Every time some debutante decides to dazzle the world there's another flop due on Broadway. But the thing that makes me maddest is the way people condescend. I remember one season on the road—all the small-town social leaders inviting you to parties and then whispering and snickering in the corner. Snickering at Gladys Knowles!" Evelyn's voice rang with indignation: "When Gladys goes to Europe she dines with the most prominent people in every country, the people who don't know these back-woods social leaders exist—"

"Does she dine with their wives too?" asked Colonel Cary.

"With their wives too." She glanced sharply at Mrs. Ives. "Let me tell you that girls on the stage don't feel a bit inferior, and the really fashionable people don't think of patronizing them."

The silence was there again heavier and deeper, but this time excited by her own words Evelyn was unconscious of it.

"Oh, it's American women," she said. "The less they have to offer the more they pick on the ones that have."

She drew a deep breath, she felt that the room was stifling.

"I'm afraid I must go now," she said.

"I'll take you," said George.

They were all standing. She shook hands. She liked George's mother, who after all had made no attempt to patronize her.

"It's been very nice," said Mrs. Ives.

"I hope we'll meet soon. Good-night."

With George in a taxi she gave the address of a theatre on Broadway.

"I have a date," she confessed.

"I see."

"Nothing very important." She glanced at him, and put her hand on his. Why didn't he ask her to break the date? But he only said:

"He better go over 45th Street."

Ah, well, maybe she'd better go back to England—and be Mickey Mouse. He didn't know anything about women, anything about love, and to her that was the unforgivable sin. But why in a certain set of his face under the street lamps did he remind her of her father?

"Won't you come to the picture?" she suggested.

"I'm feeling a little tired—I'm turning in."

"Will you phone me tomorrow?"

"Certainly."

She hesitated. Something was wrong and she hated to leave him. He helped her out of the taxi and paid it.

"Come with us?" she asked almost anxiously. "Listen, if you like—"

"I'm going to walk for a while!"

She caught sight of the men waiting for her and waved to them.

"George, is anything the matter?" she said.

"Of course not."

He had never seemed so attractive, so desirable to her. As her friends came up, two actors, looking like very little fish beside him, he took off his hat and said:

"Good-night, I hope you enjoy the picture."

"George—"

—and a curious thing happened. Now for the first time she realized that her father was dead, that she was alone. She had thought of herself as being self-reliant, making more in some seasons than his practice brought him in five years. But he had always been behind her somewhere, his love had always been behind her— She had never been a waif, she had always had a place to go.

And now she was alone, alone in the swirling indifferent crowd. Did she expect to love this man, who offered her so much, with the naive romantics of eighteen. He loved her—he loved her more than anyone in the world loved her. She wasn't ever going to be a great star, she knew that, and she had reached the time when a girl had to look out for herself.

"Why, look," she said, "I've got to go. Wait—or don't wait."

Catching up her long gown she sped up Broadway. The crowd was enormous as theatre after theatre eddied out to the sidewalks. She sought for his silk hat as for a standard, but now there were many silk hats. She peered frantically into groups and crowds as she ran. An insolent voice called after her and again she shuddered with a sense of being unprotected.

Reaching the corner she peered hopelessly into the tangled mass of the block ahead. But he had probably turned off Broadway so she darted left down the dimmer alley of 48th Street. Then she saw him, walking briskly, like a man leaving something behind—and overtook him at Sixth Avenue.

"George," she cried.

He turned; his face looking at her was hard and miserable.

"George, I didn't want to go to that picture, I wanted you to make me not go. Why didn't you ask me not to go?"

"I didn't care whether you went or not."

"Didn't you?" she cried. "Don't you care for me any more?"

"Do you want me to call you a cab?"

"No, I want to be with you."

"I'm going home."

"I'll walk with you. What is it, George? What have I done?"

They crossed Sixth Avenue and the street became darker.

"What is it, George? Please tell me. If I did something wrong at your mother's why didn't you stop me?"

He stopped suddenly.

"You were our guest," he said.

"What did I do?"

"There's no use going into it." He signalled a passing taxi. "It's quite obvious that we look at things differently. I was going to write you tomorrow but since you ask me it's just as well to end it today."

"But why, George?" she wailed. "What did I do?"

"You went out of your way to make a preposterous attack on an old gentlewoman who had given you nothing but courtesy and consideration."

"Oh, George, I didn't, I didn't. I'll go to her and apologize. I'll go tonight."

"She wouldn't understand. We simply look at things in different ways."

"Oh—h-h." She stood aghast.

He started to say something further, but after a glance at her he opened the taxi door.

"It's only two blocks. You'll excuse me if I don't go with you."

She had turned and was clinging to the iron railing of a stair.

"I'll go in a minute," she said. "Don't wait."

She wasn't acting now. She wanted to be dead. She was crying for her father, she told herself—not for him but for her father.

His footsteps moved off, stopped, hesitated—came back.

"Evelyn."

His voice was close beside her.

"Oh, poor baby," it said. He turned her about gently in his arms and she clung to him.

"Oh yes," she cried in wild relief. "Poor baby—just your poor baby."

She didn't know whether this was love or not but she knew with all her heart and soul that she wanted to crawl into his pocket and be safe forever.

# LO, THE POOR PEACOCK!

*"Lo, the Poor Peacock!" began as a "Gwen" story, meant to be part of a series of stories about an adolescent girl named Gwen Bowers and her father Bryan—these characters based on Scottie Fitzgerald and her father. Two of these stories appeared in the* Post: *"Too Cute for Words" (18 April 1936) and "Inside the House" (13 June 1936). Both are included in the Cambridge edition of* The Basil, Josephine, and Gwen Stories *(2009). "Peacock" was offered by Ober without success to the* Post *and, in revised form, with names changed, to* Ladies' Home Journal. *The story remained unpublished until September 1971 when it appeared in* Esquire, *in a version heavily cut and altered by an* Esquire *editor. The "Gwen" text of the story is not known to survive. The version sent to* Ladies' Home Journal *is published here; it survives at Princeton in a 30-page typescript with Fitzgerald's revisions. This text first appeared in* Price, 591–607.

Miss McCrary put the leather cover over the typewriter. Since it was the last time, Jason came over and helped her into her coat, rather to her embarrassment.

"Mr. Davis, remember if anything comes up that I didn't cover on the memorandum, just you telephone. The letters are off; the files are straight. They'll call for the typewriter on Monday."

"You've been very nice."

"Oh, don't mention it. It's been a pleasure. I'm only sorry—"

Jason murmured the current shibboleth: "If times pick up—"

A moment after her departure her face reappeared in the doorway.

"Give my love to the little girl. And I hope Mrs. Davis is better."

At once it was lonely in the office. Not because of Miss McCrary's physical absence—her presence often intruded on him—but because she was gone *for good*. Putting on his coat Jason looked at the final memorandum—it contained nothing that need be done today—or in three days. It was nice to have a cleared desk, but he remembered days when business was so active, so pulsating that he telephoned instructions from railroad trains, radiographed from shipboard.

At home he found Jo and two other little girls playing Greta Garbo in the living room. Jo was so happy and ridiculous, so clownish with the childish smudge of rouge and mascara, that he decided to wait till after luncheon to introduce the tragedy.

Passing through the pantry he took a slant-eyed glance at the little girls still in masquerade, realizing that presently he would have to deflate one balloon of imagination. The child who was playing Mae West—to the extent of saying 'Come up and see me sometime'— admitted that she had never been permitted to *see* Mae West on the screen; she had been promised that privilege when she was fourteen.

Jason had been old enough for the war; he was thirty-eight. He wore a salt-and-pepper mustache; he was of middle height and well-made within the first ready-made suit he had ever owned.

Jo came close and demanded in quick French:

"Can I have these girls for lunch?"

"Pas aujourd'hui."

"Bien."

But she had to be told now. He didn't want to give her bad news in the evening, when she was tired.

After luncheon when the maid had withdrawn, he said:

"I want to talk, now, about a serious matter."

At the seriousness of his tone her eyes left a lingering crumb.

"It's about school," he said.

"About school?"

He plunged into his thesis.

"There've been hospital bills and not much business. I've figured out a budget—You know what that is: It's how much you've got, placed against how much you can spend. On clothes and food and education and so forth. Miss McCrary helped me figure it out before she left."

"Has she *left*? Why?"

"Her mother's been sick and she felt she ought to stay home and take care of her. And now, Jo, the thing that hits the budget hardest is school."

Without quite comprehending what was coming, Jo's face had begun to share the unhappiness of her father's.

"It's an expensive school with the extras and all—one of the most expensive day schools in the East."

He struggled to his point, with the hurt that was coming to her germinating in his own throat.

"It doesn't seem we can afford it any more this year."

Still Jo did not quite understand, but there was a hush in the dining room.

"You mean I can't go to school this term?" she asked, finally.

"Oh, you'll go to school. But not Tunstall."

"Then I don't go to Tunstall Monday," she said in a flat voice. "Where will I go?"

"You'll take your second term at public school. They're very good now. Mama never went to anything but a public school."

"Daddy!" Her voice, comprehending at last, was shocked.

"We mustn't make a mountain out of a mole-hill. After this year you can probably go back and finish at Tunstall—"

"But *Daddy!* Tunstall's supposed to be the best. And you said this term you were satisfied with my marks—"

"That hasn't anything to do with it. There are three of us, Jo, and we've got to consider all three. We've lost a great deal of money. There simply isn't enough to send you."

Two advance tears passed the frontier of her eyes, and navigated the cheeks.

Unable to endure her grief, he spoke on automatically:

"Which is best—spend too much and get into debt—or draw in our horns for a while?"

Still she wept silently. All the way to the hospital where they were paying their weekly visit she dripped involuntary tears.

Jason had undoubtedly spoiled her. For ten years the Davis household had lived lavishly in Paris; thence he had journeyed from Stockholm to Istamboul, placing American capital in many enterprises. It had been a magnificent enterprise—while it had lasted. They inhabited a fine house on the Avenue Kleber, or else a villa at Beaulieu. There was an English Nanny, and then a governess, who imbued Jo with a sense of her father's surpassing power. She was brought up with the same expensive simplicity as the children she played with in the Champs Élysées. Like them, she accepted the idea that luxury of life was simply a matter of growing up to it—the right to precedence, huge motors, speed boats, boxes at opera or ballet; Jo had early got into the habit of secretly giving away most of the surplus of presents with which she was inundated.

Two years ago the change began. Her mother's health failed, and her father ceased to be any longer a mystery man, just back from Italy with a family of Lenci dolls for her. But she was young and adjustable and fitted into the life at Tunstall school, not realizing how much she loved the old life. Jo tried honestly to love the new life too, because she loved things and people and she was prepared to like the still newer change. But it took a little while because of the fact that she loved, that she was built to love, to love deeply and forever.

When they reached the hospital Jason said:

"Don't tell mother about school. She might notice that it's hit you rather hard, and make her unhappy. When you get—sort of used to it we'll tell her."

"I won't say anything."

They followed a tiled passage they both knew to an open door.

"Can we come in?"

"*Can* you?"

Together husband and daughter embraced her, almost jealously, from either side of the bed. With a deep quiet, their arms and necks strained together.

Annie Lee's eyes filled with tears.

"Sit down. Have chairs, you all. Miss Carson, we need another chair."

They had scarcely noticed the nurse's presence.

"Now tell me everything. Have some chocolates. Aunt Vi sent them. She can't remember what I can and can't eat."

Her face, ivory cold in winter, stung to a gentle wild rose in spring, then in summer pale as the white key of a piano, seldom changed. Only the doctors and Jason knew how ill she was.

"All's well," he said. "We keep the house going."

"How about you, Jo? How's school? Did you pass your exams?"

"Of course, Mama."

"Good marks, *much* better than last year," Jason added.

"How about the play?" Annie Lee pursued innocently. "Are you still going to be Titania?"

"I don't know, Mama."

Jason switched the subject to 'the farm,' a remnant of a once extensive property of Annie Lee's.

"I'd sell it if we could. I can't see how your mother ever made it pay."

"She did though. Right up to the day of her death."

"It was the sausage. And there doesn't seem to be a market for it any more."

The nurse warned them that time was up. As if to save the precious minutes Annie Lee thrust out a white hand to each.

As they got into the car, Jo asked:

"Daddy, what happened to our money?"

Well—better tell her than to have her brood about it.

"It's complicated. The Europeans couldn't pay interest on what we lent them. You know interest?"

"Of course. We had it in the Second Main."

"My job was to judge whether a business showed promise, and if I thought so we loaned them money. When bad times came and they couldn't pay, we wouldn't loan any more. So my job was played out and we came home."

He went on to say that the money he had invested in the venture—oh, many thousands, oh, never mind how much, Jo—and now all that money was 'tied up.'

Under the aegis of the old shot tower they slowed by a garage to fill the tank.

"Why do you like to stop at this station, Daddy? Beside that ugly old chimney over there?"

"That's not a chimney. Don't you know what it is? During the Revolution they had to drop lead down to make the bullets to fire at the British. This is a Historical Monument."

... They rounded the corner of the Confederate dead. Jo spoke again suddenly:

"Americans have a hard time, don't they, Daddy? Always fights about nothing."

"Oh well, we're a fighting race. That's what brought us here in the first place."

"But it's not happy—like in Europe."

"They have their troubles. Anyhow you were just a child and all shielded." And he added as they stopped in front of their house, "What of it?"

"Mummy has heart trouble, and you lost your money, and—"

"For heaven's sake don't get sorry for yourself!" he said gruffly. "That spoils people for good. We have a nice house, at least." He felt a pang at knowing that they were going to have to give it up, but he did not want to put too much upon her in one day.

But in the hall Jo was still absorbed in her inner story.

"Daddy, we're like the characters in Little Orphan Annie, only we haven't got that dog that says *Arp* all the time. I never heard a dog say *Arp* did you? They always have dogs in the funny papers now that say 'Arp' or 'Woof,' and I never heard a dog say either."

He was relieved at the turn the conversation had taken.

"I only like the Gumps. Except when I feel mean I like Dick Tracy and X-9."

Jo sighed as she started to her room.

"Nothing seems so bad—when you only have to read about it," she said ruefully.

## II

Almost before Jo was adjusted to public school the news broke to her of their impending move. It was a far cry from the spacious house with the mutual, free-rolling lawns of the new suburbs, to the little apartment. Into which the big sofa and the big bed simply wouldn't go and had to repose instead at storage, along with many other things. Jo derived a melancholy consolation from being allowed to act as interior decorator. With some difficulty her father restrained his hilarity.

"I think it's *beau*tiful, Baby."

"Oh, I know you don't. But Daddy, I thought I'd get tinfoil at the five-and-ten and make the whole room silver, like a room in the

'House Beautiful'. But it *rum*pled. And now it won't come *off*—no matter what I do makes it worse!"

During Washington's Birthday vacation she repainted her furniture. The man from the Cleaning and Dyeing Company looked aghast at the rug he was expected to restore. And that evening at dancing school mothers warned their children away from the violent rashes on her arms—and were appalled—no understatement is possible—by the clearly leprous quality of the green or purple patches that glared like menacing eyes—dull and sinister eyes—from her hair. There had been nothing to do about it; hair is not washed in tears. The patches remained, remained indeed for weeks. After a fortnight they took on a not unattractive hue—attractive, that is to say, to anyone but Jo—of the roofs of many European villages washed down by an avalanche. And mingled. Thoroughly mingled.

The catastrophe discouraged Jo so much that she no longer wanted to go to the Beacon's Barn dancing class.

Jason argued for it—it was not expensive.

"But there's no *use*," she said, "—now I don't go to Tunstall any more. They have secrets. I like a lot of people at school now."

"You'd better," her father said.

"Why do you say I'd *better*?"

In their new isolation these two talked and fought against each other like adults, almost the old sempiternal dispute of man and wife.

Jason hated that it should be that way, hated her to see him in moments of discouragement.

"Let's go out to the farm," he said one Saturday at breakfast. "You've never been there."

"Can we afford to run the car?"

"Jo, can't you forget for a minute that I'm poor? I've explained; in the textile business there're only three or four accounts that pay commissions. That's like interest. You said you understood that."

"Yes."

"And the brokers who have them are naturally hanging on—they had them before I came here. As long as I have to sell second-class merchandise to—Let's forget it and like the ride."

"It certainly can go fast, Daddy. Can we really afford to run it?"

"It's cheaper running fast. I want to get there before they finish making the first batch of sausage."

It was seventy miles between fields of frosty rubble, between the ever-dividing purple shoulders of the Appalachians, between villages he had never wanted to ask the names of, so much did he cherish the image of them in his heart....

But Jo's heart was still in France. She was less regarding than thinking.

"Daddy—why couldn't we just make a lot of money out of the farm? Like grandmother did. And just live on that. And get rich."

"But there isn't any farm any more, I tell you. There's just a—just a large pig-sty!"

He retreated from his coarseness as he saw her face contract.

"It isn't quite all that, Baby. Young Seneca does a little truck farming—"

"Who's Young Seneca?"

"There was an Old Seneca and now there's a Young Seneca—"

"When it was a big farm how big was it, Daddy?"

"As far as you can see."

"Far as the mountains?"

"Not quite."

"It was a big farm, wasn't it?"

"It was good and big—even for these parts," he answered, falling into the vernacular.

After a time Jo asked:

"How do they make the sausage, Daddy?"

"I kind of forget. I think—let's see—I think the formula is sixteen pounds of lean meat and sixteen of fat meat. And then they grind it all together. Then they knead in the seasoning—nine tablespoons of salt, nine pepper, nine sage—"

"Why *nine*?"

"That's what your grandmother did."

—Jason had fed Jo's insatiable curiosity with as much as he remembered of the process as they turned into the washed-out lane that led to the farm.

Young Seneca, plunged into work, hurried over to greet them.

"How goes?" Jason asked.

"Just startin', Mr. Davis. We butchered last night. Then a couple of boys thought they had a right to sleep all day. Have I got to pay 'em for that time? They just keep the dogs off."

"The *dogs*?" Jo demanded.

He acknowledged her presence.

"That's right, Missy. Dogs down here are up to anything. We say: 'It's a poor dog that can't keep his own self.'"

Getting out of the car they walked toward the smokehouse.

"We pay those hands well," Jason said. "They still get the chitlings and cracklings and hogs' heads?"

"They gets the regular, Mr. Davis. Even them ditchers work right hard. You take now Aunt Rose that worked for your mother-and-law—she's been kneadin' that seasoning till her arms like to fall off."

The Negress in question greeted them cheerfully.

"Day! Mr. Davis. Day! young lady."

She left her job momentarily to inspect the child, wiping her hands of the sharp spices on a big old kitchen towel.

"And *don't* you look like your mother did?"

Jo wandered into the smokehouse. She passed barrels of flour, salt, lard—of brown sugar, of cut sugar, of sugar granulated. Coming out she ran into a colored girl with a bucket of milk on her head.

"I'm sorry."

Without losing a bit of her balance the young woman laughed hilariously.

"Don't need to be sorry. There's chits been threatnin' to push me down three years, and none ov'em ever do it."

. . . Jo emerged from the smokehouse to find her father in argument with Young Seneca, who broke off from time to time to call instructions to his helpers.

"That there's a flour sifter you're using, Aunt Jinnie. You ought to use a cornmeal sifter for getting out them sage stems."

Jo's interest was divided between the sausage grinding and her father's conversation with Young Seneca.

"We're not making a cheap sausage and listen to this."

He took a letter from his pocket and read aloud: "'We cannot undertake to distribute your product any longer because of the cancellations.' Now I can't believe that's just hard times. This used to be the best-known stuff of its kind in the East. It's fallen off in quality. So where's your pride, man? They didn't use to be able to keep up with the orders. Something's missing."

"Sure I don't know what it is, Mr. Davis."

When they started back a hickory fire flamed against the white sycamores and it was cold.

"Daddy, if the farm was mine I'd try to find out what's the matter about the sausage."

Every day Jo lost a little faith in her father. Father had been "wonderful" once, and she went on, because she had been correctly tuned to the idea that duty is everything. She had been early made to put her back and wrists into that great realization—work isn't all enthusiasm, though that is an essential part of it—in the long stress and strain of life it is more often what one doesn't want to do any longer.

### III

At high school Jo was behind in some subjects but in language classes her only difficulty was to bring her accent down to the level of the rest; her weak spot was Ancient History, which she had never studied—her remark that Julius Caesar was King of Egypt, remembered vaguely from a quick reading of "Anthony and Cleopatra," became a teacher's legend in the school. She made only a few friends at school; she was at the age of existing largely in her imagination.

On Jason's part it was no help in the dull late winter to know that Jo was losing faith in him. Her right to security and to special privilege as well—this, that was as much a part of her as her sense of responsibility—made a friction between them. But something was gone—Jo's respect for the all-wise, all-just, all-providing.

He tried to keep up his morale with exercise, and with ceaseless pursuit of better textile accounts. His thin stream of commission money scarcely sufficed to keep his head above water. With one of the big ones he would be on safe ground, for he was favorably known here. Well disposed wholesalers tried to slant in his direction, but they were prevented by a class of merchandise they did not care to carry.

There came the black day when he cracked—the blue black, the purple black, the green black of those unused to it. In the morning the grocer's wife came; she said loud in the living room that she and her husband did not care to carry the account any longer.

"Be quiet!" Jason warned her. "Wait till the little girl gets off to school."

"Your little girl! What about mine. One hundred ten dollar—"

Jo's feet sounded on the stairs.

"Morning Daddy. Oh! Morning Mrs. Deshhacker."

"Good morning."

Temporarily, Jo's imperturbability disarmed Mrs. Deshhacker, but after she had gone into the dining room, she delivered her ultimatum more firmly. Jason could only say:

"I'll try.... Middle of next week.... Anyhow a partial payment."

There was the silver: Certain pieces were inviolate—the Supreme Court Bowl, the Lee spoons with the crest of his grandfather—

Jason had seen the sign many times. Mr. Cale would take any security—was most generous, most reliable.

"How do you do, sir?"

With the infallible good manners of the Marylander, even of the humbler denominations, he stood waiting. His venality scarcely showed through his mask.

Jason mumbled something with a shamed face. Mr. Cale was used to that and stopped him.

"You want to raise some money?"

"Yes—on some silver."

"What kind?"

"Table silver. Some goblets that have been a long time—" He broke off—the indignity was intolerable— "and a coffee set."

"Well naturally you have to show me."

"Of course. There may be other things—some furniture. A few pieces—I'll redeem them in a month or so."

"Oh, I'm sure you will."

Big chance he will, he added from his own experience....

At the hospital Jason was stopped in the hall and made to sit down by the floor nurse. Doctor Keyster was finishing his rounds and wanted to talk to him before he went into his wife's room.

"About what?"

"He didn't say."

"She's *worse?*"

"I don't know, Mr. Davis. He just wants to talk to you—"

She was cleaning thermometers as she talked.

Half an hour later in a little reception room Dr. Keyster spoke his mind.

"She doesn't respond. There's nothing before her but years of rest, that's all I can say—years of rest. We've all got fond of her here but there'd be no service to you in kidding you."

"She'll never get well?"

"Probably never."

"You don't think she'll ever be well?" Jason asked again.

"There *have* been cases—"

... Then the spring was gone out of life, April, May and June. That was all gone.

... April when she came to him like a rill of sweetness. May when she was a hillside. June when they held each other so close that there was nothing more except the lashes flicking on their eyes....

Dr. Keyster said:

"You might as well make up your mind to it, Mr. Davis."

Going home once more from one of the many pietas to his love, Jason's taxi passed through an agitated meat market; a labor agitator was addressing the crowd; when he saw Jason in his taxi he shifted the burden of his discourse to him.

"Here is one! And here *we* are! We'll turn them upside down and shake them till the dimes and quarters roll out!"

Jason wondered what would roll out of him. He had just enough to pay the taxi.

Up in his bedroom he felt for the third time the balance of the thirty-eight revolver—life insurance all paid up.

"Help me to kill myself!" he prayed. "No fooling now. Put it in the mouth."

—The phone rang sharp and he tossed the gun onto the empty twin bed.

A woman's voice said: "Is this Mr. Davis? This is Principal McCutcheon's secretary. Just one moment."

Then came a man's voice, level and direct.

"This is Mr. McCutcheon at the High School. It's an unfortunate matter, Mr. Davis. We have to ask you to withdraw your daughter Josephine from school."

Jason's tense breath caught in his throat.

"I thought you'd rather know before she reached home. I tried your office. We're compelled, much against our sensibilities, to expel three of the girls for conduct that can't be condoned. When a pupil falls below the tone of the school the individual must be sacrificed to the good of the majority. I called a committee of teachers, Mr. Davis, and they saw eye-to-eye with me."

"What was the nature of the offense?"

"That I don't care to go into on the phone, Mr. Davis. I shall be glad to see you by appointment any afternoon except Thursday between two and four. I must add that we were more than surprised to find Josephine linked up to this matter. She's held herself—well, I must say, a little aloof; she hasn't ingratiated herself with her teachers, but—well, there we are."

"I see," Jason said dryly.

"Good afternoon, sir."

Jason reached for the revolver and began taking the cartridges out of the magazine.

—I've got to stick around—a little longer, he thought.

Jo arrived in half an hour, her usually mobile mouth tight and hard. There were dark strips of tears up and down her cheeks.

"Hello."

"Hel*lo*, darling." He had been waiting for her downstairs; he waited till she had taken off her coat and hat.

"What's it all about anyhow?"

Furiously she turned to him.

"I *won't* tell you! You can shake me, Daddy! You can beat me!"

"For *God's* sake—what's this all about? When did I ever beat you?"

"They wanted to this morning because I wouldn't say what they wanted."

Jo flung herself into a corner of the big couch and wept into it. He walked around the room, concerned and embarrassed.

"I don't want to know, Jo. Whatever you do is all right with me. I trust you, Baby, all the way. I'm not even making any inquiries."

She turned tired eyes up at him.

"You won't? You promise, word of honor?"

"Yes. I've got an idea, a real hunch. Unless—or say till I get the Gehrbohm account, I have lots of time in the afternoon. Suppose I be your private tutor for a while. I was pretty good once in Latin and Algebra. For the languages we'll get a reading list from the library."

She sobbed again deep into the big cushions.

"Oh Baby! Stop that. We're not defeatists, you and me. Take a bath and then we'll get up some dinner."

When she had gone into her room Jason tried to think of something outside himself. Then he remembered what Annie Lee had said in their short quarter hour this morning.

"I can't understand about the farm—it was all so simple. There was the seasoning—nine tablespoons of salt, then nine of hickory ash, then the pepper and sage. And of course always the tenderloin—"

"Hickory ash?" Jason had exclaimed. "Tenderloin?"

Stirred by his surprise she lifted herself up in bed, so that he had to ease her gently down again. "Don't tell me Young Seneca isn't using tenderloin—isn't putting in the tablespoons of *hic*kory ash?"

—In the living room of the apartment Jason sat down and wrote Young Seneca.

When Jo came downstairs he said, "Take this over to the post office, will you? It's about the farm."

After examining the address Jo demanded:

"Father—do you mean *ser*iously you're going to teach me?"

"Am I? You bet! Teach you all I know."

"All right."

But in the grey dusk he was still bent over the ragged text-book.

"Caesar," he said over the first text. "It's addressed to the damn Swiss!"

He translated:

"In Switzerland they necked the Gods and the men—"

"*What*, Daddy?"

"Wait now: In Switzerland they necked the men and then they necked the Gods—This is difficult now—Latin didn't seem like that in *my* day."

Jason turned to Jo with exasperation. "Don't they give you sentences to construe? *Helvētiī quī nec dēos nec hominēs verēbantur*—That means quiver I think—*magnum dolorem*. That means it all ends up very sad. Why did you ask me to translate it in the first place?"

"I *did*n't ask you. I knew that part. It means the Helvetians who feared neither Gods nor men came to great grief because they were restrained on all sides by mountains."

He read again: "*Patiēbantur quod ex omnibus partibus*, and that means a rampart of ten feet," he cried exultantly across the lamplight.

"Yah! You saw that in a footnote."

"I did not," he lied.

"Give me your word of honor?"

"Let's talk about something else."

"You fancy yourself as a teacher."

That was the end of the first night's Latin.

Thumbing over the book Jo found her place and read aloud slowly:

"If the government revenue from taxes increased from one billion dollars in 1927 to five hundred billion dollars in 1929, what was the increased percent?"

"Go on," said Jason.

"Go on yourself, Daddy. You're this wonderful mathematician. And try this one!"

"Let me read it myself: 'If the sum of the reciprocals of two consecutive even numbers is zero. Then the sum of two other consecutive numbers is 11/60. What are the numbers?'"

Jason said, "There's always for the X an unknown quantity. You have to have some system—haven't you?"

"Swell system."

"Got to start somewhere." He bent over it again: "If the government revenue increased from five billions in 1927 to—"

He was temporarily at the end of his resources.

"Darling," he said. "In a week I'll know more about this—"

"Yes, Daddy."

"Time for you to go to bed."

There was a pregnant silence between them.

"I know."

She came over to him and pecked briefly at an old baseball scar on his forehead.

### IV

To keep the chronicle going one must skip through the days when Annie Lee's farm came to life again—when Young Seneca realized that Mr. Davis *act*ually wanted *tenderloin* put into the sausage—the day he recalled that an important appendage was *nine tablespoons of hickory ash*.

Orders for the buckets began to increase. From merely paying for itself, the farm began to dribble a trickle of profit.

V

Some nights Jason used to go to her bedside and sit. Not tonight, though. He picked up in the living room the copy of "Caesar's Gallic Wars."

*The Swiss, who feared neither Gods nor men, suffered....*

"Who am I to be afraid?" Jason thought. He who had led eight Ohio country boys to death in a stable in France and come out of it with only the loss of the tip of his left shoulder!

*The Swiss who feared neither Gods nor men suffered—*

He pulled the lamp closer.

The night wore on in a melange of verbs and participles. Toward eleven the phone rang.

"This is Mr. McCutcheon."

"Oh, yes."

"There's a serious injustice been done your daughter."

It seems that there had been some wild excursion into the boys' locker-room—during which someone was posted as sentry outside. The sentry had run away but Jo was there trying to warn them at the moment when the monitors appeared.

"I'm sorry, Mr. Davis. There isn't much we can do in these cases—except offer our sincere apology."

"I know."

The phone put on the voice of Mr. Halklite.

Here it was! The Pan-American Textile account.

"He*llo*, Mr. Davis! I'm in Philadelphia. We've had some correspondence—I'll be down in your part of the world tomorrow and I thought I'd drop in. Sorry to call so late...."

Breakfast was waiting when, having made a journey to his office and back, Jason went to his bedroom—almost immediately Jo, who had heard him come in, knocked at the door and demanded in alarm:

"What's the matter?"

"I'm just tired. I've been working all night. Say, if you have those girls to lumpshun—" the words seemed extraordinarily hard and long—"then fix up the room afterwards. Very important. Business meeting."

"I understand, Daddy."

Holding to the bed-post he swayed precariously. "Whole future depends on this man. Make it nice for him."

With no more warning he pitched forward across the bed.

## VI

Unexpectedly at eleven o'clock the colored girl admitted Mr. Halklite. On his tour of inspection Mr. Halklite had become, perforce, less and less kind, though he was kindly by nature. Keenness was his valuable business asset—exercising the quality had temporarily become dull—there was the necessity of weeding out the exhausted and the inefficient. Halklite could tell the dead from the living, and that was half of why he had just been elected a vice-president of Pan-American Textile. Only half, though. The other half was because he was kind.

A little girl came into the room.

"Good morning. Is your father in? I think he expected me."

"Won't you come in? Father's got a cold—he's lying down."

In Jason's bedroom Jo shook and shook the exhausted body without result. She went back into the living room.

"Daddy'll be getting up presently," she said. "He's sorry he wasn't dressed to meet you."

"Oh, that's all right. You're Mr. Davis' little girl?" Mr. Halklite said.

Jo crossed as if casually to the piano bench and turned back to him with sudden decision.

"Mr. Halklite, father's had flu, and the doctor doesn't want him to get up. He's going to try to."

"Oh, we can't let him!"

"The doctor didn't want him to. But Daddy's like that. If he says he'll do something, he does. Daddy needs a woman to take care of him. And I'm so busy at school—"

"Tell him not to get up," Halklite repeated.

"I don't even know whether he can."

"Then tell him it doesn't matter."

She went to her father's room and presently returned.

"He sent you best regards. He was sorry not to see you."

Her heart was in agony. Keeping that agony out of her expression was the hardest thing she had ever had to do.

"I'm good and sorry," Mr. Halklite said. "I wanted to talk to him. How old is your father, young lady?"

"I don't know. I guess he's about thirty-eight."

"Well a man can be young at thirty-eight," he protested. "Isn't your father still young?"

"Daddy's young. But he's serious." She hesitated.

"Go on," Halklite said. "Tell me about him. I'll leave you to your lessons as soon as I finish my cigarette. But I think you ought to stay out of your father's room while he's ill."

"Oh, I do."

"You're fond of your daddy?"

"Yes—everybody is."

"Does he go around much?"

"Not much—Oh, he does though. He goes out to see Mama once a week. And he goes to walk half an hour when I go to bed. He starts out when I start to bed and then I call down to him when I hear him open the door coming in—*pour dire bon soir*."

"You speak French?" She regretted that she had mentioned it, but she admitted, "I grew up in France."

"So did your daddy, didn't he?"

"Oh no, Daddy's very American. He can't even speak French much, really."

Halklite stood up, made his decision suddenly, perhaps irrationally.

"You tell your father we want to put our account in his hands. Maybe that'll cheer him up and help him get well. 'Pan-Am-Tex.' Can you remember that? He'll understand."

### VII

It was April again and they walked in the zoo.

"It's been a hard year, Jo."

"I know that, Daddy. But look at the peacocks!"

"This is your education, Jo. It's most of what you'll ever know about life. You'll understand later."

"I know we've had bad times, Daddy. Everything's better again, isn't it? Look at the peacocks, *mon père*. *They* don't worry."

"Well, if you insist, let's sit on the bench and stare at them."

Jo sat silent for a moment. Then she said:

"We were peacocks once, weren't we?"

"What?"

"They probably have sorrows and troubles sometimes, when their tails don't grow out."

"I guess so. What school do you want to go to next year? You can have your choice."

"That doesn't seem to matter anymore. Look at the peacock—Look! the one that's trying to peck outside the cage. I love him—do you?"

Jason said, "After all, considering everything, it wasn't such a bad year."

"What?" Jo turned from the cage where she had gone to try, unsuccessfully, to feed the bird a shelled peanut.

"Daddy, let's stop worrying. I thought we stopped months ago. Mother's coming home next week. Maybe some day we'll be three peacocks again."

Jason came over to the wire.

"I suppose peacocks have their problems."

"I suppose so. Look, *Daddy*! I've got this one eating the popcorn."

# THE END OF HATE

*Fitzgerald dictated this story to his secretary in August 1936 while he was recovering from a broken shoulder, suffered in a diving accident in Asheville, North Carolina. Over a period of six years Fitzgerald cut, recast, retitled, and rewrote the story several times, finally selling it to* Collier's *in May 1937. It was first published, under the title "The End of Hate," in* Collier's *105 (22 June 1940): 9–10, 63–64. For an account of the writing and revision of the story, see Justin Mellette, "Of Empresses and Indians: A Compositional History of 'The End of Hate,'" F. Scott Fitzgerald Review 12 (2014): 108–23. Two earlier versions of the story, "Thumbs Up" and "Dentist Appointment," are included in Anne Margaret Daniel, ed.,* I'd Die for You *(New York: Scribners, 2017).*

The buggy progressed at a tired trot and the two occupants were as warm and weary as the horses. The girl's hair was a crackly yellow and she wore a dress of light blue bombazine—the first really grownup dress she had ever known. She was going to be a nurse in a wartime hospital, and her brother complained that she was arrayed like a woman of the world.

"We're now almost in the District of Columbia," said Captain Doctor Pilgrim. "We will stop and get water at the next farmhouse."

The two Pilgrims were probably the only adults thereabout who did not know that southern Maryland was suddenly and surprisingly in Confederate hands. To ease the pressure on Lee at Petersburg, General Jubal Early had marched his corps up the valley in a desperate threat at the capital, had thrown shells into the suburbs, and then unwillingly turned back toward the west. His last infantry columns had scarcely slogged along this road, leaving a stubborn dust behind.

The Pilgrims, who had driven down from Ohio, were unaware of the situation; and as the buggy turned into the Washington Pike, Josie was puzzled by a number of what seemed to be armed tramps who limped past. And there was something about two men who galloped toward the buggy from the farmhouse that made her ask alertly, "What are those people, Brother? Secesh?"

To anyone who had not been at the front, it would have been hard to place the men as soldiers—Tib Dulany, who had once written verse for the "Lynchburg Courier," wore a planter's hat, a rag of a coat, blue pants originally issued to a Union trooper, and a cartridge belt stamped C.S.A. The riders drew up beside the buggy and Tib saluted Pilgrim.

"Hi there, Yank!"

"Tell us where we can get water—" began Josie haughtily. Suddenly she saw that Captain Doctor Pilgrim's hand was at his holster—but it stayed there—the second rider held a carbine at his heart.

Captain Pilgrim raised his hands.

"Is this a raid?" he demanded. "Are you guerrillas?"

"Turn in yonder at the farmhouse," said Tib politely. "You can get water there."

He addressed Josie, who was driving. He observed that her skin had a peculiar radiance as if phosphorus had touched it, and around her eyes was that veiled expression sometimes described as starry.

"Nobody's going to hurt you," he said. "You're inside Lee's lines."

"Lee's lines!" Captain Pilgrim cried indignantly as he turned the carriage. "Every time you Mosby cutthroats come out of your hills and cut a telegraph—"

The team jolted to a stop—the second trooper had grabbed the reins, and turned white eyes upon the doctor.

"One more peep about Mosby—"

"He just doesn't know the news, Wash," said Tib. "He doesn't recognize the Army of Northern Virginia."

Wash released the reins and the buggy drove up to the farmhouse. Only as the doctor saw a dozen horses tied by the porch did he realize that he was several days behind the times.

"Right now," continued Tib, "Grant is washing the dishes and Old Abe is upstairs making the beds." He turned to Wash: "I sure would like to be in Washington tonight when Mr. Davis rides in. That Yankee rebellion didn't last long, did it?"

Josie suddenly believed it and her world crashed around her— the Boys in Blue—the Union forever—Mine eyes have seen the glory...

"You can't take my brother prisoner—he's not really an officer, he's a doctor."

"Doctor, eh? Don't know about teeth, does he?" asked Tib, dismounting at the porch.

"That's his specialty."

"He's just what we're looking for. Doctor, if you'll be so kind as to come in you can pull a tooth of a Bonaparte, a cousin of Napoleon the Third. He's attached to General Early's staff and he's been carrying on for an hour but the ambulances have gone on."

An officer came out on the porch, gave a nervous ear to a crackling of rifles in the distance, and bent an eye upon the buggy.

"We found a tooth specialist, Lieutenant," said Tib. "The Lord sent him into our lines and if Napoleon still needs help—"

"Bring him in," the officer exclaimed. "We didn't know whether to take the prince along or leave him."

Suddenly Josie had a glimpse at the Confederacy on the vine-covered verandah. There was an egress from the house: a spidery man in a shabby riding coat adorned with faded stars, followed by two younger men cramming papers into a canvas sack. Then a miscellany of officers, one on a crutch, one stripped to his undershirt with the gold star of a general pinned to a bandage on his shoulder. There was disappointment in their tired eyes. Seeing Josie, they made a single gesture: their dozen right hands rose to their dozen hats and they bowed in her direction.

Josie bowed back stiffly. In a moment they swung into their saddles and General Early looked for a moment toward the city he had not taken. Then he spoke to the aide at his stirrup: "I want couriers from Colonel Mosby every half hour till we reach White's Ford."

"Yes, sir."

The general's sun-strained eyes focused on Dr. Pilgrim in the buggy.

"I understand you're a dentist," he said. "Pull out Prince Napoleon's tooth or whatever he needs. Do well by him and these troopers will let you go without parole."

The clop and crunch of mounted men moved down the lane, and in a minute the last sally of the Army of Northern Virginia faded into the distance. A French aide-de-camp came out of the farmhouse.

"The prince is still in agony," he announced.

"This Yank is a doctor," Tib said. "One of us'll go along while he's operating."

The stout invalid in the kitchen, a gross miniature of his world-shaking uncle, tore his hand from his mouth and sat upright.

"Operation!" he cried. "*Quel horreur!*"

Dr. Pilgrim looked suspicious.

"My sister—where will she be?"

"In the parlor, Doctor. Wash, you stay here."

Prince Napoleon groaned again.

"I am a trained surgeon," Pilgrim reassured him stiffly. "Now, sir, will you take off that hat?"

The prince removed the white Cordoba which topped a costume of red tail-coat, French uniform breeches and dragoon boots.

"Prince, if he doesn't do well we got some apple trees outside and plenty rope."

Tib went into the parlor where Miss Josie sat on the edge of a sofa.

"The general said not to harm my brother," she reminded him.

"I'm more worried about what he's about to do to the prince," said Tib, sorry for her lovely anxious face.

An animal howl arose from the library.

"You hear that?" Tib said. "Napoleon's the one to worry about. And then, after our cavalry pickets pass, you and your brother can resume your journey."

Josie relaxed and looked at him with a certain human interest.

"What did my brother mean when he said you were a gorilla?"

"It's '*guer*rilla,' not '*gorilla*,'" he objected. "When a Yankee's on detached service they call him a scout, but they pretend we're only part-time soldiers, so they can hang us."

"A soldier not in uniform is a spy, isn't he?"

"I *am* in uniform—look at my buckle. And, believe it or not, Miss Pilgrim, I was a smart-looking trooper when I rode out of Lynchburg four years ago."

He told her how he had been dressed that day, and Josie listened—it wasn't unlike the first volunteers leaving Youngstown, Ohio.

"—with a big red sash that belonged to my mother. One of the girls stood in front of the troop and read a poem I had published."

"Say the poem," Josie urged him. "I would so enjoy hearing it."

Tib considered. "All I remember is: 'Lynchburg, thy guardsmen bid thy hills farewell.' I—"

Came a scream from across the hall and a medley of French. Wash appeared in the door.

"Say, Tib—the Yank got the tooth."

"Fine," said Tib. He turned back to Josie.

"I certainly would like to write a few lines sometime to express my admiration of you."

"This is so sudden," she said lightly.

She might have spoken for herself, too.

Presently Wash turned from the window:

"Tib, the patrols have started shootin' back from the saddle."

"Will you leave without *us*?" the French aide demanded suspiciously.

"We sure will," said Tib. "The prince can observe the war from the Yankee side for a while. Miss Pilgrim, I bid you a most unwilling goodbye."

Peering hastily into the kitchen, Tib saw the prince so far recovered as to be sitting upright.

Now Wash called from outside:

"Hey, Tib!"

There were shots very near. The two scouts were unhitching their horses when Wash muttered, "Hell's fire!" and pointed down the drive where five Federal troopers were in view at the far gate. Wash swung his carbine one-handed to his right shoulder.

"I'll take the two on the left."

"Maybe we could run for it," Tib suggested.

"They got seven-rail fences."

Leisurely the file of cavalry trotted up the drive. Even after four years, Tib hated to shoot from ambush, but he had no choice.

"Get your mark, Wash. When they break we'll ride through 'em."

But the ill luck of Southern arms that day was with them. Before they could loose a shot a man's body flung against Tib and pinioned him—a voice shouted beside his ear:

"Men! There're rebels here!"

As Tib wrestled desperately with Pilgrim, the Northern patrol stopped, drew pistols. Wash was bobbing from side to side trying to get a shot at Pilgrim but the doctor maneuvered Tib's body in between.

In a few seconds it was over. Wash fired once, but the Federals were around them before he was in his saddle. Panting, the two young men faced the Federals. Dr. Pilgrim spoke sharply to their corporal: "These are Mosby's men."

Those years were bitter on the border. And nothing was more bitter than Mosby's name. Wash dodged suddenly, ran and sprawled dead on the grass in a last attempt to get away. Tib, still struggling, was trussed up at the porch rail.

"There's a good tree," said a soldier.

The corporal glanced at Dr. Pilgrim.

"You know he's one of Mosby's men?"

"I'm in the Seventh Virginia Cavalry," said Tib.

"Are you one of Mosby's men?"

Tib didn't answer.

"All right, boys, get the rope."

Dr. Pilgrim's austere presence asserted itself again.

"I don't want to hang him, but this type of irregular must be discouraged."

"We string 'em up by their thumbs sometimes," suggested the corporal.

"Then do that," said Dr. Pilgrim.

By seven that evening the road outside was busy again. Mail and fresh vegetables were moving toward the capital—the diversion was over, except for the stragglers along the Pike.

In the farmhouse it was quiet. Prince Napoleon was waiting for an ambulance from Washington. There was no sound—except from Tib, who, as his skin slipped off his thumbs, repeated aloud to himself fragments of his own political verses.

When it was late and the provost guard was dozing on the porch, someone came who knew where the stepladder was—she had heard them dump it after they strung up Tib. When she had half sawed through the rope she went back to her room for pillows and moved the table under him and laid the pillows on it. She did not need any precedent for what she was doing. When Tib fell with a grunting gasp, murmuring deliriously, "Nothing to be ashamed of," she poured a bottle of sherry over his hands.

It was a hot, sultry morning, with sleeping dust from the fields and leaves. Since midnight Josie had been driving in the direction that Tib indicated before he lapsed into a broken sleep beside her; but as they approached the village she reined in and woke him gently.

Tib sat up with a jerk, stared at his hands wrapped in the tearings of a petticoat, and remembered.

"We've got to find a doctor," Josie said. "I think we're in Virginia."

Tib stared around. "It looks like Loudoun County. Leave me anywhere."

"Not before we find a doctor."

That was the last thing he heard as his tired heart tried once more to leap out of his body. His knees buckled....

When he awoke hours later, everything was changed—they were in a glade of trees, with the horses hitched and standing. His hands burned like fire.

"I know a doctor—" he murmured.

"We found a doctor and he fixed your hands. I wanted him to put you to bed—it seems that our cavalry—the Union cavalry are all over here. He didn't dare hide one of Mosby's men."

Her hand touched his hot forehead.

"You're exactly like an angel," he whispered drunkenly. "That's a fact."

"You don't know me," said Josie, but her fingers stayed on his forehead, pushed back the damp strands.

"If I could just get to one of our houses—" Tib fretted indiscreetly. "We have a chain of sympathizers' houses right through the Yankee lines. Or else I could go due east to Georgetown."

"Georgetown!" Josie exclaimed. "That's part of Washington."

"If you think I haven't been in Washington often enough—" He stopped himself and added cryptically, "Not as a spy, mind you—as a dispatch carrier."

"It seems so risky to go there."

"Longest way around, shortest way home."

He closed his eyes—then surprisingly he added: "We can get married in Lynchburg."

In the dim world of the journey it seemed to him that he had proposed to Josie somewhere and she had accepted.

"Try to sleep until it's dark," she whispered.

As he slept she watched him. Then, exhausted herself, she lay down beside him, moving his head till it rested on her shoulder.

When she awoke it was dark; she felt that he was awake, too, but she did not speak. Why not wait a while—wait like this—alive through the very recklessness of her protest and its unknown consequence. Who was she now? What had she done with herself in twenty hours?

After an hour a faint chill from the uplands sifted through the glade.

"What are you?" he demanded suddenly. "You're a good girl, I know—"

"Just another human being."

He considered for a moment. "You're coming on South with me. When we get to our lines we can be married."

"That's not a good idea. I must go to Washington. My brother'll understand—in his own way."

They got up and walked to where the horses had stood patiently through the hours. Before they got into the buggy, Josie turned to him suddenly and for a moment they faded into the sweet darkness, so deep that they were darker than the darkness—darker than the black trees—then so dark that when she tried to look up at him she could but look at the black waves of the universe over his shoulder and say, "Yes, I'll go with you if you want—anywhere. I love you too."

It was a long night. Somewhere outside the first ring of Washington forts they stopped the horses; Tib went into a farmhouse he knew and came out in civilian clothes with the papers of a Kentucky deserter. Josie gave her own name at the barriers and showed a letter from the hospital where she was to nurse.

Then along the sleeping streets of Georgetown with the horses nodding and drowsing in their traces.

"That house on the corner," he said. "This is the only possible danger. Sometimes they get on to the Southern stations and set traps. I'll go in alone first—"

He pulled with his teeth at the bandage on one hand and she cried out in protest.

"I'll just free this one. In case of any trouble I'd like to be able to use one hand. It won't hurt."

"It will!" she said in agony. "I wanted to wait till you were safe before I told you—the doctor had to amputate your thumbs."

"Oh."

With an odd expression, Tib stared down at the bandages.

"In order to save your hands."

"I can feel my thumbs."

"It's the nerves you feel."

Tib was out of the buggy like a flash—stood beside it trembling.

"Drive on," he said in a strange voice.

"What?"

"You were trying to pay for what your brother did. Drive on!"

In the brightening dawn she looked at him once more, all other feeling washed by a great surge of compassion. Then he was no longer there—and a sense of utter ruin crept slowly over her. She slapped the reins on the horse and drove down the street, aghast and alone.

April, 1865. And Tib Dulany—by two days an ex-trooper of Confederate cavalry—looking into the bar of the Willard Hotel—in Washington, now a busy, noisy world. He had come on a desperate chance—turned his back on the dark years—to get a job in the West. It was for a test of his ability to forget the past that he had ridden penniless into the capital—the day after Lee's surrender. His story was the story of men who have fought in wars—at the newspaper offices:

"We're saving our jobs for our own men." In the printing shops they stared at his thumbs: "How do you set type with a mutilation—"

Tib went into a shop and bought gloves, as a sort of disguise; he got a trial at one place—but he was no good now as a journeyman printer. No good as a printer—no good now.

The atmosphere of the Willard bar—a boom-town atmosphere—depressed him. Upstairs, in the plush corridors, he quivered at the sight of women in fine clothes; he became conscious of his hand-me-down suit, bought in Alexandria, Virginia, that morning.

Then he saw Josie Pilgrim coming out of a dining room on the arms of two officers—more beautiful than he had remembered. She was a ripe grape, she was ready to fall for the shaking of a vine....

But it wasn't quite this that made him turn around and walk blindly in the other direction—it was rather that she was the same, she was the girl of those old nightmare hours, the girl whose brother's face he had conjured up in the last cavalry action.

And this had made her beauty a reminder of cruelty and pain.

In the past months, Tib had been trying to belittle her into a species of impressionable gamin—a girl who might have ridden off with *any* man. To certain people the symbolism of women is intolerable. Because Josie's face represented a dream and a desire it took him back to the very hour of his torture....

Later when a fellow boarder in Georgetown buttonholed him on the stairs, he shook him off.

"Mr. Dulany, I ask only a little of your time," the man said. "I know you were *one* of Mosby's men—a true Southerner—that you came to this house several times during the war—"

"Very busy," Tib said.

They were a ruined lot—Tib hadn't liked the spies with whom he had been in contact during the war—now, anyhow, he was absorbed in an idea of his own:

To get a fresh start one had to even things up. Spew forth in a gesture the hate and resentment that made life into a choking muddle. He went upstairs and took a derringer out of his haversack.

An hour later Josie Pilgrim's carriage drew up in front of the boarding house. A woman held the front door half open and looked at her suspiciously.

"I saw a friend, Mr. Tib Dulany, in the Willard," she said.

She kept looking at the flounce on her French skirt.

"You want to see him?" the woman asked. "Please step inside." She took Josie by the arm like a doll, spinning her into the hall.

"Wait," she said.

As Josie waited obediently she was conscious of a scrutiny from the parted double doors of a parlor—first one pair of eyes, then another.

The woman came down the stairs.

"He's gone," she said. "Maybe he's gone for good."

Josie went back to her carriage—back to the state of mind where she lived between two worlds. Her beauty had not gone unnoticed in Washington. She had danced at balls with young men on government pay, and now in this time of victory she should be rejoicing—but she had seen the Glory of the Lord hung up by the thumbs—and then left her heart in the street in front of this house eight months ago.

Dr. Pilgrim was busy packing when the housekeeper told him he had a patient below.

"Tell him I'm busy. Tell him I'm leaving the city—tell him it's nine o'clock at night."

"I did tell him. He said he was from another town—that you once operated on him."

The word operate aroused Pilgrim's curiosity. Patients seldom spoke of the new dental work as "operating."

"Tell him I'll be right down."

He did not recognize the young man wearing black gloves who sat in his parlor. He did not remember any previous transaction—moreover he didn't like the young man—who took some time getting to the point.

The doctor was starting next day for France, on a special invitation from a cousin of Napoleon the Third, to take up plutocratic practice in Paris.

"You're a Southerner," he said, "and I have never practiced my profession in the South."

"Yes, you have," Tib reminded him. "Once you practiced within the Southern lines."

"That's true! I did. Thanks to that I am going to France—" He broke off suddenly—he knew who Tib was—he saw death looking at him from across the room.

"Why—it's you!" he said. "You're that rebel."

Tib held his pistol loosely in his hand pointing at the floor. He slipped off his right-hand glove.

"There are servants in the house—and my sister—"

"She's at the theatre."

"What are you going to do?"

With a sudden surge of hate up into his throat:

"I'm going to shoot your thumbs off. You won't be much use in your profession, but you may find something else to do."

"They'll hang you—whatever I did to you was in discharge of my duty. Why—the war's practically over—"

"Nothing's over. Things won't begin till you and I start life on the same terms. Even this won't be as bad as what you did to me.... I think we'll close the windows."

He got up without taking his eyes off Pilgrim. There were loud voices in the street now but in his preoccupation Tib did not at first hear what they were calling. A window was flung up across the street and someone shouted from a passing carriage.

"The President's been shot! Lincoln's been shot!"

The carriage went on—the shouting voices multiplied—the quality of panic in them chilled Tib before he realized the import of the words.

"Abe Lincoln has been shot," he repeated aloud. Automatically he pulled down the last window.

"Oh!" groaned Pilgrim. "You people allowed to run loose in Washington!"

Into Tib's bedeviled head came the thought that the plot had been formed in the boardinghouse where he had laid his head last night—half-heard conversations became plain to him—that must have been the private business of the man who tried to speak to him on the stairs.

On the porch outside there were footsteps—Tib had scarcely put away his gun when Josie Pilgrim, a young officer by her side, hurried into the room.

"Brother, have you heard?" Seeing Tib, Josie's voice looped down: "The President was shot and killed in the theatre—" Now her voice was high, flicking at the lower edge of panic.

Dr. Pilgrim stood up, trembling with relief at the interruption.

"It's a reign of terror!" he said. "This man—"

Josie crossed the room and stood beside Tib.

"So glad you're here," she said.

"So am I," Dr. Pilgrim said. "Perhaps Captain Taswell will put him under arrest."

Confused, the officer hesitated.

"Captain Taswell," Josie said, "when you asked me to marry you I told you there was someone else, didn't I?"

He nodded.

"This is the man. He and my brother have quarreled. Nothing that my brother says about him can be believed."

"He came here to kill me!" Pilgrim announced with certain civility—sobered way down. He walked to the window, came back, sat down, and listened to Tib's voice speaking loud and fierce:

"No. Not to kill you."

"My brother is afraid," Josie said, with calculated scorn. "He's bothered by something he did months ago."

Dr. Pilgrim made himself speak coolly:

"This man happens to be a Mosby guerrilla."

As Captain Taswell's belief wavered between brother and sister, Josie did something irrevocable, crossed a bridge as definite as the rivers that mark the Virginia border.

"We ran away together," she said to Captain Taswell. "We were going to get married, but it seemed better to wait till the war was over."

Captain Taswell nodded.

"In that case, I'm afraid I'm in the way."

As he went out, Dr. Pilgrim started to call after him, but his lips closed without sound. Josie looked earnestly at Tib. "I guess now you've *got* to marry me."

"You seem to be doing things for me always," Tib answered.

It has been whispered that there are only two kinds of women—those who take and those who give—and it was plain which kind Josie was. Even though his country was a desert of hate Tib was no longer a soul lost by wandering in it.

The shocking news of the evening—still only faintly appreciated—had made a sea change. The strongest man had taken the burden upon his great shoulders, given life its impetus again even in the accident of his death.

Dr. Pilgrim realized something of the sort, for in the silence that ensued he made no comment; nor did he voice any objection when Josie made another decision:

"Tib, dear, I don't know where you're going—I don't know where we're going, but Brother and I would be awfully happy if you'd sleep in this house tonight."

# A FULL LIFE

*Fitzgerald wrote this story in the spring of 1937, incorporating into the narrative three pages of typescript from an earlier story entitled "The Vanished Girl," that had been rejected by* Redbook. *It's possible that Fitzgerald wrote "A Full Life" as a private gesture; there is no record of its being submitted to any magazine by the Ober agency. It is also possible that Fitzgerald intended to revise the story further and to send it to* Esquire. *(The story would have put an emphatic end to his famous heroine—not with a whimper but a bang.) "A Full Life" survives among the Marie Shank Additions, F. Scott Fitzgerald Papers, Princeton University Library. It was first published, with commentary, in the* Princeton University Library Chronicle *49 (Winter 1988): 167–72. For remarks on the composition of the story and speculation about Fitzgerald's further plans, see Horst H. Kruse, "F. Scott Fitzgerald in 1937: A Manuscript Study of 'A Full Life,'" in* F. Scott Fitzgerald in the Twenty-First Century, *ed. Jackson R. Bryer, Ruth Prigozy, and Milton R. Stern (Tuscaloosa: University of Alabama Press, 2003): 153–72.*

At twilight on September 3rd, 1923, a girl jumped from the fifty-third-story window of a New York office building. She wore a patented inflatable suit of rubber composition which had just been put on the novelty market for purposes of having fun—the wearer by a mere jump or push could supposedly sail over fences or street intersections. It was fully blown up when she jumped. The building was a set-back and she landed on the projecting roof of the fiftieth floor. She was bruised and badly shaken but not seriously hurt.

She recovered consciousness in the ambulance and gave the name Gwendolyn Davies but in the emergency room when the intern so addressed her she denied it, and insisted on leaving the hospital after necessary stitches had been taken. Several inquiries that were undoubtedly for this girl asked for a different name. The intern, Dr. Wilkinson, gathered that a little orgy after hours had been taking place in the office at the time.

A week later Dr. Wilkinson took out a library book that he had borrowed there some time before. It was a collection of mysterious cases re-written from contemporary newspaper accounts, and the third story, entitled "The Vanished Girl," read as follows:

*In 1915 Delphis, N.Y., was an old town of large, faded houses, built far back on shady lawns—not at all like the Long Island and New Jersey villages where even Sunday is only a restless lull between the crash of trains. During the war there was a murder there, and in 1922 bandits held up a garage.*

*After that nothing happened for a long time till Gwendolyn Davies walked out of her father's house one day and disappeared off the face of the earth.*

*She was the daughter of a poor doctor and the prettiest girl in town. She had a brave, bright face that made you look at her, yellow hair and a beggar's lips that would not beg in vain. The last person who ever laid eyes on Gwen Davies was the station master who put her suitcase on the train. She told him lightly that she was leaving for her family's own good— she didn't want to "raise the roof," but no scandal ever developed about her. When she reached New York she was to go directly to a recommended boarding house adjacent to the college. She didn't appear there—she simply melted like a shadow into the warm September night.*

*"Height, five feet five inches, weight, one hundred and sixteen pounds. Features, regular and pleasing. Left eye slightly larger than the right. Wearing a blue traveling suit and a red, leather-trimmed hat. Bright personality. We ask everyone to keep an eye out for this girl whose parents are prostrated by her disappearance."*

*She was one of many thousands of lost girls, but her beauty and the fact that her father was a reputable physician made it news. There was a "ring" said the tabloids; there was original sin, said the pulpit; and "mark my words," said the citizens of Delphis, their words being wild suppositions about somebody knowing something more than he or she saw fit to tell. For awhile the town of Delphis was as sad as the village of Hamlin after the Pied Piper had come and gone—there were young men who forgot their partners entirely when the orchestra played "Babes in the Woods" or "Underneath the Stars," and fancied they had loved Gwen and would never love another.*

*After a few years a New York judge walked away into the blue and the case of Gwen Davies was revived for a day in the newspapers, with a note that someone had lately seen her or her double in a New York surface car; after that the waters closed over her, apparently forever.*

Dr. Wilkinson was sure it was the same girl—he thought for awhile of trying to trace her by going to a newspaper with the story but he was a retiring young man and the idea became shelved like the play he was always going to write and the summer he was going to spend on the Riviera.

But he never forgot—he was forever haunted by the picture of the girl floating slowly out over the city at dusk, buoyed up by delicious air, by a quintessence of golden hope, like a soaring and unstable stock issue. She was the girl for whom a part of him was always searching at cafés and parties and theatres, when his practical wife would ask:

"Why are you staring around, Harvey? Do you see anybody we know?"

He did not explain.

## II

Five years later the following story appeared in the New York papers:

*This afternoon at four o'clock the Comptesse de Frejus jumped from the deck of the liner* Stacia *one day out from New York. She was rescued after the ship had turned around and searched for two hours through a fortunately calm sea. The Comptesse is an American, the former Mrs. Cornelius B. Hasbrouk, who obtained her divorce in Reno last year and then married René, Compt de Frejus, in Paris. She gave out no statement but said to an officer of the cutter which picked her up that her chief thought in the water was to beat off the huge birds who attempted to perch on her head and peck at her eyes. The passengers with whom she had been talking had no warning of her sudden act nor any explanation.*

There were no pictures of the Comptesse de Frejus and when Dr. Wilkinson went to the newspaper files at the public library he found that there were no pictures of Mrs. Cornelius B. Hasbrouk either, save with her arm covering her face. But there were a great many columns about Mrs. Hasbrouk's first marriage and one of them mentioned a scar on her forehead—a scar that corresponded to a suture he had performed himself.

The columns had been written two years before. Mrs. Hasbrouk's first marriage had begun stormily. The groom, a junior at Harvard, was twenty and had just inherited a fortune of twenty million dollars from his father, the powder manufacturer. The bride was a young lady of no background, not even the stage. The story ran that when Mr. Hasbrouk was located the next morning in a barber shop he had to be shown his picture in the paper before he realized that he was married.

The new Mrs. Hasbrouk was the cross of the cameramen but the reporters did rather well by her. She was described as lovely, modest, well-bred, and charming. There was a vague impression that she was either from the South, North or West, though one paper announced her birthplace as New York City. She said rather cryptically that she had married the young munitions magnate because she had "always really belonged to him" but that she would give him up if he preferred. Pending an annulment the couple departed for a trip to the South Seas.

Dr. Wilkinson was rather relieved that this marriage had not lasted and that her subsequent union with a member of the French nobility had led her to jump into the Atlantic. He felt that he knew her, in some such manner as one might know a composer or a writer one had never seen—he knew her though she had written only on air and there was a mysterious compulsion that made him follow her career with admiration and curiosity. He made certain notes from these newspaper files and settled down to wait for her to become news again.

### III

At two o'clock on a June afternoon in 1937 Dr. Wilkinson, now a stout baldish man of forty, parked his car by a circus which had pitched on the shores of Long Island. The performance was not to begin until three but there were certain preliminary attractions and it was one of these which had attracted him to the spot. A little aside from the main tent stretched a large white banner on which was lettered:

### The Human Shell

*At two-thirty this afternoon
the Countess of Frejus will
be fired out of this cannon.*

A crowd of intellectuals was already inspecting the enormous piece of ordinance but Dr. Wilkinson stationed himself beside the net which was to catch the living bullet at the end of its trajectory.

In a few minutes a little group approached the cannon and Dr. Wilkinson's heart put-putted like a motor boat. There, not a hundred feet away, dressed in the costume of an aviatrix, stood the girl whose life he had followed in the headlines. For him this was the high point of a somewhat humdrum and defeated life—he felt a great excitement, almost a reverence, in the face of the moment.

There was a sudden deep booming sound and a great puff of smoke from the mouth of the cannon; on the instant the form of the Countess of Frejus, née Gwendolyn Davies, arched gracefully into the air, described a perfect parabola and plumped gently into the net beside which he stood. In a moment she had clambered out and the doctor advanced toward her.

"Good afternoon," he said and introduced himself as a doctor who had once attended her.

"So it was you," she said politely. "I'm afraid I must have seemed ungracious in leaving the hospital so quickly."

"But I understand," he assured her. "In fact I have been greatly interested in your career."

"You're not a reporter too."

"No indeed. My interest is personal. I do want to ask you a few questions."

Her lovely face clouded.

"I hate questions," she said.

"But I have waited so long. Come, Countess—I simply want you to explain certain remarks you made here and there. For instance when you ran away from Delphis you said you 'did not want to raise the roof,' and when you got married you said you had 'always really belonged to Mr. Hasbrouk.' But you never said anything about why you jumped out the window or off the boat. Couldn't you give me a little clue for my own satisfaction?"

She looked at him closely.

"And if I won't tell you?"

He had his trump in reserve.

"Then, Countess, I shall be forced to give information to the police of Delphis and collect the reward for information leading to your whereabouts. While I have conceived a great admiration for you, there are others who might judge otherwise. It would be a salutory story for prospective runaways to find you ending up as an artificial shell."

She gave a little laugh.

"But I'm not an artificial shell," she said. "The joke's on you—I'm full of dynamite so I always thought I'd go off."

Even as this explanation issued from her lips she exploded with a tremendous bang, which was heard as far as New York City.

There were headlines in all the papers but Dr. Wilkinson was unfortunately killed by the concussion and did not see them. And so another glamor girl passes into history.

# DISCARD

*This story was written under the title "Director's Special" in July of 1939. It was declined by the* Post, *revised by Fitzgerald, again turned down by the* Post, *and rejected also by* Collier's *and* Cosmopolitan. *After Fitzgerald's death the story was published under the title "Discard" in* Harper's Bazaar 82 *(January 1948): 103ff.*

The man and the boy talked intermittently as they drove down Ventura Boulevard in the cool of the morning. The boy, George Baker, was dressed in the austere gray of a military school.

"This is very nice of you, Mr. Jerome."

"Not at all. Glad I happened by. I have to pass your school going to the studio every morning."

"What a school!" George volunteered emphatically. "All I do is teach peewees the drill I learned last year. Anyhow I wouldn't go to any war—unless it was in the Sahara or Morocco or the Afghan post."

James Jerome, who was casting a difficult part in his mind, answered with "Hm!" Then, feeling inadequate, he added:

"But you told me you're learning math—and French."

"What good is French?"

"What good—say, I wouldn't take *any*thing for the French I learned in the war and just after."

That was a long speech for Jerome; he did not guess that presently he would make a longer one.

"That's just it," George said eagerly. "When you were young it was the war, but now it's pictures. I could be getting a start in pictures, but Dolly is narrow-minded." Hastily he added, "I know you like her; I know everybody does, and I'm lucky to be her nephew, but—" he resumed his brooding, "but I'm sixteen and if I was in pictures I could go around more like Mickey Rooney and the Dead-Ends—or even Freddie Bartholomew."

"You mean act in pictures?"

George laughed modestly.

"Not with these ears; but there's a lot of other angles. You're a director; you know. And Dolly could get me a start."

The mountains were clear as bells when they twisted west into the traffic of Studio City.

"Dolly's been wonderful," conceded George, "but gee whizz, she's arrived. She's got everything—the best house in the valley, and the Academy Award, and being a countess if she wanted to call herself by it. I can't imagine why she wants to go on the stage, but if she does I'd like to get started while she's still here. She needn't be small about that."

"There's nothing small about your aunt—except her person," said Jim Jerome grimly. "She's a '*grande cliente*.'"

"A what?"

"Thought you studied French."

"We didn't have that."

"Look it up," said Jerome briefly. He was used to an hour of quiet before getting to the studio—even with a nephew of Dolly Bordon. They turned into Hollywood, crossed Sunset Boulevard.

"How do you say that?" George asked.

"'*Une grande cliente*,'" Jerome repeated. "It's hard to translate exactly but I'm sure your aunt was just that even before she became famous."

George repeated the French words aloud.

"There aren't very many of them," Jerome said. "The term's misused even in France; on the other hand it *is* something to be."

Following Cahuenga, they approached George's school. As Jerome heard the boy murmur the words to himself once more he looked at his watch and stopped the car.

"Both of us are a few minutes early," he said. "Just so the words won't haunt you, I'll give you an example. Suppose you run up a big bill at a store, *and* pay it; you become a '*grand client*.' But it's more than just a commercial phrase. Once, years ago, I was at a table with some people in the Summer Casino at Cannes, in France. I happened to look at the crowd trying to get tables, and there was Irving Berlin with his wife. You've seen him—"

"Oh, sure, I've met him," said George.

"Well, you know he's not the conspicuous type. And he was getting no attention whatever and even being told to stand aside."

"Why didn't he tell who he was?" demanded George.

"Not Irving Berlin. Well, I got a waiter, and he didn't recognize the name; nothing was done and other people who came later were getting tables. And suddenly a Russian in our party grabbed the head waiter as he went by and said 'Listen!'—and pointed: 'Listen! Seat that man immediately. *Il est un grand client—vous comprenez?—un grand client!*'"

"Did he get a seat?" asked George.

The car started moving again; Jerome stretched out his legs as he drove, and nodded.

"I'd just have busted right in," said George. "Just grabbed a table."

"That's one way. But it may be better to be like Irving Berlin—and your Aunt Dolly. Here's the school."

"This certainly was nice of you, Mr. Jerome—and I'll look up those words."

That night George tried them on the young leading woman he sat next to at his aunt's table. Most of the time she talked to the actor on the other side, but George managed it finally.

"My aunt," he remarked, "is a typical '*grande cliente.*'"

"I can't speak French," Phyllis said. "I took Spanish."

"I take French."

"I took Spanish."

The conversation anchored there a moment. Phyllis Burns was twenty-one, four years younger than Dolly—and to his nervous system the oomphiest personality on the screen.

"What does it mean?" she inquired.

"It isn't because she *has* everything," he said, "the Academy Award and this house and being Countess de Lanclerc and all that...."

"I think that's quite a bit," laughed Phyllis. "Goodness, I wish *I* had it. I know and admire your aunt more than anybody I know."

Two hours later, down by the great pool that changed colors with the fickle lights, George had his great break. His Aunt Dolly took him aside.

"You did get your driver's license, George?"

"Of course."

"Well, I'm glad, because you can be the greatest help. When things break up will you drive Phyllis Burns home?"

"Sure I will, Dolly."

"Slowly, I mean. I mean she wouldn't be a *bit* impressed if you stepped on it. Besides I happen to be fond of her."

There were men around her suddenly—her husband, Count Hennen de Lanclerc, and several others who loved her tenderly, hopelessly—and as George backed away, glowing, one of the lights playing delicately on her made him stand still, almost shocked. For almost the first time he saw her not as Aunt Dolly, whom he had always known as generous and kind, but as a tongue of fire, so vivid in the night, so fearless and stabbing sharp—so apt at spreading an infection of whatever she laughed at or grieved over, loved or despised—that he understood why the world forgave her for not being a really great beauty.

"I haven't signed anything," she said explaining, "—East or West. But out here I'm in a mist at present. If I were only *sure* they were going to make 'Sense and Sensibility,' and meant it for me. In New York I know at least what play I'll do—and I know it will be fun."

Later, in the car with Phyllis, George started to tell her about Dolly—but Phyllis anticipated him, surprisingly going back to what they had talked of at dinner.

"What was that about a *cliente*?"

A miracle—her hand touched his shoulder, or was it the dew falling early?

"When we get to my house I'll make you a special drink for taking me home."

"I don't exactly drink as yet," he said.

"You've never answered my question." Phyllis' hand was still on his shoulder. "Is Dolly dissatisfied with who she's—with what she's got?"

Then it happened—one of those four-second earthquakes, afterward reported to have occurred "within a twenty-mile radius of this station." The instruments on the dashboard trembled; another car coming in their direction wavered and shimmied, side-swiped the rear fender of George's car, passed on nameless into the night, leaving them unharmed but shaken.

When George stopped the car they both looked to see if Phyllis was damaged; only then George gasped: "It was the earthquake!"

"I suppose it was the earthquake," said Phyllis evenly. "Will the car still run?"

"Oh, yes." And he repeated hoarsely, "It was the earthquake—*I held the road all right.*"

"Let's not discuss it," Phyllis interrupted. "I've got to be on the lot at eight and I want to sleep. What were we talking about?"

"That earth—" He controlled himself as they drove off, and tried to remember what he had said about Dolly. "She's just worried about whether they are going to do 'Sense and Sensibility.' If they're not she'll close the house and sign up for some play—"

"I could have told her about that," said Phyllis. "They're probably not doing it—and if they do, Bette Davis has a signed contract."

Recovering his self-respect about the earthquake, George returned to his obsession of the day.

"She'd be a '*grande cliente,*'" he said, "even if she went on the stage."

"Well, I don't know the role," said Phyllis, "but she'd be unwise to go on the stage, and you can tell her that for me."

George was tired of discussing Dolly; things had been so amazingly pleasant just ten minutes before. Already they were on Phyllis' street.

"I would like that drink," he remarked with a deprecatory little laugh. "I've had a glass of beer a couple of times and after that earthquake—well, I've got to be at school at half past eight in the morning."

When they stopped in front of her house there was a smile with all heaven in it—but she shook her head.

"Afraid the earthquake came between us," she said gently. "I want to hide my head right under a big pillow."

George drove several blocks and parked at a corner where two mysterious men swung a huge drum light in pointless arcs over paradise. It was not Dolly who "had everything"—it was Phyllis.

Dolly was made, her private life arranged. Phyllis, on the contrary, had everything to look forward to—the whole world that in some obscure way was represented more by the drum light and the red and white gleams of neon signs on cocktail bars than by the changing colors of Dolly's pool. He knew how the latter worked—why, he had seen it installed in broad daylight. But he did not know how the world worked and he felt that Phyllis lived in the same delicious oblivion.

After that fall, things were different. George stayed on at school, but this time as a boarder, and visited Dolly in New York on Christmas and Easter. The following summer she came back to the Coast and opened up the house for a month's rest, but she was committed to another season in the East and George went back with her to attend a tutoring school for Yale.

"*Sense and Sensibility*" was made after all, but with Phyllis, not Bette Davis, in the part of Marianne. George saw Phyllis only once during that year—when Jim Jerome, who sometimes took him to his ranch for week-ends, told him one Sunday they'd do anything George wanted. George suggested a call on Phyllis.

"Do you remember when you told me about '*une grande cliente?*'"

"You mean I said that about *Phyl*lis?"

"No, about Dolly."

Phyllis was no fun that day, surrounded and engulfed by men; after his departure for the East, George found other girls and was a personage for having known Phyllis and for what was, in his honest recollection, a superflirtation.

The next June, after examinations, Dolly came down to the liner to see Hennen and George off to Europe; she was coming herself when the show closed—and by transatlantic plane.

"I'd like to wait and do that with you," George offered.

"You're eighteen—you have a long and questionable life before you."

"You're just twenty-seven."

"You've got to stick to the boys you're traveling with."

Hennen was going first-class; George was going tourist. At the tourist gangplank there were so many girls from Bryn Mawr and Smith and the finishing schools that Dolly warned him.

"Don't sit up all night drinking beer with them. And if the pressure gets too bad slip over into first-class, and let Hennen calm you."

Hennen was very calm and depressed about the parting.

"I shall go down to tourist," he said desperately. "And meet those beautiful girls."

"It would make you a heavy," she warned him, "like Ivan Lebedeff in a picture."

Hennen and George talked between upper and lower deck as the ship steamed through the narrows.

"I feel great contempt for you down in the slums," said Hennen. "I hope no one sees me speaking to you."

"This is the cream of the passenger list. They call us tycoon-skins. Speaking of furs, are you going after one of those barges in a mink coat?"

"No—I still expect Dolly to turn up in my stateroom. And, actually, I have cabled her *not* to cross by plane."

"She'll do what she likes."

"Will you come up and dine with me tonight—after washing your ears?"

There was only one girl of George's tone of voice on the boat and someone wolfed her away—so he wished Hennen would invite him up to dinner every night, but after the first time it was only for luncheon and Hennen mooned and moped.

"I go to my cabin every night at six," he said, "and have dinner in bed. I cable Dolly and I think her press agent answers."

The day before arriving at Southampton, the girl whom George liked quarreled with her admirer over the length of her fingernails or the Munich Pact or both—and George stepped out, once more, into tourist class society.

He began, as was fitting, with the ironic touch.

"You and Princeton amused yourself pretty well," he remarked. "Now you come back to me."

"It was this way," explained Martha. "I thought you were conceited about your aunt being Dolly Bordon and having lived in Hollywood—"

"Where did you two disappear to?" he interrupted. "It was a great act while it lasted."

"Nothing to it," Martha said briskly. "And if you're going to be like that—"

Resigning himself to the past, George was presently rewarded.

"As a matter of fact I'll show you," she said. "We'll do what we used to do—before he criticized me as an ignoramus. Good gracious! As if going to Princeton meant anything! My *own* father went there!"

George followed her, rather excited, through an iron door marked "Private," upstairs, along a corridor, and up to another door that said "First-Class Passengers Only."

He was disappointed.

"Is *this* all? I've been up in first-class before."

"Wait!"

She opened the door cautiously, and they rounded a lifeboat overlooking a fenced-in square of deck.

There was nothing to see—the flash of an officer's face glancing seaward over a still higher deck, another mink coat in a deck chair; he even peered into the lifeboat to see if they had discovered a stowaway.

"And I found out things that are going to help me later," Martha muttered as if to herself. "How they work it—if I ever go in for it I'll certainly know the technique."

"Of what?"

"Look at the deck chair, stupe."

Even as George gazed, a long-remembered face emerged in its individuality from behind the huge dark of the figure in the mink coat. And at the moment he recognized Phyllis Burns he saw that Hennen was sitting beside her.

"Watch how she works," Martha murmured. "Even if you can't hear you'll realize you're looking at a preview."

George had not been seasick so far, but now only the fear of being seen made him control his impulse as Hennen shifted from his chair to the foot of hers and took her hand. After a moment, Phyllis leaned forward, touching his arm gently in exactly the way George remembered; in her eyes was an ineffable sympathy.

From somewhere the mess call shrilled from a bugle—George seized Martha's hand and pulled her back along the way they had come.

"But they *like* it!" Martha protested. "She lives in the public eye. I'd like to cable Winchell right away."

All George heard was the word "cable." Within half an hour he had written in an indecipherable code:

HE DIDN'T COME DOWN TOURIST AS DIDN'T NEED TO BECAUSE SENSE AND SENSIBILITY STOP ADVISE SAIL IMMEDIATELY

GEORGE<br>(COLLECT)

Either Dolly didn't understand or just waited for the clipper anyhow, while George bicycled uneasily through Belgium, timing his arrival in Paris to coincide with hers. She must have been forewarned by his letter, but there was nothing to prove it, as she and Hennen and George rode from Le Bourget into Paris. It was the next morning before the cat jumped nimbly out of the bag, and it had become a sizable cat by afternoon when George walked into the situation. To get there he had to pass a stringy crowd extending from one hotel to another, for word had drifted about that *two* big stars were in the neighborhood.

"Come in, George," Dolly called. "You know Phyllis—she's just leaving for Aix-les-Bains. She's lucky—either Hennen or I will have to take up residence, depending on who's going to sue whom. I suggest Hennen sues me—on the charge I made him a poodle dog."

She was in a reckless mood, for there were secretaries within hearing—and press agents outside and waiters who dashed in from time to time. Phyllis was very composed behind the attitude of "please leave me out of it." George was damp, bewildered, sad.

"Shall I be difficult, George?" Dolly asked him. "Or shall I play it like a character part—just suited to my sweet nature. Or shall I be primitive? Jim Jerome or Frank Capra could tell me.

Have you got good judgment, George, or don't they teach that till college?"

"Frankly—" said Phyllis getting up, "frankly, it's as much a surprise to me as it is to you. I didn't know Hennen would be on the boat any more than he did me."

At least George had learned at tutoring school how to be rude. He made noxious sounds—and faced Hennen who got to his feet.

"Don't irritate me!" George was trembling a little with anger. "You've always been nice till now but you're twice my age and I don't want to tear you in two."

Dolly sat him down; Phyllis went out and they heard her emphatic "Not now! Not now!" echo in the corridor.

"You and I could take a trip somewhere," said Hennen unhappily.

Dolly shook her head.

"I know about those solutions. I've been a confidential friend in some of these things. You go away and take it with you. Silence falls—nobody has any lines. Silence—trying to guess behind the silence—then imitating how it was—and more silence—and great wrinkles in the heart."

"I can only say I am very sorry," said Hennen.

"Don't be. I'll go along on George's bicycle trip if he'll have me. And you take your new chippie up to Pont-à-Dieu to meet your family. I'm alive, Hennen—though I admit I'm not enjoying it. Evidently you've been dead some time and I didn't know it."

She told George afterward that she was grateful to Hennen for not appealing to the maternal instinct. She had done all her violent suffering on the plane, in an economical way she had. Even being a saint requires a certain power of organization, and Dolly was pretty near to a saint to those close to her—even to the occasional loss of temper.

But all the next two months George never saw Dolly's eyes gleam silvery blue in the morning; and often, when his hotel room was near hers, he would lie awake and listen while she moved about whimpering softly in the night.

But by breakfast time she was always a *"grande cliente."* George knew exactly what that meant now.

In September, Dolly, her secretary and her maid, and George moved into a bungalow of a Beverly Hills hotel—a bungalow crowded with flowers that went to the hospitals almost as fast as they came in. Around them again was the twilight privacy of pictures against a jealous and intrusive world; inside, the telephones, agent, producers, and friends.

Dolly went about, talking possibilities, turning down offers, encouraging others—considered, or pretended to consider, a return to the stage.

"You *dar*ling! Everybody's *so* glad you're back."

She gave them background; for their own dignity they wanted her in pictures again. There was scarcely any other actress of whom that could have been said.

"Now, *I've* got to give a party," she told George.

"But you *have*. Your being anywhere *makes* it a party."

George was growing up—entering Yale in a week. But he meant it too.

"Either very small or very large," she pondered, "—or else I'll hurt people's feelings. And this is not the time, at the very start of a career."

"You ought to worry, with people breaking veins to get you."

She hesitated—then brought him a two-page list.

"Here are the broken veins," she said. "Notice that there's something the matter with every offer—a condition or a catch. Look at this character part; a fascinating older woman—and me not thirty. It's either money—lots of money tied to a fatal part, or else a nice part with no money. I'll open up the house."

With her entourage and some scrubbers, Dolly went out next day and made ready as much of the house as she would need.

"Candles everywhere," George exclaimed, the afternoon of the event. "A fortune in candles."

"Aren't they nice! And once I was ungrateful when people gave them to me."

"It's magnificent. I'm going into the garden and rehearse the pool lights—for old times' sake."

"They don't work," said Dolly cheerfully. "No electricity works—a flood got in the cellar."

"Get it fixed."

"Oh, no—I'm dead broke. Oh yes—I am. The banks are positive. And the house is thoroughly mortgaged and I'm trying to sell it."

He sat in a dusty chair.

"But how?"

"Well—it began when I promised the cast to go on tour, and it turned hot. Then the treasurer ran away to Canada. George, we have guests coming in two hours. Can't you put candles around the pool?"

"Nobody sent you pool-candlesticks. How about calling in the money you've loaned people?"

"What? A little glamor girl like me! Besides, now they're poorer still, probably. Besides, Hennen kept the accounts except he never put things down. If you look so blue I'll go over you with this dustcloth. Your tuition is paid for a year—"

"You think I'd go?"

Through the big room a man George had never seen was advancing toward them.

"I didn't see any lights, Miss Bordon. I didn't dream you were here, I'm from Ridgeway Real Estate—"

He broke off in profound embarrassment. It was unnecessary to explain that he had brought a client—for the client stood directly behind him.

"Oh," said Dolly. She looked at Phyllis, smiled—then she sat down on the sofa, laughing. "*You're* the client; you want my house, do you?"

"Frankly, I heard you wanted to sell it," said Phyllis.

Dolly's answer was muffled in laughter but George thought he heard: "It would save time if I just sent you all my pawn checks."

"What's so very funny?" Phyllis inquired.

"Will your—family move in too? Excuse me; that's not my business." Dolly turned to Ridgeway Real Estate. "Show the Countess around—here's a candlestick. The lights are out of commission."

"I know the house," said Phyllis. "I only wanted to get a general impression."

"Everything goes with it," said Dolly, adding irresistibly, "—as you know. Except George. I want to keep George."

"I own the mortgage," said Phyllis absently.

George had an impulse to walk her from the room by the seat of her sea-green slacks.

"Now *Phyl*lis!" Dolly reproved her gently. "You know you can't use that without a riding crop and a black moustache. You have to get a Guild permit. Your proper line is 'I don't have to listen to this.'"

"Well, I *don't* have to listen to this," said Phyllis.

When she had gone, Dolly said, "They asked *me* to play heavies."

"Why, four years ago," began George, "Phyllis was—"

"Shut up, George. This is Hollywood and you play by the rules. There'll be people coming here tonight who've committed first degree murder."

When they came, she was her charming self, and she made everyone kind and charming so that George even failed to identify the killers. Only in a washroom did he hear a whisper of conversation that told him all was guessed at about her hard times. The surface, though, was unbroken. Even Hymie Fink roamed around the rooms, the white blink of his camera when he pointed it, or his alternate grin when he passed by, dividing those who were up from those coming down.

He pointed it at Dolly, on the porch. She was an old friend and he took her from all angles. Judging by the man she was sitting beside, it wouldn't be long now before she was back in the big time.

"Aren't you going to snap Mr. Jim Jerome?" Dolly asked him. "He's just back in Hollywood today—from England. He says they're making better pictures; he's convinced them not to take out time for tea in the middle of the big emotional scenes."

George saw them there together and he had a feeling of great relief—that everything was coming out all right. But after the party, when the candles had squatted down into little tallow drips, he detected a look of uncertainty in Dolly's face—the first he had ever seen there. In the car going back to the hotel bungalow she told him what had happened.

"He wants me to give up pictures and marry him. Oh, he's set on it. The old business of *two* careers and so forth. I wonder—"

"Yes?"

"I don't wonder. He thinks I'm through. That's part of it."

"Could you fall in love with him?"

She looked at George—laughed.

"Could I? Let me see—"

"He's always loved you. He almost told me once."

"I know. But it would be a strange business; I'd have nothing to do—just like Hennen."

"Then don't marry him; wait it out. I've thought of a dozen ideas to make money."

"George, you terrify me," she said lightly. "Next thing I'll find racing forms in your pocket, or see you down on Hollywood Boulevard with an oil well angle—and your hat pulled down over your eyes."

"I mean honest money," he said defiantly.

"You could go on the stage like Freddie and I'll be your Aunt Prissy."

"Well, don't marry him unless you want to."

"I wouldn't mind—if he was just passing through; after all every woman needs a man. But he's so *set* about everything. Mrs. James Jerome. No! That isn't the way I grew to be and you can't help the way you grow to be, can you? Remind me to wire him tonight—because tomorrow he's going East to pick up talent for 'Portrait of a Woman.'"

George wrote out and telephoned the wire, and three days later went once more to the big house in the valley to pick up a scattering of personal things that Dolly wanted.

Phyllis was there—the deal for the house was closed, but she made no objections, trying to get him to take more and winning a little of his sympathy again, or at least bringing back his young assurance that there's good in everyone. They walked in the garden, where already workmen had repaired the cables and were testing the many-colored bulbs around the pool.

"Anything in the house she wants," Phyllis said. "I'll never forget that she was my inspiration and ideal, and frankly what's happened to her might happen to any of us."

"Not exactly," objected George. "She has special things happen because she's a '*grande cliente*.'"

"I never knew what that meant," laughed Phyllis. "But I hope it's a consolation if she begins brooding."

"Oh, she's too busy to brood. She started work on 'Portrait of a Woman' this morning."

Phyllis stopped in her promenade.

"She did! Why, that was for Katharine Cornell, if they could persuade her! Why, they swore to me—"

"They didn't try to persuade Cornell or anyone else. Dolly just walked into the test—and I never saw so many people crying in a projection room at once. One guy had to leave the room—and the test was just three minutes long."

He caught Phyllis' arm to keep her from tripping over the board into the pool. He changed the subject quickly.

"When are you—when are you two moving in?"

"I don't know," said Phyllis. Her voice rose. "I don't like the place! She can have it all—with my compliments."

But George knew that Dolly didn't want it. She was in another street now, opening another big charge account with life. Which is what we all do after a fashion—open an account and then pay.

# LAST KISS

*Fitzgerald wrote this story (entitled "Pink and Silver Frost" in another version) during the summer of 1939. It was rejected by* Collier's *and* Cosmopolitan *and was "stripped" by Fitzgerald for* The Last Tycoon. *An early version of "Last Kiss" was published after Fitzgerald's death in* Collier's *123 (16 April 1949): 16–17ff. The final revision of the story, which is published here, appeared first in* Short Stories: *757–72.*

It was a fine pure feeling to be on top. One was very sure that everything was for the best, that the lights shone upon fair ladies and brave men, that pianos dripped the right notes and that the young lips singing them spoke for happy hearts. All these beautiful faces, for instance, must be absolutely happy.

And then in a twilit rhumba, a face passed Jim's table that was not quite happy. It had gone before Jim decided this, but it remained fixed on his retina for some seconds thereafter. It belonged to a girl almost as tall as he was, with opaque brown eyes and cheeks as delicate as a Chinese tea-cup.

"There you go," said his hostess, following his glance. She sighed. "It happens in a second and I've tried for years."

Jim wanted to answer:

—But you've had your day—three husbands. How about me? Thirty-five and still trying to match every woman with a lost childhood love, still finding in all girls the similarities and not the differences.

The next time the lights were dim he wandered through the tables toward the entrance hall. Here and there friends hailed him—more than the usual number of course, because his contract as a producer had been noticed in the "Hollywood Reporter" that morning, but Jim had made other steps up and he was used to that. It was a charity ball and by the bar ready to perform was the man who imitated wall paper and Bob Bordley with a sandwich board on his back which read:

AT TEN TONIGHT
IN THE HOLLYWOOD BOWL
SONJA HENIE
WILL SKATE ON
HOT SOUP

Nearby Jim saw the producer whom he was displacing tomorrow, having an unsuspecting drink with the agent who had contrived his ruin. Next to the agent was the girl whose face had seemed sad as she danced by in the rhumba.

"Oh, Jim," said the agent, "Pamela Knighton—your future star."

She turned to him with professional eagerness. What the agent's voice had said to her was: "Look alive! This *is* somebody."

"Pamela's joined my stable," said the agent. "I want her to change her name to Boots."

"I thought you said Toots," the girl laughed.

"Toots or Boots. It's the oo-oo sound. Cutie shoots Toots. Judge Hoots. No conviction possible. Pamela is English. Her real name is Sybil Higgins."

Jim felt the deposed producer looking at him with an infinite something in his eyes—not hatred, not jealousy but a profound and curious astonishment that asked "Why? Why? For God's sake, why?" More disturbed by this than by enmity, Jim surprised himself by asking the English girl to dance. As they faced each other on the floor he felt a rising exultation.

"Hollywood's a good place," he said, as if to forestall any criticism from her. "You'll like it. Most English girls do—they don't expect too much. I've had luck working with English girls."

"Are you a director?"

"I've been everything—from press agent on. I've just signed a producer's contract that begins tomorrow."

"I like it here," she said after a minute. "You can't help expecting things. But if they don't come I could always teach school again."

Jim leaned back and looked at her—the impression was of pink and silver frost. She was so far from a school marm, even a school marm in a Western, that he laughed. But again he saw that there was something sad and a little lost within the triangle formed by lips and eyes.

"Who are you with tonight?" he asked.

"Joe Becker," she answered naming the agent. "Myself and three other girls."

"Look—I have to go out for half an hour. To see a man—this is not phoney. Believe me. Will you come along for company and night air?"

She nodded.

On the way they passed his hostess who looked inscrutably at the girl and shook her head slightly at Jim. Out in the clear California night he liked his big new car for the first time, liked it better than driving himself. The streets through which they rolled were quiet at this hour and the limousine stole silently along the darkness. Miss Knighton waited for him to speak.

"What did you teach in school?" he asked.

"Sums. Two and two are five and all that."

"It's a long jump from that to Hollywood."

"It's a long story."

"It can't be very long—you're about eighteen."

"Twenty." Anxiously she asked: "Do you think that's too old?"

"Lord, no! It's a beautiful age. I know—I'm twenty-one myself and the arteries are only beginning to harden."

She looked at him gravely, estimating his age and keeping it to herself.

"I want to hear the long story," he said.

She sighed.

"Well, a lot of old men fell in love with me. Old, old men—I was an old man's darling."

"You mean old gaffers of twenty-two?"

"They were between sixty and seventy. This is all true. So I became a gold-digger and dug enough money out of them to come to New York. I walked into '21' the first day and Joe Becker saw me."

"Then you've never been in pictures?" he asked.

"Oh yes—I had a test this morning."

Jim smiled.

"And you don't feel bad taking money from all those old men?" he inquired.

"Not really," she said, matter-of-fact. "They enjoyed giving it to me. Anyhow it wasn't really money. When they wanted to give me presents I'd send them to a jeweler I knew and afterwards I'd take the present back to the jeweler and get four fifths of the cash."

"Why, you little chiseller!"

"Yes," she admitted placidly. "Somebody told me how. I'm out for all I can get."

"Didn't they mind—the old men I mean—when you didn't wear their presents?"

"Oh, I'd wear them—once. Old men don't see very well, or remember. But that's why I haven't got any jewelry." She broke off. "I understand you can rent jewelry here."

Jim looked at her again and then laughed.

"I wouldn't bother about it. California's full of old men."

They had twisted into a residential district. As they turned a corner Jim picked up the speaking tube.

"Stop here." He turned to Pamela, "I have some dirty work to do." He looked at his watch, got out and went up the street to a building with the names of several doctors on a sign. He went past the sign walking slowly, and presently a man came out of the building and followed him. In the darkness between two lamps Jim went close, handed him an envelope and spoke concisely. The man walked off in the opposite direction and Jim returned to the car.

"I'm having all the old men bumped off," he explained. "There're some things worse than death."

"Oh, I'm not free now," she assured him. "I'm engaged."

"Oh." After a minute he asked, "To an Englishman?"

"Well—naturally. Did you think—" She stopped herself but too late.

"Are we that uninteresting?" he asked.

"Oh, no." Her casual tone made it worse. And when she smiled, at the moment when an arc light shone in and dressed her beauty up to a white radiance, it was more annoying still.

"Now you tell *me* something," she said. "Tell me the mystery."

"Just money," he answered almost absently. "That little Greek doctor keeps telling a certain lady that her appendix is bad—we need her in a picture. So we bought him off. It's the last time I'll ever do anyone else's dirty work."

She frowned.

"Does she really need her appendix out?"

He shrugged.

"Probably not. At least that rat wouldn't know. He's her brother-in-law and he wants the money."

After a long time Pamela spoke judicially.

"An Englishman wouldn't do that."

"Some would," he said shortly, "—and some Americans wouldn't."

"An English gentleman wouldn't."

"Aren't you getting off on the wrong foot," he suggested, "if you're going to work here?"

"Oh, I like Americans all right—the civilized ones."

From her look Jim took this to include him, but far from being appeased he had a sense of outrage.

"You're taking chances," he said. "In fact I don't see how you dared come out with me. I might have had feathers under my hat."

"You didn't bring a hat," she said placidly. "Besides Joe Becker said to. There might be something in it for me."

After all he was a producer and you didn't reach eminence by losing your temper—except on purpose.

"I'm *sure* there's something in it for you," he said, listening to a stealthy treacherous purr creep into his voice.

"Are you?" she demanded. "Do you think I'll stand out at all—or am I just one of the thousands?"

"You stand out already," he continued on the same note. "Everyone at the dance was looking at you."

He wondered if this was even faintly true. Was it only he who had fancied some uniqueness?

"You're a new type," he went on. "A face like yours might give American pictures a—a more civilized tone."

This was his arrow—but to his vast surprise it glanced off.

"Oh, do you think so?" she cried. "Are you going to give me a chance?"

"Why certainly." It was hard to believe that the irony in his voice was missing its mark. "Except, of course, after tonight there'll be so much competition that—"

"Oh, I'd rather work for you," she declared; "I'll tell Joe Becker—"

"Don't tell him anything," he interrupted.

"Oh, I won't. I'll do just as you say."

Her eyes were wide and expectant. Disturbed, he felt that words were being put in his mouth or slipping from him unintended. That so much innocence and so much predatory toughness could go side by side behind this gentle English voice.

"You'd be wasted in bits," he began. "The thing is to get a fat part—" He broke off and began again. "You've got such a strong personality that—"

"Oh don't!" He saw tears blinking in the corners of her eyes. "Let me just keep this to sleep on tonight. You call me in the morning—or when you need me."

The car came to rest at the strip of red carpet in front of the dance. Seeing Pamela, the crowd bulged forward grotesquely in the spilt glare of the drum lights. They held their autograph books at the ready, but failing to recognize her, they sighed back behind the ropes.

In the ballroom he danced her to Becker's table.

"I won't say a word," she whispered. From her evening case she took a card with the name of her hotel penciled on it. "If any other offers come I'll refuse them."

"Oh no," he said quickly.

"Oh yes." She smiled brightly at him and for an instant the feeling Jim had had on seeing her came back. There was an impression in her face, at least, of a rich warm sympathy, of youth and suffering side by side. He braced himself for a final quick slash to burst the scarcely created bubble.

"After a year or so—" he began. But the music and her voice overrode him.

"I'll wait for you to call. You're the—you're the most civilized American I've ever met."

She turned her back as if embarrassed by the magnificence of her compliment. Jim started back to his table—then seeing his hostess talking to someone across his empty chair, he turned obliquely away. The room, the evening had gone raucous—the blend of music and voices seemed inharmonious and accidental and his eyes covering the room saw only jealousies and hatreds—egos tapping like drum beats up to a fanfare. He was not above the battle as he had thought.

He started for the coat-room thinking of the note he would dispatch by waiter to his hostess: "You were dancing so I—" Then he found himself almost upon Pamela Knighton's table, and turning again he took another route toward the door.

## II

A picture executive can do without creative intelligence but not without tact. Tact now absorbed Jim Leonard to the exclusion of everything else. Power should have pushed diplomacy into the background, leaving him free, but instead it intensified all his human relations—with the executives, with the directors, writers, actors and technical men assigned to his unit, with department heads, censors and "men from the East" besides. So the stalling off of one lone English girl, who had no weapon except the telephone and a little note that reached him from the entrance desk, should have been no problem at all.

*Just passing by the studio and thought of you and of our ride. There have been some offers but I keep stalling Joe Becker. If I move I will let you know.*

A city full of youth and hope spoke in it—in its two transparent lies, the brave falsity of its tone. It didn't matter to her—all the money and glory beyond the impregnable walls. She had just been passing by—just passing by.

That was after two weeks. In another week, Joe Becker dropped in to see him.

"About that little English girl, Pamela Knighton—remember? How'd she strike you?"

"Very nice."

"For some reason she didn't want me to talk to you." Joe looked out the window. "So I suppose you didn't get along so well that night."

"Sure we did."

"The girl's engaged, you see, to some guy in England."

"She told me that," said Jim, annoyed. "I didn't make any passes at her if that's what you're getting at."

"Don't worry—I understand those things. I just wanted to tell you something about her."

"Nobody else interested?"

"She's only been here a month. Everybody's got to start. I just want to tell you that when she came into '21' that day the barflies dropped like—like flies. Let me tell you—in one minute she was the talk of Cafe Society."

"It must have been great," Jim said dryly.

"It was. And Lamarr was there that day too. Listen—Pam was all alone, and she had on English clothes I guess, nothing you'd look at twice—rabbit fur. But she shone through it like a diamond."

"Yeah?"

"Strong women wept into their vichyssoise. Elsa Maxwell—"

"Joe, this is a busy morning."

"Will you look at her test?"

"Tests are for make-up men," said Jim, impatiently. "I never believe a good test. And I always suspect a bad one."

"Got your own ideas, eh."

"About that. There've been a lot of bad guesses in projection rooms."

"Behind desks too," said Joe rising.

A second note came after another week.

*When I phoned yesterday one secretary said you were away and one said you were in conference. If this is a run-around tell me. I'm not getting any younger. Twenty-one is staring me in the face—and you must have bumped off all the old men.*

Her face had grown dim now. He remembered the delicate cheeks, the haunted eyes, as from a picture seen a long time ago. It was easy to dictate a letter that told of changed plans, of new casting, of difficulties which made it impossible....

He didn't feel good about it but at least it was finished business. Having a sandwich in his neighborhood drugstore that night, he looked back at his month's work as good. He had reeked of tact. His unit functioned smoothly. The shades who controlled his destiny would soon see.

There were only a few people in the drugstore. Pamela Knighton was the girl at the magazine rack. She looked up at him, startled, over a copy of the "Illustrated London News."

Knowing of the letter that lay for signature on his desk, Jim wished he could pretend not to see her. He turned slightly aside, held his breath, listened. But though she had seen him, nothing happened, and hating his Hollywood cowardice he turned again presently and lifted his hat.

"You're up late," he said.

Pamela searched his face momentarily.

"I live around the corner," she said. "I've just moved—I wrote you today."

"I live near here too."

She replaced the magazine in the rack. Jim's tact fled. He felt suddenly old and harassed and asked the wrong question.

"How do things go?"

"Oh very well," she said. "I'm in a play—a real play at the New Faces Theatre in Pasadena. For the experience."

"Oh, that's very wise."

"We open in two weeks. I was hoping you could come."

They walked out the door together and stood in the glow of the red neon sign. Across the autumn street newsboys were shouting the result of the night football.

"Which way?" she asked.

—The other way from you, he thought, but when she indicated her direction he walked with her. It was months since he had seen Sunset Boulevard, and the mention of Pasadena made him think of when he had first come to California ten years ago, something green and cool.

Pamela stopped before some tiny bungalows around a central court.

"Good-night," she said. "Don't let it worry you if you can't help me. Joe has explained how things are, with the war and all. I know you wanted to."

He nodded solemnly—despising himself.

"Are you married?" she asked.

"No."

"Then kiss me good-night."

As he hesitated she said, "I like to be kissed good-night. I sleep better."

He put his arms around her shyly and bent down to her lips, just touching them—and thinking hard of the letter on his desk which he couldn't send now—and liking holding her.

"You see it's nothing," she said, "just friendly. Just good-night."

On his way to the corner Jim said aloud, "Well, I'll be damned" and kept repeating the sinister prophecy to himself for some time after he was in bed.

### III

On the third night of Pamela's play Jim went to Pasadena and bought a seat in the last row. He entered a tiny auditorium and was the first arrival except for fluttering ushers and voices chattering amid the hammers backstage. He considered a discreet retirement but was reassured by the arrival of a group of five, among them Joe Becker's chief assistant. The lights went out; a gong was beaten; to an audience of six the play began.

Jim watched Pamela; in front of him the party of five leaned together and whispered after her scenes. Was she good? He was sure of it. But with pictures drawing upon half the world for talent there was scarcely such a phenomenon as a "natural." There were only possibilities—and luck. He was luck. He was maybe this girl's luck—if he felt that her pull at his insides was universal. Stars were no longer created by one man's casual desire as in the silent days, but stock girls were, tests were, chances were. When the last curtain dropped, domestically as a Venetian blind, he went backstage by the simple process of walking through a door on the side. She was waiting for him.

"I was hoping you wouldn't come tonight," she said. "We've flopped. But the first night it was full and I looked for you."

"You were fine," he said shyly.

"Oh no. You should have seen me then."

"I saw enough," he said. "I can give you a little part. Will you come to the studio tomorrow?"

He watched her expression. Out of her eyes, out of the curve of her mouth gleamed a sudden and overwhelming pity.

"Oh," she said. "Oh, I'm terribly sorry. Joe brought some people over and next day I signed up with Bernie Wise."

"You did?"

"I knew you wanted me and at first I didn't realize you were just a sort of Supervisor. I thought you had more power—" She broke off and assured him hastily, "Oh, I like you better *per*sonally. You're much more civilized than Bernie Wise."

He felt a stab of pain and protest. All right then, he was civilized.

"Can I drive you back to Hollywood?" he asked.

They rode through an October night soft as April. When they crossed a bridge, its walls topped with wire screens, he gestured toward it and she nodded.

"I know what it is," she said. "But how stupid! English people don't commit suicide when they don't get what they want."

"I know. They come to America."

She laughed and looked at him appraisingly. Oh, she could do something with him all right. She let her hand rest upon his.

"Kiss tonight?" he suggested after a while.

Pamela glanced at the chauffeur, insulated in his compartment.

"Kiss tonight," she said.

He flew East next day, looking for a young actress just like Pamela Knighton. He looked so hard that any eyes with an aspect of lovely melancholy, any bright English voice, predisposed him. It seemed rather a desperate matter that he should find someone exactly like this girl. Then when a telegram called him impatiently back to Hollywood, he found Pamela dumped in his lap.

"You got a second chance, Jim," said Joe Becker. "Don't miss it again."

"What was the matter over there?"

"They had no part for her. They're in a mess. So we tore up the contract."

Mike Harris, the studio head, investigated the matter. Why was a shrewd picture man like Bernie Wise willing to let her go?

"Bernie says she can't act," he reported to Jim. "And what's more she makes trouble. I keep thinking of Simone and those two Austrian girls."

"I've seen her act," insisted Jim. "And I've got a place for her. I don't even want to build her up yet. I want to spot her in this little part and let you see."

A week later Jim pushed open the padded door of Stage III and walked anxiously in. Extras in dress clothes turned toward him in the semi-darkness; eyes widened.

"Where's Bob Griffin?"

"In that bungalow with Miss Knighton."

They were sitting side by side on a couch in the glare of the make-up light, and from the resistance in Pamela's face Jim knew the trouble was serious.

"It's *nothing*," Bob insisted heartily. "We get along like a couple of kittens, don't we, Pam?"

"You smell of onions," said Pamela.

Griffin tried again.

"There's an English way and an American way. We're looking for the happy mean—that's all."

"There's a nice way and a silly way," Pamela said shortly. "I don't want to begin by looking like a fool."

"Leave us alone, will you Bob?" Jim said.

"Sure. All the time in the world."

Jim had not seen her in this busy week of tests and fittings and rehearsals, and he thought now how little he knew about her and she of them.

"Bob seems to be in your hair," he said.

"He wants me to say things no sane person would say."

"All right—maybe so," he agreed. "Pamela, since you've been working here have you ever blown up in your lines?"

"Why—everybody does sometimes."

"Listen, Pamela—Bob Griffin gets almost ten times as much money as you do—for a particular reason. Not because he's the most brilliant director in Hollywood—he isn't—but because he never blows up in his lines."

"He's not an actor," she said puzzled.

"I mean his lines in real life. I picked him for this picture because once in a while I blow up. But not Bob. He signed a contract for an unholy amount of money—which he doesn't deserve, which nobody deserves. But he earns it because smoothness is the fourth dimension of this business and Bob has learned never to say the word 'I'. People of three times his talent—producers and troupers and directors—go down the sink because they can't learn that."

"I know I'm being lectured to," she said uncertainly. "But I don't seem to understand. An actress has her own personality—"

He nodded.

"And we pay her five times what she could get for it anywhere else—*if* she'll only keep it off the floor where it trips the rest of us up. You're tripping us all up, Pamela."

—I thought you were my friend, her eyes said.

He talked to her a few minutes more. Everything he said he believed with all his heart, but because he had twice kissed those lips he saw that it was support and protection they wanted from him. All he had done was to make her a little shocked that he was not on her side. Feeling rather baffled, and sorry for her loneliness he went to the door of the bungalow and called:

"Hey, Bob!"

Jim went about other business. He got back to his office to find Mike Harris waiting.

"Again that girl's making trouble."

"I've been over there."

"I mean in the last five minutes," cried Harris. "Since you left she's made trouble! Bob Griffin had to stop shooting for the day. He's on his way over."

Bob came in.

"There's one type you can't seem to get at—can't find what makes them that way."

There was a moment's silence. Mike Harris, upset by the situation, suspected that Jim was having an affair with the girl.

"Give me till tomorrow morning," said Jim. "I think I can find what's back of this."

Griffin hesitated but there was a personal appeal in Jim's eyes—an appeal to associations of a decade.

"All right, Jim," he agreed.

When they had gone Jim called Pamela's number. What he had almost expected happened but his heart sank none the less when a man's voice answered the phone.

### IV

Excepting a trained nurse, an actress is the easiest prey for the unscrupulous male. Jim had learned that in the background of their troubles or their failures there was often some plausible confidence man, who asserted his masculinity by way of interference, midnight nagging, bad advice. The technique of the man was to belittle the woman's job and to question endlessly the motives and intelligence of those for whom she worked.

When Jim reached the bungalow hotel in Beverly Hills where Pamela had moved, it was after six. In the court a cold fountain plashed senselessly against the December fog and he heard Major Bowes' voice loud from three radios.

When the door of the apartment opened Jim stared. The man was old—a bent and withered Englishman with ruddy winter color dying in his face. He wore an old dressing gown and slippers and he asked Jim to sit down with an air of being at home. Pamela would be in shortly.

"Are you a relative?" Jim asked wonderingly.

"No, Pamela and I met here in Hollywood, strangers in a strange land. Are you employed in pictures, Mr.— Mr.—"

"Leonard," said Jim. "Yes. At present I'm Pamela's boss."

A change came into the man's eyes—the watery blink became conspicuous, there was a stiffening of the old lids. The lips curled down and backward and Jim was gazing into an expression of utter malignity. Then the features became old and bland again.

"I hope Pamela is being handled properly?"

"You've been in pictures?" Jim asked.

"Till my health broke down. But I am still on the rolls at Central Casting and I know everything about this business and the souls of those who own it—"

He broke off. The door opened and Pamela came in.

"Well hello," she said in surprise. "You've met? The Honorable Chauncey Ward—Mr. Leonard."

Her glowing beauty, borne in from outside like something snatched from wind and weather, made Jim breathless for a moment.

"I thought you told me my sins this afternoon," she said with a touch of defiance.

"I wanted to talk to you away from the studio."

"Don't accept a salary cut," the old man said. "That's an old trick."

"It's not that, Mr. Ward," said Pamela. "Mr. Leonard has been my friend up to now. But today the director tried to make a fool of me and Mr. Leonard backed him up."

"They all hang together," said Mr. Ward.

"I wonder—" began Jim. "Could I possibly talk to you alone?"

"I trust Mr. Ward," said Pamela frowning. "He's been over here twenty-five years and he's practically my business manager."

Jim wondered from what deep loneliness this relationship had sprung.

"I hear there was more trouble on the set," he said.

"Trouble!" She was wide-eyed. "Griffin's assistant swore at me and I heard it. So I walked out. And if Griffin sent apologies by you I don't want them—our relation is going to be strictly business from now on."

"He didn't send apologies," said Jim uncomfortably. "He sent an ultimatum."

"An ultimatum!" she exclaimed. "I've got a contract, and you're his boss, aren't you?"

"To an extent," said Jim, "—but of course making pictures is a joint matter—"

"Then let me try another director."

"Fight for your rights," said Mr. Ward. "That's the only thing that impresses them."

"You're doing your best to wreck this girl," said Jim quietly.

"You can't frighten us," snapped Ward. "I've seen your type before."

Jim looked again at Pamela. There was exactly nothing he could do. Had they been in love, had it ever seemed the time to encourage the spark between them, he might have reached her now. But it was too late. He seemed to feel the swift wheels of the industry turning in the Hollywood darkness outside. He knew that when the studio opened tomorrow, Mike Harris would have new plans that did not include Pamela at all.

For a moment longer he hesitated. He was a well-liked man, still young, and with a wide approval. He could buck them about this girl, send her to a dramatic teacher. He could not bear to see her make such a mistake. On the other hand he was afraid that somewhere people had yielded to her too much, spoiled her for this sort of career.

"Hollywood isn't a very civilized place," said Pamela.

"It's a jungle," agreed Mr. Ward. "Full of prowling beasts of prey."

Jim rose.

"Well, this one will prowl out," he said. "Pam, I'm very sorry. Feeling like you do, I think you'd be wise to go back to England and get married."

For a moment a flicker of doubt was in her eyes. But her confidence, her young egotism, was greater than her judgment—she did not realize that this very minute was opportunity and she was losing it forever.

For she had lost it when Jim turned and went out. It was weeks before she knew how it happened. She received her salary for some months—Jim saw to that—but she did not set foot on that lot again. Or on any other. She was placed quietly on that black list that is not written down but that functions at backgammon games after dinner, or on the way to the races. Men of influence stared at her with interest at restaurants here and there but all their inquiries about her reached the same dead end.

She never gave up during the following months—even long after Becker had lost interest and she was in want, and no longer seen in the places where people go to be looked at. It was not from grief or discouragement but only through commonplace circumstances that in June she died.

V

When Jim heard about it, it seemed incredible. He learned accidentally that she was in the hospital with pneumonia—he telephoned and found that she was dead. "Sybil Higgins, actress, English. Age 21."

She had given old Ward as the person to be informed and Jim managed to get him enough money to cover the funeral expenses, on the pretext that some old salary was still owing. Afraid that Ward might guess the source of the money he did not go to the funeral but a week later he drove out to the grave.

It was a long bright June day and he stayed there an hour. All over the city there were young people just breathing and being happy and it seemed senseless that the little English girl was not one of them. He kept on trying and trying to twist things about so that they would come out right for her but it was too late. That pink and silver frost had melted. He said good-bye aloud and promised that he would come again.

Back at the studio he reserved a projection room and asked for her tests and for the bits of film that had been shot on her picture. He sat in a big leather chair in the darkness and pressed the button for it to begin.

In the test Pamela was dressed as he had seen her that first night at the dance. She looked very happy and he was glad she had had at least that much happiness. The reel of takes from the picture began and ran jerkily with the sound of Bob Griffin's voice off scene and with prop boys showing the number blocks for the takes. Then Jim started as the next-to-last one came up, and he saw her turn from the camera and whisper:

"I'd rather die than do it that way."

Jim got up and went back to his office where he opened the three notes he had from her and read them again.

*...just passing by the studio and thought of you and of our ride.*

—just passing by. During the spring she had called him twice on the phone, he knew, and he had wanted to see her. But he could do nothing for her and could not bear to tell her so.

"I am not very brave," Jim said to himself. Even now there was fear in his heart that this would haunt him like that memory of his youth, and he did not want to be unhappy.

Several days later he worked late in the dubbing room, and afterwards he dropped into his neighborhood drugstore for a sandwich. It was a warm night and there were many young people at the soda counter. He was paying his check when he became aware that a figure was standing by the magazine rack looking at him over the edge of a magazine. He stopped—he did not want to turn for a closer look only to find the resemblance at an end. Nor did he want to go away.

He heard the sound of a page turning and then out of the corner of his eye he saw the magazine cover, the "Illustrated London News."

He felt no fear—he was thinking too quickly, too desperately. If this were real and he could snatch her back, start from there, from that night.

"Your change, Mr. Leonard."

"Thank you."

Still without looking he started for the door and then the magazine closed and dropped to a pile and he heard someone breathe close to his side. Newsboys were calling an extra across the street and after a moment he turned the wrong way, her way, and he heard her following—so plain that he slowed his pace with the sense that she had trouble keeping up with him.

In front of the apartment court he took her in his arms and drew her radiant beauty close.

"Kiss me good-night," she said. "I like to be kissed good-night. I sleep better."

—Then sleep, he thought as he turned away—sleep. I couldn't fix it. I tried to fix it. When you brought your beauty here I didn't want to throw it away, but I did somehow. There is nothing left for you now but sleep.

# NEWS OF PARIS—FIFTEEN YEARS AGO

*Fitzgerald composed this beginning for a story in 1940. The narrative remained uncompleted at his death in December of that year. "News of Paris" survives in typescript among his papers at Princeton. It was first published in* Furioso 3 (Winter 1947): 5–10, *with an explanatory note by Arthur Mizener, pp. 11–12.*

"We shouldn't both be coming from the same direction," Ruth said. "A lot of people know we're at the same hotel."

Henry Haven Dell smiled and then they both laughed. It was a bright morning in April and they had just turned off the Champs Élysées toward the English Church.

"I'll walk on the other side of the street," he said, "and then we'll meet at the door."

"No, we oughtn't even to sit together. I'm a countess—laugh it off but anything I do will be in that damn 'Boulevardier.'"

They stopped momentarily.

"But I hate to leave you," he said. "You look so lovely."

"I hate to leave you too," she whispered. "I never knew how nice you were. But goodbye."

Half way across the street, he stopped to a great screech of auto horns playing Debussy.

"We're lunching," he called back.

She nodded, but continued to walk looking straight ahead on her sidewalk. Henry Haven Dell continued his crossing and then walked quickly, from time to time throwing a happy glance at the figure across the way.

—I wonder if they have telephones in churches, he thought. After the ceremony he would see.

He stood in a rear row, catching Ruth's eye from time to time, teasing her. It was a very fashionable wedding. As the bride and groom came down the aisle the bride caught his arm and took him along with them down the street.

"Isn't it fun," the bride said. "And just think, Henry, I almost married you."

Her husband laughed.

—at what, Henry thought. I could have had her if she'd really been the one.

Aloud he said:

"I have to telephone before the reception."

"The hotel's full of phones. Come and stand beside me. I want you to be the first to know."

He got to a phone only after an hour.

"The *Paris* is delayed," said the Compagnie Transatlantique. "We can't give you an exact hour. Not before four. Oh, no, Monsieur—not possibly."

Good. In the lobby he joined a party of wedding guests and repaired to the Ritz on the man's part of the bar. You couldn't be with women incessantly.

"How long will you be in Paris, Henry?"

"That's not a fair question. I can always tell you how long I'll be in London or New York."

He had two cocktails—each at a different table. A little before one when the confusion and din were at their height he went out into the Rue Cambon. There was not a taxi to be had—the doormen were chasing them all the way up to the Rue de Rivoli. One sailed into port with a doorman on the running board but a lovely little brunette in pale green was already waiting.

"Oh, look," begged Henry. "You're not by any chance going near the Bois."

He was getting into the cab as he spoke. His morning coat was a sort of introduction. She nodded.

"I'm lunching there."

"I'm Henry Dell," he said, lifting his hat.

"Oh, it's you—at last," she said eagerly. "I'm Bessie Wing—born Leighton. I know all your cousins."

"Isn't this nice," he exclaimed and she agreed.

"I'm breaking my engagement at luncheon," she said. "And I'll name you."

"Really breaking your engagement?"

"At the Café Dauphine—from one to two."

"I'll be there—from time to time I'll look at you."

"What I want to know is—does he take me home afterward. I'm not Emily Posted."

On impulse he said:

"No, I do. You may be faint or something. I'll keep an eye on you."

She shook her head.

"No—it wouldn't be reverent this afternoon," she said. "But I'll be here weeks."

"This afternoon," he said. "You see, there's a boat coming in."

After a moment's reluctance she answered:

"I do *almost* know you. Leave it this way. If you see me shaking a spoon back and forth I'll meet you in front in five minutes."

Ruth was sitting at table. Henry talked lazily to her for ten minutes, watching her face and the spring light upon the table. Then with a casual glance he located Bessie Wing across the room, deep in conversation with a man of twenty-six, his own age.

"We'll have this afternoon—and then goodbye," said Ruth.

"Not even this afternoon," he answered solemnly. "I'm meeting the boat in an hour."

"I'm sorry, Henry. Hasn't it been fun?"

"Lots of fun. So much fun." He felt sincerely sad.

"It's just as well," said Ruth with a little effort. "I have fittings that I've postponed. Remember me when you go to the Opera or out to Saint-Germain."

"I'll do my best to forget you."

A little later he saw the spoon waving.

"Let me go first," he said. "I somehow couldn't bear to sit here and see you walk off."

"All right, I'll sit here and think."

Bessie was waiting under a pear tree in front—they crammed hastily into a taxi like escaping children.

"Was it bad?" he asked. "I watched you. There were tears in his eyes."

She nodded.

"It was pretty bad."

"Why did you break it?"

"Because my first marriage was a flop. There were so many men around that when I married I didn't know who I loved anymore. So there didn't seem to be any point if you know what I mean. Why should it have been Hershell Wing?"

"How about this other man?"

"It would have been the same way only now it would be my fault because I know."

They sat in the cool American drawing room of her apartment and had coffee.

"For anyone so beautiful—" he said, "there must be many times like those. When there isn't a man—there's just men."

"There was a man once," she said, "when I was sixteen. He looked like you. He didn't love me."

Henry went and sat beside her on the fauteuil.

"That happens too," said Henry. "Perhaps the safest way is 'Ships that pass in the night.'"

She held back a little.

"I don't want to be old-fashioned but we don't know each other."

"Sure we do—remember—we met this morning."

She laughed:

"Sedative for a broken engagement!"

"The specific one," he said.

It was quiet in the room. The peacocks in the draperies stirred in the April wind.

Later they stood on her balcony arm in arm and looked over a sea of green leaves to the Arc de Triomphe.

"Where is the phone?" he asked suddenly. "Never mind—I know."

He went inside, picked up the phone beside her bed.

"Compagnie Générale? ... How about the boat train from the *Paris*?"

"Oh, she has not docked in Havre yet, Monsieur. Call in several hours. The delay has been at Southampton."

Returning to the balcony Henry said:

"All right—let's go to the Exposition."

"I have to, you see," she said. "This woman, Mary Tollifer I told you about—she's the only person I can go to with what I did at luncheon. She'll understand."

"Would she understand about us too?"

"She'll never know. She's been an ideal of mine since I was sixteen."

She was not much older than Bessie, Henry thought as they met her in the Crillon lobby—she was a golden brown woman, very trim and what the French call "*soignée*"—which means washed and something more. She had an American painter and an Austrian sculptor with her and Henry gathered that they were both a little in love with her, or else exploiting her for money—money evident in the Renault town car that took them to the exhibition of decorative arts that ringed the Seine.

They walked along through the snow, passed the chromium rails, the shining economy of steel that was to change the furniture of an era. Henry, once art editor of the "Harvard Lampoon," was not without a seeing eye but he let the painter and sculptor talk. When they sat down for an *aperitif* afterwards, Bessie sat very close to him—Mary Tollifer smiled and saw. She looked appraisingly at Henry.

"Have you two known each other long?" she asked.

"Years," said Henry. "She is a sister to me. And now I must leave you all—after a charming afternoon."

Bessie looked at him reproachfully, started to rise with him—controlled herself.

"I told you there was a boat," he said gently.

"Ships," she answered.

As he walked away he saw the painter move to the chair he had vacated by her side.

The *Paris* was still delayed at Southampton and Henry considered what to do. When you have been doing nothing in a pleasant way a long time it is difficult to fill in stray hours. More difficult than for one who works. In the country he might have exercised—here there were only faces over tables. And there must continue to be faces over tables.

—I am become a contemptible drone, he thought. I must give at least a thought to duty.

He taxied over to the Left Bank—to the Rue Notre Dame des Champs—to call on a child he had endowed just after the war. A beautiful little orphan who begged in front of the Café du Dôme. Henry had sent her for three years to a convent. He saw her once or twice each summer—not now for almost a year.

"Hélène is out," said a new concierge whom Henry did not know. "How should I guess where she is? At the Café de Lilas? At Lipps?"

He was faintly shocked—then faintly reassured when he found her at Lipps, the beer place, which was, at least, a step more respectable than the Dôme or the Rotonde. She left the two Americans with whom she was sitting and embraced him shyly.

"What are you preparing to do, Hélène?" he demanded kindly. "What profession do the nuns teach you?"

She shrugged her shoulders.

"I shall marry," she said. "A rich American if I can. That young man I just left for example—he is on the staff of the 'New York Herald Tribune.'"

"Reporters are not rich," he reproved her, "and that one doesn't look very promising."

"Oh, he is drunk now," said Hélène, "but at times he is all one would desire."

Henry had been a romantic four years ago—right after the war. He had in no sense brought up this girl to marry or for anything else. Yet the thought was in his mind then: "What if she could continue to be a great beauty?" And now as he looked at her he felt a surge of jealousy toward the reporter.

# PUBLIC LETTERS

## THE CLAIMS OF THE *LIT*.

The Editor of
The Alumni Weekly,

Dear Sir: I read with interest the letter of Mr. Edmund B. Wilson, Jr., '16, in The Alumni Weekly for Feb. 25, and I most heartily concur in his plea that the claims of the *Nassau Literary Magazine* to endowment should be prior to those of the Philadelphian Society. A scant fourth of every class, the more immature, impressionable, and timid fourth, are swept up yearly by the drag-net of the Philadelphian Society. By senior year most of them realize that the point of view therein camouflaged under the name of "social service" has little connection with modern life and modern thought—except with the present kill-joy spirit sweeping the Chautauquas—and the swarm of earnest youths diminishes to a mere scattering of mild and innocuous uplifters. But I believe that during the first three years inestimable harm is done to the impressionable fourth. Nothing could be less stimulating to that quickening of interest and intellectual curiosity which is the aim of all education than the depressing conviction of sin distilled by those prosperous apostles who go the rounds of the colleges frightening amiable freshmen. That a man such as the famous "bad example" should be permitted to sit smugly upon a Princeton lecture platform to be pointed at by the raucous lecturer as a reformed rake, and hence as an ideal, is a custom too ridiculous to be disgraceful but also too absurd to be endowed.

It seems inevitable that this herd of blue-nosed professional uplifters, at present at large in America appealing to the intellect of farmers' wives and pious drug-clerks, shall have a breeding place in Princeton, but that men to whom such ideas are distasteful and revolting should have to contribute to keep it alive and bawling when the *Lit*. goes unendowed is really too much.

---

*Princeton Alumni Weekly* 20 (10 March 1920): 514. This is the first of the public letters (some serious, some humorous) that Fitzgerald sent to *PAW* and to other Princeton publications. The Philadelphian Society, mentioned in the first paragraph of this letter, was a campus religious organization.

It is an unnecessary truckling to the mediocre religious fanaticism of a dull and earnest minority. Princeton lives by its statesmen and artists and scientists—even by its football teams—but not by its percentage of puritans in every graduating class.

F. Scott Fitzgerald '17.

## THE CREDO OF F. SCOTT FITZGERALD

Dear Boyd: It seems to me that the overworked art-form at present in America is the "history of a young man." Frank Norris began it with "Vandover and the Brute," then came Stephen French Whitman with "Predestined" and of late my own book and Floyd Dell's "Moon Calf." In addition I understand that Stephen Benét has also delved into his past. This writing of a young man's novel consists chiefly in dumping all your youthful adventures into the readers' lap with a profound air of importance, keeping carefully within the formulas of Wells and James Joyce. It seems to me that when accomplished by a man without distinction of style it reaches the depth of banality as in the case of "Moon Calf." \*\*\* Up to this year the literary people of any pretensions—Mencken, Cabell, Wharton, Dreiser, Hergesheimer, Cather and Charles Norris—have been more or less banded together in the fight against intolerance and stupidity, but I think that a split is due. On the romantic side Cabell, I suppose, would maintain that life has a certain glamour that reporting—especially this reporting of a small Midwestern town—cannot convey to paper. On the realistic side Dreiser would probably maintain that romanticism tends immediately to deteriorate to the Zane Grey-Rupert Hughes level, as it has in the case of Tarkington, fundamentally a brilliant writer. \*\*\*

It is encouraging to notice that the number of pleasant sheep, i.e., people who think they're absorbing culture if they read Blasco Ibanez, H. G. Wells and Henry Van Dyke—are being rounded into shape. This class, which makes up the so-called upper class in every American city, will read what they're told and now that at last we have a few brilliant men like Mencken at the head of American letters, these amiable sheep will pretend to appreciate the appreciable

---

*St. Paul Daily News*, 20 February 1921, Feature Section, p. 8. This letter, to Fitzgerald's literary friend Thomas Boyd, was untitled in its first appearance. It was reprinted as "The Credo of F. Scott Fitzgerald" in the *Chicago Daily News*, 9 March 1921, and appeared under other titles in other newspapers.

of their own country instead of rushing to cold churches to hear noble but unintelligible words, and meeting once a week to read papers on the aforementioned Blasco Ibanez. Even the stupidest people are reading "Main Street," and pretending they thought so all the time. I wonder how many people in St. Paul ever read "The Titan" or "Salt" or even "McTeague." All this would seem to encourage insincerity of taste. But if it does it would at least have paid Dreiser for his early struggles at the time when such cheapjacks as Robert Chambers were being hailed as the "Balzacs of America."

— F. Scott Fitzgerald

## CONFESSIONS

*F. Scott Fitzgerald, the first chronicler of the flapper, in "This Side of Paradise" makes this explanatory reply when I asked him what book he would rather have written than any other:*

Dear Miss Butcher:

I'd rather have written Conrad's "Nostromo" than any other novel. First, because I think it is the greatest novel since "Vanity Fair" (possibly excluding "Madame Bovary"), but chiefly because "Nostromo," the man, intrigues me so much. Now the Nostromo who exists in life and always has existed, whether as a Roman centurion or a modern top sergeant, has often crept into fiction, but until Conrad there was no one to ponder over him. He was dismissed superficially and abruptly even by those who most admired his efficient handling of the proletariat either in crowds or as individuals. Kipling realized that this figure, with his almost autocratic disdain of weakness, is one of the most powerful props of the capitalistic system, and under various names he occurs in many of Kipling's stories of Indian life—but always as a sort of glorified servant. The literary attitude toward him has been that of an officer sitting in his club with a highball during drill.

"Well, I've got nothing to worry about. Sergt. O'Hare has the troop and—" this with a patronizing condescension— "I believe he knows just about as much about handling them as I do."

Now Conrad didn't stop there. He took this man of the people and imagined him with such a completeness that there is no use of any one else pondering over him for some time. He is one of the most important types in our civilization. In particular he's one that always made a haunting and irresistible appeal to me. So I

---

*Chicago Daily Tribune*, 19 May 1923, p. 9. A public letter to Fanny Butcher, who was beginning her tenure as the literary editor of the *Tribune*.

would rather have dragged his soul from behind his astounding and inarticulate presence than written any other novel in the world.

                    Sincerely,

                    F. Scott Fitzgerald

## LETTER TO A. PHILIP RANDOLPH

Great Neck, L.I.
May 25, 1923.

Dear Mr. Randolph:

I read THE MESSENGER from cover to cover and thoroughly enjoyed its intelligent editing and its liberal point of view. Many congratulations to you, and many thanks for sending it to me.

                Sincerely,

                F. Scott Fitzgerald

---

*The Messenger* 5 (June 1923): 749. The letter is addressed to A. Philip Randolph, one of the editors of *The Messenger*, an African American literary and political magazine that played an important role in the Harlem Renaissance during the 1920s. Fitzgerald's letter appeared with eleven others under the heading "The Thinking World Commends Messenger." Among the other letter-writers were J. E. Spingarn, a literary critic and civil rights activist; Heywood Broun, a columnist for the *New York World*; and Oswald Garrison Villard, who wrote for the *New York Evening Post* and *The Nation*.

## IN LITERARY NEW YORK

F. Scott Fitzgerald Says Appearance in January of Mencken and Nathan's American Mercury Will Be Event of the Year—Tom Boyd Writing for Scribner's Magazine.

GREAT NECK, L. I.

DEAR BERNARD: You ask me for the news from literary New York. Outside of the fact that Rebecca West and Frank Swinnerton are in town, there isn't any. Tom Boyd, after being feted on all sides by admirers of his books, got off for France and is sending back short stories for Scribner's Magazine by every boat.

The books of the fall seem to have determined themselves as "A Lost Lady," Thomas Beer's life of Stephen Crane and Eleanor Wylie's "Jennifer Lorn," a remarkable period romance which just misses—but misses—being a classic. Floyd Dell's new book ("Janet March") is a drab, dull statistic throughout. How such an intelligent, sophisticated man can go on year after year turning out such appalling novels is a question for the psychoanalysts, to whom, I understand, he resorts.

Aldous Huxley's "Antic Hay," while a delightful book, is inferior on all counts to Van Vechten's "The Blind Bow-Boy."

But the real event of the year will, of course, be the appearance in January of the American Mercury. The Smart Set without Mencken and Nathan is already on the stands, and a dreary sight it is. In their nine years' association with it those two men had a most stupendous and far reaching influence on the whole course of American writing. Their influence was not so much on the very first-rate writers, though even there it was considerable in many cases as on the cultural background. Their new venture is even more interesting. We shall see what we shall see.

---

*St. Paul Daily News*, 23 December 1923, Section 2, p. 5. A public letter to Bernard Vaughan, a St. Paul journalist.

You ask for news of me. There is little and that bad. My play ("The Vegetable") opened in Atlantic City and foundered on the opening night. It did better in subsequent performances, but at present is laid up for repairs.

—Scott Fitzgerald.

## WHO'S WHO IN THIS ISSUE

F. SCOTT FITZGERALD ("Wait Till You Have Children of Your Own!") writes us: "A word as to my article. A little while ago every magazine in the country carried two or three 'flapper' or 'anti-flapper' stories, all equally silly, usually written by some wild young devil of forty-five and with most of the data obtained, so far as I can understand, not from life but from a careful perusal of a novel and some short stories that I was so misguided as to write back in 1920. So, naturally, I feel a certain responsibility toward a generation which started life under so many warning fingers. This article is not a defense of the legendary 'wild young person'; it is an attempt to formulate some of the ideas abroad in my generation—in particular as to the education of their own children. These may be the opinions of only two parents out of every two thousand but, in the world of ideas, the opinion of the vast dull majority is of no possible importance anyhow."

---

*Woman's Home Companion* 51 (July 1924): 110. This excerpt from a Fitzgerald letter appears in a section called "Brief Notes about Our Authors." Fitzgerald's article "'Wait Till You Have Children of Your Own!" is included in the Cambridge volume *My Lost City* (2005).

## LETTER TO CLASS SECRETARY

### '17

Mr. Fitzgerald's latest and hitherto unpublished opus follows:

"No news. We are spending a month here in the Pyrenees near Pau—then on March 1 we go to the Riviera, probably Nice, to remain until I finish my new novel. Owen Davis' dramatization of *The Great Gatsby* has opened in New York and looks like a hit. It appears (the novel I mean) in England this month, and in French translation next fall. A book of short stories, *All the Sad Young Men*, appears in New York this month. Last summer we made a tour through Burgundy and Provence with Sap Donahoe. Nonny Jackson writes that he has a new daughter. Townsend Martin and John Bishop are with Famous Players, and that is all the news I know."

---

*Princeton Alumni Weekly* 26 (14 April 1926): 718. Fitzgerald's letter appears with other letters and reports from members of his class (1917).

## F. SCOTT FITZGERALD IS BORED BY EFFORTS AT REALISM IN 'LIT'

**Not Flesh and Blood Characters but Petulant Phantoms Appear in Stories in March Issue.**

POETRY EARNS MORE PRAISE

Griswold's Sonnets Outstanding Feature of Issue—Careful Work by Barnouw and Day Is Noted.

By F. Scott Fitzgerald '17.

In my days stories in the *Lit* were about starving artists, dying poilus, the plague in Florence and the soul of the Great Khan. They took place, chiefly, behind the moon and a thousand years ago. Now they all take place on Nassau Street, no longer back than yesterday. Playing safe they are more "real", but by reason of their narrow boundaries they are desperately similar to each other.

There is the sensitive under-graduate who, perhaps because he is the author, is never given a recognizable skin; there is mention of Nassau Street and Gothic towers; without once seeing or feeling the visual world, without being fresh or tired, without being desperate or ecstatic, neither eating nor loving, and drinking only as a mannerism of the day, this petulant ghost moves through a vague semi-adventure with a girl, a parent, the faculty or another shadow labelled his room-mate. Acted upon but never acting, limp and suspicious, he lacks even the normal phosphoresence of decay.

He drifts through the two best stories in this month's *Lit*—in one he barely attains a stale-mate with his father, due to the latter's advantage of being flesh and blood, since he is observed, however superficially from the outside. *Stranger* by Charles Yost is really a pretty good story, though like all tales of futility and boredom it

---

*Daily Princetonian*, 16 March 1928, pp. 1, 3. A review, for the student newspaper, of the March 1928 issue of the *Nassau Literary Magazine*. Fitzgerald wrote for the *Nassau Lit* during his undergraduate years.

unavoidably shares the quality of its subject—but it is intelligent, restrained and with some but not enough excellent writing.

A. Z. F. Wood's *St. George and the Dragon* is even a little better. Offended by the manners of his home town the ghost grows angry and knocks down not a yokel but another ghost by mistake. We are left to imagine his humiliation. If the author had been a little less facile about Jim's real motives the story would have carried a great deal of conviction, for it is credible, well written and interesting throughout.

H. M. Alexander's *Peckham's Saturday Night* is a good story. *Waking Up* by A. S. Alexander is below the author's standard. *The Old Meeting House* by H. A. Rue is Gray's Elegy copiously watered—it might have come out of the *Lit* of forty years ago.

The poetry is better. Griswold's two sonnets show imagination and power and, I dare say, a great deal of honest toil. They are incomparably the best thing in the issue, cheering even exciting. Erik Barnouw's lighter piece is excellent. So is Price Day's poem—it has feeling, not a few real felicities and, again, welcome signs of patience and care. Wilfred Owen's *Brass Moon* has quality—his shorter pieces are trite; we have such feeble lines as "walk solemnly single file", "piquant turned-up nose", "creep in upon the window sill" etc. *Harlem and the Ritz* by H. T. B. is trivial but I like the form of his long poem. *Defiance* by Grier Hart is fair. The remaining verse is of no interest.

To conclude: This is a dignified but on the whole unadventurous number of the oldest college magazine in America. The present reviewer's strongest reaction is his curiosity as to the fate of Mr. Yost's and Mr. Wood's phantoms. One is sure, of course, that they will in a few years refuse to go into their fathers' businesses, one hardly blames them—but what then? The American father, under the influence of his wife, will immediately yield and the ghost will carry his pale negatives out into the world. Those to whom life has been a more passionate and stirring affair than one must suppose it now is at Princeton will not envy him his hollow victory.

## UNFORTUNATE "TRADITION"

Editor, the *Weekly*
Sir:

It seems to me a pity that the *Alumni Weekly* and the Press Club keep harping on the "tradition" that a lineman shall captain Princeton football teams. It is not a very hoary or venerable tradition—as late as 1922 Halfback Gilroy was Captain-elect, and at any moment it might be necessary to honor it in the breach. There are fine linesmen whose nerves go to pieces under strain, and there are backs with temperaments as steady and imperturbable as sergeants of Marines—I need only mention Buell of Harvard and Mallory of Yale.

My point is that a star prep school back with quite justifiable ambitions for glory—say a born quarterback with a gift for leading and driving—might read of this "tradition" and say to himself "What's the use of bucking up against that kind of discrimination?" Imagine the effect of an annual boast that only outfielders could captain the nine, or that sprinters were too unreliable to lead a track team!

Why not put a quietus on this "tradition" until it has the endorsement of at least a decade?

Nineteen-Seventeen

February 4, 1929.

---

*Princeton Alumni Weekly* 29 (15 February 1929): 562. This is the first of Fitzgerald's communications about the Princeton football team.

## FITZGERALD SETS THINGS RIGHT ABOUT HIS COLLEGE

Dear Mr. Olmsted:

Your article in The Washington Herald of May 9th is inaccurate in that it places the Princeton freshman enrollment at 2200. That is the total enrollment. The freshmen are limited to about 600 less than at Yale and Harvard: and Princeton is still the hardest institution to get in to and stay in (and leave!) in America.

Sincerely,

F. Scott Fitzgerald.

---

*Washington Herald*, 28 June 1929, Section 2, p. 1. A letter to Stanley Olmsted, published as part of a longer article by Olmsted on Fitzgerald.

## FALSE AND EXTREMELY UNWISE TRADITION

*Graduate Finds Cause for Fear in Advertisement of Erroneous "Sacred Old Football Tradition."*

To the Editor of the Princetonian:

Sir:—I see that the fact of a lineman being elected Football Captain is still being sent out to the papers as a "sacred old tradition." As the present writer pointed out in the *Alumni Weekly* last winter, there is no such tradition—Ralph Gilroy was Captain-elect in 1922—and the report serves merely to fill two lines of space for unimaginative Press Club members each year. The point is that I believe it directly responsible for the fact that no first class backs have entered Princeton for four years; where Roper used to make tackles out of extra halfbacks he is now compelled to make fullbacks out of guards and quarterbacks out of air. If anyone believes that rival colleges don't make full use of this alleged discrimination in winning over prospective triple threats, he is simply an innocent; for American boys have a pretty highly developed desire for glory.

It will take five years to kill this rumor, but the Athletic Association has obviously done nothing—and no matter what steps are taken now we can scarcely expect any more Slagles, Miles, Wittmers and Caulkins until 1940.

"Seventeen."

Paris, January 24, 1930.

---

*Daily Princetonian*, 27 February 1930, p. 2. The letter, signed "Seventeen" (Fitzgerald's class at Princeton), was clipped and pasted into one of his scrapbooks—hence the attribution.

## LETTER TO H. N. SWANSON

The latest word I have from Scott Fitzgerald is a note written from Paris and done with his usual restraint: "I want you," he says, "to head a new magazine I want to start. *Undergraduate Underwear* is its name. Let me know immediately through my agent, or through the mail, or *Through the Sepoy Rebellion With Sir Robert Baden-Powell*, or *Through the Wheat*, or *Through the Afghan Passes* by G. A. Henty, or threw a curve when he thought he'd throw a fast one. If you don't, I'm through with you forever."

---

*College Humor*, no. 76 (April 1930): 134. H. N. Swanson, then the editor of *College Humor*, later became a literary agent in Hollywood and represented Fitzgerald on various pieces of movie business during the 1930s. Among Swanson's other clients were James M. Cain, William Faulkner, Pearl Buck, and Raymond Chandler.

## CONFUSED ROMANTICISM

Editor, the *Weekly*
Sir:

I have just been reading the debate between Mr. Casement and Mr. Van Arkel in the *Alumni Weekly*. I am enlightened rather than astonished by Mr. Casement's indifference to any conception of education more modern than the British public school spirit of the middle 'nineties. The two men are talking across a chasm, as the resignation in both their rebuttals clearly shows. It has become a truism that the salient points of character are fixed before the age of twelve. At eighteen you can change a young man's superficial habits, teach him the ethics of a profession, expose him to broadening or narrowing influences—but the deeper matters of whether he's weak or strong, strict or easy with himself, brave or timid—these things are arranged in the home, almost in the nursery. It is preposterous to ask a university to take over such a task.

Is it required of Oxford, Cambridge, Göttingen, Heidelberg, Paris? The Honor System, to take an example, was and is successful as a *contract* ("You don't watch us and we won't cheat you"). When it was extended into a headmaster's harangue ("Now, boys, you won't copy your themes, will you—you give me your word of honor, don't you, boys"), it showed signs of going to pieces. The Honor System is a fine thing precisely because it is not the sort of paternalism Mr. Casement seems to advocate. And I may add that the students lost their cars chiefly because the cars had become a nuisance to the university at large.

Mr. Casement's attitude reminds me of that of the father who sends his timid son to a military school "to make a man out of him." To a boy who grew up as I did—playing at football and baseball and going through the average rough and tumble—the rushes and their like were only a good roughhouse. To other boys they were a nuisance, and one would be blind not to admit after fifteen years that these boys included some of the best.

---

*Princeton Alumni Weekly* 32 (22 April 1932): 647–48.

Modern Princeton cannot devote itself primarily to moulding the regimented Samurai that Mr. Casement admires, without sacrificing the intellectual freedom and choice which distinguishes a university from a prep school. It does not interfere with such men; but it merely insists that they shall be, intellectually, officers and not privates. It gives a special break to those who will presumably be scholars, scientists, and artists, and this Mr. Casement simply can't understand. Nevertheless, his argument would not seem so intemperate if he would admit that there are many human instruments of good and his ideal is just possibly not the only one. Kingdoms have been built by consumptives and hunchbacks, and the "well rounded man" of the 'nineties—the Roosevelt-Churchill-Soldier-of-Fortune type—takes on with time an increasing aspect of papier mâché. It survives as an ideal for the eternally juvenile and the latest immigrants in such legends as "Knute Rockne, Builder of Men." It is a type valuable in time of war, especially when stiffened with a rigorous technical training. That it should have the preempted place in a great university, dedicated to preserving "what the world will not willingly let die"—well, Mr. Casement believes that it should have such a place. To younger men he seems to be merely voicing the confused romanticism of that generation into which he was born.

*F. Scott Fitzgerald '17*

Baltimore.

## AN OPEN LETTER TO FRITZ CRISLER

*By F. Scott Fitzgerald '17*

Dear Fritz: You write me again demanding advice concerning the coming season. I hasten to answer—*again* I insist that using a member of the Board of Trustees at left tackle to replace Charlie ("Asa") Ceppi and Christian ("Dean") Eisenhart, would be a mistake. My idea is a backfield composed of Kipke, Eddie Mahan, President Lowell and anybody we can get for the left side—Pepper Einstein in the center—and then either bring back Light Horse Harry Lee, or else you fill in yourself for the last place. Or else shift Kadlic to center and fill in with some member of the 75-lb. team.

Failing that, it *is* as you suggest in your round-robin, a question of using a member of the Board of Trustees. Then who? and where? There is "Hack" Kalbaugh. There is the late President Witherspoon—but where is he? There is Harkness Hall, but we can't get it unless we pay for the whole expressage *at this end!*

The best suggestion is probably to put Rollo Rulon Roll-on at full, and return to the Haughton system.

Now Fritz, I realize that you and I and Tad know more about this thing than I do—nevertheless I want to make my suggestion: all the end men and backfield men and members of the Board of Trustees start off together—then they all reverse their fields led by some of the most prominent professors and alumni—Albie Booth, Bob Lassiter, etc., and almost before we know it we are up against the Yale goal—let me see, where was I? I meant the Lehigh goal—anyhow some goal, perhaps our own. Anyhow the main thing is

---

*Princeton Athletic News* 2 (16 June 1934): 3. Krisler was the head football coach at Princeton from 1932 to 1937. Later in his career, while coaching at the University of Michigan, he developed one of the earliest systems of two-platoon football. The Haughton system, mentioned midway through the letter, was developed at Harvard under the tutelage of its coach Percy Haughton. The offense relied on deception; on defense Haughton used a five-man line with three linebackers—an innovation. His teams won thirty-three games in a row between 1912 and 1915.

that the C.W.A. is either dead, or else just beginning, and to use again that variation of the "Mexican" shift that I suggested last year will be just *disastrous*. Why? Even I can follow it! Martineau comes out of the huddle—or topples back into it—he passes to some member of past years' teams—(who won't be named here because of the eligibility rules) and then—well, from then on we go on to practically anything.

But not *this* year, Fritz Crisler, if you take my advice!

The Team.

## ANONYMOUS '17

*The second of the alumni contributions is written by a man who prefers that his name not be mentioned\* inasmuch as he is revealing the secrets of the 1917 team. It is in the author's words "an account of activities of 1916–17" and may be taken as the general prologue to this history.*

The 1916–17 team was perhaps the strongest in Princeton history with an undefeated record of six issues and no suppressions. At quarterback Edmund B. Wilson using an open style of play used notable headwork in his mingling of straight stuff and trick plays. At fullback John Peale Bishop starred. Already represented in the *Century* he could always be counted on to pick up a few meters. F. Scott Fitzgerald was perhaps the fastest of the halfbacks though there have been faster ones since. His mate John Biggs Jr. plunged brilliantly close to center in a way that prophesied his legal success. Charlie Bailey alternated with him at the position.

At one end we had Hamilton Fish Armstrong, later an All-American Book-of-the-Month man. At the other was Townsend Martin whose later life as a playrite was featured by his connection with "A Most Immoral Lady." Herbert Agar, the critics' choice as American Pulitzer Prize winner, Alexander McKaig, later producer of "The Racket", and Elliot Springs, the War Bird, turned out for the tackle posts, while at guard the poets Hardwick Nevin, Henry Chapin, and Harry Keller could be depended upon to plug up any holes in the line. Stephen Benét's team at Yale was easily snowed under, though the charges of professionalism against the Tigers were easily proved a few years later.

Needless to say the above account is not typical of the style employed, which is why the sports writer remains anonymous.

---

\* The editors are privileged to say that this sporting information is given by a member of the team named above. There is no prize for solution, but the editors, who have read "This Side of Paradise", can make a guess.

---

*Nassau Literary Magazine* 95 (June 1934): 9.

## LETTER TO HARVEY H. SMITH (1938)

*Scott Fitzgerald* writes (on the illustrated stationery of The Garden of Allah, Hotel and Villas, Hollywood—Cable Address: Gardallah): "I'm out here with Metro doing a script of *Three Comrades* for Taylor and Crawford. Lots of old Triangle men here—Jimmy Stewart, who may be in my picture, Phillips Holmes, Dick Foran et al, but I seem to be the only representative of our times."

Speaking of "our times," Gertrude Stein, in *The Autobiography of Alice B. Toklas*, says that Scott started a new generation with *This Side of Paradise* and *The Great Gatsby*, and that she thinks he will be read when most of his contemporaries are forgotten!

---

*Princeton Alumni Weekly* 38 (28 January 1938): 372. Smith was the secretary for Fitzgerald's class at Princeton. Fitzgerald received his only Hollywood screen credit for his work on *Three Comrades* (1938). *The Autobiography of Alice B. Toklas* was first published in 1933.

## LETTER TO HARVEY H. SMITH (1939)

January 9, 1939

Dear Harvey: —

...only a note from Sap Donohoe at Coronado and a short visit with Bert Hormone whom I hadn't seen since Triangle Days. He came out here first with the Federal Theatre project, was spotted by Selznick I believe and took a test for the part of Rhett Butler. The rumor is that they wanted somebody with a more roguish face and Bert still has the same bland innocence of twenty years ago. New Year's I saw him again in the front row at the Trojan-Duke game. He was cheering on his sophomore son who is Tipton's substitute and expected to be a big shot next year. When I asked Bert about the disloyalty he gave the usual alibi "Princeton was too hard to get in to." I understand how he feels because my off-spring couldn't get into Princeton either—so this fall she went to Vassar instead.

Best wishes always,

*Scott Fitzg*

---

*Princeton Alumni Weekly* 39 (3 February 1939): 369–70.

# JOURNALISM

# THE CRUISE OF THE ROLLING JUNK

### PART ONE

The sun, which had been tapping for an hour at my closed lids, pounded suddenly on my eyes with broad, hot hammers. The room became crowded with light and the fading frivolities on the wall paper mourned the florid triumph of the noon. I awoke into Connecticut and a normal world.

Zelda was up. This was obvious, for in a moment she came into my room singing aloud. Now when Zelda sings soft I like to listen, but when she sings loud I sing loud too in self-protection. So we began to sing a song about biscuits. The song related how down in Alabama all the good people ate biscuits for breakfast, which made them very beautiful and pleasant and happy, while up in Connecticut all the people ate bacon and eggs and toast, which made them very cross and bored and miserable—especially if they happened to have been brought up on biscuits.

So finally the song ended and I inquired whether she had asked the cook—

"Oh, she doesn't even know what a biscuit is," interrupted Zelda plaintively, "and I wish I could have some peaches anyhow."

Then a wild idea came to me and paraded its glittering self around.

"I will dress," I said in a hushed voice, "and we will go downstairs and get in our car, which I note was left in the yard last night as it happened to be your turn to put it away and you were too busy. Seating ourselves in the front seat we will drive from here to Montgomery, Alabama, where we will eat biscuits and peaches."

I discovered to my satisfaction that she was properly impressed. But she only stared at me, fascinated, and said, "We can't. The car won't go that far. And besides we oughtn't to."

I perceived that these were mere formalities.

"Biscuits," I said suggestively. "Peaches! Pink and yellow, luscious—"

---

*Motor* 41 (February, March, April 1924).

"Don't! Oh, don't!"

"Warm sunshine. We can surprise your father and mother. We can just not write that we're coming, and then, one week from today we can just roll up to their front door and say that we couldn't find anything to eat up in Connecticut, so we thought we'd drop down and get some bis—"

"Would it be good?" begged Zelda, demanding imaginative encouragement.

I began to draw an ethereal picture—of how we would roll southward along the glittering boulevards of many cities, then, by way of quiet lanes and fragrant hollows whose honeysuckle branches would ruffle our hair with white sweet fingers, into red and dusty-colored country towns, where quaint fresh flappers in wide straw lids would watch our triumphant passage with wondering eyes....

"Yes," she objected sorrowfully, "if it wasn't for the *car*." And so we arrive at the Rolling Junk.

The Rolling Junk was born during the spring of 1918. It was of the haughty make known as the Expenso, and during its infancy had sold for something over thirty-five hundred dollars. Of course, while nominally engaged in being an Expenso, it was, unofficially, a Rolling Junk, and in this second capacity it was a car that we have often bought. About once every five years some of the manufacturers put out a Rolling Junk, and their salesmen come immediately to us because they know that we are the sort of people to whom Rolling Junks should be sold.

Now this particular Rolling Junk had passed its prime before it came into our hands. To be specific, it had a broken backbone unsuccessfully reset, and the resultant spinal trouble gave it a rakish list to one side; it suffered also from various chronic stomach disorders and from astigmatism in both lamps. However, in a nerve-wracking and rickety way it was exceedingly fast.

As to its appendages, it had been so careless about itself as to dispense with all tools except a decrepit jack and a wrench which upon proper application could effect the substitution of one wheel with tire attached for one wheel with tire blown out or punctured.

But to offset these weaknesses, which amounted to general debility, it *was* an Expenso, with the name on a little plate in front, and this was a proud business. Zelda was hesitating. She became depressed. She sat on the side of my bed and made some disparaging remarks about the cost of such a trip and about leaving the house for so long. Finally she got up and went away without any comment and presently I heard the sound of a suitcase being dragged out from under a bed.

And that's the way it started. Within half an hour after the birth of the Idea we were ambling along a Connecticut country road under the July sunshine. Three large grips crunched in the back seat, and Zelda's hand clutched a four-inch map of the United States torn from the circular of the "More Power Grain and Seed Co." This, together with the two mournful tools and a pair of goggles with the glass out of one eye, was our equipment for the trip.

In Westport we stopped at our favorite garage and were filled with the usual liquids, gasoline, water and oil of juniper—or no! I was thinking of something else. During this process a number of individuals noted the suitcases and clustered about the car, and in nonchalant tones we explained to the dispenser of liquids that we were touring to Alabama.

"My golly!" exclaimed one of the onlookers in an awed voice, "that's way down in Virginia, ain't it?"

"No," I said coldly, "it's not."

"It's a state," said Zelda, giving him what might be termed a mean look. "I come from it."

The geographic person was subdued.

"Well," said the garage man cheerfully, "you going to stay all night there, I see."

He pointed to the bags.

"All night!" I cried passionately. "Why, it takes a week to get there."

The garage man was so startled that he dropped the filling pipe and the gasoline flowed over his shoes.

"You mean to say you're going somewhere in this Rolling Junk that it takes a week to get to?"

"You heard me say Alabama, didn't you?"

"Yeah. But I thought that was the name of a hotel up to New York."

Somebody in the crowd began to snicker.

"Which half the car you going in?" demanded an obnoxious voice, "the high half or the low half?"

"Race you there in Schneider's milk wagon."

"What you goin' to do, coast down?"

The atmosphere was growing oppressive. I was sorry we hadn't said merely that we were running down the post road to New York. We had difficulty in being properly haughty when the garage man, who had been consulting physician to the Rolling Junk for several months, looked at us with his head shaking solemnly and remarked in a funereal tone:

"God help you!"

I threw the gear lever into first.

"Don't worry!" I said sharply.

"You better have a hearse body put on."

I took my foot off the clutch, intending to shoot away from this distasteful scene with a triumphant rush, mowing down, if possible, several of the rapidly swelling throng. Unfortunately the Rolling Junk chose this moment to give a little sneeze and doze off.

"That car knows its business," commented the garage man. "This here 'Alabama' talk is like asking an old man's home to get up a football team."

By this time I had coaxed the engine into a loud erratic cackle, and with a great groan we sped away and went galloping down the post road to New York.

Now if I were Mr. Burton Holmes I would describe in detail all the places we passed between Westport and New York—of how in one place the natives all wear blue hats and waistline suits, and how in another they wear no clothes at all, but spend their days swimming in the sunshine in an old mud-hole not more than a hundred yards from the road. These places you may find detailed in any automobile guide book with their pop, and their points of interest, together with how to jog left into and jog right out of them. You may take them for granted—the educational part of this article begins a little farther on.

There was a race course near New York, I remember, or perhaps it was an aerodrome, and there were many tall bridges leading somewhere, and then there was the city. Streets, crowds in the streets, a light wind blowing, the sunshine between tall buildings, faces splashing and eddying and swirling like the white tips of countless waves, and, over all, a great, warm murmur.

Enormous policemen with the features of Parnell, of De Valera, of Daniel O'Connell, gigantic policemen with the features of Mr. Mutt, of Ed Wynn, of ex-President Taft, of Rudolph Valentino, grave features, roly-poly features, melancholy features, —all slid past us like blue mileposts, contracted and shortened, dropped far off, graduated themselves in a descending line like a sketch for a lesson in perspective. Then the city itself moved off, moved away from us and fell behind, and we, vibrating in involuntary unison with the Jersey ferry, were sorry for all the faces back there, could almost have wept for them, who could not taste the sunshine we were going to taste, nor eat the biscuits nor the peaches, nor follow the white roads from dawn to early moonlight.... To be young, to be bound for the far hills, to be going where happiness hung from a tree, a ring to be tilted for, a bright garland to be won— It was still a realizable thing, we thought, still a harbor from the dullness and the tears and disillusion of all the stationary world.

## II

Across the river it was four o'clock. The marsh in which New Jersey floats glided by us, followed closely by the three ugliest cities in the world. We tore down a yellow ribbon of a road under one of those soft suns I had known so well for four years—suns that were meant to shine on the svelte tan beauty of tennis courts and on the green fairways of shining country clubs. Most of all they were the suns of Princeton, the white and gray and green and red town where youth and age nourish their respective illusions year upon lazy year.

We followed the yellow ribbon. The sun sliced itself into trigonometric figures, became a luminous cloud and was suddenly gone. Twilight came up out of New Brunswick, out of Deans, out of Kingston. Hamlets, nameless in the dark, turned yellow squares on us from scattered windows and then dark skies leaned over the road and the fields, and we were lost.

"Look for towers," I said to Zelda. "That'll be Princeton."

"It's too dark."

A sign passed us at a crossroads—stretched out the plaintive white arms of a ghost. We stopped and, dismounting, I struck a match. Four names stared momentarily out of the dark. One only was familiar—New York, 30 miles. This was a relief—at least we were still on our way *from* New York—or, depressing thought, perhaps *to* New York. At least we were not *in* New York, nor on the other side of it—though of this last fact I was not certain.

I turned to Zelda, who was placidly enjoying the set table of the sky.

"What'll we do?"

"Well," she answered finally, "we can't tell by the map of the More Power Seed Company, because all over this part of New Jersey it just has a big white circle that says, 'More Power Seeds used exclusively in this section.'"

"It's after nine o'clock."

"Look at that moon," she pointed avidly. "It's the—"

"Yes, but we want to get to Princeton, and eat and sleep."

"Do you mean to say that you went to Princeton for four years and don't know the names around here well enough to recognize places right near it?"

"For all I know, these villages may be near Atlantic City—sort of suburbs. Listen! By Golly, we *are* on the shore. Listen to the surf—"

Then we begun to laugh. The surf, if it was the surf, was mooing. In the dark, the heavy, velvet dark, we laughed aloud, and the cow with a grassy flourish and a kittenish kulump of her hoofs, galloped away to play ocean at the other end of the pasture. Then silence save for the steady lament of the Rolling Junk's motor and our voices that were still and small now, like well-behaved consciences.

"Do you really think" — her tone was sincerely curious — "that we're near Atlantic City? If we are I'd like to go there."

The cow mooed again, far away; the moon without any apology passed under a cloud. I re-entered the Rolling Junk and began to feel uneasy.

"We can camp out," proposed Zelda dreamily.

"An excellent idea," I agreed. "I can turn the car upside down and we can sleep under it."

"Or we can build here," she suggested. "You can take the tools and build a house. Or do you think you can build a house with only a tire wrench—but then you've got the jack too—"

Zelda began to sing a hymn, hoping for Divine intervention. Then she gave up and began to sing the Memphis Blues. But the song had not the faintest effect on the implacable heavens, so we started down the road looking for a house. We decided that if we found one that did not have the unmistakable aspect of a criminal's den or of a place where a witch lived, we would stop and inquire our way. If the house we chose happened to be a hell-hole I would pretend that the tire-wrench was a revolver and soon bring the wretches to terms.

But we stopped at no house, for when we had gone a hundred yards we came to a stone bridge and beneath it there flowed a stream. The moon came out and there in silver tranquility the Stony Brook meandered along past its Corot elms. We were within a mile of Princeton. Over the bridge with a solemn rumble, past the Gothic boathouse with its dreams of faded Junes, up through a short rising wood into midsummer Princeton, asleep as surely as if General Mercer had still to writhe on its memorable hill under a British bayonet.

Nassau Street was desolate—it was too early for the tutoring schools to draw down their netfuls of the ambitious, the lazy, the dull—and the Nassau Inn was almost as dark as its haughty crony Nassau Hall across the street.

Entering I discovered the stout and cynical Louie behind the counter, Louie who trusts without believing. It is his tragedy to have seen his famous bar grow dark—a bar where Aaron Burr had sipped the wine of conspiracy, where ten generations of fathers and sons had reveled, and where now, alas, the walls, made of the carved tops of a hundred immemorial tables, will ring no more to the melodies of Rabelaisian song.

"O thou beyond surprise," I said to Louie, "give me a room and a bath for self and wife. We journey to the equator in quest of strange foods and would sleep once more beneath an Aryan roof before consorting with strange races of men such as the cotton-tailed Tasmanians and the pigmies."

Louie knew me not, though he divined that I had once been of the elect. He agreed that I could have a room and whispered to me that town and college were quiet as the dead. We rolled to the garage, where the colored man in charge seemed, to my chagrin, to take our arrival quite as a matter of course. He actually told me that upon payment of a nominal sum I could leave the car there all night.

We returned, walking slowly under a gentle cheerful rain, to the Nassau Inn, and all night the quiet water fell on the blue slate roofs and the air was soft and damp.

### III

Then it was morning, and after the rain the grass on the college campus was very green. It was patterned grass, a lake very smooth and cool, and out of it gray castles rose softly to a low Gothic and faded out against the grayness of the sky. There were dozens of these granite islands in the great lakes of grass—some were poised upon terraces that were huge static waves, some were strung along in graceful isthmuses and peninsulas, weaving here and there, and joined up eventually to other peninsulas by bridge-like cloisters over the green, green water.

At nine-thirty, the sun leaned into sight above Nassau Hall and in the luxurious garage we inquired for the health of the Rolling Junk.

The garage man stared at it skeptically.

"How fah you goin'?"

I did not repeat the mistake I had made in Westport.

"To Washington."

"Well," he said slowly, "you may make it, but I wouldn't bet you no good money on it—"

"There was nothing said about betting!" I retorted crisply.

"—because I never bet on no long shots like this-a-one. You may make it and then you may not."

Upon receipt of this information, I stepped on the self-starter and the Rolling Junk filled the garage with a great roar and clamor. Then we were sailing down Nassau Street in the direction of Trenton.

Lawrenceville School's lazy red brick was asleep in the sun as we went past. We looked at the seed-catalogue map, but when we found that Trenton was covered by the legend about "More Power Seeds" we tossed the map to a passing pig who was trotting briskly toward Princeton with the obvious intention of enrolling himself in the freshman class.

In Trenton we made our first horrible mistake. Having dispensed with the More Power Seed Map of the United States which, despite its hiatuses, did at least give us an idea of our direction, we purchased "Dr. Jones's Guide Book for Autoists." From that point onward the cadence of Dr. Jones's prose rang in our ears all day; the mysteries of his mileage, his knowledge of pop, and finally his ability to state all his conclusions forward or backward, were to us the powers of a demoniac spirit as infallible as the Pope.

To begin with, we referred to three indexes, and from their combined evidence we discovered that Philadelphia lay somewhere between New York and Washington—a fact which I had long suspected. This discovery was followed by a long search—"Let *me* look." "Wait a minute—you've had it for hours." . . . "I have not. If you'd just let me alone for a *minute!*" . . . "Oh, all right, but you're not doing it like it *says*."—until we made the further discovery that the first thing to do was to jog left along turnpike.

"What does 'jog' mean?" inquired Zelda.

"Jog? I think it means to put on all the gas and skid around the corners."

She looked at me solemnly.

"I think it means to run in second."

"What it really means," I explained, "is to turn round and round in big circles until we get out of a place."

"Maybe it means to sort of bounce. How do we know a Rolling Junk *can* jog, anyhow? Maybe it takes a special kind of a car."

Whether our course out of Trenton can be described as a jog or not, I do not know. Zelda held Dr. Jones's Guide Book on her lap and gave me turning instructions as soon as—or at least almost immediately after—we reached each turning. Pretty soon the page which told how to get from Trenton to Philadelphia tore out and blew away, so we turned to the page which told how to get from Philadelphia to Trenton and read it backward, which did almost as well—almost, but not quite, because once we somehow got turned all the way around, and started back toward Trenton. Then luckily, that page came out and blew away also, and we reached Philadelphia in the orthodox manner—that is, by inquiring the way from the sages who sit in front of country stores and are paid by the tire manufacturers to give wrong directions.

The day was still a callow youth when we entered the birthplace of Benjamin Franklin—or was it William Penn?

Just as we were disembarking from the car, a squad of policemen charged up and told us that this was a one-way street, but was liable to be changed to another-way street at any moment, in which case we would have to stand there until the following week, when it would be changed back to a one-way street again. So we drove up a mean-looking alley where there were no rules. There was a ragged individual hanging about, and as soon as I was able to catch his eye, which was so shifty as to be almost irretrievable, I told him that we were leaving valuable suitcases in the car and would be much obliged if he would tell anyone who came along not to take them. He said he would, so we walked away.

After luncheon we returned to the mean-looking alley. All was as we had left it except that the shifty-eyed man had disappeared. This was puzzling, but just as I was about to start the motor we heard a voice from a back window close by.

"Hey Mister," the speaker's face was dark with hair and grime, "you better set that old junk upto a stein of gasoline."

We thought of course that this was merely more of that same ribald wit which seemed to be rife in Connecticut. But we were in error.

"Yes, sir. She did you one good turn 'bout an hour ago."

I scowled at him.

He leaned farther out of the window and the grime on his face shone enthusiastically as he talked.

"There was a bum with a mean eye snoopin' around her and he'd peek in at them satchels you got in there an' then he'd look up an' down the alley, and then he stuck in his paw kind of slow when all of a sudden, *Bang!*—an' he give an awful jump and yelled out 'Don't shoot!' an' tore up the alley like he thought the whole police force was after him."

"Did you shoot a gun at him?" demanded Zelda.

"Not me. Your car there blew out a tire at him."

I dismounted. Sure enough! The right rear tire was kneeling down.

"Did someone steal the tire?" inquired Zelda anxiously.

"No—it blew out. All the air came out."

"Well, we've got another, haven't we?"

We did have another. Its name was Lazarus. It was scarred and shiny and had had innumerable operations upon its bladder. We used it only for running to the nearest garage whenever one of the other four was incapacitated. When we reached a garage our custom was to have the incapacitated tire repaired and replaced, while Lazarus would be returned to his sleeping porch in the rear.

After twenty minutes I assembled the jack and elevated the groaning ruin four inches from the ground—Zelda meanwhile giving out such helpful texts as "If you don't hurry we'll never get to Washington tonight," and "Why didn't you leave the jack under the rear seat so I wouldn't have to *move* every two minutes?" By the time I had replaced the blown-out tire with the wheel to which Lazarus was attached, she had become frightfully depressed.

At length we rolled cautiously out of the alley and began searching the neighborhood for a garage. A policeman gave us voluminous directions in terms of east and west, and on my assuring him that I had forgotten my compass he interpreted himself in terms of left and right. And so by and by we found ourselves in a strangely familiar locality, sounding our horn in front of a sign which read "Bibelick's Family Garage."

"Well, look what I see," said Zelda in an awed voice. "The alley back of this must be where we started from."

For from the garage had stepped our late acquaintance, the man whose face was dark with hair and grime.

"Come back?" he growled cynically.

"You might have told us this was a garage," I retorted with some heat.

Mr. Bibelick eyed me pugnaciously.

"How'd I know you wanted a garage?"

"I want to get that tire repaired."

"And we've got to hurry," added Zelda, "because we're going to—"

"Yes," I interrupted hastily. "We've got to get out in the suburbs right away. Just put a new tube in that casing and pump it up and put it on in back."

After a gay spasm of cursing Mr. Bibelick set to work. He took off the injured tire and contemptuously showed me a large hole I'd overlooked in the casing. I assented weakly to his assertion that I'd have to have a whole new tire. While he effected the necessary substitution Zelda and I amused ourselves by naming the rest of the tires. The two in front we called Sampson and Hercules, because of their comparative good health. The rear axle was guarded on the right by the aged Lazarus, covered with sores, and on the left by an affair of mulatto-colored rubber and uncertain age in which, nevertheless, we reposed considerable confidence. It was freckled but not bruised. I was for calling it Methuselah, but for some inscrutable reason Zelda named it Santa Claus. There was reserved for Santa Claus that very day an adventure so grotesque that, had we been granted premonition of it we would have named it something quite different.

The new tire affixed to the rear was designated as Daisy Ashford; at the same moment Mr. Bibelick announced by a great burst of expectoration that his travail was at an end. By this time I felt that we had lived in Philadelphia for many days, that the Rolling Junk had become a house and would roll no longer and that we had best settle down and advertise for a cook and a maid.

"How about this old inner tube?" demanded Mr. Bibelick scornfully. "I'll throw it in back an' you can use it for a life-preserver if you get in any floods."

"Don't bother," retorted Zelda, who had become fidgety to an extent that would have delighted St. Vitus. "You can cut it up into oblongs and sell it for chewing gum."

"Have I got water?" I asked.

Ostensibly answering me but obviously looking at Zelda, Mr. Bibelick replied:

"You got plenty on the brain."

The incredible cheapness of this repartee was revolting to both Zelda and me, so I started the motor and filled the air with smoky blue vapor. A little later we had left Philadelphia behind and, still under a glittering sunshine, were running along the white roads of Delaware.

## IV

South across the Brandywine we wandered, along a plum-blossomed zigzag lined with copses white as snow. The sun fell west before us across freckled orchards. It hovered in the half sky, silhouetting, in gray against gold, ancient Dutch manor houses and stone barns that had been standing when Cornwallis, his black boots gleaming, came out of a crumbling town and yielded up an empire to a swollen posse of farmers—before that, when Braddock, the rash, died with a fashionable curse in a wood that was spitting flame. South we went—over little rivers and long gray bridges to placid Havre de Grace, a proud old lady with folded hands who whispered in faded dignity that she had once been under consideration for capital of the nation.

But she had married a plumber instead of a President and the fruit of the union was a large "boomer" sign which swayed in blatant vulgarity over the street by which we entered, like a beggar holding out his cap for pennies.

Then through Maryland, loveliest of states, the white-fenced rolling land. This was the state of Charles Carroll of Carrollton, of colonial Annapolis in its flowered brocades. Even now every field seemed to be the lawn of a manor, every village lane was a horse market that echoed with jokes from London coffee houses and the rich ring of spurs from St. James Street—jokes and spurs more glamorous perhaps to the provincial beaux and belles for having reached them three months old. Here my great-grandfather's great-grandfather was born—and my father too on a farm near Rockville called Glenmary. And he sat on the front fence all one morning, when he was a little boy, watching the butternut battalions of Early stream by on their surprise attempt at Washington, the last great threat of the Confederacy.

On we traveled between woods lovelier than the blue woods of Minnesota in October when the mist is rising and fields as green and fresh as the fields of Princeton in May. We stopped at a little old inn, cobwebbed with climbing wild honeysuckle, and ordered—an ice cream cone and a chicken sandwich. We rested only five minutes—there was sunshine all around us now—we must make haste to go on, go down, into the warmth, into the dusky mellow softness, into the green heart of the South to the Alabama town where Zelda was born.

From the Inn of Tranquility the roads were rare—an unbroken boulevard that made a broad band over high green hills and drooped symmetrically across sunny valleys. It was twilight before we turned into the pungent, niggery streets of Baltimore and early dusk when we set face toward Washington. The boulevard melted suddenly into a suburban street.

"Hasn't it been wonderful!" exclaimed Zelda happily.

"Wonderful. We've gone a hundred and eighty-one miles today. And yesterday we went only seventy-seven."

"Gosh, we're smart!"

"And we've passed through six states and haven't had a bit of trouble—except that blow-out in Philadelphia."

"It's the best thing that ever happened," she said rapturously, "and we've been outdoors and I feel wonderful and healthy and—I'm so glad we came. How many more days before we'll get there?"

"Oh, about five—maybe four if we go awfully fast."

"Can we?" she demanded: "Oh, let's try tomorrow! All that stuff they said about the car was just silly. They were just trying to make us mad. Why—"

"Stop!" I cried fearfully. "Stop—"

But it was too late. We had tempted fate with outrageous temerity—with a crash and a roar the drone of the world changed to thunder in my ears, the car seemed to fall to pieces before our eyes and it was as though we were flat on the street and being dragged, miraculously uninjured, between immense cobblestones which pounded and ground together as we went by. Yet we were *not* in the street—some relics of rationality told us that—we were on soft leather cushions and the wheel was still in my hand. In the instant of calamity some object had flashed by us at break-neck speed, something strange yet familiar, and then passed out of sight.

After an agonized and endless period of this crazy furious bumping—the car, or whatever piece of it we were still sitting in, was jerking frantically along at twenty miles an hour—I reached for the emergency brake, but, desperate as was the emergency, it refused to function. I knew at last that the whole rear end was dragging in the street. I heard Zelda make curious incoherent sounds beside me and I expected any second to be hoisted heavenward on a pillar of flame and offered up as a gasoline holocaust.

Then, it must have been two crimson minutes after the first wrench of the catastrophe, the Rolling Junk with a horrible leaping gesture came to a full stop.

"Get out!" I cried to Zelda. "Get out! Quick! It's going to blow up!"

In the sudden quiet the fact that she neither moved nor answered, but only gave out that curious crying noise, seemed burdened with a sinister significance.

"Get out! Don't you understand? A wheel came off! We dragged! Get out!"

Suddenly my excitement changed to anger. She was laughing! She was roaring! She was bent double with uncontrollable mirth. I pushed her precipitately from the car and half dragged, half threatened her to a safe distance.

"Good God!" I stood there panting. "The wheel came off! Don't you understand? The wheel—it's gone!"

"So I notice!" cried Zelda, rocking with laughter. "It isn't there any more."

I turned from her in frantic disgust. The Rolling Junk, trembling slightly, stood in ominous silence. Behind it a trail of sparks extended back for two hundred yards. More from nervousness than from intention I started off at a rickety dog-trot in the direction that the wheel and tire—it was Santa Claus—had taken. I suspected dimly that by this time it had reached the Capitol or had announced our thunderous arrival to the doorman at the New Willard. But I was wrong. Two blocks farther up I came upon Santa Claus, lying quietly on his side in an innocent slumber, apparently uninjured.

Around him in the darkness were gathered a dozen children, staring first at the tire, then at the now starry sky, obviously under the impression that Santa Claus was a meteoric body fallen from Paradise.

I pushed my way with some importance through the group.

"See here," I said, in a brisk, efficient tone, "that's mine!"

"Who said it ain't?" I think they suspected that I had been rolling it as a hoop.

"It came off," I added, becoming rather sheepish as my excitement died. "I'll take it with me."

Hoisting it to my shoulder in as dignified a manner as is possible before young children, I staggered back the two blocks to the Rolling Junk, and found it surrounded by an enthusiastic crowd.

I joined Zelda and we stared with the rest. The car, its rear axle resting securely on the pavement, suggested a three-legged table. From all sides comments arose from the admiring Columbians, most of whom had been on nearby porches, enjoying the night in their shirt-sleeves.

"Wheel come off?"

"Gee! Lookit that there car!"

"Yeah. Wheel came off."

"What happened? Wheel come off?"

"Yeah?"

"Where'sa wheel?"

"It come off."

"It went up the street. You should of watched it go."

"I seen it go. You should of watched. Gee!"

"I says to Morgan, 'Well if I ain't a son-of-a-gun, look at that thing. It's a wheel,' I says. An' Morgan says, 'No,' and I says, 'Sure it's a wheel—all by itself,' I says."

"What happened? It come off?"

"Yeah."

"You'd of ought to seen the car go along. All of a sudden there was this noise and Violet and me looked and there was this car without no wheel, bumping along, an' the sparks shootin' off behind like they was out of a skyrocket."

"The lady in it was laughing."

"Yes, I seen she was laughing."

"She must of thought it was funny."

By this time someone had noticed me, standing modestly, tire in hand, on the outskirts of the crowd, and a more reticent mood was communicated to the onlookers. Their remarks were now confined to asking whether the wheel had come off and I told them all politely that it had. They eyed me with suspicion. There seemed to be a vague feeling that in some way I had arranged it that the wheel should come off. We stood there chatting for some time. In fact, as the host I passed around a package of cigarettes. Several matches were struck and the axle was examined by all present. They exclaimed, "Gee!" in the proper manner; one of them was kind enough to inspect the front of the car and even to try out the horn.

"The horn's all right anyhow," said he—whereat we all laughed heartily, including me and excepting Zelda. She seemed to have done all her laughing in the stress of the catastrophe and I now perceived a dangerous light gathering in her eyes. She appeared to be measuring the distance between herself and the nearest onlooker.

"I think we ought to do something," she suggested sternly.

"All right," I agreed feebly. "I'll go in a house and telephone for a garage."

She continued her menacing silence.

"They can drag it into Washington, you see." I turned to the crowd. "I wonder if there's a telephone I can use."

As though this were a prearranged signal, the crowd began to melt away. At least all of them who possessed telephones melted away, for when I repeated my question to the half dozen who remained they all answered either that they had no telephone or that they lived on the other side of the city. I was somewhat pained. It seemed to me that I had always granted the use of my telephone to castaways, even if they were strangers and it was after dark.

"Hey!"—One of the survivors was holding a lighted match to the axle—"This thing's all right. I guess your brake-band's shot to hell for sure, but the axle's O.K. You can just jack it up and put the wheel back on."

He was a young man, a returned soldier, still wearing part of his uniform. I was much encouraged. Anything mechanical from nail-hammering to applied dynamics is a great dark secret to me, and had this accident occurred in the center of the Sahara I would have walked to the Cairo garage before it would have occurred to me that the car could be patched up and driven on. Inspired by the young soldier and by another enthusiastic looker-on who immediately removed his coat, I made my usual search for the jack. Ten minutes later the Rolling Junk was assembled and so far as my inexpert eyes could determine, as good as new.

Grateful, but blundering, I took each man aside singly and attempted to "at least pay you for your time," but they would have none of it. The soldier turned me off easily—the other man, it seemed to me, was somewhat insulted.

"What on earth were you laughing at when the thing went blah?" I inquired of Zelda as we drove away, conservatively at five miles an hour.

She snickered reminiscently.

"Well—there was something about that crazy wheel shooting up the street and us bumping along and you with that silly expression on your face, tugging at the emergency and shouting something about going to blow up—"

"I saw nothing funny about it," I retorted stiffly. "Suppose *I* had laughed and *no*body had pulled on the emergency brake—where would we be now?"

"Probably just where we are."

"We would not."

"We would too. It just stopped of itself anyhow. That man said so."

"What man?"

"That soldier."

"When did he?"

"Back there. He said the emergency brake was automatically disconnected when the wheel came off. You might as well have laughed—like me."

"But I was right in principle anyhow."

"But I had more fun than you did—and that's what we came for."

Disheartened by this repudiation of my accomplishment, I drew up in front of the Willard, where a new problem immediately presented itself. Would they let us in? We—especially I—scarcely resembled the savory patrons catered to by fashionable hotels. The general effect I gave was of a black and tan ruin. My hands were two gray clots of oil and dirt, and my face was the face of a daring chimney sweep. Zelda too was draped with dust and according to her own feminine standards, infinitely less presentable than I. It took all our courage to leave the Rolling Junk under the door-porter's contemptuous eye and walk into the hotel. Walk? Rush is a better word. We tore across the lobby like pursued criminals, flung ourselves violently into the attention of a startled clerk and chattered out our apology.

"We've been turning—I mean touring," I cried passionately. "Turning down from Connecticut—I mean touring. We want a room and a bath. We've got to have one WITH A BATH!" I felt the need of impressing on him at once that we were not of the great unwashed, that from under these cocoons of dirt two gorgeous butterflies would presently emerge at the simple application of hot water.

He began to paw over a register. I felt that more pressure was necessary.

"My Expenso is outside—my EXPENSO!" I gave him time to associate the idea of incalculable wealth with the idea of an Expenso, and then I added, "Is there a garage in Washington? I mean is there one near? Not in the hotel, I don't mean, but nearby? You see, my—"

He raised his head and regarded me dispassionately. I forced my face into a conciliatory smirk. Then he beckoned a bell-boy and we made ready for forcible expulsion. But when he spoke his words were like benediction.

"Twenty-one twenty-seven," he said without hysteria. "Garage one block down and one over. They'll take any kind of a car."

I leaned hastily over the counter and shook his hand.

## PART TWO

Washington, as most Americans know, is generally considered the Capital of the United States. The population, including the diplomats from defunct governments, is estimated at—but as a matter of fact I believe it will be best to put the educational part of this article in a special appendix in the rear. I would much rather tell how we awoke in enthusiasm thinking that Virginia—the real South—was only an hour away. We ordered a gorgeous breakfast-in-bed—a joy dampened only by the news that peaches were unobtainable. Zelda, having never seen Washington before, had no desire to go sightseeing—for sightseeing is only a pleasure to those who can point and explain. However, the first public building I visited was the garage, where I went to inquire how the Rolling Junk had passed the night.

"Good morning," said the garageman who bore an unmistakable resemblance to the late Czar of all the Russias. "Is this your—car?"

I acknowledged it fearlessly. He shook his head more in sadness than in anger.

'If *I* was you," the Czar suggested lugubriously, "I'd get rid of it—if you *can*. If you can't, why you better lay up here a couple of weeks while I give her a thorough overhauling, put on new wheels and new tappets, get rid of some squeaks and groans, find some new lights, burn the carbon out of the cylinders, buy four new tires and send for another axle to put in for that bum one—"

"But she looks all right," I said persuasively. "All except that little list to the side." "Well," said the Czar with melancholy despair, "I had two men waitin' since seven o'clock. They been puttin' on new brakebands 'stead of the ones you wore off in your accident. Be ready 'bout four o'clock, maybe."

"Four o'clock! I've got to get to Richmond by tonight."

"Best we can do," sighed the Czar. "Your battery's wore out too. It ain't had no water."

"Oh, no. I can fix that." And going up to the battery I gave it a violent shake. "See?"

To his astonishment it now worked. Why, I do not know. When shaken at regular intervals it would resume its functions, and behave itself for as long as a week at a time.

"Well, look at your wheels then. That one with the hunk of rubber on it. Or is that just some old cloth wound around the wheel?"

"That's Lazarus," I suggested politely.

"—Whatever it is. I thought it was a Goodstone Cord. Anyhow that wheel's only got a few good spokes left. Some day it's just goin' to collapse on you. It's like riding on an egg."

He had me here. I seized the wheel and shook it violently as I had the battery, but there was no result. The spokes remained broken. He had me on the tappets too, but this was scarcely fair as I wasn't sure what a tappet was. The Czar explained that there were eight of them and that they held down an affair called the "blotter." If there had been thirty-two of them or even sixteen, it would have been all right—but this blotter was particularly wild and eight tappets wouldn't keep it down. I asked the Czar if he couldn't put eight more tappets on, but he said he wasn't in the manufacturing business.

Having done my best for the Rolling Junk I left the Czar to his gentle Romanoff melancholy and returned to the New Willard to find Zelda dressed and restless. I told her the lamentable news.

"Let's turn back," she suggested immediately. "We'll never get there. Never. We might as well turn back. Think of the money we're spending. Seventy-five dollars yesterday. It'll be fifty dollars more before we get out of Washington and that'll leave us only eighty out of our two hundred."

I explained that we had to get a new tire yesterday.

"But we'll probably have to get one every day. Lazarus is about to explode from old age and Santa Claus won't go another hundred miles."

"But I'm going to have the bank wire us money to somewhere in South Carolina and then we'll be perfectly safe."

Zelda, who is astonishingly naive, was amazed and cheered at the notion of money being wired about so cavalierly. We spent the morning discovering that the peach was as extinct in North America as the dinosaur. We began to doubt that we had ever eaten one—yet in the past we had seen pictures of little girls communing with them and we knew that the word, however mythical, had passed into the English language. Abandoning the search, we stopped in front of a news stand and assuaged our boredom by buying picture postcards of all Washington's churches and sending them with pious messages to our irreligious friends.

Four o'clock rolled along Pennsylvania Avenue and greeted us at the door of the Romanoff garage; in half an hour we had added one more rattle to the ancient bridge over which the fugitives from Bull Run had streamed on an afternoon of panic and terror, and our four wheels rolled onto the soil of the Old Dominion.

A cool wind blew, faint and fresh. Slow short hills climbed in green tranquility toward a childish sky. And already there were antebellum landscapes—featuring crazy cabins inhabited by blue-black gentlemen and their ladies in red-checked calico. The South now—its breath was warm upon us. The trees no longer exfloreated in wild haste, as though they feared that October was already scurrying over the calendar—their branches gestured with the faintly tired hauteur of a fine lady's hand. The sun was at home here, touching with affection the shattered ruins of once lovely things. Still, after fifty years we could see the chimneys and wall corners that marked the site of old mansions—which we peopled with pleasant ghosts. Here under the gay wistaria, life at its mellowest had once flourished—not as on Long Island with streets and haste and poverty and pain just twenty miles away, but in a limitless empire whose radius was the distance a good horse could travel in a morning and whose law was moulded only of courtesy and prejudice and flame.

And at the moment when we became aware of Virginia's picturesqueness we became aware also of its selfconscious insistence on this picturesqueness. It seemed to cherish its anachronisms and survivals, its legend of heroism in defeat and of impotence before the vulgarities of industrialism, with too shrill an emphasis. For all its gorgeous history there was something tinny and blatant in its soul.

We reached Fredericksburg about five. I tried to reconstruct the battle from memory—I was not there but I had read about it—and failed wretchedly. I located the river, the hill and the town, but they had become changed around in some curious manner since the Civil War and they no longer worked. A garrulous gasoline dispenser told us that his father had participated in the battle and gave us his idea of the position of the contending troops. But if he was correct the history books have all erred grievously, three dozen generals have perjured themselves and Robert E. Lee was defending Washington.

At sunset we plunged into the Wilderness—the Wilderness where slain boys from Illinois and Tennessee and the cities of the gulf still slept in the marshes and the wooded swamps—but over the bloody ground there was only the drone of the cicadas now and the sway of the lush vines. The road began to wind between stagnant pools and crepuscular marshes and each time we emerged for a moment into view of the open sky we found it a darker blue, and saw that the mouth of the next tunnel of gray gloom was denser and less opaque. Finally we came out of a green subway to find that it was half-past seven and full night. An uncanny nervousness began to come over me and when the next copse approached I treaded the road with breathless care—sensitive to a certain profanity when the deep hum of our great motor burst against the ominous leafy walls.

And it was at this point, with danger, had I known it, just around the corner, that Zelda decided that she wanted to drive. We stopped in the first clearing and I yielded up the wheel.

Ten minutes passed. It was necessary to drive slowly, and, as well as I could determine from Dr. Jones's Guide Book, which I fingered unsatisfactorily by the light of a recent acquisition, electric torch, we were still forty-two miles from Richmond—still well over an hour away. My uncanny predilection now resolved itself into the specific dread that Lazarus would give up the ghost with a nerve-shaking roar in the middle of a wooded swamp, and that I should have to remove him—at the mercy of bullfrogs and banshees and the dead of battles long ago.

With a sort of aching hollowness I saw the next woods approach. The leaves splashed away before us and Zelda followed a receding emptiness, confused by the cock-eyed slant of the head lights, of which one sought the road beneath and the other, with appalling perversity, illuminated the roof of the arboreal world.

We drifted down a sudden incline and, still descending slowly, were rounding the surface of a dark pool, when a man stepped suddenly into the road about twenty yards in front of us. The glare of the depressed headlight fell on him for a moment and we saw that his face, brown or white, we could not determine which, was covered with a black mask, and that in his right hand was the glint of a revolver. The impression he made, vivid and startling, endured for a moment; I remember that he uttered an indistinguishable shout and that I yelled "Look out!" to Zelda, and tried to slide us both down low in the seat—then, all in the same minute, there was a swift rush of cool air, there was a black-banded face not ten yards away—and I realized with a sort of awed exhilaration that Zelda had stepped on the accelerator. With a gasping cry the masked man took a quick sidestep and avoided the bull-like leap of the car by inches—then we were by and away, rocking blindly skidding around turns—hunched down in our seats to avoid a shot, until we could scarcely see the way.

We rounded half a dozen bends, still traveling at over forty miles an hour before I found breath to gasp: "You stepped on it!"

"Yes," sighed Zelda laconically.

"That was the thing to do but—I'd have slowed up I think—involuntarily."

"I didn't mean to step on it," she confessed surprisingly. "I was trying to stop and I got mixed up and stepped on the wrong thing."

We laughed and began to chatter feverishly as our taut nerves relaxed. But it was pitch dark, with Richmond far off, and when I discovered that there was but a single gallon of gasoline in the tank I felt again that uncanny hollowness. The shadowy phantoms of an hour before had given way to images of murderous negroes hiding in bottomless swamps and of waylaid travelers floating on their faces in black pools. I regretted violently that I had not bought a revolver in Washington.

Under the torch I looked at the guide-book map. There seemed to be but one settlement between us and Richmond, a small dot which bore the sinister name of Niggerfoot. Ah—let it lack churches and schools and chambers of commerce, but let it not lack gasoline!

Ten minutes later it came into view as a single light which divided itself presently into the half a dozen yellow windows of a country store. As we came closer we could distinguish the blurred sounds of many voices within. The weird mood into which our later experience had projected us made us loath to stop—but we had no choice. I drew up alongside, where we were immediately joined by two aged negroes and a quartet of little black boys from whom I demanded gasoline. After the manner of their race they tried to avoid the issue—the gasoline was locked up for the night; it was impossible to get at it.

They shook their heads. They mumbled melancholy and ineffectual protests. As I grew more vehement, their stubborn stupidity grew hazy rather than gave way—one of the old men vanished into the darkness to return with a yellow buck of reasonable age. Then there was more arguing until finally one of the little boys went sullenly in search of a pail. When he returned a second boy carried the pail up the road, and fifteen minutes later an absolutely new boy arrived with three quarts of gasoline.

Meanwhile I had gone into the store for cigarettes and found myself enclosed immediately in a miasmatic atmosphere which left on me a vivid and unforgettable impression. I could not say clearly even now what was going on inside that store—a moonshine orgy, a pay-day gambling bout, something more sinister than these or perhaps not sinister at all. Nor could I determine whether the man who waited on me was black or white. But this I know—that the room was simply jammed with negroes and that the moral and physical aura which they cast off was to me oppressive and obscene. I was glad to find my way outside again into the hot dark where the moon had risen and the gasoline carrier had come into sight and the two old negro men were exclaiming aloud in falsetto cackles at the size and thunder of the Expenso engine.

About nine o'clock the road became hard and smooth beneath us and trembling lights glimmered into our consciousness until the city, around which four bloody years had centered, developed on all sides of us.

But entry into Richmond was, we discovered, a difficult matter. The city was set behind impregnable barriers. The streets we tried were in various conditions of cavernous repair and adorned with romantic red lanterns—a sort of mole's carnival. I began to think that the defenses erected for the crisis of 1865 had never been removed and were still defiantly repelling the Yankee invader—but they yielded to us at last and permitted us to arrive at our inevitable destination, the Best Hotel in Town....

"Good evening," I said hastily to the clerk. "We're touring through from Connecticut and we want a room with a Bath." I smiled ingratiatingly. "We've *got* to have a bath with a room."

It was essentially the same speech that had gained us entrance to the New Willard. It served the same purpose here; it did more than that, for they gave us the bridal suite—an immense and imponderable affair as melancholy as a manufacturer's tomb. With the water steaming into the tub we discussed the day. We had left only one state—or district—behind us, but we had traversed a hundred and thirty-three miles and tasted drama. All afternoon, impression after impression had taken us by storm, leading up to the climax of the lone highwayman in the swamp. But one more happening was destined to disturb further the shattered equanimity of the day. It was not another highwayman. It was a piece of tongue.

It lay quietly and comparatively unobtrusively in the center of the carpet and after delicately stirring with the tip of a pencil I saw that it had been lying there several weeks.

Then I turned quickly away from it as I heard Zelda's voice speaking tensely, passionately, over the telephone—

"Hello! This is room two-ninety-one! What do you *mean* by renting us a room with *meat* all over the floor?"

A pause. The whole telephone system of the hotel seemed to me to be vibrating with fury—

"Yes, 'meat all over the floor'! Old dead *meat!* I think it's perfectly *terrible!*... All right! *Right* away!"

She banged up the phone and turned on me an outraged countenance.

"How utterly disgusting!"

Five minutes later, after Zelda was enveloped in the steam of her hot bath, there was a knock at the door. I opened it upon a harassed, apologetic clerk. Behind him stood three colored assistants bearing large shovels.

"Pardon me," he said deferentially. "The lady called up to complain that the floor was covered with dead meat."

I pointed sternly.

"Look!" I said.

He stared with polite eyes.

"Where?"

The tongue, being still of a reddish hue, was almost imperceptible against the lugubrious crimson carpet. At length he made it out and motioned a negro forward to secure it.

"Now, where's the rest, sir?"

"I'm sure I don't know," I answered stiffly. "You'll have to locate it yourself."

After a puzzled search behind the radiators, in the clothes closet and under the bed, the negroes reported that there was no more tongue. Shouldering their great shovels, they moved toward the door.

"Is there anything else?" asked the night clerk, anxiously. "I'm very sorry about this, sir. There's never been any old meat in any of the bedrooms before tonight, sir."

"I hope not," I said firmly. "Good night."

He closed the door.

## II

And now a day of depression—inaugurated by the garage man of Richmond. He was concise and specific in his information. The body of the Rolling Junk was split almost in two and was about to fall off the car. It must be welded on in a blacksmith's shop.

We wandered about Richmond, drenched by an unbelievable heat and humidity. We visited the Confederate museum and pored for an hour over shredded battleflags and romantic sabres and gray uniform coats, and, as we passed from room to room, the proud splendor of each state's display was dimmed only a little by the interminable lists of living women who had managed in some way to get their names linked up with these trophies. The trophies needed no sponsoring by the Miss Rachael Marys and the Mrs. Gladys Phoebes whom one pictured as large-bosomed and somewhat tiresome old ladies engaged in voluble chatter upon their ancestors in the sitting rooms and boarding houses of Macon, Georgia.

This exhausted Richmond—we discovered nothing else of any possible interest. After noon the humidity became oppressive sultriness, and the scattered curlicues of clouds began to solve a great jigsaw puzzle in the sky. We went to the blacksmith and found that he had only just begun his soldering—because the garage man had discovered that the blotter had again escaped the tappets. We sat and stewed on the blacksmith's block.

We had planned to reach Oxford, North Carolina, before night, and Oxford was over a hundred and fifty miles away. When, as we were finally rolling out of the blacksmith's, Santa Claus blew into rubber butterflies, we began to despair.

When we moved out into the sultry country-side at last the sun was in shadow and the picture before us was as dispiriting as the view out of a dentist's window. The fields were green without freshness and the villages, where lanky men and boys gathered at the gasoline tanks to stare at our motor, moved us to neither pastoral nor historical enthusiasm. We were not happy. The tyranny of tires weighed upon our spirits. There were so many weak spokes in one wheel that it was unsafe to run on it at over ten miles an hour. We used it merely for a spare wheel; upon it we limped slowly to the next garage after each catastrophe.

We talked now neither of biscuits nor of peaches. Having discussed them for one hundred and fifty hours with gradually diminishing energy, Zelda's imaginative appetite was at length satiated. And, on my part, I believe the sight of a peach or a biscuit would have gagged me. So Zelda sat all afternoon with Dr. Jones's Guide Book in her hands, turning to the wrong page, giving erroneous directions and losing the place at crucial moments.

Just after six the dark came down in earnest. There was a mutter of thunder and out of the west came one of those fierce warm dusty winds which arouse uncanny discomfort with their high, bleak moanings and the touch of their hot, humid hands. The dark hindered our progress and we began to doubt that we could make North Carolina, that night. It was still seventy miles away.

The wind was soon swollen into a dark gale and over the field toward us came the ponderous thresh of the rain. The sky was branded with a chain of flaming Z's and the thunder bowled sultry doom along the flat land. Then the rain sirened closer, washed over us, bringing with it the stinging deposits of the dust-laden wind. When the sand left our eyes Zelda hurriedly thumbed the guidebook and found a town named Clarksville about twelve miles ahead.

The name of the town was printed in large capitals and though its population was only five thousand we presupposed at least one tolerable hotel. The fact that it lay in Virginia was, of course, a moral loss—it would be the first time we had passed two nights in a single state.

I drove as fast as I dared into the blown darkness, but the way seemed interminable in the Byronic storm. We were relieved when, at last, Clarksville rolled up the road toward us. I left Zelda to register at the Dominion Hotel, and went to find a garage. For once, perhaps because we had only gone one hundred and twelve miles, I had no list of suspicions and instructions to write out and hand to a sleepy-eyed attendant.

Returning I found that we were not nearly so well housed as the Rolling Junk. No food was obtainable in the hotel, so I went into a country store and bought two unappetizing egg-sandwiches from the unappetizing proprietor. These I took up to Zelda who, with great presence of mind, threw them immediately out of the window.

Our room was bare and it had a bath with it. Into the bath ran ice-cold water. Zelda swam in it as a matter of principle, and then—chiefly out of spite—taunted me into a feeble imitation. It was a miserable, shivering, depressed pretense of a bath, but when it was over I made the usual virtue of it and strutted around the room like a dollar-a-year man after his daily dozen.

### III

Sunday morning, Zelda awoke and dressed herself in a white knickerbocker suit. Famished, we went downstairs and were served with an abominable breakfast that I nibbled at humbly but by which Zelda felt herself deliberately insulted. When we were leaving the hotel two fat ladies who were occupying the front steps stared at Zelda's knickerbockers and chattered violently to each other— whereupon Zelda, now in a raging mood, returned their stare and remarked in a perfectly audible voice, "Look at those two *horrible* women!" I am aware that this phrase is of the type usually attributed to villainesses in sloppy fiction—showing that damp cornflakes have much the same effect as a stony heart.

Sunday in Virginia is a day of rest—gasoline is almost as hard to get as cigarettes, and we were glad when the North Carolina boundary grew near. Dr. Jones's Guide Book had now resorted to sheer fiction—and cheap, trashy, sentimental fiction at that. While I favor discreetly draping many of the facts of life, I call it a pernicious optimism that tries to pass off the rocky bed of a dried-out stream as a "boulevard." And the map was ornamented with towns, pops, corner stores and good roads that could have existed only in Dr. Jones's rosy imagination.

About the time we crossed the white chalk line which divides Virginia from North Carolina, we became aware that some sort of dispute was taking place in the interior of the car. It began as a series of sullen mutters, but soon the participants were involved in a noisy and metallic altercation—I gathered that things were being thrown.... Dismounting, I crawled underneath and glared at the bottom of the car. It looked to me as it had always looked. There were some dark, mysterious rods and some dark iron pans and a great quantity of exhaust. We thought that perhaps we were out of gasoline and had the tank filled at the next station, but the pounding continued. We tried oil and water—even had the hood chamied off, but with no result. When we reached a town of some size we sought out the largest garage and demanded an inspection.

After three men in overalls—Sunday was not a day of rest in North Carolina—had played around for awhile on little wooden sidewalks that slid underneath the car, they all stood up in line and shook their heads in sad unison like a musical comedy chorus. Then they wheeled about and went away.

At this point there was a great roaring at the door, and in rode a tall young man driving a large and powerful Expenso, of the same type as ours. Without exactly looking at the young man, I began to mope disconsolately around my own car, shaking the wheels sternly and picking bits of dust off the fender—in short, giving the impression that I was only waiting for something or somebody before beginning to perform some significant mechanical action.

The young man, having parked his Expenso, strolled over to look at mine.

"Trouble?" he demanded.

"Nothing much," I answered grimly. "It's all broken inside, that's all."

"Your wheel's coming off," he remarked dispassionately.

"Oh, it's done that," I assured him. "It did that in Washington."

"It's coming off again—from the inside."

I smiled politely as though I had noticed it some time before. I took the wrench from the rear of the car and began to tighten the wheel.

"It's coming off from the *inside*. No use tightening it there—you'll have to take it off."

I was somewhat confused, as I had not been previously aware that a wheel could come off from the inside as well as just come off, but I snapped my fingers and remarked:

"Of course. How stupid of me!"

When I had removed the wheel and leaned it up against the wall of the garage, I approached the axle under the now suspicious eye of the Expenso owner. Stare as I might, it looked to me exactly like any other axle, and I failed to perceive in it any qualities which would permit the wheel to come off from the inside. I tapped it tentatively. Then, from force of habit, I shook it. These two gestures having been observed in silence by the tall young man, I turned to him mildly.

"You're right," I said. "It was coming off from the inside." Then I picked up the wheel and was about to replace it on the axle, when the Expenso owner gave a warning grunt, finished lighting a cigarette, and inquired solemnly:

"What you doing?"

"I'm putting it back."

"What did you take it off for?"

He had me there. I had taken it off solely because he had told me to, yet somehow this didn't seem the right answer to his question.

"Because—why, to see if it was coming off from the inside."

"Well, you saw, didn't you?"

This was unfair. It was not playing the game. I decided to defy him, decided not to.

"Why—no," I muttered weakly. "It looked all right to me."

The suspicion in his eye changed to certainty. He glanced in at the knickerbocker-clad Zelda, seated in nonchalant gravity in the front seat. Then he looked at me.

"Where are your tools?" he said briefly. "Get your other wrench."

"I haven't any tools."

I had thrown aside all pretense. I stood before him naked in my mechanical ignorance. But my avowal, made in sheer helplessness, had its effect. He dropped his cigarette and stared at me open-mouthed. He had a tremendous mouth.

"No *tools!*"

"I have no tools," I repeated meekly.

I had shocked him. I had stuck a sharp iron into the heart of his morality. I had offended horribly against his spotless creed of the Expenso. In one minute I had passed from a place among the privileged into an outer, darker circle. I owned an Expenso?—then so much the more blasphemous if I was not worthy of my property.

He called brusquely to a garage helper.

"Here! Let's have a C wrench."

Iron in a novel shape appeared, and I thought how wonderful is civilization. Actuated by a natural baseness, I shrank back from the car as though fearing the coolness of the metal. But he tossed the article at me relentlessly, and I took it, approached the axle, adjusted the wrench feebly and began to turn whatever there was to turn.

The Expenso expert stood over me sternly.

"No," he said indignantly. "*Tighten* it."

Had he ordered me to eat it I should have been no more helpless. I dropped the wrench to my side and stared at him with what I suspected was a silly expression. Zelda's face was hidden sleepily in her hands. She had abandoned me, without so much as a wink, to this man's devices. Even the garage force had moved off and away, lest they be called upon.

"Here!" Cato strode toward me. With a mixture of shame and relief I yielded up the wrench to him. He reached for one of the sliding floors, dropped knee upon it and, without difficulty, adjusted the wrench. I crowded up upon him, obscenely interested. Then my hopes were dashed to the ground. With a straightforward movement of his shoulders that seemed somehow to express the emotion of utter contempt which just failed to show in his face, he stood up and pointed to the wrench.

"That's the way," he said. He meant, "Get to work! You dog, you! How dare you own an Expenso!" But he said aloud: "Get some oil from over there in the corner and use it before you begin."

Then, as I moved away to get the oil, he got in his horrible, insidious touch—something so subtle that it could have sprung only from a lack of subtlety, something so utterly devastating that when Zelda told me of it later, half an hour later—my brain reeled and the world became black as death. For the man moved upon Zelda, commanded her politeness by using the advantage he held over me, and after a few misleading preliminaries said:

"It's a pity that a nice girl like you should be let to wear those clothes."

He was looking at her knickerbockers. It was fifty years of provincialism speaking; it was the negative morality of the poor white—and yet it filled me with helpless and inarticulate rage. But Zelda's coolness in the face of such a charge must have flabbergasted him. He had trusted too much in his moral advantage over me, for he did not annoy her further. If he had, I do not doubt that he would have met with the same fate as the two old women in Clarksville.

We got ourselves eventually from the garage. The wheel was no longer coming off "from the inside"; the noise had ceased; all was serene. We confided ourselves to Dr. Jones and started south through North Carolina. We attained Durham, but, due to the fact that the rain had begun to fall, we omitted to celebrate the fact that we had now gone six hundred miles and were half way to Montgomery. We ate a luscious watermelon, which cheered us a little—but we could not erase it from our minds that, so long as Zelda wore her white knickerbockers, the surrounding yokelry regarded us with cold, priggish superiority, as "sports." We were in Carolina and we had not conducted ourselves sartorially as the Carolinians.

After Durham the sun came out and shone heavily down upon the worst roads in the world. But they were the best roads, we were assured both by Dr. Jones and by a high yellow nigger with green eyes, between Durham and Greensboro. In that case the other roads must have been planted with barbed-wire entanglements. If you can imagine an endless rocky gully, rising frequently in the form of unnavigable mounds to a slope of sixty degrees, a gully covered with from an inch to a foot of gray water mixed with solemn soggy clay of about the consistency of cold cream and the adhesiveness of triple glue; if you drove an ambulance over shelled roads in France and can conceive of all the imperfections of all those roads placed within forty miles—then you have a faint conception of the roads of upper North Carolina.

With a patient fortitude we jogged left and we jogged right and we jogged both directions together; we groaned laboriously up and slid perilously down. We traversed whole stretches that would not have been fit boulevards for baby tanks. After awhile we began to meet other tourists—flivvers up to their hips in mud, immersed so deep that only the driver's eyes were visible; flivvers traveling in ruts that were deep as graves and wide as footpaths, and, most tragic of all, bubbles where flivvers had recently sunk out of sight with their intrepid crews, to be heard from no more.

"Any better along where you come from?" they would shout, unless their mouths were below the mud surface; and I would always answer, "Worse!" But I was always wrong, for the further we went the worse it grew. For the first time I felt a sort of pride in the achievements of the Rolling Junk. Erratic it might be, but it had a broad-shouldered sturdiness and an indomitable ruggedness when faced with a material obstacle. It could scale a precipice or ford a muddy stream impassible to a smaller, lighter car.

We had little else now about which to be enthusiastic. Biscuits and peaches had paled; the joy of "surprising mother and father" had been talked to a slow death; our suitcases bulged both with laundry and with the mud of eight states and a district. And, lastly, we were running short of money.

To be exact, there remained twenty-five dollars and some brown and silver change. When I had written from Washington for money I had directed, with an unjustifiable optimism, that it be sent *not* to Greens*boro*, North Carolina—which we were now approaching—but to Green*ville*, South Carolina, which was two hundred miles farther south.

At twilight we came into Greensboro, which offered the O. Henry Hotel, an elaborate hostelry, at sight of which Zelda decided to slip on a skirt over her knickerbockers. This time I instructed the garage man *not* to inspect the Rolling Junk—nay, not even to look at it closely. If there was anything the matter with it we couldn't afford to have it fixed anyhow. It was better not to know. Then we bathed in faintly reddish water which lent a pleasant crimson glow to the bath-tub, and ate a large dinner. This last, with the tip, used up four dollars and fifty cents of our money, but we were too tired to care.

## PART THREE

Greenville or starve! The Rolling Junk eyed us with reproachful lamps as though it knew that it had been cheated of its customary physical examination. We explained to it that our garage and hotel bills, our gasoline and oil, our breakfast and the black man's tip had reduced our capital to six dollars and thirty cents.

The sunshine was sparkling, and it was only half past eight.

"I'm glad the roads are good," said Zelda. "We can do two hundred miles before sunset. We've never started this early before."

Insidious roads!—brick now as though to make up for the recent gullies.

"Step on it!" urged Zelda.

"I was about to."

Two hundred miles to money, two hundred miles to tires, repairs, shelter and food.

So I stepped on it. It was the first time I had tested the speed of the Rolling Junk—the Boston Post Road was monopolized by gigantic trucks which made racing precarious. But now—the smooth brick of the road stretched seductively before us, without another automobile, or a street car or a cross-street or a turning. And slowly the indicator on the dashboard mounted to forty, to fifty, then crept slowly to fifty-five, receded to fifty-three and, as if reconsidering, climbed rapidly up to sixty-one.

"Are you stepping on it?"

"Yes."

"It's not so nice as an airplane," she remarked cryptically.

I had been saving up for an ultimate burst of speed, but at this I pressed my foot down until the accelerator was touching the floor. With almost a leap the Rolling Junk increased its pace—we seemed to be flying—the speedometer shot up to sixty-four, then, point by point, battled a hazardous course to seventy-four, where it tried to settle, reaching for seventy-five on slight downgrades and dropping to seventy-three on hills.

At that rate we would have arrived in Montgomery at half past four that day—it was unbelievable—of course we couldn't keep it up—we didn't expect to get to Montgomery until the day after tomorrow—still—the wind was roaring—the road was contracting before us like a rubber band—momentarily I expected one of the wheels to flash by us or else crush up on its spokes like an egg—Kingdom Come—

Ten, fifteen minutes passed. The road, barren of any traffic, stretched on indefinitely. We must have covered twenty miles with scarcely a change of pace. I was imagining a boulevard like this stretching between Westport and Montgomery. I was imagining that I had the fastest car ever made—it could travel three miles a minute. At that rate we could have left Westport after lunch and arrive at Montgomery in time for dinner—

After awhile excessive motion began to weary me. I saw the suspicion of a turn about two miles ahead and taking my foot slowly from the accelerator reduced our speed to forty miles an hour—at which pace we seemed to be merely crawling. It was at this point that I became aware of a new sound—a persistent and obnoxious sound, distinct and differentiated from the sound of our motor. At the same moment Zelda glanced around.

"Lord!" she cried. "It's a motorcycle policeman!"

I tried to come down as unostentatiously as possible to a modest thirty. But my efforts at camouflage were feeble—as transparent as the start of innocent surprise I gave when the policeman rode up alongside and greeted me with a prolonged grunt. At his bidding I came to a full stop.

"Well!" he said with a ferocious countenance.

"Well?" I answered brilliantly. I felt that I should have offered him a drink or at least a piece of candy or something—but I could offer him nothing.

"Going seventy miles an hour, weren't you?"

Instead of correcting him, I merely lifted my eyebrows in horror and exclaimed reproachfully, as though I could hardly believe my ears.

"Seventy miles an *hour!*"

"Seventy miles an *hour!*" he mimicked. "Tuhn around and folla me back to the codehouse."

"Officer," I said briskly, "we're in a hurry. We—"

"I saw you were in a hurry. I can tell from my own speedometeh how fast you were goin'."

"We're in a—in a *terrible hurry!*" I insisted, thinking wildly of the six dollars and thirty cents in my pocket. Suppose the fine were ten dollars! Would we have to languish in jail? A shiver passed over me. "Isn't there anything we can do?"

"Well," he said glibly, "the fine for first offense speeding is five dollahs. If you don't want to come back to the codehouse you can give me the five dollahs and I'll see it gets to the jedge."

I had my suspicions that this transaction was unofficial—that the jedge would never "hear tell" of my money. But I did believe that the fine would reach that figure, perhaps more, and the return to the "codehouse" would be an expense of both time and gasoline. So I handed over a precious bill whereat the guardian of the roads thanked me, tipped his hat and drove hastily away.

"Now how much money have we?" asked Zelda crossly.

"Dollar thirty."

"If you hadn't slowed down he couldn't have caught us."

"We'd have had to slow down eventually. And he'd have telephoned ahead or else shot at our tires."

"He couldn't have hurt them much."

We sat in stony silence between the five-dollar bill and Charlotte.

In Charlotte we lunched. We lunched on the thirty cents, reserving the dollar for an emergency. Zelda had an ice cream cone, and a hot dog and a nut bar. I digested a fifteen-cent dish which was resting on a lunch-counter, under the transparent alias of meat and potatoes. Feeling much worse we drove out of Charlotte and took the road to Greenville—or rather did not take the road to Greenville. Due to a growing vagueness on the part of Dr. Jones we started back toward New York and rode in fatuous ignorance for twelve miles. By that time it had become utterly impossible to force the road and the guide book into any sort of agreement, even though we let trees pass as telegraph poles and counted mileposts as schoolhouses. We grew nervous. We spoke to a farmer. He laughed and said he'd have to tell his wife about this.

It was all very discouraging. We passed back through Charlotte—it looked even less attractive to us than it had before. But hardly were we well in the country again when we noticed that the apparently smooth road on which we were driving had grown unaccountably rough. I dismounted suspiciously—sure enough, Hercules had given up the ghost.

I put on the spare wheel with its new tire, but no sooner had it touched the ground than one of its spokes gave way. The situation was frightful—we had one good wheel and one good tire, but they were not together. Ah, if the wheel would only keep its shape until we reached a garage, if the garage man would only make the necessary change for one dollar!

Crawling along at ten miles an hour—at which rate we would have reached Montgomery in six days—we came to a country garage at three o'clock. We were very unhappy. I told the proprietor what I wanted and when I had finished he named his price. It was—here we held our breaths—one dollar.

Greenville was still one hundred miles farther south. One drop too little of gasoline, one more puncture, and we were done.

And then five miles from the South Carolina border, we obtained a succulent revenge for the humiliation heaped upon us by the scornful and highly moral Expenso owner the day before. It was necessary that this revenge take place in North Carolina—had it occurred ten miles further south and in the sister state I would have borne the scar of the earlier encounter forever. As it is, I bear no malice.

The incident began as inauspiciously as the catastrophe of the day before. In fact, the Rolling Junk became noisily temperamental and I was compelled to stop.

"What is it?" Zelda's voice was tense with alarm. "Is the wheel coming off from the inside again?"

"I think it's the motor."

"Is it coming off?"

"I don't know. I think it's going out."

As a matter of form I raised the hood and gazed at the mass of iron and tin and grease within. Probably if I had been a giant thirty-three yards tall, with a hand three yards long, who could have taken up the Rolling Junk and given it a *real* shake, it would have started, very much on the principle of a refractory watch.

We waited fifteen minutes. A farmer rolled stiffly down the road in a flivver. I waved at him wildly, but he took me for a hold-up man and seemed not a little startled as he went by.

We waited another fifteen minutes. Another car came into sight far down the road.

"Look, Zelda—" I began—ceased, for she was in a state of unusual activity. Like lightning she produced a disk-shaped box and became absorbed in the passionate pigmentation of her face—her hands ran like serpents through her bobbed hair, giving its permanent wave a jaunty blouse.

"You go way," she said shortly.

"Go way?"

"Turn in that gate there and sit behind the wall."

"Why the—"

"Hurry up! Before that car comes over the next hill."

I had begun to get a glimmer of her idea. Obediently I ran back to the designated gate and concealed myself behind the very obligingly convenient wall.

The car dropped over the hill, grew larger, passed me with a whiff of oily dust. I saw it flash by the Rolling Junk and then, about *twenty* yards farther on, come to a precipitous stop. It backed with a scampish eagerness until it was beside the Expenso. Though I could see neither its driver nor Zelda, I gathered that they were in conversation. Then, after a moment, a figure dismounted from the other car and raised one side of the Rolling Junk's hood. He peered at the engine, nodded boastfully, comprehensively, smiled superiorly at Zelda and returned to his own car for tools. A minute later he was lying on his back underneath our car and I heard a clanking that delighted my heart.

Five minutes passed. He emerged several times to wipe the white July dew from his brow and to converse with Zelda. When he emerged the last time he buttoned up the hood. Zelda, evidently acting according to his direction, started the motor—it gave out a healthy, robust sound. The Samaritan replaced the tools in his car and, returning, set one foot on the running board of the Rolling Junk and began an animated conversation. I judged that it was time for my re-appearance—I walked out into the road and toward them, mildly whistling "The Beale Street Blues."

They both turned. The man's eyes, the eyes possibly of a country banker's son, looked upon me in dismay—they were eyes, I am glad to say, very much like those of the Expenso owner of the day before.

"Oh you're back!" exclaimed Zelda pleasantly. "Did you find a phone? It doesn't matter if you didn't because this gentleman was kind enough to fix what was wrong."

"That was mighty nice of him," I said brazenly.

The man gazed from one to the other of us with a strained stare. Then from sheer embarrassment he made the remark that put him utterly in my power.

"Oh," he ejaculated, involuntarily and in an obviously disappointed voice, "I thought you were alone."

"No," said Zelda gravely, "my husband's with me." And she added cruelly, "I never tour alone."

I climbed in beside her and took the wheel.

"It certainly was awfully kind of you, and I'm very much obliged."

The banker's son grunted, stood there staring at me wordlessly, with pendant brows. I threw the car into first.

"We've got to hurry on," I suggested.

Zelda thanked him profusely. We slid off. When we had gone fifty yards I looked back and discovered that he had turned his car completely around and started off in the direction from which he had come.

Considerably cheered we drove on, heading into a pale yellow sun which hovered over the black and green highlands in the distance.

"Gosh!" exclaimed Zelda in sudden dismay. She was staring blankly at an open page of Dr. Jones's guide book.

"What's the matter?"

"There's a toll-bridge between North and South Carolina, and we haven't a nickel!"

Almost at the same moment it came into view. For the second time that day I stepped hard on the accelerator. We flew down a short hill, thundered on to the rattling bridge and raced madly across to the friendly shore. Zelda glancing back, reported that a funny little man had come out of a funny little house and was waving his arms passionately. But we were safe in South Carolina.

Safe?—At seven o'clock we smelled the rusty metallic sweat of the engine. The oil register showed zero. We became very sad. We tried to fool the engine by running very fast—so we groaned up a hill and down into a city named for the stoical Lacedaemonians—Spartanburg. The game was up—we had no money to buy oil and we could go no farther.

"It's my birthday," said Zelda, suddenly. This somehow astonished me more than anything that had happened that day.

"I just remembered."

She had just remembered!

"Let us go to the police station and give ourselves up," she said. In conventional predicaments she is without resources.

"No," said I. "We will go to the Spartanburg telegraph office and persuade them to wire ahead to Greenville for our money."

Zelda doubted whether the Spartanburg agent would trust us. Also being from Alabama, and having therefore no confidence in Progress, she did not believe that the money was in Greenville anyhow.

We reached the telegraph office and, peering in through the windows after the immemorial manner of the poor, we saw that the station agent was a young male of kindly countenance. We entered. He consented to wire for us. We sat outside in the Rolling Junk for half an hour, enviously watching well-fed people pass, and then the operator came out and told us that we were no longer penniless, but possessed of three hundred dollars. We almost wept upon him, but he refused a gratuity.

We left the Rolling Junk to be thoroughly doctored, and dined in a Greek restaurant, where we were served by a handsome Spartan with a cake to celebrate Zelda's birthday. To conclude fittingly a day on which we had been guilty of speeding, bribery, toll-dodging and obtaining help under false pretenses, we purchased many curious postcards adorned with plush and frosting and moral messages, and sent them broadcast through the land. That day we had gone one hundred and eighty miles, and the backbone of the trip was broken at last.

## II

Next day the triumphant Rolling Junk, bulging with oil, plunged through impassable streams and surmounted monstrous crags. A garage man in Anderson told us that the Expenso had one hundred different ailments and would not last out another hundred miles, but they were all new ailments, so we laughed in his face. We were going to arrive in Montgomery in time for dinner the following evening. We even considered wiring ahead lest Zelda's parents be dangerously shocked when we appeared, but we decided against it, for we had kept our secret too long to relinquish it now.

The collapse of Sampson near the Georgia line was only a comic calamity, for was not old Lazarus clinging firmly to the left rear wheel, the last survivor of the five tires with which we had left Westport?—brave Lazarus with his bald spots and his abrasions. Santa Claus, Hercules, Sampson, as well as the tire we had abandoned to make chewing gum for Mr. Bibelick in Philadelphia, were all departed to the rubber heaven where nails and glass exist not and one is always a spare.

We crossed into Georgia by a long iron bridge and burst into a long yell of jubilation, for Georgia was next to Alabama and Zelda had often motored from Montgomery to football games in Columbus or Atlanta. The sandy roads took on a heavenly color, the glint of the trees in the sun was friendly, the singing negroes in the field were the negroes of home. In every town through which we passed, Zelda would declare enthusiastically that she knew dozens of boys who lived there if she could only just remember their names. Several times she went to the extent of entering drug stores and futilely thumbing directories in search of gallants who had once danced in the dawn at Sewanee or Tech or the University of Alabama, but the months had washed away all except a dozen fragmentary first names and a few shadowy memories.

We drew near Athens, the seat of the University of Georgia. Had we broken down irretrievably at this point I believe we would have had ourselves towed into Montgomery by horses rather than arrive without the Rolling Junk. We were only two hundred and fifty miles away, and we decided to sleep in Athens, rise before dawn and cover all the remaining distance on the morrow. We had never done two hundred and fifty miles in a day—but the roads down here were smooth and dry and we knew that we could make better time than in the Carolinas.

In the hotel we were given a salesman's display room—a huge chamber with sample tables and a business-like air, haunted by the pleasant ghosts of lazy southern commerce. In the streets, the dark balmy streets, we watched strolling girls in their stiff muslin dresses, girls with too much rouge, but cool and soft-voiced and somehow charming here under the warm southern moon. Our evening round of postcards seemed almost out of place—we were living again the life and moving in the atmosphere we had known so well in Montgomery two years before. I saw some numbers of Old King Brady and Young Wild West on a news stand, and fascinated by their colored covers I bought half a dozen. We read them in bed until nine o'clock when, in accordance with our plans for next day, we turned out the light.

The telephone tolled violently at four, and we awoke with all the excitement of early Christmas morning. We dressed in a sleepy haze and stumbled down to breakfast—but there was no breakfast! A drowsy night-clerk stared at us in scorn as we dragged our bags through the lobby. A drowsy watchman yawned and spluttered as I entered the garage across the street where burned a blue and solitary light. Then we were in the deep dusty leather seats whose feel we knew so well, tearing along through the last end of the darkness toward Atlanta.

Something more than half awake we watched the morning develop in hamlet after hamlet as we went by. In one place milk was being delivered, in the next a drowsy housewife was shaking something—perhaps a child—on the back porch. Then for an hour we passed group after group of negroes bound singing for the cotton fields and the work of the hot hours.

Just after eight there was Camp Gordon where once upon a time I had taught Wisconsin country boys the basic principles of "squads right" through two chilly months;—and, later, smiling Peachtree Street beamed upon us with a hundred mansions of opulent Atlanta set among bright groves of pine and palm.

We stopped at a little cafe for breakfast—then out on the road again and racing a flivver along the hard dust in a delirium of delight. Why not? When evening came we would have travelled twelve hundred miles, traversed the entire coast of a great nation and vindicated the Rolling Junk against all the garage-men in Christendom. Why, we were so proud now that when a drawling gasoline-jerker gaped at our Connecticut license we told him that Connecticut was five thousand miles away and that we had driven it in three days.

It was not only of ourselves that we boasted to each other, but of the Rolling Junk.

"Remember how she took those Carolina Hills?"

"And went through those muddy streams where the other cars had stopped?"

—"And ate up that stretch of road near Charlotte?"

"Oh, it's a wonderful car, I think. It has its faults, of course, but it certainly has power."

"Good old Expenso!"

At noon we came to West Point, which, contrary to general report, is not a military academy, but only the town that separates Georgia from Alabama. Over the bridge and onto the soil of Zelda's native state, the cradle of the Confederacy, the utter heart of the Old

South, the ground of our dreams and destination. But we were too maudlin with excitement now to experience a distinct territorial thrill and set it off from other and equally importunate emotions.

The afternoon began in heat. The road ran through sandy swamps full of damp evaporation and under heavy growth of Spanish moss where the atmosphere was like a conservatory. We stopped at Opelika for gasoline. Just next door was Auburn, seat of the Alabama Polytechnic Institute. Here Zelda had known the greatest gaiety of her youth, for Auburn belonged primarily to Montgomery as its sister college, the University, belonged to Birmingham. Auburn—in many hurried letters had she aroused my uneasiness with the news that she was just starting up to Auburn to attend a dance, watch a football game, or merely spend an idle day!

Through Tuskegee then as the heat of the afternoon was drifting off from the land like smoke. We left something behind us in Tuskegee. We did not know it at the time and it was better that we should not know. Into a tranquil street of the reposeful city we had dropped an intrinsic part of the Rolling Junk—from Tuskegee onward we were without the services of a battery. It had jumped with a neat and imperceptible movement from the car. Had we stopped now and shut off the motor, if only for a minute, no power we could have wielded would have started us again.

We spoke little now. When automobiles passed we craned our necks looking for familiar faces. Suddenly Zelda was crying, crying because things were the same and yet were not the same. It was for her faithlessness that she wept and for the faithlessness of time. Then into the ever-changing picture swam the little city crouching under its trees for shelter from the heat.

Simultaneously one of the most ludicrous signs that I have ever seen caught my eye. It was an enormous, faded, battered affair which hung by one ear from a post set awry by the roadside. In almost illegible letters, erratically dotted with defunct electric bulbs, it proclaimed that this was:

MONTGOMERY
"Your Opportunity"

We were in Montgomery—it was breathless, unbelievable. A journey by train is somehow convincing. Sleep bridges the mysterious gap. You feel that the intrinsic change from one locality to another has taken place in the night—but we found it impossible to believe, now, that one day's trip had been hitched securely on to another day's trip and had led us *here*. —Why, Montgomery was on another plane and we were actually rolling into it, right down Dexter Avenue as though it had been a street in Westport!

It was five o'clock. We were sure that Judge and Mrs. Sayre would be on the porch. Our hearts thumped desperately—Twelve Hundred Miles! "Oh, hello!" we would say—or would we be calm? Or would we faint dead away? Or would the Rolling Junk crumble to pieces before our eyes? Or what would express the tremendous vitality of our success—and the unexpected sadness of the journey's end, of the South itself, of the past we two had had together in this town.

We turned a last corner and craned our eyes to see. We stopped the car in front of Zelda's house.

There was no one on the porch. Fumbling at the door handles we descended from the car and ran up the front steps. My eye caught sight of half a dozen newspapers on the porch rolled into cylinders for quick delivery and a horrible presentiment swept over me. Zelda was at the closed door, her hand was on the knob.

"Why," she cried, "it's locked! Why, it's locked!"

I was thunderstruck.

"It's locked!" her voice was quite wild. "They're not here!"

I tried the door. I counted the papers.

"They've been gone three days."

"How terrible." Her lip was trembling. I tried to think of a possible hope.

"They're probably at—out in the country or something. They'll probably be back tomorrow." But the blinds were down. There was an air of desertion about it all.

"Why, my own house is locked!" Her tone was unbelieving—almost terrified.

Then a woman's voice from the lawn—Zelda turned and recognized her next door neighbor.

"Zelda Sayre, what are you doing down here?"

"My house is locked," said Zelda tensely. "What's the matter?"

"Why," exclaimed the lady in a gentle surprise. "Why, Judge and Mrs. Sayre left Sunday night for Connecticut. I thought they were going to surprise you all. Why, Zelda, child, did you ride down here in an automobile?"

Zelda sat down suddenly on the steps and leaned her head against a post.

"That's what they said," went on the lady in blue. "They said they were going up to surprise you all."

Ah, and it was bitter how well they had succeeded!

And so we came into port at last. I wonder if any such adventure is ever worth the enthusiasm put into it and the illusion lost. None but the very young or very old can afford such voluminous expectations and such bitter disappointment. And if you had asked me then if I would do it again I would have answered with an emphatic No.

And yet—I have discovered in myself of late a tendency to buy great maps and pore over them, to inquire in garages as to the state of roads; sometimes, just before I go to sleep, distant Meccas come shining through my dreams and I tell Zelda of white boulevards running between green fields toward an enchanted sunset land. We have a good car—an *In*expenso and *not* a Rolling Junk—we look at it and wonder if it is sturdy and powerful enough to scale hills and plunge through streams like the other. We say now, when our opinion is asked, that there is no car like a good Expenso—

But the night grows late and I must round out the story. After the catastrophe we tried to start the car, to go to Zelda's sister, but we discovered that the battery was gone. Weeks later we learned, accidentally, that its mangled remains had been discovered in Tuskegee. The loss of the battery was the last blow and for a time the world seemed very dark. But the word blew around that Zelda was home and in a few minutes automobiles began to drive up to the door and familiar faces clustered around us—faces amused, astonished, sympathetic, but all animated by a sincere pleasure in her return. So after a while our disappointment dimmed and faded away like all things.

We sold the Rolling Junk in Montgomery—we had decided, needless to say, to return to Westport by train. Of its subsequent history I know less than I would like to. It was passed on from a man I knew slightly to a man I did not know at all, and so I lost sight of it forever. Who knows? Perhaps it is still bowling along between Durham and Greensboro with faithful Lazarus resting on the rack at last. Perhaps, less erratic and as robust as ever, it is still giving the lie to garage men and frightening highwaymen in Virginia swamps. Perhaps it is resolved into its component parts and has lost its identity and its mortal soul—or perished by fire or been drowned in the deep sea. My affection goes with you, Rolling Junk—with you and with all the faded trappings that have brightened my youth and glittered with hope or promise on the roads I have travelled—roads that stretch on still, less white, less glamorous, under the stars and the thunder and the recurrent inevitable sun.

## THE HIGH COST OF MACARONI

Like most other Americans we are in Europe. We came over here a year and a half ago to try and save money. We are going to try it for another year and a half and then if we haven't succeeded any better we're coming home and get something to eat.

If you like such travel articles as "A Merry Two Years Ramble in Europe" you have opened at the wrong page. Turn on. This is an unpleasant story with all sorts of sinister characters in it whose business is to take money away from noble and good-hearted Americans. Whenever we hear of another couple who have come over here to lay something by we bend our heads and weep into whatever is at hand—usually macaroni.

When we first came over we went down to Southern France where we worried along for six months trying to support a large and constantly increasing French family who jokingly referred to themselves as our "servants." By the end of that time we had salted down in the bank and in various stocks and bonds and development schemes a little over one hundred dollars. This was the all too familiar experience that confronted us at the end of our first half year abroad.

"I can't deal with these people," said my wife. "They know the game too well. If we're going to save anything we'll have to move on."

"Where to?"

"How about Italy?"

Now she insists to this day that I was the first to mention Italy but that is not true. She was. When we dispute the matter—which is seldom more than once a week—she is apt to become a little excited about it: "Shut up, yourself!" and all that regrettable sort of thing. The fact remains that we looked up the rate of exchange for Italy and finding it much more promising than the rate of exchange for France decided to spend a warm quiet economical winter in Rome.

This time we were taking no chances so we made an iron-bound schedule that we swore to live up to. It apportioned every possible expense and left such a wide margin for miscellaneous that life

---

*Interim* 4, nos. 1–2 (1954): 6–15.

couldn't take us unawares. It guaranteed that by the end of the winter three thousand dollars would be saved and by the end of a decade we would be secure for life. Underneath our signatures Zelda drew some flowers which were very pretty indeed and we went to bed with the feeling that we were on the right track at last. Of course it seemed a shame to leave France just as we had learned the language—we spoke it now with hardly any accent—that is hardly any French accent—but we were in deadly earnest about laying something by and the exchange pointed the way.

So one sunny October morning we filled our small French car with the one suitcase it would hold, said goodbye to our child and nurse who were to follow by train, and drove away from our pleasant Riviera villa. Perhaps my diary of our trip through sunny Italy, words set down in the heat of enthusiasm while the enchantment of the beautiful scenery was still upon me, will give you a better idea of the journey than anything I could write now.

### FRIDAY, OCTOBER 31ST.

This evening at seven o'clock we left France behind and crossed the border into the flowery land of Italy, where we immediately noticed a change in the temperature. It grew slightly colder. Zelda was homesick until she called up the nurse from San Remo, where we spent the night, and found the child alive and well. Macaroni for dinner—it was nice to be eating real Italian food.

### SATURDAY, NOVEMBER 1ST.

Lost our way and would have driven back into France but the customs officer stopped us and turned us around. Everybody looks very poor and hungry. Zelda says we passed some pretty flowers this morning but we are evidently too far north to find any warm weather, for the car froze while we were having dinner in Savona. We had macaroni with cheese, a very original idea and very good.

### SUNDAY, NOVEMBER 2ND.

This morning we bought a lap-robe to keep warm. It only cost three dollars which is very cheap and shows we are on the right track. It would have cost four times that in America. I tell Zelda it isn't fair to judge prices by these hotels on the high road. At ten o'clock we reached Pisa. Zelda says that just before dark we passed another flower.

### MONDAY, NOVEMBER 3RD.

After a nice breakfast of coffee and macaroni we started for Florence. Gasolene is rather high, about sixty cents a gallon because of the rate of exchange, but they say things are cheaper farther south. I notice that they always ask us whether we are English or American before they tell us what we owe, and some instinct tells me we should pretend to be English. Bought small but costly monocle. Zelda fretful. She has taken a curious dislike to macaroni.

The lap-robe worn out.

### TUESDAY, NOVEMBER 4TH.

Zelda has been very foolish about this macaroni thing—she says it makes her sick to eat it for breakfast and we had words somewhere between Florence and Rome. As we approached Rome we thought we saw another flower but it turned out to be an old garter. Shortly afterwards we drove into a large city where everyone was driving on the wrong side of the street, except me. The man who tried to arrest me told me this was Rome and I had better do as the Romans do. The porter at the hotel says he thinks it will stop snowing before morning.

At nine o'clock the following day I went to a Real Estate Office (*Reala Estata Uffizia*) and asked a very sleepy clerk (*clerka*) for an apartment (*apartamente*) adding that I wished to pay no more than one hundred and fifty dollars a month. At this the clerk woke up and broke into a roar of laughter. He shouted out something and immediately other clerks began to crowd into the room to take a look at me.

"What's the matter with you people?" I demanded indignantly.

"Theesa Holy Year."

"That's all the more reason why you ought to be civil and not make all that irreverent racket."

At this they all began to talk at once and to shake their first fingers at me menacingly. It was sometime before I realized the significance of what they said.

This was Holy Year. Only one year in every twenty-five is Holy Year—and we had blundered right into it. To the Roman business man, Holy Year is that period when he counts on making enough profit out of foreign pilgrims to enable him to rest for twenty-five years more. A host of speculators—army officers, black-handers, waiters, mule drivers, morticians and princes of the blood—round up every edifice that can be disguised as an apartment house and wait for the Americans. It is only considered necessary to re-paper four rooms in a rickety tenement, set up a bath tub in a clothes closet and say "two hundred a month" in a firm but pious voice. Sometimes the bath tub isn't even connected, and once, during the discouraging weeks that ensued, our prospective landlord didn't even know what it was for. He had bought it because the other speculators were buying them and he told us it was part of a new American heating system.

After a fortnight of following false clues up dreary alleys we gave up an idea of an apartment at reasonable price and settled down for the season in a small hotel. There was no coarse display or anything like that—the only jewels I ever saw were in the manager's watch and they were too small to be offensive. If our child blew a whistle in the hall the clients all rushed downstairs shouting "Where is the fire?"

The building itself had been erected over the tomb of one of the early emperors and the elevator shaft was obviously in direct communication with the open mausoleum. There was atmosphere for you! We almost resented the fact that a new dining salon was being built in one wing and that we could not continue to eat in the quaint old cloak-room which was being used temporarily. There was something very foreign and "old-world" about it all. It was awful. There was one other American among the guests but we never met him. At first we thought from his hue that he was an East Indian Rajah but he turned out to be from Georgia. My wife is from Alabama. After a long argument, I prevailed upon her to stay.

The manager had made us a special rate for the winter—eight hundred dollars a month, which was to include two double rooms, a study, a bath, heat, light, air, tips, tax and food, and anything else we could think of. We were lucky to get in at all, he said—in another month people would be sleeping in the streets and the food would give out with the rush of pilgrims. The Hotel de la Morgue, on the other hand, served six courses at every meal. I translate a sample bill of fare:

1. *Couvert*
2. Choice—Bread or butter
3. Macaroni with grated meat
4. Spaghetti with pulverized tomatoes
5. Vermicelli with annihilated cheese
6. Fruit or go hungry

But we never left the table hungry. In fact we never went to it hungry. There was some spell about that cloak-room that after you entered it you didn't care about eating.

Let us leave the Hotel de la Morgue for a few hours and saunter about the streets of Rome. Contrary to general belief Rome is not inhabited entirely by men. True the women are locked into their homes by day and by night, in a manner that would please our most violent anti-feminists, but the number of children who swarm the streets testified to their existence. After twilight groups of men loiter dismally on every corner—colorless, monotonous men with bored and dreary faces. They hope that something will happen—that a belated flapper will whisk by for a bit of color, that the United States will remove the emigrant restrictions or, failing this, that the rattle of machine guns will begin and signal in a new revolution. For the Italian is a natural anarchist. His legacy is the riotous spirit of the dark ages, that talent for violence and suspicion against which during the last hundred years a dozen champions from Mazzini to Mussolini have struggled in vain. The divine rough-house which began in the sixth century is by no means over—it first presented itself to us during a tea dance one afternoon at a fashionable hotel.

It was not our hotel. At our hotel we felt that tea dances were vulgar. It was at the Mazuma Americana, a fashionable pile where macaroni was never mentioned above a whisper. We had been shown to a small uncoveted table in the corner, ordered tea and something to take the taste of it out of our mouths and were about to rise and dance when suddenly our peace was broken by the presence of two young men at our elbow. They were thin, pale young men. Their black eyes flashed dully, their coats caught them like corsets at the waist, it was incredible that their right and left feet were headed the same way. But they were, they headed toward us, and their drooping mouths became twisted with some difficulty into expressions of scorn.

"This table," said the foremost, tapping it gently with his forefinger, "is reserved for the Princess Dumbella."

It was not, but his party, which included the Princess Dumbella, was two places shy.

"There are no other tables left," I said. "We've ordered tea and it's impossible for us to leave."

"I know there are no other tables," he said. "That's why the Princess Dumbella must have this table."

Now the Dumbellas are descendants of one of these bandit families who for six centuries robbed, wrecked, tortured, bribed, murdered, bullied and cheated their way into the control of Roman affairs. This control was taken from them, neatly but firmly, some fifty years ago, but by dint of several American marriages they have continued to hold their position among the international aristocracy. Less than any other aristocracy in the world, including the Russian, do they deserve the name, for their history is one long epic of ravage and destruction.

"This table," repeated the young man, "is reserved for the Dumbellas. You are keeping them waiting, do you hear?"

His shrill voice piped above the hot volume of American jazz. What faint memories of despotism still flickered in this ghost and made him think that that name could frighten anyone out of a two-place table!

"Who are the Dumbellas?" I inquired.

"The Dum—!" He gasped. His companion beckoned suddenly to the head waiter and a sustained conversation took place in Italian.

"I beg your pardon," said the head waiter to me. "But are you staying in this hotel?"

"No," I answered, "I am at the Hotel de la Morgue. We prefer small hotels."

They all looked a little shocked. The head waiter was the first to recover.

"I regret to say that this table is reserved."

"There was no reserved card on it," I protested. "We were shown here and our order was taken—"

"Don't argue," said my wife quietly. "Let's go. It's the rate of exchange."

"I can put up a table for you just inside the pantry door," suggested the head waiter.

We got up and stood facing them all for a moment, trying to think of some crushing remark to make. But nothing occurred to us, so, scornfully rejecting the substitute table, we swept (I believe that's the word) out the door into the cool December afternoon.

"I don't like this place," I said, as a Fascisti colonel tried to brush us from the sidewalk in token of his spontaneous admiration for my wife. "I don't like these people, or our hotel or this city. Let's go away."

"We can't."

"And why not?"

"Because we're keeping our schedule. If we moved before spring we'd get behind."

"I think we ought to get out."

"But it seems so silly—just as we begin to save something we get bored and move on."

"But what we're spending would buy more than this in New York City."

"This is Holy Year."

"Don't rub it in."

"Well, let's make the best of it. Let's read a lot of history and go to see lots of churches and ruins and—and all that, every afternoon. At least there aren't any distractions here to keep you from working."

We stayed. We bought a history book—if it hadn't opened to the name Paola Dumbella we might have read it. We plodded through the ruins. None of our guides had ever read the advertisement which says "Even his best friends won't tell him," and we tried to keep them ten feet away. We went to the movies, where they gave the first half of American pictures and announced that the second half would be shown the following week. We hissed. We were told afterwards that a hiss means applause.

A month passed. Just as I had learned to drive on the wrong side of the street the law was changed,—everyone must drive on the right. The Romans paid no attention—they kept to the left, the English and Americans kept to the right and the trolley cars fought it out up and down the center, so that every street in Rome became a one way street with the traffic going both ways.

Two months—two years—two decades passed. I was growing madder and madder. A white streak appeared in my hair, our child grew up, married, moved away. The president's iron horse wore out. The Colosseum fell down. Still the hotel dining room failed to be completed and we continued to eat macaroni in the cloak-room. Finally we discovered that the new dining room had only been a decoy to fill up the hotel—and had since been sold to a business concern next door. But we were too old to care.

Years passed. Little grandchildren played about our knees and we gaped fondly at them from toothless mouths. My wife decided at last to let her hair grow long. The last of the Dumbellas died. Sometimes we wondered if the joke wasn't on us after all. Anyone can save money if he is willing to live on dog-biscuit (that is, anyone except a dog) but the clever thing is to save money and still live on the fat of the land. Something was wrong somewhere—and one day we suddenly blew up—and found out.

It began with a handkerchief, a red handkerchief with a small blue bear in the corner, one of six which Zelda bought for the child. By one of those convenient oversights, at which the Romans are so adept, only five emerged from the package when it was opened at home.

Zelda sat down and gave three hearty groans.

"It's no use," she said. "If I don't go back I'll be cross all day because I've been cheated and if I do go back they'll swear they put six in, and I'll be even crosser."

"I'll go with you," I said sternly. "We'll go back there and they'll hand over that handkerchief or else they'll go to jail."

We went and argued. If there was one thing everyone in that store was sure of it was the fact that six handkerchiefs had been wrapped up. I told them I would never enter their store again, that I had three brothers with acute hayfever and had contemplated a large purchase of handkerchiefs next day—but they were firm. After half an hour, I was on their side—I began to think the handkerchief must have eaten its way through the paper and dropped on the street. Finally I apologized humbly for bothering them and crawled out of the store.

"Maybe you're right," I said, "but you'd never get it."

"I did get it."

She opened her hand.

From it, like one of those firework "worms" on the Fourth of July, uncurled a diminutive red handkerchief with a bear in the corner.

"It was pushed out of sight under that pile on the counter," she said.

"You *stole* it?"

"No. It jumped into my hand."

"But suppose they saw you."

"They did. And the proprietor sort of winked as if he were congratulating me. They just wouldn't give in—that was all."

I considered.

"There's something about this we don't understand—"

"We don't understand anything," she interrupted—"their way of being rude or their way of being polite, their way of being honest or their way of being dishonest. I don't think you're supposed to argue, like you are in France. I think the thing is to do just what you want—like driving on the right side of the street for instance. Everybody drives just where they want to."

And so it happened that on a cold January afternoon two puzzled Americans strolled along the somewhat odorous avenues of the Eternal City lost in thought. We knew that these people were different from us but did we remember that we were also different from them? Often when in the tourist office we had seen hordes of the more ignorant and baffled of our countrymen trying to explain to a foreign clerk that they wanted "a lower berth" or some other unobtainable commodity, we had plumed ourselves on superior cosmopolitan knowledge. When in Rome—that was the idea! This business of the handkerchiefs was the clue. It was when we decided this that the fun began.

As we entered the Hotel de la Morgue we were presented with the bill. I looked at it. I always looked at it, in the American way; now I really looked at it. Then I took out my fountain pen and ran a line through the item mineral waters.

"I won't pay that," I said.

"Why not, Signor?"

"Because one day I found the waiter filling the bottles from the tap in the hall." Again I drew a black line across the page. "And I won't pay for heat. There was no heat from Monday till Thursday. When it went on Friday we were so used to being cold that we had to open the windows."

"What's more," joined in my wife, "you know that the tourist season has been a disappointment and that you couldn't rent our rooms again. Take off twenty-five per-cent of that bill or we leave tomorrow."

I handed the bill back over the counter and stood there looking at the manager and trembling slightly.

"Some one has been talking to you," he broke out angrily, "someone in the hotel."

We exchanged a glance.

"We know the whole game," I answered. "We really ought to take off something for the missing dining room and the elevator that doesn't work and the food that doesn't work and the servants that don't work and—"

"Sh!" he whispered, "Sh-h-h!" A small crowd had gathered. "If you will come to my private office later perhaps we can arrange something."

"But how about the whole winter we've wasted," I cried. "Arrange that if you can! Give us back November, December, January. What excuse have you got for the money you've already squeezed out of us for a stable room in this disreputable barn—!"

I broke off. His lips were already muttering automatically and I did not need to listen in order to know what they were saying.

"It's the rate of exchange. The rate of exchange."

A sort of madness overtook us. We jumped into a taxicab and drove up to the Hotel Mazuma Americana. The afternoon tea dance was beginning and our eyes lighted upon the Princess Dumbella and her two cavaliers of the month before leisurely approaching the last vacant table. I rushed up to the head waiter.

"Look here," I said. "I *have* to have that table. I'm Claude Lightfoot, the great American money king and if I can't have that table I'll call the Italian loan."

"But Signor, the Princess Dumbella—"

"Enough! Get me Signor Mussolini on the telephone."

In a moment the Dumbella party was intercepted. A barricade of waiters formed in front of them, on both sides of them, jostling, tripping, apologizing. Meanwhile we were bowed to the coveted table down a quietly opened lane.

Outside it was dark and cold. The dreary mists of the Campagna had drifted in and spread through the streets like the dissolving smoke of a bombardment. Half a dozen sullen taximen lounged by the door of the cabaret smoking the tobacco that is salvaged by old women from discarded butts of cigarettes. One of them followed as we started toward the nearest taxi.

"Hotel de la Morgue," I said. My wife stepped inside.

"Fifty lira," he answered.

"Between five and six lira," I corrected him. "I've ridden this before."

"But it's after ten o'clock."

"Call it fifteen lira with the tip," I said. "But hurry up, it's cold."

"Fifty lira," he repeated.

"Don't joke," I said. "We've graduated from that class."

To my chagrin he shrugged his shoulders and walked away.

We got out and approached the next cab, but its owner, after a conference with the first man, didn't move from his lounging place and merely gave a contemptuous shake of the head. We tried them all with the same result.

"They're after big game," I thought. "They know we're wise."

I decided to try my fascisti methods. I had no castor oil handy but I approached the first chauffeur with a menacing eye.

"You're going to take us home. I'll give you twenty-five lira, which is five times the meter price and that's all."

For answer he looked at his companion and spat contemptuously upon the sidewalk. An Italian issued from the cabaret, entered a taxicab and, with no discussion beyond the giving of an address, drove away.

"You're going to take us home now, do you hear," I said in a raised voice.

"American?" he demanded.

"What's that got to do with it."

"Fifty lira."

No respectable book has been written upon the psychology of midnight—or perhaps it was the ring of the words "fifty lira," which sounds like "fifty dollars," though it's closer to two. What happened had been provided for about fifteen years previously when I took four boxing lessons from Tommy Gibbons (he wasn't famous then, he was Mike's young brother). The lessons were concerned largely with what to do in a street fight. I never intended to be in a street fight—but about two minutes after the final mention of fifty lira I was.

It lasted, with short bursts of arguments, for about ten minutes. First there was *one* taxi driver, and I had a little the best of it; then there were two and I was having a little the worst of it. But I didn't think I was, and when the meddlesome stranger stepped between us I was in no mood to have it stop there, and I pushed him impatiently out of the way. He came back persistently, lurching in between us, talking in a stream of Italian, doing his best, it seemed to me, to interrupt my offensives—and to the advantage of the taximan. Once too often he caught at my arm. Blind with anger I turned on him quickly and (with more success than I had so far had with the others) caught him under the point of the chin; whereupon, rather to my surprise, he sat down.

Immediately a murmur arose from the now-gathering crowd.

"Santa Maria!"

"Ah Dios."

"Pauvra Americano!"

"O mio culpa!"

"You done it now!" said a voice in broken English. "Better beat it while the goin's good. You knocked him down."

"Served him right!" I cried. "Why didn't he keep out of it? What business is it of his?"

"It's the only business he's got," said the voice. "That's John Alexander Borgia, the chief of the secret police of the carbonieri."

\*\*\*

Capri is a small island in the bay of Naples where the Emperor Tiberius used to go when Rome got too hot for him. People have been going there for much the same reason ever since. Because we think it will make things easier we have even asked permission to change our names. If you happen to be thumbing through the pages of this magazine sometime and you run across any stories by F. Scott Finklestien, don't be puzzled. That will be me.

## "WHY BLAME IT ON THE POOR KISS IF THE GIRL VETERAN OF MANY PETTING PARTIES IS PRONE TO AFFAIRS AFTER MARRIAGE?"

Once past the age of thirty all civilized persons realize that many of our institutions are no more than conspiracies of silence.

When the clergyman assumes for the sake of his sermon that there is a great body of men and women who "live a moral life" he does not mean, if he is a man of any intelligence, that every week and every year this body is composed of the same people. He means rather that on any given date more people are engaged in keeping the rules than are engaged in breaking them. And he also means that these people who are at the moment engaged in being virtuous will combine against the people who are outraging the morals of the time.

The libertine sits in the jury box and votes against the divorce case defendant as heartily as does the pillar of the church. Three days later the pillar of the church may elope with the sexton's wife and five hundred unfaithful husbands read the news aloud at breakfast in shocked and horrified tones.

So in discussing the question as to whether we human beings are really capable of a happy monogamy, I don't want to start from the angle that four-fifths of us are approximately lily white and the other fifth a rather dingy shade of gray. I assume that at present there are a large majority of couples on this continent who are true to each other and a minority who are at present tangled up in some fascinating but entirely illegal affair.

### MONOGAMY A THEORY

We believe, from our racial experience, that monogamy is the simplest solution of the mating instinct. It tends to keep people out of messes and less time is required to keep up a legal home than to support a chorus girl. There are disadvantages—marriage is often dull for at least one of the parties concerned and the very security of the

---

*New York American*, 24 February 1924, p. LII-3.

bond tends, not infrequently, to make an unconscious bully of the man or a shrew of the woman. But on the whole the advantages outweigh the disadvantages, and the only trouble is—that it isn't really monogamy because one party is so frequently not true to the other.

This, despite the angry denials of thousands of pew-holders, is the unfortunate truth. The more the opportunity the greater is the tendency for young men and women to experiment in new fields. Some professions are proverbially dangerous in this respect—stage people "on the road," travelling salesmen, men of great means and great leisure, poor people who are thrown, by crowding conditions, into close proximity—all these men and women drift frequently into liaisons in what seems to them the most natural way in the world.

The truth is that monogamy is not (not yet at least) the simple natural way of human life. But we are officially pledged to it as the only possible system in the western world and at present it is kept working by a series of half artificial props—otherwise it may collapse and we may drift, quite naturally, into an age of turmoil and confusion.

### A FAITHFUL COUPLE

I know a man named Harry, a girl named Georgianna (these, strange to say, are their real names) who married in those happy radical days before the war, when experiment was in the air. The understanding was that, when the first flush was over, Harry and Georgianna were to be free to ramble. They were exceptionally well-mated, exceptionally congenial, and the fascination endured well into the fourth year of their marriage.

Then they made two discoveries—that they were still in love with each other, and that they were no longer completely unaware of the other men and women in the world. Just as they made these discoveries, circumstances threw them suddenly into gayest New York. Harry, through the nature of his occupation, came into almost daily contact with dozens of charming and foot-loose young women, and Georgianna began to receive the attentions of half a dozen charming and foot-loose young men.

If ever a marriage seemed bound for the rocks this one did. We gave them six months—a year at the outside. It was too bad, we felt, because fundamentally they loved each other, but circumstances had undoubtedly doomed them—as a matter of fact, they are now in process of living happily together forever after.

### JEALOUSY AIDS LOVE

Did they decide that the best way to hold each other was to let faithfulness be entirely voluntary? They did not. Did they come to an arrangement by which neither was to pry into the other's life? They did not. On the contrary they tortured each other into a state of wild, unreasoning jealousy—and this solved the problem neatly in less than a week.

Despite the sentimentalists, jealousy is the greatest proof of and prop to love. Harry and Georgianna, with the relentless logic of jealousy—poor, abused, old jealousy—forced concessions out of each other. They decided that the only sensible course was to remain always together. Harry never goes to see a woman alone nor does Georgianna ever receive a man when Harry is not there. Women over sixty and men over eighty are excepted.

Harry does not say:

"You mind my taking Clara to the theatre? What nonsense! Why, her husband is one of my best friends."

Nor does Georgianna protest:

"Are you mad because I sat out with Augustus? What nonsense! Why, Augustus hasn't got three hairs on top of his head."

### DANGEROUS INTRUDERS

They know that the wives of best friends and the men with less than three hairs on their heads are the most dangerous of all. Any one can protect his or her household against Apollo and Venus—it is the club-footed man and the woman with honest freckles who will bear watching.

If Harry goes away on a trip Georgianna goes with him. They go to no mixed parties unless both of them are able to go—and if there is any jealousy in the air neither of them strays out of the other's sight.

As I write this it sounds like a self-enforced slavery—a double pair of apron strings—but in the case of Harry and Georgianna, two highly strung and extremely attractive young people, it had the inestimable advantage of working admirably. I think they are the happiest couple I know.

## AS TO "COMPATABILITY"

The Experience of the Race (that stupid old man who every once in a while gets a few truths through his head) has found certain things violently unfavorable to a contented monogamy. Two of the most obvious things are a great disparity in age and a surrounding atmosphere of excessive alcoholic stimulation—two factors which occur chiefly among the well-to-do classes.

A heart-balm expert, in discussing the matter of successful marriages, the other day alluded to a "spirit of kindliness" between husband and wife—as if kindliness were a thing that can be acquired by wanting to acquire it or can be turned off and on in our hearts like a water faucet.

She spoke of "intellectual compatibility." It is one of her favorite phrases. The trouble is that when people are in love it is horribly hard to find out just how intellectually compatible they are—for they will bluff and lie and conceal and pretend interests that will never materialize after the celebrated words are murmured at the altar.

## "PETTING PARTIES"

But there are several essentials to successful monogamy that are not talked about in the women's magazines. A genius may some day arise who will find a way of presenting physiological facts to youth without shocking youth's sensibilities into an infuriated disgust. The long list of current "sex books," while they may have a certain value to married people, have absolutely no effect on the young except to arouse pruriency and sometimes to kill the essence of romance. It is the toss of a coin which is the worst—knowledge so acquired, or ignorance itself. And yet should such knowledge be acquired before marriage rather than after? If so, how?

It is only recently that the "petting party" has become almost as conventional a term as "afternoon reception" among the upper and middle classes, but in some more primitive communities a sustained physical courtship has preceded marriage. Such a courtship is the natural, not the vicious; the romantic, not the sordid; the ultra-ancient, not the ultra-modern preparation, for married life.

I have heard otherwise intelligent people speak of "petting parties" as if they were accidental and immoral phenomena in an entirely non-physical world—instead of an introduction to life, intended by nature to ameliorate the change between the unmarried and married states. We have given them a new tag, tied them up in some curious way with cocktails, opium, "The Sheik" and sheer perversity, but they have always existed and, it is to be hoped, always will.

One of the favorite questions of the recent controversy was:

"What kind of wife will the girl make who has had numerous petting parties before marriage?"

The answer is that nobody knows what kind of wife any girl will make.

"But," they continue, "won't she be inclined to have petting parties after she's married?"

### "WHY BLAME THE KISS?"

In one sense she will. The girl who is a veteran of many petting parties was probably amorously inclined from birth. She'll be more prone to affairs after marriage than the girl who didn't want any parties. But why blame it on the poor kiss? It is a question of temperament. The alarmist believes not in cause and effect, but that one effect produces the other.

It may even be true that petting parties tend to lessen a roving tendency after marriage. A girl who knows before she marries that there is more than one man in the world but that all men know very much the same names for love is perhaps less liable after marriage to cruise here and there seeking a lover more romantic than her husband. She has discovered already that variety is not half as various as it sounds. But if petting parties had been so named in 1913 we would have been assured that they caused the war.

Here is a more worthy scapegoat—the one-child family. Because of our breathless economic struggle, it has become almost an American institution. Women with one child are somehow more restless, more miserable, more "nervous" and more determined to pay any price for the attention of men than women with several children or no children at all. The child often becomes a pest and a bore and a continual subject for heated discussion at the dinner table. For some reason parents do not mind losing both temper and dignity before one child. They will hesitate in the presence of two.

### FOR "EASY DIVORCE"

Now I have discussed a number of things that war against a true and enduring marriage, rather than offering remedies for making every home a paradise in twelve lessons. Believing as I do that all questions worth solving are entirely insoluble, it is the only angle from which I can sincerely approach the subject. On the constructive side I can only say that I believe in early marriage, easy divorce and several children.

All in all nothing can tarnish the cheerful fact that a sincerely happy marriage under exclusive monogamy—one marriage in five, in ten—sometimes I think one in a hundred—is the most completely satisfactory state of being in this somewhat depressing world.

## DOES A MOMENT OF REVOLT COME SOME TIME TO EVERY MARRIED MAN?

Any decent, self-respecting marriage should have a percentage of from three to seven revolts every day. Otherwise, it's not a marriage—it's a defeat. Or rather it's a sitting on the lukewarm sidelines watching somebody else play.

In the first place no sooner does a man marry his reproachless ideal than he becomes intensely self-conscious about her. In a sort of panic he tries to make her into a thorough conservative as quickly as possible. It doesn't matter how beautiful her complexion looked to him before they were married—the first time he sees her at her easel applying complicated pigments to her eyelids and the lobes of her ears, the horrible suspicion seizes him that she has an immoral streak, and what's worse that she is conspicuously overdoing it and will probably be hailed in the streets.

In consequence—a double revolt is immediately enacted before her mirror, a revolt ending with that celebrated masculine statement:

"Well, you're *not!* And that's all there is to it!"

Is he sensitive? Mr. Egg, the young husband? Horribly! Did you ever go to a young married party and see the husbands, one by one, whisper to their wives not to do what the other wives are doing?

If it's anybody else except Mrs. Egg she can do all these things and you'll be one of the husbands who gather admiringly around her. But Mrs. *Egg*—well, you'd rather she'd sit in the corner with Mrs. Yoke and discuss whether you drop four stitches when you purl.

So after awhile young Mrs. Egg begins to feel that if Mr. Egg has demands on her, she has demands on him too, and then the revolt of Mr. Egg begins.

There is, for instance, that ghastly moment once a week when you realize that it all depends on you—wife, babies, house, servants, yard and dog. That if it wasn't for you, it'd all fall to pieces like an old broken dish. That because of those things you must labor all the

---

*McCall's* 51 (March 1924): 21, 36.

days of your life, when otherwise you could go to the poorhouse or murder your office boy or spend the summer in Monte Carlo and the winter in Sing Sing prison. But you can't! How did it happen? Where is the gay young man, the length of whose rambles was measured only by the size of his pocketbook?

After awhile you forget the gay young man and enter the third stage of revolt which endures through Mrs. Egg's palmy days—that is, as long as she is still attractive to other men. These are the days of:

"Here I've been working all day and you want to go out and dance all night. Well, you can't. I'm through. I'm an old man. I want to sit by the fire and bore the very pattern off the wallpaper!"

"I wish I was dead—God forbid!" says Montague Glass. In the same spirit I have often wished that I had never laid eyes on my wife—but I can never stand for her to be out of my sight for more than five hours at a time.

## WHAT KIND OF HUSBANDS DO "JIMMIES" MAKE?

How about the sons and daughters of the rich? Those whose engagements and marriages are this day announced on society pages the country over. What kind of a success will they make of marriage and what sort of ideals are they capable of passing on to their children? Consider:

The door captain at the Mont Mihiel Restaurant approaches Eddie, the head waiter, with a distraught expression in his eyes.

"Young Mr. Jimmy Worthington is outside," he says.

"Drunk?" asks Eddie.

"He can hardly stand up."

"Is he dressed?" Eddie does not mean: Is he in his underwear?—though this would not surprise him a great deal. He means: Does he have on a dinner coat?

"Yes."

"All right," says Eddie. "Show him in."

### JIMMY'S IDEAS ABOUT LIFE

And into the Mont Mihiel cafe reels that peerless aristocrat, that fine flower of American civilization, young Mr. Jimmy Worthington. His father made a fortune hoarding food during the war but the son scorns commerce and has gone in for aristocracy on a large scale.

I have often talked to Jimmy and tried to find out his ideas about life. It is an enlightening if somewhat alarming experience, for Jimmy's conversation is chiefly a history of his more recent dissipations. He has heard his father make remarks about "these dangerous radicals," so Jimmy thinks of all the policemen and soldiers in America as a sort of bodyguard to protect his person from the "lower classes."

He thinks that when he is arrested for running his car 60 miles an hour he can always get out of trouble by handing his captor a large enough bill—and he knows that even if he has the bad luck to run over someone when he's drunk, his father will buy off the family

---

*Baltimore American* 30 (March 1924): ME-7.

and keep him out of jail. This is a complete summary of Jimmy's attitude toward the government under which he lives.

### FASHIONS IN BEHAVIOR

It has been the fashion for the last five years to blame rich girls for the "wildness" of the younger generation. Women, however, are always just what men make them. In 1840, women were required to faint to show their delicacy—in 1924, women are required to dissipate to show their sportsmanship. Occasionally the revulsion from some orgy throws Jimmy in a panic into the arms of a girl of character. But, as a rule, he marries someone like himself.

Jimmy and Mrs. Jimmy have a year of dissipation together. Mrs. Jimmy is "a good sport"—she has to be; if she ceased being one Jimmy would find another lady to be a good sport in her stead. Perhaps at the end of a year or two, there is a single child—not particularly wanted nor particularly unwanted; not the center of the household, apparently, nor the result of any scheme of life—simply a child which exists through its infancy in a sort of vacuum; not unloved but, somehow, an incongruity inasmuch as its parents, though they may have three houses, have not yet succeeded in establishing anything in the nature of a home.

On the contrary, they are already drifting apart. Their bonds were never very close, for in the world of continual stimulation in which they moved they never really regarded marriage as a permanent thing.

### JIMMY'S CHILDREN

The psychological effect of the child on Mrs. Jimmy begins a new era in their marriage. Something is wrong and she knows it. She is torn between her natural love for the child and the idea that she's got to keep up with Jimmy. But the problem is solved for her by Jimmy, who has learned to amuse himself without her. To all intents and purposes their marriage is over.

Let us suppose though that Jimmy and Mrs. Jimmy remain together after a fashion and have a series of three children over an interval of 10 years. Is Jimmy in any position to supervise their education? Not he. He hasn't even the wisdom to leave them intelligently alone.

He knows by this time that there is something wrong with his life and his one idea is that his children shall be unlike himself. And of all the intolerant, mean and unjust parents in the world, an ex-libertine is the worst. He looks with horror on the mildest escapade.

While at no period in the world's history, perhaps, has a larger proportion of the family income been spent upon display, an even worse phenomenon is observable in those who come into direct contact with the irresponsible rich. Every wealthy set in the big cities has many couples who, from their inability to pay the heavy financial cost of post-prohibition entertaining, have become nothing more than sponges and parasites.

I know dozens of boys who have never been able to live down expensive educations—who have come into contact with the rich, wasting class at the big prep-schools and universities and never realized that what young Midas wastes today was once paid for by old Midas, his grandfather, and that what he himself wastes is going to be sweated out of his parents' inadequate bank book. He sees young Midas reel through life like Jimmy, or if he wants to work, become a director in six companies on his twenty-fifth birthday. So the poor but lazy young man gets a confused, jealous and distorted picture of the world.

Is Jimmy, lasting a month in Wall Street, to blame for his failure to hold a job? What possible attraction can Wall Street hold for him? Joy in the work? He hates the work—he is too dull and slow for it. Money? He knows there's plenty of money at home and his for the asking. Pride? But he need feel no shame in being a parasite since half the rich young men he knows are just as lazy and useless as himself. Responsibility?

Here we come to something that sets the American "leisure class" off from the leisure class of all other nations—and makes it probably the most shallow, most hollow, most pernicious leisure class in the world. It has frequently no consciousness that leisure is a privilege, not a right, and that a privilege always implies a responsibility.

Look for a minute at the so-called English aristocracy, a favorite butt of American comics. Mention it, and you bring up before the small town eye a picture of an anaemic, weak-chinned individual with a small coronet on the side of his head. This picture is, of course, about as lifelike as the antiquated British idea that Americans were engaged in a permanent buffalo hunt.

### SONS OF THE NEWLY RICH

In the first place, the young Englishman of wealth heretofore has made an honest attempt to go into politics and run his government. He may not have been brilliant at it, but he was rich and he didn't need bribes and stock presents and tips on the market—and that's why the British Government has been incomparably the cleanest government in the world. Compared to it, recent developments would make the American Government appear to be a barnyard of scandal and corruption. Can you imagine the Teapot Dome oil disclosures or wounded-veteran graft having happened in the British Isles?

There is, of course, the Jimmy in England too, but he is in a minority there. Here, since the war, at least, Jimmy has become a majority of the rich boys of the land. He occurs most frequently among the newly rich. The older families often have some tradition of responsibility. Their boys go into politics if they can afford it or into law or one of the arts. They are sent to carefully chosen schools—schools which realize that the rich boy must be broken into habits of work and discipline when he is young. And they are given no such allowances as the Jimmies are given.

There was a boy in my class at Princeton who was the son of one of the oldest and wealthiest families in the Middle West. During his freshman year he kept an account book with a record of every dollar he spent. I make no comment on the value of this particular practice, but it shows how necessary it seemed to this boy's father that he should have a sense of responsibility—if not to the country, at least to the fortune he was some day to control.

### ONE ENCOURAGING FACT

Probably the most encouraging thing about the Jimmies is that they don't survive—survive, I mean, as rich men. The largest purse has a bottom, and though Jimmy never works while he can bluff and sponge and borrow his way along, his children will have to take what scraps remain and start again in the middle class.

Since I was seven years old, just 20 years ago, I have seen in my own experience the break up of five sizable fortunes. Out in St. Paul, where I was born, a dozen houses still stand that were once inhabited by one-generation "aristocrats." The "aristocrats" are dead now and their fortunes have melted away; their children, who had no sense of responsibility, even toward their fathers' money, are bad examples around the streets or, at best, starting life over again with nothing but their own talents and a pioneer name.

This phenomenon, remember, is peculiarly American. English families seldom, if ever, decay with such rapidity, because they are founded not on sand but on aristocracy. And real aristocracy, whatever its faults, is willing to undergo a discipline of its own.

### A PRETENTIOUS MOCKERY

The leisure class of England are not soft. They have their scandals, their wastrels, their roués—but in London one never gets the impression that one does sometimes in New York, that all society is a silly, pretentious, vicious mockery of a defunct feudal regime.

Let the American rich have their summer and winter places which tower over our suburban bungalows; let them keep 12 suits and servants to our one. The founder of a great family has been shrewd and successful and bought his descendants soft, fine things that no relative has seen fit to provide for us.

Theoretically, at least, we have the same chance for a marble mausoleum as all the Astors in England and America. It is not so much what the rich do as what they don't do that becomes more and more deplorable each year. They grow softer and softer—and Jimmy's father is now just as soft as Jimmy. Let two dozen workmen meet behind a barn and he bursts out in a cold sweat, casts aside eight centuries of justice and tries to get half a dozen bewildered foreigners sent to Leavenworth for 10 years. He stocks his cellar with liquor and then votes righteously for prohibition "for the good of the masses."

And Jimmy's father after a hard office day looks for his ideals—to his wife.

The effect of this on the children of the rich has been enormous. Women are not public-spirited and they are not natural idealists— they are too "practical" to be concerned with anything that is not their own. When they make standards they are inclined to make violently selfish and unchivalric standards.

Can you imagine the usual very rich woman urging her son to go into politics for the good of the country—if, say, he were making a big success in business? The thing is inconceivable. Women do have vast dreams for their children, but when it comes down to cases their desire is that their children shall take no chances and, at all costs, keep out of trouble.

Many American rich boys of this generation get what ideals they have from their mothers. The boy watches his mother's almost insane strivings toward a social position commensurate with her money. He sees her change her accent, her clothes, her friends, her very soul, as she pushes her way up in life, pulling her busy husband with her. Jimmy's idea of politics becomes the remembrance of some preposterous women's club that met at his mother's house one day. Politics, he thinks, is a thing where ugly women read long dull papers made up out of the month's newspaper editorials.

By the time he is twenty-one Jimmy is about as public-spirited as a rattle-snake. He is not told that his father grew rich because America is the richest country in the world and his father was somewhat shrewder and more industrious than other men. He is told that his father is an unselfish individual who "helped develop the country." He is told that because his father has done this noble work he can now look down on everyone less rich than he. This privilege, the boy gathers from his mother, is the highest inspiration of which a citizen is capable.

So, as it turns out, our rich boy grows up in one of two ways. Either he learns a set of intensely soft, intensely selfish ideals at his mother's knee and spends his life busily adding to the fortune that his father made; or he learns no ideals at all, and assuming that aristocracy is a sort of drunken reel between two long lines of bribed policemen, spends his life and money in a riot of extravagance and petty vice.

### FIVE HUNDRED OF RICHEST

What a waste! Think of the hundreds of first-rate men who have come out of the British leisure class—statesmen, poets, painters, architects, soldiers, scientists, physicians, philosophers, empire builders—men who have made life easier and more beautiful by having lived. And then look at the American leisure class and note that it has produced—well, two Presidents out of twenty-seven! The greatest Americans have come almost invariably from the very poor class—Lincoln, Edison, Whitman, Ford, Mark Twain.

All that leisure—for nothing! All that wealth—it has begotten waste and destruction and dissipation and snobbery—nothing more. Three generations of chorus girls and racetrack touts and one generation of bootleggers have profited from it—that is all.

Is this to go on forever? Are the rich to breed 10,000 Jimmies until they become a race apart—or will they find that if they want to survive they must realize what really is the responsibility toward the country? Otherwise it will be brought home to them in the decay and failure of their own begotten sons.

## OUR YOUNG RICH BOYS

A few years ago there were so many experts on the younger generation, like for instance, the lady who wrote "Dancing with the Darkies" (which I may say I have never seen done in my own city), and Madame Glyn who said that young ladies always checked their corsets at dances. So every time I went to a dance in those days I always inquired for the corset check-room because I wanted to see a lot of corsets all hung up in a row. I even asked young ladies, while entering a dance, if there was anything they would like to check, but they never handed me anything immoral—even when I shut my eyes and held out my hand in case they should be embarrassed.

Then came the kind of younger generation who were all dressed up in bell-bottom trousers. The excitement was at fever heat. The newspapers in my town were afraid that the bell-bottoms would seize the city hall, raise a pair of trousers on the flag-staff and kill all the he-men.

Personally it made me nervous to have bells or any sort of musical instruments attached to my trousers, but I had no objections to anyone else doing it if he liked.

If you want to read about any of these kinds you had better lay this down right now. This is about the young man who was once saddled with the ghastly name of "male flapper"—a name that is as depressing as "lady wrestler," and was about as popular with the young man as "Liberty Lads" was with the doughboys.

The midland cities have changed. Apartment houses have risen on the vacant lots where football teams composed of wealthy boys once played against football teams composed of "muckers." At fourteen the wealthy boy is no longer anxious to have enormous

---

*McCall's* 53 (October 1925): 12ff. Fitzgerald's article appeared alongside an article by Zelda entitled "What Became of the Flappers?" The joint title was "What Becomes of Our Flappers and Sheiks?" Illustrations were by John Held, Jr., who executed drawings for the dust jackets of *Tales of the Jazz Age* and *The Vegetable*.

muscles and be Ted Coy of Yale, but to own a sport car and be Ben Lyon—or even Michael Arlen. The cheap literature of daring, of Nick Carter and Young Wild West, has vanished. It is a conquered world into which the post-war boy grows up; there are no outposts of civilization to grasp his imagination. He gets the impression that everything has been done. Instead of the Henty books he reads the moving picture magazines.

If by the time he is fifteen he hasn't a car of his own, some one else in his crowd is sure to have one—some one a little older or some one whose parents are too careless or too new to their money to think what having a car may mean. With a car one can be downtown, across a city, out of sight in fifteen minutes. So young Tommy gets his car and the fun begins. What could be more harmless than for Tommy to take Marjorie to the movies? Why Marjorie's mother and Tommy's mother have known each other all their lives. Besides, it's done—other children do it. So Tommy and Marjorie are licensed to drift where they will through the summer night.

The probabilities are that Tommy and Marjorie will never so much as kiss. He tells her how he once "picked up a chicken" and took her to ride, and Marjorie is impressed with his temerity. Sometimes there is a faint excitement, a faint glow between them. Usually—not always, but usually—there is nothing more.

Tommy becomes sixteen. He goes out every night now—to the movies, to a dance, to a gathering on a girl's porch. It seems to his parents that there is always something and that the something always sounds harmless and is always what the other boys are doing. In fact, what worries Tommy's parents is what he is *not* doing. He was bright, as a little boy, but now, because he never has time to work at night, his report cards from his local private school are invariably unsatisfactory. There remains a solution of course—the prep-school. Smiles of relief from the parents. The prep-school will do the trick. Nothing easier than passing it off on somebody else. It is discovered, however, that most of the stricter and more thorough prep-schools have an annoying habit of asking for the boy before fifteen—and refusing to take him any older. So he is sent instead to some small prep-school in New York state or New Jersey that is not so particular.

A year passes. The popular Tommy takes his preliminary examinations for college. The examinations are an absurd hodge-podge and as the preparations for them have failed to intrigue Tommy's interest he scratches through, say, one out of five. He is glad to be home for the summer. He has his car again, and with the other boys of his age, is beginning to go to dances at various country clubs. He finds this most amusing—an unbearably pleasant contrast to the childish restraint of his prep-school. In fact, when autumn comes he persuades his father to send him to one of those curious institutions that are springing up all over the east—the tutoring schools.

Now the tutoring school has neither the discipline of a prep-school nor any of the restraining force that lies in the modeled public opinion of a great university. Theoretically the fact that there is no football team gives the boy time to concentrate on cramming. Actually it gives him time to do what he likes. The masters are smarter and better-paid than the masters in the small prep-schools. In fact they are so smart and they explain everything so clearly that they completely cure Tommy of any faculty of working things out for himself. It is notorious that although the tutoring school boys generally get into college they seldom survive the first mid-year examinations.

Meanwhile the lack of athletic activities in the school drives Tommy to express his vitality in other ways. He smokes incessantly and experiments with alcohol. Some of the boys are twenty and twenty-one years old. They are dull and unimaginative or they would long since have passed their examinations, so, for stimulus and amusement they turn to—New York. And Tommy does too. Many of the boys have automobiles because their parents realize how bored they would otherwise be.

We are almost all newly rich in America, and the number of millionaires who have any definite idea of a modern education is so small as to be negligible. They are aware, however, that their sons require an astonishing lot of money to keep up with the "other boys." An Englishman goes through an Eton and Oxford that are not so different from what they were in his father's time. The Harvard graduate of 1870 could keep a pretty good tab on his

Harvard son of 1900. But all that Mr. Thomas senior in San Francisco knows about his son's school is that it promises to get Tommy into college.

Tommy is now eighteen. He is handsomely dressed and an excellent dancer, and he knows three chorus girls in the Follies by their first names. He takes this side of life much more seriously than does the college man—he has no senior societies or upper class clubs to hold up a warning finger. His life is one long weekend.

Coming home for another summer Tommy resumes his country-club existence in a somewhat haughty manner. His home town, if it happens to be in the middle west, bores him now. With a rather pathetic wistfulness he still reads the moving-picture magazines and thinks naively that he would like to have a test taken for the screen. He sees in the newspaper that the younger generation has been debauched by the movies and corrupted by jazz music, and in a dim way he supposes that the newspapers are right. He finds that the only things which do not seem to have given his friends a shove downward are the pie-eating contest and the penny arcade. Mingled with such nonsense he finds the statement that the boy of today is a great deal less courteous than his older brother in the preceding generation. And this, despite Tommy's ease of manner and his apparent worldliness, is quite true. It is due in some measure to modern dancing—not, as our local Savonarolas think, to the steps that are danced, but to the "cutting in" system which has cut the ground from under the unattractive girl.

In the age of the program, two or three dances were always devoted to the fat girl or the female Ben Turpin because Tommy's father and her father were friends. It wasn't anything to look forward to, even then, but nowadays if Tommy should ask her to dance he would have to dance with her until the musicians packed up their sandpaper and went home.

Tommy has never learned courtesy. He has no faith in any conventions but his own. If you tell him that his manners or his dance are "common," are borrowed from the lower classes, he will laugh at you and be right. He knows that if he wants to see close dancing forbidden or steps censored he must go to the cheap dance halls, the amusement park pavillions or the cabarets in small cities where the bouncer and the policewoman are on the alert to enforce the proprieties and keep the patrons from being—"common."

He is now nineteen. By this time he has managed to pass off almost enough examinations to get into college. But his ambition to enter college is on the wane—at least it fails to inspire him to successful effort. Perhaps the war occurred when he was at tutoring school and in the attendant disorganization of the universities he came to feel that it was the natural thing to give up going or leave in mid-term or find one's educational status in a sort of bizarre jumble. Besides, he thinks that he has had all the college has to offer—except the curriculum. So he comes home at twenty, perhaps after a hectic half-year at New Haven or Princeton, having now assumed to himself all the privileges of aristocracy without any of its responsibilities. He is a complete parasite, polished without being cultured, and "fast" without being vicious. There is nothing effeminate about him. He is healthy, good looking, a bit vacuous—perfectly useless.

I like Tommy personally. He interests me. He is pleasant company. And if he is useless, he knows it and makes a joke of it, says he is "dumb" and blames himself. He is convinced that he wasn't smart enough to get through college. He prefers married women to flappers, who rather bore him. You couldn't call him a "male flapper" to his face because he would probably knock you down—golf and boxing are liable to be his two accomplishments. He is simply a boy who under different circumstances might have been what is known in the editorials as "a useful member of society." He might have done more than cornered the wheat or manufactured a new potato peeler. If the wilderness is conquered there is a whole world of science, theoretical and applied, calling out for recruits who have money and time to spare.

I must admit that personally I have passed on. I am not even part of the younger generation. I have reached the stage where I ask, "How is the food?" instead of "How is the music?" And I have learned my dance. Once I was always among those two or three couples who stand up at the overture and hesitate and look at other couples to see who will begin—and finally get off that world famous remark: "We don't want to give an exhibition!"

But that was back before the civil war when we used to do the good old lancers and the shimmee. Since then I have learned my dance. It is not much—in fact it is so out of date that I have been asked if it is something new—but I am going to stick to it.

And I can still watch the comedy from the chaperone's bench.

I have no solutions, although I am profoundly interested. Perhaps it is just as well that we cannot produce an aristocracy that is capable of surviving. Perhaps Tommy's ineffectuality is some indirect economic re-assertion of the principle of equality. Who knows? Perhaps he will turn about at thirty and reshape the world upon his own desire. It's little we can guess.

# MISCELLANEOUS

# THE AUTHOR'S APOLOGY

### The Author's Apology

I don't want to talk about myself because I'll admit I did that somewhat in this book. In fact, to write it took three months; to conceive it—three minutes; to collect the data in it—all my life. The idea of writing it came on the first of last July: it was a substitute form of dissipation.

My whole theory of writing I can sum up in one sentence: An author ought to write for the youth of his own generation, the critics of the next, and the schoolmasters of ever afterward.

So, gentlemen, consider all the cocktails mentioned in this book drunk by me as a toast to the American Booksellers Association.

MAY, 1920

*Sincerely,*
*F. Scott Fitzgerald*

---

Some 500 copies of this single-leaf item, all signed by Fitzgerald, were prepared for a meeting of the American Booksellers Association in May 1920. The leaves were tipped into copies of the third trade printing of *This Side of Paradise* (April 1920) for distribution to those who attended. Parts of "The Author's Apology" were used by Fitzgerald in "An Interview with Mr. Fitzgerald," which follows after the next item in this section. The copy reproduced here in facsimile is from the Princeton collections.

## CONTRIBUTIONS TO *THE AMERICAN CREDO*

### 22

That all male negroes can sing.

### 51

That George Bernard Shaw doesn't really believe anything he writes.

### 193

That whenever a vaudeville comedian quotes a familiar commercial slogan, such as "His Master's Voice," or "Eventually, why not now?", he is paid $50 a performance for doing so.

### 199

That all men named Clarence, Claude or Percy are sissies.

### 248

That a man of fifty-five is always more experienced than a man of thirty-five.

### 262

That John D. Rockefeller would give his whole fortune for a digestion good enough to digest a cruller.

---

From H. L. Mencken and George Jean Nathan, *The American Credo: A Contribution Toward the Interpretation of the National Mind* (New York: Knopf, 1920). For this collection, Mencken and Nathan solicited quips and witticisms from their literary friends. Fitzgerald marked his contributions in his personal copy of the book, which is among his papers at Princeton. See James L. W. West III, "F. Scott Fitzgerald's Contributions to *The American Credo*," *Princeton University Library Chronicle* 34 (Autumn 1972): 53–58.

## 429

That all the schoolboys in Boston have bulged brows, wear large spectacles and can read Greek.

## 433

That all the cheaper brands of cigarettes are sophisticated with drugs, and in time cause those who smoke them to get softening of the brain.

## 442

That lighting three cigarettes with one match will bring some terrible calamity upon one or other of the three smokers.

## 449

That all the great writers of the world now use typewriters.

## 450

That all Presidents of the United States get many hot tips on the stock-market, but that they are too honourable to play them, and so turn them over to their wives, who make fortunes out of them.

## 455

That George M. Cohan and Irving Berlin can only play the piano with one finger.

## AN INTERVIEW WITH MR. FITZGERALD

### by F. Scott Fitzgerald

With the distinct intention of taking Mr. Fitzgerald by surprise I ascended to the twenty-first floor of the Biltmore and knocked in the best waiter-manner at the door. On entering my first impression was one of confusion—a sort of rummage sale confusion. A young man was standing in the center of the room turning an absent glance first at one side of the room and then at the other.

"I'm looking for my hat," he said dazedly. "How do you do. Come on in and sit on the bed."

The author of *This Side of Paradise* is sturdy, broad-shouldered and just above medium height. He has blond hair with the suggestion of a wave and alert green eyes—the mélange somewhat Nordic—and good-looking too, which was disconcerting as I had somehow expected a thin nose and spectacles.

We had preliminaries—but I will omit the preliminaries. They consisted in searching for things: cigarettes, a blue tie with white dots, an ash tray. But as he was obviously quite willing to talk, and seemed quite receptive to my questions, we launched off directly on his ideas of literature.

"How long did it take to write your book?" I began.

"To write it—three months, to conceive it—three minutes. To collect the data in it—all my life. The idea of writing it occurred to me on the first of last July. It was sort of a substitute form of dissipation."

---

*Saturday Review* 43 (5 November 1960): 26, 56. Fitzgerald fabricated this self-interview a few weeks after the publication of *This Side of Paradise* and gave it to the publicity department at Charles Scribner's Sons. The department sent a copy to the book critic Heywood Broun; he quoted from it in his *New York Tribune* column for 7 May 1920, p. 14. The full text of the self-interview, from Fitzgerald's manuscript, appeared for the first time in the *Saturday Review* in 1960, as cited above. Robert Hichens, mentioned near the end of the interview, was an English novelist, short-story writer, and satirist.

"What are your plans now?" I asked him.

He gave a long sigh and shrugged his shoulders.

"I'll be darned if I know. The scope and depth and breadth of my writings lie in the laps of the gods. If knowledge comes naturally, through interest, as Shaw learned his political economy or as Wells devoured modern science—why, that'll be slick. On study itself—that is in 'reading up' a subject—I haven't anthill-moving faith. Knowledge must cry out to be known—cry out that only I can know it, and then I'll swim in it to satiety as I've swum in—in many things."

"Please be frank."

"Well, you know if you've read my book. I've swum in various seas of adolescent egotism. But what I meant was that if big things never grip me—well, it simply means I'm not cut out to be big. This conscious struggle to find bigness outside, to substitute bigness of theme for bigness of perception, to create an objective *magnum opus* such as *The Ring and the Book*—well, all that's the antithesis of my literary aims.

"Another thing," he continued. "My idea is always to reach my generation. The wise writer, I think, writes for the youth of his own generation, the critic of the next and the schoolmasters of ever afterward. Granted the ability to improve what he imitates in the way of style, to choose from his own interpretation of the experiences around him what constitutes material, and we get the first-water genius."

"Do you expect to be—to be—well, part of the great literary tradition?" I asked, timidly.

He became excited. He smiled radiantly. I saw he had an answer for this. "There's no great literary tradition," he burst out. "There's only the tradition of the eventual death of every literary tradition. The wise literary son kills his own father."

After this he began enthusiastically on style.

"By style, I mean color," he said. "I want to be able to do anything with words: handle slashing, flaming descriptions like Wells, and use the paradox with the clarity of Samuel Butler, the breadth of Bernard Shaw and the wit of Oscar Wilde. I want to do the wide sultry heavens of Conrad, the rolled-gold sundowns and crazy-quilt skies of Hichens and Kipling as well as the pastel dawns and twilights of Chesterton. All that is by way of example. As a matter of fact I am a professed literary thief, hot after the best methods of every writer in my generation."

The interview terminated about then. Four young men with philistine faces and conservative ties appeared and, looking at each other, exchanged broad winks. Mr. Fitzgerald faltered and seemed to lose his stride.

"Most of my friends are—are like those," he whispered as he showed me to the door. "I don't care for literary people much—they make me nervous."

It was really rather a good interview, wasn't it!

## ON THE GIRL SCOUTS

> # Ruggiero Auto and Cycle Co.
> Donate this space to the Girl Scouts this week
>
> I am glad of the chance to march along with the Girl Scouts. —James Hay, Jr.
>
> I know the work the Girl Scouts are doing and it has my enthusiastic approval. It will certainly make them all better voters, wives and mothers. — Arthur Train.
>
> **Gertrude Atherton** writes from Culver City, California, where she is working on the production of a movie from one of her books: "I heartily endorse the Girl Scout idea and you are welcome to use my name."
>
> Don't you think that after being hymned in the press as the creator of a particularly villainous type of flapper that it would be somewhat ironic for me to come out for the Girl Scouts?
>
> Nevertheless as I passed two very beautiful Girl Scouts on Fifth Avenue today I am inclined to feel rather friendly toward the organization.
> 
>       Very sincerely,
> *Daily*       (Signed)  F. Scott Fitzgerald."

---

This statement, from an unidentified newspaper, was clipped and pasted by Fitzgerald into one of his scrapbooks. James Hay, Jr., was a journalist and author of detective novels; Arthur Train, an attorney, wrote a popular series of legal thrillers published by Scribners; Gertrude Atherton, a middlebrow novelist, is remembered for *Black Oxen* (1923).

## THIS IS A MAGAZINE

### A Group of Familiar Characters from the American Periodical World

### By F. Scott Fitzgerald

*The scene is the vast and soggy interior of a magazine—not powder or pistol, but paper and popular. Over the outer curtain careens a lady on horseback in five colours. With one hand she raises a cup of tea to her glossy lips while with the other she follows through on a recent mashie shot, meanwhile keeping one rich-tinted, astounding eye upon the twist of her service and its mate on the volume of pleasant poetry in her other hand. The rising of the curtain reveals the back-drop as a patch-work of magazine covers. The furniture includes a table on which lies a single periodical, to convey the abstraction 'Magazine', and around it your players sit on chairs plastered with advertisements. Each actor holds a placard bearing the name of the character represented. For example, the Edith Wharton Story holds a placard which reads "By Edith Wharton, in three parts."*

*Near (but not in!) the left hand stage box is stationed a gentleman in underwear holding a gigantic placard which announces that "THIS IS A MAGAZINE".*

*As the Curtain rises the audience discovers the Edith Wharton Story attempting a* tête à tête *with a somewhat arrogant British Serial.*

THE EDITH WHARTON STORY (*a bit bitterly*): And before I could so much as shoot a saucy subtlety, there I was plumped down between an odious fable in broken Yiddish and this—this affair next to me.

> *'This affair' is a very vulgar and proletarian Baseball Yarn who sprawls colloquially in his chair.*

---

*Vanity Fair* 15 (December 1920): 71. The "mashie" (mentioned in the third sentence) was a golf club with approximately the loft of a five-iron. The "Penrod Story" on p. 388 would be by Booth Tarkington.

THE BASEBALL YARN: Was you speakin' to me, lady?
> (*On the lady's part a frigid and Jamesian silence. She looks, by the way, like a lady who has lived all her life in three-room apartments and had her nerves ruined by impulsive elevator boys.*)

THE BASEBALL YARN (*in brutal soliloquy*): If they could jes' stick a guy in a magazine where he could borrer one good chewter-backer!

A DETECTIVE STORY (*in a tense whisper*): There's one in my third paragraph. But be quiet and be careful not to break any retorts.

THE BASEBALL STORY (*facetiously*): Or make any, eh? Ha! Ha! Ha!

THE BRITISH SERIAL (*to* The Edith Wharton Story): I say, who's that little story over near the Editorial? Don't fancy I've seen her before since I've been running.

THE EDITH WHARTON STORY (*lowering her voice*): My Dear Man, she's a nobody. Seems to have no family—nothing but a past.

THE BRITISH SERIAL: She has a certain charm, but a deuced vulgar plot. (*He yawns.*)

THE BASEBALL YARN (*in a rude aside to the Detective Story*): The noble Duke looks a bit padded his own self. Say! Pipe the old grampa asleep on his advertisements.

THE DETECTIVE STORY: That's the Robert Chambers Serial. He's through this issue.

THE BASEBALL YARN: Kinda like that little thing next to him. New in here ain't she?

THE DETECTIVE STORY: New and scared.

THE BASEBALL YARN: Looks as if she was wrote with a soft pencil.

THE DETECTIVE STORY: Overdressed! Her illustrations cost more than she did.
> (*Several chairs down, a little Love Poem leans tenderly across a story to another Love Poem.*)

THE FIRST LOVE POEM: I adore your form.

THE SECOND LOVE POEM: You've got a good figure yourself—in your second line. But your meter looks a little strained.

THE FIRST LOVE POEM: You are the caesura in the middle of all my lines. Alas! someone will cut you out and paste you on a mirror—or send you to his sweetheart with "Isn't this lovely!" scrawled across you—or passepartout you.

THE SECOND LOVE POEM (*coyly*): Now you just get right back to your own page.

> (*At this point, the Robert Chambers Story awakens with a start, and walks rheumatically over to the Edith Wharton Story.*)

THE ROBERT CHAMBERS STORY (*asthmatically*): May I join you?

THE EDITH WHARTON STORY (*acidly*): You seemed well content to flirt with that sentimental little piece, behind the advertisements.

THE ROBERT CHAMBERS STORY: On the contrary, she bores me. Every character in her is born in wedlock. Still she's a relief from the Commercial yarns.

THE BRITISH SERIAL: You can be thankful you haven't got your feet between two smelly soap advertisements. (*He points to what appears to be a paralytic dwarf at his feet.*) Look! There's my Synopsis of Preceding Chapters all tangled up again.

THE ROBERT CHAMBERS STORY: Thank heavens, I'm published! I've had some annoying experiences in the last eight months. In one issue there was a Penrod Story next to me making so much noise that I couldn't hear my own love scenes.

THE EDITH WHARTON STORY (*cruelly*): Never mind. The shopgirls could fill them in with their eyes closed.

THE ROBERT CHAMBERS STORY (*sourly*): My dear lady, your climax is on crooked.

THE EDITH WHARTON STORY: At least I have one. They tell me you drag horribly.

THE BASEBALL YARN: Well, if the swells ain't scrappin' with each other!

THE EDITH WHARTON STORY: No one invited your comments.

THE BASEBALL YARN: Go on! You're full of dots!

THE EDITH WHARTON STORY: At least, I'm not full of mixed metaphors!

THE ROBERT CHAMBERS STORY: Weak repartee! Columnist's humor.

*(A new voice, very oratorical and sonorous, breaks in. It is—)*

THE POLITICAL ARTICLE: Come! There's nothing irreconcilable there. There's no knot so tight that there isn't a way out of the labyrinth.

THE LITTLE STORY WITHOUT A FAMILY (*timidly*): Dear folks, it's a sweet cosy world. So don't poison your little lungs with naughty, unkind words.

THE BRITISH SERIAL: Shades of those Porter women!

THE LITTLE STORY WITHOUT A FAMILY: You don't know what abuse is until you've been returned with "Join the Navy" stamped on your envelope.

THE BRITISH SERIAL: If I had been fished out of the waste-basket, I shouldn't boast about it!

THE BASEBALL YARN: Let her alone! She's a honest Gurl. I'll kick you one in the conclusion!

*(They rise and square off, eying each other menacingly. A contagious excitement springs up; the Basil King Revelation forgets its credulous queens and tears over; an Efficiency Article loses its head and runs wildly through the issue, and even the illustrations leap out of their borders, the half-tones vying democratically with the Ben Days, in reaching the scene. The excitement spreads to the advertisements. Mr. Madison Whims of Seattle falls into a jar of No-Hairo Cold Cream. A Health and Strength Giant arrives clinging to an earphone; a Short Story Course becomes covered with Rat Poison. The Circulation increases.*

*In fact, for a minute everything is something awful! Just as the number's minutes seem as numbered as its pages, a stentorian voice proceeds from the Table of Contents, an efficient-looking gentleman with a megaphone who has been sitting unnoticed in the orchestra: "Places! A Reader!" A hush falls; everyone scurries back into position, just as a thick and impenetrable dark descends upon the stage through which emerge, as an emanation from limbo, the large glossy eyes of the cover girl, on horseback in five colours.*

*A voice comes out of the dark and, in the great quiet, it is like the voice of God.)*

THE VOICE: Wonder if there's anything in this worth readin'. Sure is some queen on the cover!

AN INSERT JOKE (*laughing feebly*): Hee! Hee! Hee! (*It is the grotesque and horrible cackle of an old man.*)

*The lights go on to show that the curtain is now down. In front of it sits a reader, a lone stage hand. He wears an expression of tremendous and triumphant boredom. He is reading the magazine.*

## THREE CITIES

It began in Paris, that impression—fleeting, chiefly literary, unprofound—that the world was growing darker. We carefully reconstructed an old theory and, blond both of us, cast supercilious Nordic glances at the play of the dark children around us. We had left America less than one half of one per cent American, but the pernicious and sentimental sap was destined to rise again within us. We boiled with ancient indignations toward the French. We sat in front of Anatole France's house for an hour in hope of seeing the old gentleman come out—but we thought simultaneously that when he dies, the France of flame and glory dies with him. We drove in the Bois de Boulogne—thinking of France as a spoiled and revengeful child which, having kept Europe in a turmoil for two hundred years, has spent the last forty demanding assistance in its battles, that the continent may be kept as much like a bloody sewer as possible.

In Brentano's near the Café de la Paix, I picked up Dreiser's suppressed "Genius" for three dollars. With the exception of "The Titan" I liked it best among his five novels, in spite of the preposterous Christian Science episode near the end. We stayed in Paris long enough to finish it.

Italy, which is to the English what France is to the Americans, was in a pleasant humor. As a French comedy writer remarked we inevitably detest our benefactors, so I was glad to see that Italy was casting off four years of unhealthy suppressed desires. In Florence you could hardly blame a squad of Italian soldiers for knocking down an Omaha lady who was unwilling to give up her compartment to a Colonel. Why, the impudent woman could not speak Italian! So the *Carabinieri* can hardly be blamed for being incensed. And as for knocking her around a little—well, boys will be boys.

---

*Brentano's Book Chat* 1 (September–October 1921): 15, 28. From the Fitzgeralds' first trip to Europe, May–July 1921. The first three novels mentioned in the fifth paragraph are by Booth Tarkington. *Moon-Calf* is by Floyd Dell. In the final paragraph Fitzgerald means High Street, a major thoroughfare in Oxford. The Via Appia, or Appian Way, was an important road of the ancient Roman republic.

The American ambassadorial tradition in Rome having for some time been in the direct line of sentimental American literature, I do not doubt that even they found some compensating sweetness in the natures of the naughty *Bersaglieri*.

We were in Rome two weeks. You can see the fascination of the place. We stayed two weeks even though we could have left in two days—that is we *could* have left if we had not run out of money. I met John Carter, the author of "These Wild Young People," in the street one day and he cashed me a check for a thousand lira. We spent this on ointment. The ointment trust thrives in Rome. All the guests at the two best hotels are afflicted with what the proprietors call "mosquitoes too small for screens." We do not call them that in America.

John Carter lent us "Alice Adams" and we read it aloud to each other under the shadow of Caesar's house. If it had not been for Alice we should have collapsed and died in Rome as so many less fortunate literary people have done. "Alice Adams" more than atones for the childish heroics of "Ramsey Milholland" and for the farcical spiritualism in "The Magnificent Ambersons." After having made three brave attempts to struggle through "Moon-Calf" it was paradise to read someone who knows how to write.

By bribing the ticket agent with one thousand lira to cheat some old General out of his compartment—the offer was the agent's, not ours—we managed to leave Italy.

"*Vous avez quelque chose pour déclarer?*" asked the border customs officials early next morning (only they asked it in better French).

I awoke with a horrible effort from a dream of Italian beggars.

"*Oui!*" I shrieked. "*Je veux déclare que je suis très, très heureux a partir d'Italie!*" I could understand at last why the French loved France. They have seen Italy.

We had been to Oxford before—after Italy we went back there, arriving gorgeously at twilight when the place was fully peopled for us by the ghosts of ghosts—the characters, romantic, absurd or melancholy, of "Sinister Street," "Zuleika Dobson" and "Jude the Obscure." But something was wrong now—something that would never be right again. Here was Rome—here on The High were the shadows of the Via Appia. In how many years would our descendents approach this ruin with supercilious eyes to buy postcards from men of a short, inferior race—a race that once were Englishmen. How soon—for money follows the rich lands and the healthy stock, and art follows begging after money. Your time will come, New York, fifty years, sixty. Apollo's head is peering crazily, in new colors that our generation will never live to know, over the tip of the next century.

## REMINISCENSES OF DONALD STEWART

By F. Scott Fitzgerald
(In the Manner of . . . . . . . . . . .)

Sitting surrounded by my children and fortified by many tons of coal at $20 a ton, against the northern winter, it pleases me to look back upon the days of my youth. Back and back, as the flames flicker, I seem to gaze upon those very first moments of my literary career and the years give up a certain name to be pondered upon—the name of a companion of my youth, now, like me, a white-beard grown old in the service of letters—his name, Donald Ogden Stewart.

How well do I remember our first meeting! It was at a dinner of Sidney Strong's at the University club. Donald Ogden Stewart said:

"How do you do?"

And quick as a flash I answered.

"Very well thank you."

With these first words we seemed to understand that there was a kinship between us. We were not monkeys, but MEN. There was no doubt about it. We could talk, we could laugh, we could shimmee—

Ah, the old days! Those quaint old fashioned dances like the shimmee—How different from the rough boisterous steps I see performed by the youngsters of today. But I depart from the subject, the old man's mind is feeble and it wanders.

The first thing he said to me, I think, was: "Let's commit a burglary!"

Oh the simple hearts of those days, the pleasures!

Then he wanted us to break the windows of an undertaker just established on Summit ave. I remember the smile of amusement that this quaint old idea aroused. But that was Don—innocent, trying

---

*St. Paul Daily News*, 11 December 1921, City Life Section, p. 6. Stewart, a writer whom Fitzgerald had befriended in St. Paul in 1919, had published "The Courtship of Miles Standish—In the Manner of F. Scott Fitzgerald" in his book *A Parody Outline of History* (1921). Fitzgerald's reminiscence is a rejoinder. Fitzgerald and Stewart worked together as screenwriters in Hollywood in 1939.

# Last Kiss

always to see things for the best. After that, I remember him at a party. He caused to be thrown on a white screen, upside down, a picture of a religious revival in South Africa and in his naive and gullible way he thought, he believed, mind you, that this was the photograph of the reunion of a certain family well known in St. Paul. He believed it! And of course everybody was laughing at him. Nobody believed it was that family. Why, the people in the picture were upside down. It was absurd.

Then at another party he pretended that he was a ventriloquist. That's what he told everybody. And anybody who was at the party could see that he was not. All it took was common sense to see that he wasn't. The doll that he was supposed to have in his lap was not a doll. It was a real fellow. How he thought he'd get away with it I don't know. Everybody that came knew it wasn't a doll even when it moved its mouth and head. So they gave poor Don the laugh as usual and made a guy of him. He felt pretty cheap after that.

How cheerful was St. Paul while he was here. He made all the women feel beautiful and all the men feel witty. He went to the opening of a "one-building university" down in southern Minnesota, enrolled as a freshman, made the football team and was initiated into the Delta Omicron Psi fraternity. Then his vacation was over and he came back to St. Paul to his position—putting up telephone wires or tearing them down or something.

When the snow came he would throw snowballs against my window about midnight and we would stroll out Summit ave. wondering if we had the nerve to call on Father Barron and start a small hours discussion as to the ascetic ideals of the 13th century or whether, after all, we hadn't better break the undertaker's window to assert the sacro-sanctity of Summit ave. against the invasions of mortuary commerce.

Sometimes, when the snow covered boulevard was deserted, we would give his favorite Colgate college cheer: "Comes out like a ribbon, lies flat on the brush"—or he would speculate as to how he could inject his synthetic gin of humor into an imitation vermouth party that promised to be awfully dull.

It's not the same town without him—so say many of us. A scandal is only a scandal, but he could turn a Sunday school picnic into a public holiday. But we were all young then. And as I look around at my white haired compatriots I wonder that the old days have gone. Ah, that was away back before the arms conference, when Fatty Arbuckle was still respectable, when bobbed hair was considered daring. Sic transit. The author of "A Parody Outline of History" and I are old men. I realize at last that our work is behind us and our day is done.

## WHAT I WAS ADVISED TO DO—AND DIDN'T

By F. Scott Fitzgerald
Author of "The Beautiful and Damned," etc.

> "Good morning, Mr. Fitzgerald," said the man with horn-rimmed spectacles. "I was asked to come down to the copy department and speak to you about writing. I understand that you received $30 for a story. Now I have had five stories in the Saturday Evening Post during the last ten years and I know the game from A to Z. There's nothing in it. It's all right for picking up a little spare cash, but as for making a living at it, it won't do. You're dreaming. It would take ten years before you'd even begin to get a start. In the meanwhile, you'd starve. Take my advice, give up writing and stay at your job."
>
> I didn't!

---

*Philadelphia Public Ledger*, 22 April 1922, p. 11.

## HOW I WOULD SELL MY BOOK IF I WERE A BOOKSELLER

By F. Scott Fitzgerald

*Author of "This Side of Paradise" "Flappers and Philosophers" and "The Beautiful and the Damned."*

*Mr. Fitzgerald (unusually fortunate in instantaneous popularity) was born in St. Paul, Minn., in the fall of 1896. After his graduation from Princeton University, he served in the war as first lieutenant of the 45th Infantry as aide-de-camp to General T. A. Ryan. He worked at advertising for five months and so cordially hated it that he gave it up, went back to St. Paul and wrote "This Side of Paradise," which was accepted before his 23rd birthday. His writing career began at eleven years of age. Nothing else really interested him. He wrote two Triangle Club plays at Princeton, but the impetus which produced "This Side of Paradise" and the eight short stories in "Flappers and Philosophers," written in the short space of five months, was the desire to get married, which he did in 1921.*

I believe that a book by a well-known author should be given a full window display—I don't believe a mixed window display of four books for four days is nearly as effective as that of one book for one day. To attract attention it might be a coy idea to set all the books upside down and to have a man with large spectacles sitting in the midst of them, frantically engrossed in the perusal of a copy. He should have his eyes wide with rapt attention and his left hand on his heart.

Seriously, the above title puzzles me. If I were a bookseller I should probably push the most popular book of the season, whether it was trash or not.

---

*Bookseller and Stationer* 18 (15 January 1923): 8. In the third paragraph, Fitzgerald is mentioning his contemporaries John V. A. Weaver, John Peale Bishop, and Thomas Boyd. The "average bob-skirted 'Dulcy'" in paragraph five is the flapper character in *Dulcy: A Comedy in Three Acts* (1921), by George S. Kaufman and Marc Connelly.

The vogue of books like mine depends almost entirely on the stupendous critical power at present wielded by H. L. Mencken. And it is his influence at second hand that is particularly important. Such men as Weaver, in *The Brooklyn Eagle*; Bishop, in *Vanity Fair*; Boyd, in the *St. Paul News*, and dozens of others, show the liberal tendencies which Mencken has popularized.

The growing demand for likely American books is almost directly created by these men, who give no room to trash in their columns and, city by city, are making the work of living writers acceptable to the wavering and uncertain "better public."

I did not know "This Side of Paradise" was a flapper book until George Jean Nathan, who had read parts of it before publication, told me it was. However, I do not consider any of my heroines typical of the average bob-skirted "Dulcy" who trips through the Biltmore lobby at tea time. My heroine is what the flapper would like to *think* she is—the actual flapper is a much duller and grayer proposition. I tried to set down different aspects of an individual—I was accused of creating a type.

I think that if I were a bookseller with a real interest in better books I would announce the new good books as the publisher announced them to me and take orders from customers in advance.

"See here," I would say; "this is a novel by Fitzgerald; you know, the fella who started all that business about flappers. I understand that his new one is terribly sensational (the word 'damn' is in the title). Let me put you down for one."

And this would be approximately true. I am not in love with sensationalism, but I must plead guilty to it in this instance. And I feel quite sure that, though my books may annoy many, they will bore no one.

## SOME STORIES THEY LIKE TO TELL AGAIN

F. Scott Fitzgerald:
"The following story, which from interior evidence I judge to be at least twenty-five years old, has amused me more than any I've heard in years:

"The scene is a banquet in Victorian England. Wine is flowing freely. Dinner is at last over and the chief speaker arises unsteadily to begin his oration with a toast.

"The chief speaker (holding a wavering glass on high): 'Gen'lemen—the queal!'

"I can hear the editors of THE HERALD protest that I have a curious sense of humor. None the less it's my favorite story."

---

*New York Herald*, 8 April 1923, Magazine Section, p. 11.

## 10 BEST BOOKS I HAVE READ

by F. Scott Fitzgerald

(Author of "This Side of Paradise," "The Beautiful and Damned," etc.)

Samuel Butler's "Note Books." The mind and heart of my favorite Victorian.

"The Philosophy of Friedrich Nietzsche" (H. L. Mencken). A keen, hard intelligence interpreting the Great Modern Philosopher.

"Portrait of the Artist as a Young Man" (James Joyce). Because James Joyce is to be the most profound literary influence in the next fifty years.

"Zuleika Dobson" (Max Beerbohm). For the sheer delight of its exquisite snobbery.

"The Mysterious Stranger" (Mark Twain). Mark Twain in his most sincere mood. A book and a startling revelation.

"Nostromo" (Joseph Conrad). The great novel of the past fifty years, as "Ulysses" is the great novel of the future.

"Vanity Fair" (Thackeray). No explanation required.

"The Oxford Book of English Verse." This seems to me a better collection than Palgrave's.

"Thaïs" (Anatole France). The great book of the man who is Wells and Shaw together.

"Seventeen" (Booth Tarkington). The funniest book I've ever read.—

*Jersey City Evening Journal*, 24 April 1923, p. 9. Syndicated by North American Newspaper Alliance.

## CENSORSHIP OR NOT

Then Mr. Fitzgerald:

"The clean-book bill will be one of the most immoral measures ever adopted. It will throw American art back into the junk-heap where it rested comfortably between the Civil War and the World War. The really immoral books like 'Simon Called Peter' and 'Mumbo Jumbo' won't be touched, they'll attack Hergesheimer, Dreiser, Anderson and Cabell, whom they detest because they can't understand. George Moore, Hardy and Anatole France who are unintelligible to children and idiots will be supprest at once for debauching the morals of village clergymen."

---

*Literary Digest* 77 (23 June 1923): 31, 61. Fitzgerald wrote this piece for a symposium; other contributors included the writers George Ade, Sherwood Anderson, Owen Johnson, Irvin S. Cobb, and H. L. Mencken; the churchmen S. Parkes Cadman and Thomas Nicholson; the librarian Flora Warren Seymour; and the editor Henry Seidel Canby. The occasion was the effort in 1923 by Justice John Ford of the New York State Supreme Court to suppress D. H. Lawrence's *Women in Love* after his daughter had brought the book home from a public library. Together with John Sumner of the New York Society for the Suppression of Vice, Ford founded the Clean Books League.

## THE MOST DISGRACEFUL THING I EVER DID

### THE INVASION OF THE SANCTUARY

It was Christmas eve. In a fashionable church were gathered the great ones of the city in a pious swoon. For the hour bankers had put out of their weary minds the number of farmers on whom they must foreclose next day in order to make their twenty per cent. Real Estate men had ceased worrying what gaudy lies should embellish their prospectuses on the following Monday. Even fatigued flappers had turned to religion and were wondering if the man two pews ahead really looked like Valentino, or whether it was just the way his hair was cut in the back.

And at that moment, I, who had been suppering heavily in a house not two doors from the church, felt religion descend upon me also. A warm current seemed to run through my body. My sins were washed away and I felt, as my host strained a drop or so from the ultimate bottle, that my life was beginning all over again.

"Yes," I said softly to myself, drawing on my overshoes, "I will go to church. I will find some friend and, sitting next to him, we will sing the Christmas hymns."

The church was silent. The rector had mounted to the pulpit and was standing there motionless, conscious of the approving gaze of Mrs. T. T. Conquadine, the wife of the flour king, sitting in the front row.

I entered quietly and walked up the aisle toward him, searching the silent ranks of the faithful for some one whom I could call my friend. But no one hailed me. In all the church there was no sound but the metallic rasp of the buckles on my overshoes as I plodded toward the rector. At the very foot of the pulpit a kindly thought

---

*Vanity Fair* 21 (October 1923): 53. This was one of ten "disgraceful" acts recounted anonymously in this *Vanity Fair* issue. The magazine offered prizes to readers who could identify the authors. Fitzgerald clipped the item and saved it in a scrapbook. The event took place over Christmas vacation during one of the years he was a student at Princeton.

struck me—perhaps inspired by the faint odor of sanctity which exuded from the saintly man. I spoke.

"Don't mind me," I said, "go on with the sermon."

Then, perhaps unsteadied a bit by my emotion, I passed down the other aisle, followed by a sort of amazed awe, and so out into the street.

The papers had the extra out before midnight.

## THE MOST PAMPERED MEN IN THE WORLD

Talking the other day with a Prominent Business Man who had just visited an eastern moving picture studio, he remarked that never in his life had he seen so much waste and inefficiency in a single day.

"Why, look here—" he began, and with such a pretty flow of words, told us how it could all be systematized, that we forgot for a moment that this was an old, old story. When Prominent Business Men go through moving picture studios they always come out feeling very superior and contemptuous—because they imagine that turning strips of celluloid into visible stories is as simple a matter as turning western cattle into Eastern roast beef.

The real fallacy of the business man's attitude lies, of course, in Vera Lafollette's eyes. When Vera has a cold—and Vera *will* take cold, even when she's under a two hundred thousand dollar contract—her eyes grow red and dim just like yours and mine, and the lids swell. You can hardly blame her, when she's in this condition, for refusing to go before the camera. She imagines that, if she does, every inch of red-eyed film will lose her one admirer, one silver dollar, one rung on the ladder she's been climbing for years.

"Fire her!" says the Business Man with a bold air, "Why, last week when my superintendent disobeyed an order—"

But his superintendent was not the mainspring of a picture in which was tied up two hundred thousand dollars. In short, the

---

Published initially under the title "The Pampered Men" in *Egoists*, pp. 152–53. Republished under Fitzgerald's title in the *F. Scott Fitzgerald Review* 5 (2006): 22–25. Fitzgerald was invited to write this article in April 1924 by Myron Zobel, the editor of *Screenland*, a movie magazine. Fitzgerald wrote the piece en route to Europe on the *Minnewaska* and mailed it to Harold Ober. Zobel rejected the article; Fitzgerald attempted to interest the *Saturday Evening Post* in an expanded version but without success. See "Polishing Up 'Pampered,'" *F. Scott Fitzgerald Review* 5 (2006): 13–21. The name "Vera Lafollette" in the third paragraph is fictitious. Fitzgerald might have been thinking of Laura La Plante, a blonde comedienne who was a top female star at Universal. The text here is from Fitzgerald's typescript, published without emendation of accidentals.

moving picture is not a good profession for the efficiency bully. It is more often confronted with the human, the personal, the incalculable element than any other industry in the world.

But in one respect, there is much truth in the Business Man's criticism of the movie. He wants to see centralization and authority, and he sees none. Is the responsibility with the producer? No—for he seems to be dependent on the director, who, in his turn, is apparently at the mercy of his story and his star. If in movie circles, you mention a successful picture, "Tol'able David", for example, you will hear the credit for its success claimed for the producer, the director, the star, the author, the continuity writer and Lord knows how many technical artisans who have aided in the triumph. Mention a failure and you will hear the blame heaped on each one of these in turn—and finally on the public itself, for not being "intelligent" enough to like what they get.

Well, I am going to venture three opinions on the subject—three opinions that I think more and more people are coming to hold.

First—that the moving picture is a director's business, and there never was a good picture or a bad picture for which the director was not entirely responsible.

Second—that with half a dozen exceptions, our directors are an utterly incompetent crew. Most of them entered the industry early and by accident, and the industry has outgrown them long ago.

Third—Any director worth the price of his puttees should average four commercial successes out of five attempts in every year.

Let me first discuss his responsibility. In most of the big companies the director can select his own stories—the scenario departments are only too glad when a director says, "I want to do this picture and I know I can." The director who undertakes pictures he doesn't believe in is merely a hack—some ex-barnstormer, who directed an illustrated song back in 1909 and is now hanging around Hollywood with nothing left except a megaphone.

The director chooses his cast, excepting the star, and he has control over the expenditure of the allotted money and over the writing and interpretation of the continuity. This is as it should be. Yet I have heard directors whining because they couldn't find a story they wanted, and the whine had the true ring of incompetence.

An author who whines for a plot at least has the excuse that his imagination has given out—the director has no excuse at all. The libraries are full of many million volumes ready to his hand.

In addition, directors sometimes complain of "incompetent actors". This is merely pathetic, for it is the director's business to *make* actors. On the spoken stage the director may justly cry that once rehearsals are over the acting is out of his power. But the movie director labors under no such disadvantage. He can make an actor go through a scene twenty times and then choose the best "take" for the assembled film. And in a fragmentary affair like a movie where the last scenes may be taken first, the director *must* do the thinking for the actor. If he is unable to, he does not belong on the platform of authority. After seeing what Chaplin did with that ex-cigarette-villain, Adolphe Menjou, and what Von Stroheim accomplished with the utterly inexperienced Mary Philbin, I believe that the alibi of incompetent acting will fall upon deaf ears.

Now directing, as the hack director understands it, is to be privy to all the outworn tricks of the trade. The hack director knows how to "visualize" every emotion—that is, he knows the rubber stamp formula, he knows how every emotion has been visualized *before*. If, in a picture, the hero departs from the heroine and the heroine wants him back, the hack director knows that she must take a step after him, hold out her hands toward him and then let them drop to her side. He knows that when someone dies in the street, this is always "visualized" by having a kneeling bystander take off his hat. If someone dies in a house, a sheet is invariably drawn over his face.

Very well, let us see how Chaplin, greatest of all directors, conveyed this latter event in "A Woman of Paris". He realized that the old convention was outworn, that it no longer had the power of calling the emotions to attention, so he invented a new way. The audience does not see the dying man at all; it sees the backs of the surrounding crowd and suddenly a waiter pushes his way out of that crowd, shaking his head. At once the whole horrible violence of the suicide is plain to us. We even understand the human vanity of the waiter in wanting to be first to convey the news.

We may forget that incident because the picture is full of spanking new effects but, when it is over, every bit of it, despite the shoddy mounting and the sentimentalized story seems vastly important. Chaplin has a fine imaginative mind and he threw himself hard into his picture—it is the lazy man, the "wise old-timer", in other words, the hack, who takes the timeworn easy way.

All I am saying comes down to this—The chief business of a director is *to invent new business to express the old emotions.*

An "original" picture is not a story of a lunatic wanting the north star. It is the story of a little girl wanting a piece of candy—but our attention must be called with sharp novelty to the fact that she wants it. The valuable director is not he who makes a dull "artistic" transcription of Conrad's "Victory"—give me the fellow who can blow the breath of life into a soggy gum-drop like Pollyanna.

Perhaps such men will appear. We have Griffith—just when he seems to be exhausted, he has a way of sitting up suddenly in his grave. We have Cruze, who can be forgiven "The Covered Wagon" if only for the amazing dream scene in "Hollywood". We have Von Stroheim, who has a touch of real civilization in his make-up and, greatest of all, Chaplin, who almost invented the movies as a vehicle for personal expression. There are half a dozen others I could name—Sennett, Lubitsch, Ingram, Cecil DeMille, Dwan—who in the last five years have made two or three big successes interspersed with countless reels of drooling mediocrity, but I have my doubts about them; we must demand more than that.

As for the rest of the directors—let a thick, impenetrable curtain fall. Occasionally, a picture made by some jitney Griffith is successful because of the intelligence of self-directing stars—but beware of such accidents. The man's next effort is likely to show the true barrenness and vulgarity of his mind.

One more remark—I doubt if successful directors will ever be found among established authors—though they may, perhaps, among playwrights and not-too-seasoned continuity men. Author-directors have a way of condescending to their audiences. Bad as Rupert Hughes' books are, they are seldom as silly and meretricious as his pictures. I suspect that his mind is on Minnie McGlook, the girl-fan of North Dakota, and not on his work—

which is—

to believe in his story, to keep his whole story in his head for ten weeks and, above all, *to invent new business to express old emotions*. All we ask from any of them is a little imagination and a little true feeling for the joys and the hopes and the everlasting struggles of mankind.

## MY OLD NEW ENGLAND HOMESTEAD
## ON THE ERIE

It was some ten years ago that, as I trundled my wife along on one of our annual jaunts into the country, her eyes fell eagerly upon it—the house of our dreams.

"Jack!" she cried, gazing over the side of the wheelbarrow. "Jack, or whatever your name is, I must have it!"

I went inside and picked it up for a song.

At first sight it would seem that I got the worst of my bargain for the lovely old Colonial lines of the place had been almost obliterated by successive generations of vandals—the shingles of the roof were covered with cross-word puzzles, fine old windows were defaced by bars (my treasure was now the local jail), and the pre-Braddock bathroom had been padlocked by some rustic board of health these fifty years.

The price agreed upon included our wheelbarrow, several strings of bright beads, half a dozen Confederate bonds and about seventy-five cents in cash. As I handed it over a foreboding seized me and I said to the owner, who was none other than a shrewd New England Yankee:

"How about the old hand-made nails?"

He failed to understand.

Glancing around I percieved a fine Chippendale toothpick-holder on the table—and in it were the old hand-made nails. They had been used to cheat the dentist these two hundred years! I could scarcely restrain my incredulous laughter. My wife couldn't either. Neither of us could scarcely restrain our incredulous laughter.

"By the by," he said (interpolating some such rustic expression as "Oh, shucks"), "Do you want it delivered?"

"No," I said firmly, "I want it left where it is. We will move in tomorrow."

And move in we did. Never will I forget those first eight years—such a sound of hammers and nails and chisels and corkscrews was

---

*College Humor* 6 (August 1925): 18–19.

never heard in that quiet neighborhood before. I have since been told that the noise caused some nasty talk in the boiler factory half a mile away.

We began at the beginning. First we had the whole modernized inside taken out and replaced with a quaint interior that we picked up at an auction in Atlantic City. When that was done we removed the outer walls and built them up again out of old bricks. We kept, of course, the old shape; we were offered something nice for that but we refused it. The next step was to lift up the house on four automobile jacks of wrought iron, dig out the overlay of modern soil and replace it with some more lovable dirt that we had stumbled upon in one of our rambles through the older and more putrid parts of Virginia. Winter was almost upon us. With desperate haste we gouged out the steam heat—the last pipe was thrown from the window on the day the first snow fell.

There was our house. What to put in it—that was the question. We had the hand-made nails but, as my wife humorously remarked, they were no good to sit on. Besides that we had an old Haig and Haig bottle bought from a professional man—he had a set which he hated to break but I prevailed upon him—a sewing machine run by acetylene (ah, but they built well in those days!) and a left-handed diaval [sic] set. But that was only a start. To be sure—just a start!

Meanwhile we tore up the ugly and monotonous macadam pavement that ran in front of our door and replaced it with some historic cobblestones discovered on a remnant counter in New York. At first we had some unpleasantness from passing motorists, but as their crossing usually left them in a dazed condition they generally drove right on.

We were hindered a little by our lack of funds—sometimes we let the household bills run for years at a time in order to pick up an old fishhook on which we had set our eyes—but the notice that began to be taken of our acquisitions was very flattering. Even the grocer, a philistine, once remarked that we had a fine lot of brass up at our house. Also we had a nice compliment on an eight-pound gong which had once called farmhands to dinner and which our baby played with all day long in the hall. Our neighbors clubbed together and bought it at the fabulous price I demanded.

As I look over my accounts for that period I find the following typical items which I set down for the benefit of those other two hundred millions who have since joined me in the quest for American antiques.

Tearing the motor from the Ford and putting shafts on it ................................................ 50.00
Fine Example of the old horse .................... 100.00
Two-door Colonial Stove with balloon tires (ah, but they built well in those days!) .............................. 25.00

Gala years! Yes, and happy years. Will I soon forget the week we had the doorways narrowed—and how we laughed when the baby got wedged into one and had to be chopped out; or the day I traded my copy of Ulysses for a first edition of Henry Ward Beecher's *Sermons*; or the afternoon we stood cobwebbed bottles of "Old Jim's Mother's Remedy" and "Davy Crockett's Colic Cure" in the Medicine chest or the day it was finished and I could really stand out in front and admire the old Colonial lines of the place—and think how my wife would hang the washing on them when Spring came. The Spring!

"Has it been worth it?" you ask. I say "Yes." That faint echoing voice is my wife's. When we sit around our table in the evening inhaling the deep rancid odor of antique brass, eating fine old mouldy potatoes and a steak that was once rejected by Washington's starving army at Valley Forge—all washed down by some stagnant green water from our well—

But come in and join us some day! Come in by the cellar door, please, and close it tight behind you. The good old air that was good enough for our forefathers is good enough for us!

## FROM *THREE YEARS* (TESTIMONIAL)

*F. Scott Fitzgerald:*
The real event of the year (1924) will, of course, be the appearance in January of *The American Mercury*.

---

Fitzgerald's contribution to *Three Years, 1924 to 1927: The Story of a New Idea and Its Successful Adaptation, with a Postscript by H. L. Mencken* (New York: The American Mercury, 1927). The first issue of *The American Mercury*, edited by Mencken and George Jean Nathan, and published by Alfred A. Knopf, appeared in January 1924. *Three Years* is an account of the founding and success of the magazine.

## TEN YEARS IN THE ADVERTISING BUSINESS

"Well, Mr. Fitzgerald, what can I do for you today?" It was in a high office with a view of that gold building.

"I want a raise, Mr. Cakebook," I said.

"Why?"

"I'm about to get married. You're only paying me Ninety-Five Dollars a month and, of course, with a family to support I've got to think of money."

Into his grey eyes came a far away look.

"Ninety-Five Dollars is a pretty good salary. By the way, let me see that laundry slogan as it stands now."

"Here it is," I said, with eager pride. "Listen: 'We keep you clean in Muskateen.' How's that? Good, isn't it. 'We keep—'"

"Wait a minute," he interrupted. "Look here, Mr. Fitzgerald. You're too temperamental. Your ideas are too fancy, too imaginative. You ought to keep your feet on the ground. Now let me see that layout."

He worked over it for a moment, his large brain bulging a little from time to time; his lips moving as to melody.

"Now listen to this," he said, "I've got something good: 'Muskateen Laundry—we clean and press.' Listen Miss Schwartz, take that down right away. 'Muskateen Laundry—we clean and press.'"

Obsequiously I congratulated him—when he began to beam I returned to my thesis.

"Well, how about money?" . . . . . . .

. . . "I don't know," he mused. "Of course we try to be fair. How much do you want?"

I thought for a moment.

---

*Princeton Alumni Weekly* 29 (22 February 1929): 585. Fitzgerald is referring toward the end of the article to a Woodbury Soap Beauty Contest for which he was named a judge (with Cornelius Vanderbilt, Jr.). Advertisements for the competition appeared in the *Ladies' Home Journal* from February to December 1929.

"Suppose you name an amount."

"I'll tell you, Mr. Fitzgerald," he said, "we don't like to argue about money with anybody. You let us use your picture and your name as one of the judges in this contest and we'll call it a thousand dollars."

"But it'll take a couple of hours," I objected, "and, of course, with a family to support I've got to think of money."

"I realize that. We'll call it fifteen hundred."

"And it's understood that I'm in no sense to endorse this product."

"Perfectly. You merely pick the prettiest girl."

We stood up and I looked out the window at that gold building.

"Did I understand you to say you're about to get married?" he asked.

"Oh, no, I've been married ten years. That was back before those little dots."

"It must have been some other couple."

"It was," I assured him. "Only the names were the same. The tissues change every decade. Good-bye, Mr. Cakebook."

"Good-bye, Mr. Fitzgerald."

## SALESMANSHIP IN THE CHAMPS-ÉLYSÉES

To work for the Company Automobile is a *métier* exacting. There of them are many of the world who, wanting to purchase an automobile, enter and say "I want to purchase an automobile," whereupon this affair begins. Now one has at the outset the information that this man wishes well to purchase a car and has already decided on this mark—otherwise he would not have entered here. One can then, naturally, amuse oneself by for a moment mocking of him, giving him to wonder if of them there are after all. During this quarter of an hour one can discover much of the type with which one is dealing at the moment and thus in any further dealing one has provided himself with resources or even established a certain dominance of character, one on top of the other.

It there has been several days when an American entered and demanded me to make him see a car. I was engaged standing in a spot thinking of affairs of one's own; presently I demanded:

"What is it that it is?"

"A car."

"But what kind of car," I demanded sharply.

"A six-cylinder touring car."

"We have not one here."

I had the man there, and for a moment he looked stupefied—but then he made:

"Can you have one here for me to see this afternoon?"

This fantastic request I only answered with a bitter and short laugh.

"And how much is it?" he continued. "As a matter of fact I'm pretty sure I want one, so I can write you a cheque."

This was becoming wearying. I drew in my breath and made: "Listen, monsieur, it is not the trouble to talk when I have told you I have now no car of that kind in the house. Nothing! Nothing! Nothing! It does not exist here. Look for yourself."

---

*New Yorker* 5 (15 February 1930): 20. Fitzgerald's working title for this piece was "Salesman of the Boulevard."

"When will you have?"

"How should I know? Perhaps in eight days. Perhaps in a month."

"I don't think you want to sell me a car," he said. "As a matter of fact they carry a make next door that I begin to think will do just as well."

He turned and went out suddenly and I stood looking after the impolite. But thinking to profit himself he is in the end deceived, because Mr. Legoupy, the seller next door, will no more sell him without making a proper study of his sincerity and his character and the extent of his desire for the car than I myself. The impolite will end himself by being able to get no car at all.

## THE DEATH OF MY FATHER

Convention would make me preface this with an apology for the lack of taste of discussing an emotion so close to me. But all my criteria of taste disappeared when I read Mrs. Emily Price Post's Book of Etiquette some months ago. Up to that time I had always thought of myself as an American gentleman, somewhat crazy and often desperate and bad but partaking of the sensitivity of my race and class and with a record of many times having injured the strong but never the weak. But now I don't know—the mixture of the obvious and the snobbish in that book—and it's an honest book, a frank piece of worldly wisdom written for the new women of the bull market—has sent me back again to all the things I felt at twenty. I kept wondering all through it how Mrs. Post would have thought of my father.

I loved my father—always deep in my subconscious I have referred judgments back to him, to what he would have thought or done. He loved me—and felt a deep responsibility for me—I was born several months after the sudden death of my two elder sisters and he felt what the effect of this would be on my mother, that he would be my only moral guide. He became that to the best of his ability. He came from tired old stock with very little left of vitality and mental energy but he managed to raise a little for me.

We walked downtown in the summer to have our shoes shined, me in my sailor suit and father in his always beautifully cut clothes, and he told me the few things I ever learned about life until a few years later from a Catholic priest, Monsignor Fay. What he knew he had learned from his mother and grandmother, the latter a bore to me—"If your Grandmother Scott heard that she would turn over in her grave." What he told me were simple things.

---

*Princeton University Library Chronicle* 12 (Summer 1951): 187–89. This piece, unfinished, was written by Fitzgerald shortly after his father died on 26 January 1931.

"Once when I went in a room as a young man I was confused, so I went up to the oldest woman there and introduced myself and afterwards the people of that town always thought I had good manners." He did that from a good heart that came from another America—he was much too sure of what he was, much too sure of the deep pride of the two proud women who brought him up, to doubt for a moment that his own instincts were good. It was a horror to find the natural gesture expressed with cynical distortion in Mrs. Price Post's book.

We walked downtown in Buffalo on Sunday mornings and my white ducks were stiff with starch and he was very proud walking with his handsome little boy. We had our shoes shined and he lit his cigar and we bought the Sunday papers. When I was a little older I did not understand at all why men that I knew were vulgar and not gentlemen made him stand up or give the better chair on our verandah. But I know now. There was new young peasant stock coming up every ten years and he was of the generation of the colonies and the revolution.

Once he hit me. I called him a liar—I was about thirteen, I think, and I said if he called me a liar he was a liar. He hit me—he had spanked me before and always with good reason, but this time there was ill feeling and we were both sorry for years, I think, though we didn't say anything to each other. Later we used to have awful rows on political subjects on which we violently disagreed but we never came to the point of personal animosity about them but if things came to fever heat the one most affected quitted the arena, left the room.

I don't see how all this could possibly interest anyone but me.

I ran away when I was seven on the Fourth of July—I spent the day with a friend in a pear orchard and the police were informed that I was missing and on my return my father thrashed me according to the custom of the nineties—on the bottom—and then let me come out and watch the night fireworks from the balcony with my pants still down and my behind smarting and knowing in my heart that he was absolutely right. Afterwards, seeing in his face his regret that it had to happen, I asked him to tell me a story. I knew what it would be—he had only a few, the story of the spy, the one about the man hung up by his thumbs, the one about Early's march.

Do you want to hear them? I'm so tired of them all that I can't make them interesting. But maybe they are because I used to ask Father to repeat and repeat and repeat.

## ON "FAMILY IN THE WIND"

### F. Scott Fitzgerald

Once upon a time F. Scott Fitzgerald was the head and front of "the younger generation"; today, at thirty-seven, he is one of the best-known short-story writers in America. A native of St. Paul, Minn., and a graduate of Princeton, he changed literary manners overnight in 1920, with "This Side of Paradise." Commenting on "Family in the Wind" he writes: "It is one of my favorite stories, as I actually went through a part of the cyclone which it describes."

---

From O. *Henry Memorial Award Prize Stories of 1933*, ed. Harry Hansen (Garden City, N.Y.: Doubleday, Doran & Co., Inc., 1933): 138. Fitzgerald's story "Family in the Wind" (1932) is included in the volume, pp. 139–61. He based the story on a series of tornadoes that occurred in the Deep South on 21–22 March 1932. Much damage occurred in Alabama, Zelda's native state. Fitzgerald and Zelda were living in Montgomery, Alabama, at the time.

## FITZGERALD'S LIST OF NEGLECTED BOOKS

F. Scott Fitzgerald has just finished a book of his own, "Tender is the Night," his first novel since 1925. From Baltimore he sends a list of "the books that seem to me to have cashed in least on their intrinsic worth in recent years":

"Miss Lonelyhearts," by Nathanael West (Liveright, 1933)—though it's really a long short story.
"Sing Before Breakfast," by Vincent McHugh (Simon and Schuster, 1933).
"I Thought of Daisy," by Edmund Wilson (Scribner's, 1929).
"Through the Wheat," by Thomas Boyd (Scribner's, 1927).

He also mentions "a book called 'Spring Flight,' by whom I've forgotten—he never appeared again," and "the detective stories of Raoul Whitfield, who I think is as good as Hammett—in fact I once suspected he was Hammett under another name." We could find no trace of "Spring Flight" or its author—perhaps Fitzgerald remembered the wrong title. As for Raoul Whitfield's detective stories, most of them are published by Knopf, and "Danger Circus," which appeared last year, is the most recent.

"There are probably other neglected books," Fitzgerald continues, "but these occur to me especially. When the most violent emotional hysteria takes place over any rehash of Lenin's 'Imperialism,' any story about a steel mill made out of the dry bones of Upton Sinclair and Jack London, or any version of Hamsun's 'Growth of the Soil,' I think the novels above certainly deserve a good reading. In each case they are the men who did it first and that means a lot to me in my valuation of people's artistic merit.... Meanwhile I am waiting for the crash down on 'Tender is the Night.' I expect a lot of good pokes from the wise boys for not having written the Odyssey."

---

From Malcolm Cowley, "Good Books That Almost Nobody Has Read," *New Republic* 78 (18 April 1934): 283. The book mentioned by Fitzgerald in the second paragraph is Lee J. Smits, *The Spring Flight* (New York: Knopf, 1925).

## THE TRUE STORY OF APPOMATTOX

# THE TRUE STORY OF APPOMATTOX

### Columnist Discovers That It Was Grant Who Surrendered To Lee Instead Of Lee Surrendering To Grant

### Circumstances Divulged For The First Time By Captain X

We have learned that when Grant had decided to surrender his milk-fed millions to Lee's starving remnants and the rendezvous was arranged at Appomattox Court House, Lee demanded that Grant put his submission into writing. Unfortunately Grant's pencil broke, and, removing his cigar from his mouth, he turned to General Lee and said with true military courtesy: "General, I have broken my pencil; will you lend me your sword to sharpen it with?" General Lee, always ready and willing to

---

Fitzgerald had this version of Lee's surrender typeset and printed at the plant of the *Baltimore Sun* in late July 1934. He sent a copy to Maxwell Perkins on 30 July and sent a copy also to Elizabeth Lemmon, who lived near Middleburg, Virginia, and with whom Perkins frequently corresponded. See Fitzgerald to Perkins, 30 July 1934, *Scott/Max*, p. 203.

oblige, whipped forth his sword and tendered it to General Grant.

It was unfortunately just at this moment that the flashlight photographers and radio announcers got to work and the picture was erroneously given to the world that General Lee was surrendering his sword to General Grant.

The credulous public immediately accepted this story. The bells that were prepared to ring triumphantly in Loudoun county were stilled while the much inferior Yankee bells in Old North Church in Boston burst forth in a false pæan of triumph. To this day the legend persists, but we of the Welbourne *Journal* are able to present to the world for the first time the real TRUTH about this eighty-year-old slander that Virginia lost its single-handed war against the allied Eskimos north of the Mason and Dixon line.

## 'MY TEN FAVORITE PLAYS.'
### NO. 152.—
#### F. Scott Fitzgerald.

F. Scott Fitzgerald, who achieved a startling success with "This Side of Paradise," who added to his prestige with "The Great Gatsby" (which Owen Davis dramatized) and whose latest (and some readers say best) novel is "Tender Is the Night," writes from Park avenue, town of Baltimore, listing the following as his outstanding impressions in the theater:

1— Charles Chaplin in "The Pilgrim."
2— Performance of an obscure stock company actor in Gillette's "Secret Service," about 1906.
3— My own performance in a magicians' show at the age of nine.
4— Greta Garbo in her first big role.
5— E. H. Sothern as Lord Dundreary in "Our American Cousin."
6— George M. Cohan in "The Little Millionaire."
7— Ina Claire in "The Quaker Girl."
8— The Theatre Guild actress who played the stage role in "Grand Hotel" that Joan Crawford played in the movies. I've seen her twice and I think she's one of the greatest actresses in the world. (Ed. note: This actress was Hortense Alden.)
9— Ernest Truex's face when he was carrying through bravely in a flop of my own that opened cold in Atlantic City.
10— David W. Griffith's face as I imagine it during the filming of "The Birth of a Nation" when he was "forging in the smithy of his soul" all the future possibilities of the camera.

*New York Sun*, 10 September 1934, p. 19.

## THE BROADCAST WE ALMOST HEARD LAST SEPTEMBER

Folks, here's Poke McFiddle bringing you the big battle in Central Europe. Take it away, Poke.

Good morning, folks—it's just dawn over here but everybody's up—yes, sir, everybody's on hand—a cast of twenty million—the greatest ever assembled. Before I begin I want to tell you who's in this corner. Folks, I'm five miles behind the lines in a dug-out with some of the finest men I ever met. I'll just introduce you before the boys get going—here's a delegation of cabinet ministers and half a dozen generals and presidents and a couple of stuffed Kings all just as eager to see the sport as you are, gentlemen—just as near to it as a periscope will let them get.

Set your clocks by that bomb, folks, it's zero hour minus one minute—and now boy! are they laying down a hot barrage! Here, I'm going to turn you over to the heavy artillery for a minute. *BOOM!* That was a big one—sounded like the Fourth, eh? Ha-ha-ha.

While the boys are waiting to go over, every one of them happy as jack rabbits, I'm going to let you hear this military band swinging the lads into battle. Take it, Tony. *BOOM!* I'm sorry, folks. That band doesn't exist any more. You see, the enemy are putting down a barrage, too. Incidentally, just before the boys go over, I'm going to turn the mike over to our commercial man who's got some Big News for you. I'll be back in a flash with a crash....

Hello, America. This program, the first battle ever broadcast, comes to you through the courtesy of the Jitka Arms Works, who are supplying the ammunition for both sides. You can't fight battles with duds—you need a Cool Clean Burst. I want to remind you of our little prize contest: you simply buy a package of our cartridges at your sporting store, tear off the top and write your guess at the number of casualties for the day. Whoever is nearest—

---

*Furioso* 3 (Fall 1947): 8–10. Written in 1935 but not published during Fitzgerald's lifetime.

Sorry to interrupt, folks, we'll hear more from Jitka later—about that Clean Cool Burst. But just now the boys are going over—and are they hitting that front line! This *is War!* They're piling in, and watching them through this periscope is a sight to see. They're down—they're up, they're up—they're down for good. But that's only one wave, folks, and they're plenty more. Incidentally, the noise isn't static, it's machine-gun fire coming to you courtesy of—

Let me tell you, the men in this dugout are *wild!* They'd give *any*thing to be in there, but they're too old and they're needed back here to run things. Or else, how could we be bringing you this fine broadcast, courtesy of A.B.C. and the Jitka Arms Company.............. Folks, the show seems to be over for the day and now we're going to take you out on the battlefield where all the Red Cross people are doing a fine job picking up some of the boys. Take it, Ned...

Hello, America. I'm going to let one boy speak for twenty thousand of them. Here he is, a fine boy—or he was this morning—and glad and proud he had the chance to do it. Speak up, son, you're talking to half a billion people.

"Hello, Mother—goodbye, Mother."

Thanks, son. Oh-oh! That was too much for him. Take it away, Poke.

Folks, we're having a little champagne dinner back here outside the dugout—and do we need it! But it seems to be getting suddenly misty in this neighborhood, very misty. And it's beginning to smell funny. I don't like it—it's GAS, folks—*GAS!* And I can't find my mask! Hey, my job is giving it out, not taking it................. The time is eight o'clock. All you truckers on your toes! Prince Paul Obaloney of Dance Hall Society will give us a lesson in the Slinky-winky Blues.

## FROM *THESE STORIES WENT TO MARKET*

F. Scott Fitzgerald has supplied these comments in regard to the origin of four of his best-known short stories: "Baby Party: Went to one—saw just a moment of bitterness between two women. Was drawn in spiritually on wife's side. Imagined the same scene among stupid people with less self-control—and its consequences. Also Maupassant's 'Piece of String.' Imagination.

"Rags Martin Jones: Struck by personality of girl just home from Europe and hating America. Also gossip about Prince of Wales. Invention.

"Absolution: Memory of time when as a boy told a lie in confession. Also glimpse of a very bored passionate celibate priest one day. Imagination.

"Winter Dreams: Memory of a fascination in a visit paid to very rich aunt in Lake Forest. Also my first girl 18–20 whom I've used over and over and never forgotten. Imagination."

---

From the introduction to *These Stories Went to Market*, ed. Vernon McKenzie (New York: McBride, 1935): xviii. McKenzie, a teacher of journalism and creative writing, had written to Fitzgerald for comments on some of his most famous stories. Fitzgerald's "first girl," mentioned in his comment on "Winter Dreams," is Ginevra King.

## HUCKLEBERRY FINN

Huckleberry Finn took the first journey *back*. He was the first to look *back* at the republic from the perspective of the west. His eyes were the first eyes that ever looked at us objectively that were not eyes from overseas. There were mountains at the frontier but he wanted more than mountains to look at with his restless eyes—he wanted to find out about men and how they lived together. And because he turned back we have him forever.

F. Scott Fitzgerald.

---

Fitzgerald wrote this statement, at the request of the International Mark Twain Society, for a banquet held in celebration of the centenary of Twain's birth, 30 November 1935. The typescript of the statement is in the Bruccoli collection at the University of South Carolina. A facsimile of the typescript was published in *Own Time*, p. 176.

## A BOOK OF ONE'S OWN

In this age of drastic compression, it is the ambition of all the publishers I know to get everything worth reading into one little book no bigger than a Reuben's sandwich. I've been playing with this idea off and on for a year, and finally worked out a new super-anthology that over a single weekend should make the conscientious reader as nearly omniscient as a man can be. It ought to make its fortunate publisher (and me) rather rich, I think. This is my prospectus:

### AT LAST!

All you want to read in One Pocket-size Volume! A miracle of Book Making. Large Type—Thick Paper.

### SOME OF THE SPLENDID CHAPTERS

Burton's Anatomy, Gone with the Wind, Steinbeck, Remnants of Modern Literature.

10,000 Words oft. mispronounced (Condensed), Nurses' Hand Book and Indian Sex Love (Orig. 6 vol.), Sheet Welding, Manual Univ. Hist. (Cond.), Mrs. Rorer's Cooking.

---

*New Yorker* 13 (21 August 1937): 19. Some of the references are now obscure. "Macfadden's Body" is *Macfadden's Encyclopedia of Physical Culture* (rev. ed. 1920); "Tony Adverse" is the bestselling 1933 novel *Anthony Adverse* by Hervey Allen, later made into a successful movie; "Tif Thayer" is Tiffany Thayer, actor and author of sexually suggestive novels; "Bryce's Am. Comintern" is a reference to James Bryce, *The American Commonwealth* (1888); "Voliva," under "Great Leaders," is Wilbur Glenn Voliva, an evangelist and advocate of Flat Earth doctrine; "Doc Dafoe" is Dr. Allan Roy Dafoe, physician to the Dionne quintuplets, who published an account of his experiences in the *Saturday Evening Post*; "Margot Asquith" is Margaret Asquith, author and wit, wife of H. H. Asquith, prime minister of the United Kingdom from 1908 to 1916; "van Dyke" is Henry van Dyke, Princeton alumnus, clergyman, and author of *The Story of the Other Wise Man* (1896).

# Last Kiss  431

All You Want to Know in Swedish (Cond.), Soc. Register Western States, Gotha's Almanac, Macfadden's Body, Famous Operas, Tolstoi, Mike Gold, Marx (Leaflet edition).

Shakespeare (Laughs from), Plastic Age, Ten Atlantic Prize Novels condensed in one, Sears-Roebuck, Bradstreet, Tony Adverse.

Memoirs of a Statistician (Cond.), Cath. Index, Readers' Digest (Cond.), Sorrows of Grand Dukes (Compressed), Orph. Annie (Selects.), Scenario Writing, quick course, Elements of Brewing, Familiar Quots., Apostles' Creed.

Plato, Adam Smith, Tif Thayer, Bryce's Am. Comintern, Bladder and Intest.

Great Leaders: Nathan Bedford Forrest, Artemus Ward (Bill Nye), Washington, Voliva, Dante, Doc Dafoe, etc.

Audubon's Birds, Astrology (Simp.), Caesar & Virgil Trots, Ten Commandments.

Bible (Cond.), New Test. Stories, Moses, Abraham's Sac., Serm. on Mount, Noah's Ark, Dorian Gray.

Tales of Wayside Inn (Unexpurg.), Rover Boys (Summary), Shirley Temple Cutouts, Painting Thru Ages, Fish of Labrador.

Famous Clowns of Bygone Days, Unsolved Murders (Cond.), Margot Asquith, Al Capone, Donald Duck, Tank Corps, etc., etc., etc.

ONE HANDY VOLUME
Bound in Boards $2.00
Compressed Morocco $3.50

As an added inducement, the publisher might give with it a set of O. Henry or van Dyke in ten volumes. This gets the buyer both ways, for if he happens to have a bookshelf, then the set will fill it up. The book needs no shelf of its own, but it might be bound to look like a small radio. Then, if the purchaser has a radio that looks like a set of books—but I become too visionary; it is time for some practical man to take hold.

—*F. Scott Fitzgerald*

## FOREWORD TO *COLONIAL AND HISTORIC HOMES OF MARYLAND*

The undersigned can only consider himself a native of the Maryland Free State through ancestry and adoption. But the impression of the fames and the domains, the vistas and the glories of Maryland followed many a young man West after the Civil War and my father was of that number. Much of my early childhood in Minnesota was spent in asking him such questions as:

"—and how long did it take Early's column to pass Glenmary that day?" (That was a farm in Montgomery County.)

and:

"—what would have happened if Jeb Stuart's cavalry had joined Lee instead of raiding all the way to Rockville?"

and:

"—tell me again about how you used to ride through the woods with a spy up behind you on the horse."

or:

"Why wouldn't they let Francis Scott Key off the British frigate?"

And since so many legends of my family went west with father, memories of names that go back before Braddock's disaster such as Caleb Godwin of Hockley-in-ye-Hole, or Philip Key of Tudor Hall, or Pleasance Ridgely—so there must be hundreds and hundreds of families in such an old state whose ancestral memories are richer and fuller than mine.

But time obliterates people and memories and only the more fortunate landmarks survive. In the case of this fine book, it is upon the home above all that Don Swann has concentrated his talents and his painstaking research—the four walls (or sixteen as it

---

Foreword to Don Swann, *Colonial and Historic Homes of Maryland* (Baltimore: Etchcrafters Art Guild, 1939): 1.

may be) of Baronial Maryland, or the artistic result of the toil and sweat that some forever anonymous craftsman put into a balcony or a parquet. And outside this general range, the etcher has also paused here and there to jot down some detail of plainer houses that helps to make this a permanent record of the history of the Free State.

His work, naturally, will speak for itself, and, to allow it to do so, I cut short this prelude with the expression of high hopes for this venture by one of the State's adopted sons.

F. Scott Fitzgerald

# RECORD OF VARIANTS

The *Thoughtbook* is presented in an unemended type facsimile. *The Vegetable* is published as an historical document with two emendations, recorded below, but with no restyling of accidentals. For Poems, Book Reviews, Public Letters, Journalism, and items in the Miscellaneous section, typographical errors have been silently emended but no substantive emendations introduced. An account of the surviving evidence is provided for each of the narratives in the Short Fiction section; emendations are recorded. The following symbols and sigla have been employed:

| | |
|---|---|
| ~ | the same word |
| ˰ | absence of punctuation |
| ed | an editorial emendation |
| TS/TSS | typescript/s |
| FSF | Fitzgerald |

The initial reading in each emendation entry is that of the Cambridge text, keyed by page and line number. This reading is followed by a left-pointing bracket which can be read as "emended from." The second or rejected reading is from the base text, always the serial text unless otherwise indicated. Editorial emendations are signaled by "ed" followed by a semicolon.

## *The Vegetable*

The base text is the 1923 Scribners first (only) impression.

| | |
|---|---|
| 47.29 | *down from* ] ed; *down* |
| 100.4 | DeMille ] ed; Demille *and subsequent occurrences* |

## "Lamp in a Window"

| | |
|---|---|
| 129.7 | got holy, then got mad ] argued stubbornly, got mad *Emendation by FSF, first published in* The Crack-Up *(1945): 163.* |

## "On Your Own"

The text published in this volume is that of a surviving 28-page TS, among the holdings of Fitzgerald's grandchildren.

# 436    Record of Variants

172.22    Ann ] ed; Anne
173.10    Charmed, ] ed; ~ ˆ

## "Lo, the Poor Peacock"

This story survives in a single exemplar, a 30-page TS with Fitzgerald's corrections and revisions, preserved among his papers at Princeton. This text is published here with no substantive emendation.

## "The End of Hate"

The text published in the Cambridge edition is FSF's final revision, a 27-page TS entitled "When This Cruel War—" that is preserved among his papers at Princeton. This text is published without substantive emendation. Three earlier TSS (entitled "Thumbs Up," "Dentist Appointment," and "When This Cruel War—") are among the holdings at the University of South Carolina.

## "A Full Life"

The text published here, without substantive emendation, is that of the only surviving exemplar, a mixed holograph and TS document among the Fitzgerald Papers at Princeton.

## "Discard"

Five versions of this story, all in TS, are present in the collections at Princeton; an early TS, entitled "Director's Special," is among a group of documents in the possession of Fitzgerald's grandchildren. The text published in this volume, without substantive emendation, is that of the latest of the five versions at Princeton.

## "Last Kiss"

The Carl A. Kroch Library at Cornell University holds a 25-page carbon TS of this story; this is the version that was published in *Collier's*, 16 April 1949. At Princeton are four typescripts, the last of these post-dating the Cornell document and representing Fitzgerald's final work on the narrative. The text of this last TS is given in the present volume, with one substantive emendation:

258.2    Or ] ed; Nor

# Record of Variants

## "News of Paris—Fifteen Years Ago"

The text in the Cambridge edition is that of an 8-page ribbon TS among the holdings of Fitzgerald's grandchildren. No substantive emendations have been introduced.

## "The High Cost of Macaroni"

The text here is that of a mixed TS and holograph draft (the only surviving exemplar) at Princeton. Two passages, omitted in the *Interim* text, have been restored:

346.33–37     ¶ There were . . . to stay.
355.10–14     Because we . . . be me.

# EXPLANATORY NOTES

Annotated below are references to persons, places, political figures, literary and dramatic works, stage actors, cinema stars, hotels and restaurants, popular songs, and terms unfamiliar to a current reader.

## THE VEGETABLE

### 38.2 Katherine Tighe and Edmund Wilson, Jr.

Katherine Tighe was a friend from St. Paul who read and marked the holograph of *This Side of Paradise* (1920), calling attention to misspellings, grammatical infelicities, and what she considered to be lapses in taste. Fitzgerald's Princeton friend Edmund Wilson read *The Beautiful and Damned* (1922) in typescript and recommended revisions and cuts. For Tighe's influence on *This Side of Paradise*, see the Cambridge edition of the novel (1995): xxx–xxxiii; for Wilson's work on *The Beautiful and Damned*, see the Cambridge edition (2008): xv–xvi.

### 39.8 "Ben Hur"

*Ben-Hur: A Tale of Christ* was an enormously popular novel by General Lew Wallace, published originally in 1880 by Harper & Brothers. The book stayed near the top of American bestseller lists until well into the twentieth century.

### 39.17–22 *the Fauntleroy nineties . . . Imitation Gibson girls*

The Reginald Birch illustrations for the first edition of Frances Hodgson Burnett's sentimental novel *Little Lord Fauntleroy* (1886) inspired a style of boys' clothing—black velvet suit, flowing tie, lace collar, broad-brimmed hat. Fitzgerald was dressed by his mother in a modified Fauntleroy outfit as a child. The Gibson Girl, as rendered in pen and ink by the illustrator Charles Dana Gibson during the 1890s and early 1900s, represented an ideal of feminine beauty for Fitzgerald's generation until the advent of the flapper. The Gibson Girl had upswept hair, a long neck, and a haughty demeanor; she was often depicted in evening clothes or a sporting costume.

### 40.11–12 *the little Victrola*

This small wind-up phonograph, called the "Vic," was marketed by the Victor Talking Machine Company. It played vinyl discs and featured a concealed speaker inside the cabinet.

### 40.15 "Some little bug..."

From the popular 1915 gimmick song "Some Little Bug Is Going to Find You," also known as "The Germ Song"—with music by Silvio Hein and lyrics by Benjamin Hapgood Burt and Roy Atwell. The first stanza: "In these days of indigestion, it is often times a question, / Of what to eat, and what to leave alone; / Every microbe and bacillus has a different way to kill us, / And in time they all will claim you for their own."

### 42.21–22 Just one gallon is all I want.

*The Vegetable* is set during Prohibition, which went into effect in January 1919 and remained in force until December 1933. Those who wished to imbibe were compelled to drink the decoctions of bootleggers, or to manufacture their own potations.

### 45.11–12 feel all the bumps on your head

Charlotte has in mind the pseudo-science of phrenology, popular in England and the US during the nineteenth century. Phrenologists used calipers and other instruments to measure the skulls of their human subjects, paying special attention to bumps or other oddities, and claiming to predict personality and intelligence from their findings.

### 47.31 *"Dada"*

Fitzgerald is satirizing Dada, an avant-garde movement in art and literature that flourished in the US and Europe from 1913 onward. Key figures included Marcel Duchamp, Francis Picabia, Tristan Tzara, and Max Ernst.

### 53.16 Rudolph Valentine

Charlotte has in mind Rudolph Valentino (1895–1926), the first of the "Latin lover" screen stars of the period, famous for his profile. Valentino is still remembered for his role in *The Sheik*, a popular 1921 silent film mentioned by Doris several lines along in the play. The movie is also cited elsewhere in this volume in "Why Blame It on the Poor Kiss?"

### 55.2–13 Mae Murray... Motion Picture Magazine... Marilyn Miller

The actress and dancer Mae Murray (1889–1965), a star at Universal Pictures, appeared on screen with most of the popular leading men of the period. She was known in the press as "The Girl with Bee-Stung Lips." *Motion Picture Magazine*, founded by John Stuart Blackton and Eugene Brewster in 1914, was an early movie rag that continued its run until 1977. Marilyn Miller (1898–1936), a Broadway star, was famous for her tap dancing and singing. She drew much attention for her performance in Florenz Ziegfeld's production of *Sally* (1920), with music by Jerome Kern.

### 62.20 It's cloudy.

Murkiness or cloudiness in moonshine was a sign of impurities, including lead, which could cause brain damage and (in sufficient quantity) paralysis and death.

### 64.21 it's easier for a camel...

Dada is remembering Matthew 19:24. "And again I say unto you, it is easier for a camel to go through the eye of a needle, than for a rich man to enter into the kingdom of God."

### 71.8 JERRY FROST, PRES.

Jerry, as president, is a satirical version of Warren Gamaliel Harding (1865–1923), the 29th president of the United States. Harding served from 4 March 1921 until his death on 2 August 1923, some three months after the publication of *The Vegetable*. Harding was a favorite whipping-boy for H. L. Mencken, who derided Harding's abuse of the English language in his speeches. Mencken dubbed the president's style "Gamalielese." (See, e.g., p. 100 of this edition.) Harding was a popular leader during his term in office, but subsequent revelations about high-level corruption during his term, including the "Teapot Dome" scandal, diminished his standing. He died in office and was succeeded by Calvin Coolidge (1872–1933). The Teapot Dome scandal is mentioned elsewhere in this volume in "What

Kind of Husbands Do 'Jimmies' Make?"—and in *Tender Is the Night*, p. 113 of the Cambridge edition.

## 78.19 Major-General Pushing

Fitzgerald would have expected his readers to think here of General John J. "Black Jack" Pershing (1860–1948), chief commander the American Expeditionary Forces in Europe during the First World War. In the presidential election of 1920 Pershing was mentioned as a possible candidate for the Republicans, but he refused to campaign for the nomination, which went to Warren G. Harding (see above). In 1923, when *The Vegetable* was published, Pershing held the position of Chief of Staff of the United States Army.

## 83.9–10 in the Ku Klux

The second incarnation of the Ku Klux Klan (to which this newsboy would belong) flourished in the US during the early and mid-1920s. It was a fraternal organization which, at its peak, enrolled between four and five million members. The 1920s version of the Klan was anti-Catholic and favored Prohibition.

## 84.29–30 that one they impeached

Jones is thinking of Andrew Johnson (1808–1875), who became the US President after Abraham Lincoln's assassination in 1865. Johnson, unpopular with Congress, was impeached by the House of Representatives in the spring of 1868; he fell one vote short of being convicted by the Senate and served out the remainder of his term. He was succeeded by Ulysses S. Grant (1822–1885), commander-in-chief of the Union forces during the Civil War. Grant is probably the "other fellow—I forget his name" mentioned by Jerry several lines along. Grant is often mentioned as one of the least effective of the American presidents; his administration was marked by widespread dishonesty and corruption. Grant's propensity for cigar-smoking might be behind Jerry's comment that he "might as well go down and get a cigar."

## 100.4 Cecil B. DeMille

The Hollywood director Cecil B. DeMille (1881–1959) was famous for making films on an epic scale, with numerous extras and elaborate scenery. He was one of the first directors to shoot the same scene from multiple angles simultaneously. Many of his movies were based on stories from the Bible, Roman history, or the American West. *The Ten Commandments*, his best-remembered silent film, was released on 4 December 1923, eight months after the publication of *The Vegetable*. DeMille is mentioned elsewhere in this volume in "The Most Pampered Men in the World."

### 100.22 I seem to see Columbia

Jerry means the female personification of the United States, familiar to readers in the 1920s from newspaper and magazine illustrations. Columbia was usually dressed in flowing robes with breastplate, armored helmet, spear, and shield—some or all of these decorated in the stars-and-stripes motif. "Hail, Columbia!" was a popular patriotic song before Congress adopted "The Star-Spangled Banner" as the official national anthem in 1931.

### 103.31 "*The Bee's Knees.*"

This popular instrumental song was recorded for Columbia Records on 27 September 1922 by Ted Lewis and His Band. It reached number 5 on the pop charts in the early months of 1923. Ted Lewis (a.k.a. "Mr. Entertainment") was known for adapting Dixieland Jazz tunes for big-band performance.

### 108.14 "A good man is hard to find..."

Lyrics from "A Good Man Is Hard to Find," a blues tune by the African American singer-songwriter Eddie Green (1896–1950). Green composed and recorded the song in 1918. Recordings by other singers followed in the early 1920s. Bessie Smith's version became a national hit in 1927, four years after the publication of Fitzgerald's play. Flannery O'Connor used the title for one of her most famous short stories, first published in 1953.

### 114.34 Douglas Fairbanks

The screen idol Douglas Fairbanks (1883–1939) was known for his swashbuckling roles in such films as *The Mark of Zorro* (1920) and *The Thief of Bagdad* (1924). He married the film actress Mary Pickford in 1920 and, with her, was a founding member of United Artists. On one of their visits to Hollywood, the Fitzgeralds were entertained at the couple's estate, called Pickfair.

## SHORT FICTION

### "On Your Own"

**169.17 the German Prince**

In 1931, when Fitzgerald composed this story, Louis Ferdinand, Prince of Prussia (1907–1994), was third in line for the throne of the German Empire—a nominal position, because the monarchy had been abolished after the First World War. Handsome and well-educated, Louis Ferdinand was keen to become involved in American life and culture; in the early 1930s he befriended Henry Ford and aspired to manage Ford's automotive interests in Western Europe. The prince was linked romantically during the 1920s with the French movie actress Lili Damita, who later married the American film actor Errol Flynn.

**170.16 breaking into an "Off to Buffalo"**

"Shuffle Off to Buffalo" was a tap-dance step invented by the late nineteenth-century terpsichore Pat Rooney, a master of the shuffle style. A song by the same title was included in the 1933 Broadway musical *42nd Street* and became popular that year in a recording by the Andrews Sisters.

**172.22 Ann Pennington, Helen Morgan**

Evelyn is impersonating Ann Pennington (1893–1971), a dancer and singer known during the 1920s for her "Shake and Quiver" dance and for her version of the Black Bottom. Helen Morgan (1900–1941) was a torch singer during the 1920s and 1930s; she starred in the first Broadway production of *Show Boat* (1927).

**175.30 *O staunch old heart...***

William McFee (1881–1966) was a prolific and popular writer of sea stories. The quotation here, which has not been located, appears also in *This Side of Paradise*, p. 227 of the Cambridge edition.

**180.13 *Lady play your mandolin...***

The first two lines of "Lady Play Your Mandolin," a fox-trot (with a Latin beat) by Oscar Levant and Irving Caesar. The song was recorded by Ben Selvin and His Orchestra for Columbia Records and released in early 1931.

The first stanza: "Lady play your mandolin, / Lady let that tune begin; / When you sing your song of sin, / I'm a sinner too."

### 180.33–34  a startling gown from Vionnet

Evelyn is wearing a dress designed by Madeleine Vionnet (1876–1975), a leading French *couturier* of the inter-war period. Vionnet popularized the bias cut in the fashion industry; she was known for her elegant Grecian-style gowns.

### 183.8  a Peter Arno cartoon

Peter Arno (1904–1968), who drew satirical cartoons for the *New Yorker*, was famous for the series "The Whoops Sisters," published in the magazine during the 1920s, and for his drawings of haughty socialites.

## "Lo, the Poor Peacock!"

### 188.7–8  Mae West

The actress, singer, and personality Mae West (1893–1980) was near the top of her screen popularity in the 1930s. She was famous for her risqué double entendres: e.g., "I used to be Snow White, but I drifted." Her best-known line, which Jo has been mimicking, is from the movie *She Done Him Wrong* (1933), in which West played opposite Cary Grant.

### 190.7  a family of Lenci dolls

These Italian dolls were popular with collectors; many were "portrait dolls," with the faces of famous entertainers painted onto porcelain heads. Lenci dolls are mentioned in *Tender Is the Night* (p. 254 of the Cambridge edition).

### 191.26  the old shot tower

This is the Phoenix Shot Tower, also called the Old Baltimore Shot Tower, erected in East Baltimore in 1828 (too late for its ammunition to have been used in the American Revolution, as Jason seems to think). From the date of its completion until 1846 it was the tallest structure in the US. Molten lead was dropped from the top of the tower into a vat at the bottom filled with cold water. The balls of lead, when dried and polished, provided ammunition for rifles and pistols and for small artillery pieces.

### 191.33 the corner of the Confederate dead

Fitzgerald is probably thinking of the Confederate Soldiers and Sailors Monument, which stands in the Bolton Hill area of Baltimore, near the Francis Scott Key Monument and the shot tower annotated just above. The inscription on the monument is "Gloria Victis" ("Glory to the Vanquished").

### 192.13–19 Little Orphan Annie... the Gumps... Dick Tracy and X-9

Popular national comic strips of the period. *Little Orphan Annie*, drawn by Harold Gray, began appearing in 1924; it followed the adventures of Annie, her dog Sandy, and her protector, the millionaire Daddy Warbucks. *The Gumps*, which made its debut in 1917, was the creation of the cartoonist Sidney Smith; the strip recounted the lives of an entirely ordinary family—father, mother, children, a wealthy uncle named Jim, and a sharp-tongued maid named Mary. *Dick Tracy*, a comic strip about a police detective in a big city, appeared first in 1931 in the *Detroit Mirror*; it was drawn by Chester Gould and featured secondary characters with amusing names: e.g., Dick's girlfriend Tess Trueheart, the villain Flattop Jones, and the odoriferous B. O. Plenty. *Secret Agent X-9*, a comic conceived in 1934 by the hardboiled writer Dashiell Hammett and the artist Alex Raymond, concerned a nameless agent (X-9) who solved crimes and engaged in espionage.

### 192.33–193.1 like a room in the 'House Beautiful'

Jo has been reading *House Beautiful*, a venerable magazine of interior decoration that began appearing in 1896 and continues to be published today. Each issue featured photographs of tastefully appointed rooms.

### 197.26–27 the Supreme Court Bowl

A detail borrowed by Fitzgerald from his and Zelda's life together. When they were married in 1920, the associate justices of the Alabama Supreme Court gave them a silver bowl as a wedding present. Zelda's father, Anthony Sayre, served on the court.

### 201.16 Caesar

Fitzgerald is quoting not from Caesar but from a schoolbook exercise entitled "Caesar and the Helvetians," in Benjamin L. D'Ooge, *Elements of*

# Explanatory Notes

*Latin* (Boston: Ginn and Company, 1921): 205. The Latin was presumably written by the author of the textbook, who provided hints for translation.

## "The End of Hate"

### 207.22 General Jubal Early

Jubal A. Early (1816–1894), a prominent Confederate general in the Civil War, served under Stonewall Jackson and Robert E. Lee for most of the conflict. "The End of Hate" is set in early July 1864, during the last days of Early's march on Washington, D.C. Confederate soldiers reached the outskirts of the city, causing considerable panic among residents there. Early, however, realized that he did not have the troops and equipment necessary to take and occupy Washington. He therefore withdrew to the Valley of Virginia. Early's march is mentioned elsewhere in this volume in "The Cruise of the Rolling Junk" and "The Death of My Father."

### 207.32 Secesh?

Josie is asking whether the men are secessionists—i.e., Southern soldiers or sympathizers.

### 208.20 you Mosby cutthroats

The cavalry battalion commanded by Colonel John Singleton Mosby (1833–1916) caused considerable difficulty for Union troops during this period of the war. Mosby's command, the 43rd Battalion, 1st Virginia Cavalry, was a partisan ranger unit; it was known as "Mosby's Raiders" and was famous for lightning-quick attacks on Federal communication lines and infantry units.

### 210.13 the white Cordoba

A generic name for a wide-brimmed hat made in the style of the *sombrero cordobés*, a hat manufactured in Cordoba, Spain, and worn throughout the region of Andalusia.

### 215.29–30 April, 1865 . . . the Willard Hotel

Lee surrendered to Grant at Appomattox Court House on 9 April 1865, thereby ending the Civil War. Tib would therefore have been free to ride into Washington and to enter the Willard, a well-known hotel at

Pennsylvania Avenue and 14th Street, originally built in 1847. Many senators and congressmen stayed at the Willard, as did prominent writers, entertainers, and other visitors to Washington.

## "A Full Life"

### 222.32–33 *"Babes in the Woods" or "Underneath the Stars"*

Jerome Kern and Schuyler Greene collaborated on "Babes in the Wood," a duet from the 1915 Broadway musical *Very Good Eddie*. Fitzgerald used the title (changing "Wood" to "Woods") for a short story that he published first in the *Nassau Lit* (May 1917) and later in the *Smart Set* (September 1919). The narrative had a third outing as a section of *This Side of Paradise* (1920). "Underneath the Stars," a slow fox-trot with words by Fleta Jan Brown and music by Herbert Spencer, was a hit song of 1915. The refrain: "Jack-O'Lantern in the lilac tree dances, / Perfume from the garden wall entrances; / Love of mine, I pine for one of your glances, / Underneath the stars I wait."

## "Discard"

### 227.29–30 Mickey Rooney and the Dead-Ends—or even Freddie Bartholomew

Child actors of the 1930s. Mickey Rooney (1920–2014) was famous for his series of Andy Hardy films and for his appearance in *Boys Town* with Spencer Tracy in 1938. The Dead-End Kids were a group of child actors who played New York street urchins in a series of movies made by Samuel Goldwyn beginning in 1937. Freddie Bartholomew (1924–1992) gained popularity for his roles in *Little Lord Fauntleroy* (1936) and *Captains Courageous* (1937).

### 228.33 Irving Berlin with his wife

Songwriter Irving Berlin (1888–1989) and his wife Ellin Mackay (1903–1988) were among the most famous American couples of the 1920s and 1930s. In January 1926 they eloped, against the wishes of Ellin's father, the New York millionaire socialite Clarence Mackay. He severed all relations with his daughter for five years, but eventually the two were reconciled.

Berlin wrote many of his most famous songs for Ellin, including "Always" (1925).

### 231.16 Bette Davis

The stage and film actress Bette Davis (1908–1989) was one of the best-known cinema stars of the 1930s and 1940s. She was versatile, playing in comedies, melodramas, and historical films. Davis was known to be difficult and temperamental; she often clashed with studio heads, directors, and other stars.

### 233.10–11 Ivan Lebedeff

The darkly handsome, mustachioed movie actor Ivan Lebedeff (1894–1953) was a native of Russia. He specialized in supporting roles, often playing a cad or con-man or villain. His films include *Sin Town* (1929), *Conspiracy* (1930), and *Wise Girl* (1937).

### 233.32 the Munich Pact

This agreement (dated 29 September 1938) among Germany, France, England, and Italy allowed Nazi Germany to annex the portions of Czechoslovakia known as the Sudetenland. The pact was a failed attempt to appease Adolf Hitler; it set the stage for the German invasion of Poland one year later, an act of military aggression that ignited the Second World War.

### 235.8 I'd like to cable Winchell

Martha means Walter Winchell (1897–1972), a newspaper and radio gossip commentator famous (and feared) for destroying the careers of celebrities and other public figures. Winchell wrote a syndicated column for the *New York Daily Mirror* and broadcast a weekly program on the New York radio station WABC.

### 235.36 Frank Capra

The movie director, producer, and writer Frank Capra (1897–1991) made several films still famous in cinema history. These include *It Happened One Night* (1934), *You Can't Take It with You* (1938), and *Mr. Smith Goes to Washington* (1939).

### 240.20–21 Aunt Prissy

Fitzgerald is conflating Aunt Pittypat and Prissy, two characters from the novel (and the movie version) of Margaret Mitchell's *Gone with the Wind*. In January 1939, toward the end of his time with Metro-Goldwyn-Mayer, Fitzgerald worked on the script for this film. By his own account he was dismissed from the project because he could not invent a way to make Aunt Pittypat sufficiently quaint. His copy of the script is among his papers at Princeton.

### 241.11 Katharine Cornell

The American stage actress, writer, and producer Katharine Cornell (1893–1974) starred on Broadway in serious dramas and historical plays. She was best known for her performances in *The Barretts of Wimpole Street* (1931), *Romeo and Juliet* (1934), and *St. Joan* (1936).

## "Last Kiss"

### 242.28–243.3 "Hollywood Reporter" ... Bob Bordley ... SONJA HENIE

*The Hollywood Reporter*, founded in 1930, was a daily trade newspaper for the movie business; its chief competitor was *Variety*, which began publication in 1905. Fitzgerald might have lifted "Bob Bordley" from the *Princeton Alumni Weekly* issue of 8 January 1937, in which a freshman hockey player of that name is mentioned, p. 292. The Norwegian figure-skater Sonja Henie (1912–1969) won the Olympics three times in Ladies' Singles; she became a popular Hollywood actress, starring in a series of skating movies in the 1930s.

### 244.34 walked into '21'

This famous New York restaurant, at 21 West 52nd Street, was and is still frequented by celebrities, authentic and would-be. Fitzgerald probably knew the club in its earlier incarnation as "Jack and Charlie's 21"—a Prohibition speakeasy equipped with a system for dumping its liquor bottles down a chute and into the city sewer system whenever the police arrived for a raid.

Explanatory Notes 451

249.19–23 Lamarr... Elsa Maxwell

The glamorous Hedy Lamarr (1914–2000), a popular film actress during the late 1930s and the 1940s, starred opposite many of the leading men of her day, including Charles Boyer, Spencer Tracy, and Clark Gable. Elsa Maxwell (1883–1963) was an author, songwriter, and gossip columnist. She played herself in the films *Stage Door Canteen* (1943) and *Rhapsody in Blue* (1945).

250.12 "Illustrated London News"

This weekly news magazine, founded in 1842, provided readers with information about British culture and politics. While serving in army training camps during the First World War, Fitzgerald read the magazine for reportage, analysis, and casualty lists. He also encountered some of the essays of Gilbert Chesterton in its pages.

255.24–25 Major Bowes' voice

The denizens of the bungalows are listening to *Major Bowes Amateur Hour*, a popular talent show of the 1930s and 1940s, hosted by Edward Bowes (1874–1946), formerly the manager of the Capitol Theatre in New York City. Major Bowes would dismiss untalented performers by striking a loud gong.

"News of Paris—Fifteen Years Ago"

261.10 the English Church

Fitzgerald is possibly thinking of the Cathedral Church of the Holy Trinity, known familiarly as the American Church in Paris, where interdenominational services were performed in the English language. This church, located on the Seine at 65 Quai d'Orsay, was a popular place of worship for fashionable Americans. It is mentioned in Fitzgerald's story "The Bridal Party" (1930).

261.14 'Boulevardier'

This English-language magazine, published by Arthur Moss (1889–1969) and Erskine Gwynne (1899–1948), was patterned after the *New Yorker*. In addition to serious writing, the magazine published gossip about American expatriates in Paris, as the reference here implies. Among the contributors were Michael Arlen, Louis Bromfield, and Ernest Hemingway.

### 261.19–20 auto horns playing Debussy

Charlie Wales, the protagonist of Fitzgerald's 1931 story "Babylon Revisited," imagines that the Paris taxis are "playing endlessly the first few bars of 'La Plus que Lente.'" This waltz for piano by the composer Claude Debussy (1862–1918) was first performed in 1910.

### 262.13 to the Ritz on the man's part of the bar

The bar of the Ritz Hotel on the Place Vendôme plays an important role in "Babylon Revisited" and in *Tender Is the Night* (1934), in which the character Abe North spends an entire day there. Like most fashionable bars of the period, the Ritz maintained a separate space for unaccompanied women, sometimes referred to as the "sit-down" bar.

### 263.2 Emily Posted

Emily Post (1873–1960) became a frequently cited authority on social behavior after the appearance of her book *Etiquette* in 1922. She was known for assuring the American bourgeoisie that common sense would supply the answer to nearly all questions about proper behavior. Fitzgerald mentions her in his essays "Pasting It Together" and "My Lost City."

### 264.36 the Exposition

The Exposition Internationale des Arts Décoratifs et Industriels Moderne, held in Paris from April to October 1925, was an occasion for the French to display luxury goods in the Art Deco style and to show architectural designs by Konstantin Melnikov and Le Corbusier. The Fitzgeralds visited the Exposition while living in Paris in 1925; it is mentioned in *Tender Is the Night*, p. 71 of the Cambridge edition.

### 265.8 the Crillon lobby

The Crillon, a Right-Bank establishment on the Place de la Concorde at the foot of the Champs-Élysées, was a luxury hotel. In *Tender Is the Night*, Dick Diver steps into the bar of the Crillon to drink "a small coffee and two fingers of gin" (p. 120 of the Cambridge edition).

## JOURNALISM

### "The Cruise of the Rolling Junk"

#### 296.17 the Expenso

The Fitzgeralds were traveling in a Marmon roadster, manufactured in 1917. The Marmon Company built only about five hundred of the vehicles before ceasing production. Very few Marmons were still on the road after the war; because the parent company was out of business, it was difficult for owners to find parts for service and repair.

#### 297.15 thinking of something else

Oil of juniper was sometimes used as an ingredient in Prohibition moonshine, to mask the taste of the alcohol. The bootlegger in *The Vegetable* adds oil of juniper to his product.

#### 298.25 Mr. Burton Holmes

The American travel lecturer and photographer Elias Burton Holmes is credited with coining the word "travelogue." He made his living as an itinerant lecturer, projecting hand-tinted glass slides through the "magic lantern." Later he made short travel films for Paramount and MGM.

#### 299.4 Enormous policemen

Most of the names are those of politicians and entertainers. The first three were Irish political leaders; Mr. Mutt was a cartoon character; Ed Wynn was a comedian famous for his goofy antics; William Howard Taft was the US president from 1901 to 1913; Rudolph Valentino (mentioned in *The Vegetable*) was a "Latin-lover" movie star.

#### 301.15–16 Stony Brook . . . Corot elms

Stony Brook, a picturesque stream familiar to Princeton undergraduates, meets the Millstone River just east of the university. The elm trees remind Fitzgerald of similar trees in the paintings of the nineteenth-century French artist Jean-Baptiste-Camille Corot.

### 301.19–20 General Mercer

Hugh Mercer, a brigadier general in the Continental Army, was mortally wounded at the Battle of Princeton on 3 January 1777. The event is commemorated in a painting by the artist John Trumbull.

### 301.22–25 Nassau Street...Nassau Inn...Nassau Hall

Nassau Street is the main thoroughfare running east–west through the town of Princeton. Some students at the university partook of strong drink at the Nassau Inn, a hotel and tavern at 52 Nassau Street. Nassau Hall, the oldest building at Princeton (erected 1756), was located almost directly across the street from this first incarnation of the Nassau Inn (not the current establishment on Palmer Square).

### 301.28 Aaron Burr

Fitzgerald has in mind the traitor and duelist Aaron Burr, a famous alumnus of Princeton. His father, Aaron Burr, Sr., was the second president of the university.

### 306.22 Daisy Ashford

The British child author Daisy Ashford published a popular novel entitled *The Young Visiters* in 1919. Her misspellings were preserved from the manuscript, as the title suggests. Because the first edition of *This Side of Paradise* was marred by numerous misspellings, some waggish reviewers referred to Fitzgerald as "the Princeton Daisy Ashford."

### 307.10–12 Cornwallis...Braddock

Charles Cornwallis and Edward Braddock, British generals who suffered defeats in the American Revolution and the French and Indian War.

### 307.23 Charles Carroll of Carrollton

This Maryland planter and patriot was the only Catholic to sign the Declaration of Independence. Carroll was involved in the burning of the British ship *Peggy Stewart* in the Annapolis harbor on 19 October 1774—an act

# Explanatory Notes

connected with the more famous events of the Boston Tea Party on 16 December 1773.

### 308.10 Inn of Tranquility

Fitzgerald is borrowing this name from *The Inn of Tranquillity* (1912), a collection of short fiction and essays by John Galsworthy. The Fitzgeralds took tea with Galsworthy in London in May 1921, during their first visit to Europe.

### 309.35 the New Willard

This incarnation of the Willard Hotel, erected in Washington, D.C., in 1904, was known as the "New Willard." It was the first skyscraper in the city, at twelve stories. The previous Willard Hotel is mentioned in "The End of Hate." Like the Old Willard, the New Willard was an important gathering place for politicians and those who sought to influence them.

### 314.15 the late Czar

Nicholas II, who assumed rule on 1 November 1894, was forced to abdicate on 15 March 1917. He was put to death on 17 July 1918, together with his wife, children, doctor, and some family servants.

### 316.32–33 reconstruct the battle

The Battle of Fredericksburg took place on 11–15 December 1862, with fighting between Confederate forces under Robert E. Lee and Union troops commanded by Ambrose Burnside. Lee's men withstood several assaults by Burnside's soldiers; Union casualties were heavy. The Battle of the Wilderness, mentioned in the next paragraph, took place near Fredericksburg in Spotsylvania County on 5–7 May 1864. Union troops under Ulysses S. Grant fought a bloody but inconclusive engagement against Lee's Army of Northern Virginia.

### 320.2 Best Hotel in Town

This was the Jefferson Hotel in Richmond, an imposing establishment in the Spanish Baroque style that had opened for business in 1895. The hotel is still in operation: an old guest register bearing the Fitzgeralds' signatures has sometimes been on display there in recent years.

### 321.24 the Confederate museum

The Museum of the Confederacy, with much Civil War weaponry and memorabilia, opened in 1896 at a location near the state capitol grounds. In its earliest years this museum was very much a memorial to the Lost Cause. It was founded and maintained by a group of Richmond society women. Fitzgerald mentions this museum also in the story "I Got Shoes" (1933), included in the Cambridge volume *A Change of Class* (2016), p. 203.

### 324.23 the hood chamied off

Fitzgerald means that the hood was cleaned with chamois cloth—a soft, absorbent cotton fabric used for polishing.

### 327.1 Cato strode toward me.

Cato the Censor, an austere and frugal Roman politician of the 2nd century BC, was known for fierce denunciation of his foes. Fitzgerald mentions him also in *The Beautiful and Damned*, p. 244 of the Cambridge edition (2008); and in the short story "'What a Handsome Pair!'" (1932), included in the Cambridge volume *A Change of Class* (2016), p. 134.

### 329.7–8 the O. Henry Hotel

This Greensboro hotel was named for William Sydney Porter, a native of the city, who wrote under the pen name "O. Henry." The establishment, erected in 1919, offered over three hundred rooms for guests, along with many modern conveniences.

### 334.16 "The Beale Street Blues"

This classic blues song, written in 1916 by W. C. Handy, was first sung on Broadway by Gilda Gray, performing in the 1919 variety show *Schubert's Gaieties*. A sample stanza: "If Beale Street could talk, if Beale Street could talk, / Married men would have to take their beds and walk, / Except one or two who never drink booze, / And the blind man on the corner singing 'Beale Street Blues'!"

# Explanatory Notes

### 337.29–30 Old King Brady and Young Wild West

These were two popular dime-novel series from Fitzgerald's youth. The first published detective stories; the second specialized in tales of the frontier West. Fitzgerald mentions the Old King Brady series in his story "A Short Trip Home" (1927), included in the Cambridge edition of *Taps at Reveille* (2014).

### 338.12 Camp Gordon

Fitzgerald was stationed with the 45th Infantry Regiment at Camp Gordon, in Augusta, Georgia, from April to June 1918. From Camp Gordon he was transferred to Camp Sheridan near Montgomery, Alabama; in July he would meet Zelda Sayre at a country club dance in Montgomery.

## "The High Cost of Macaroni"

### 347.9 *Couvert*

The French term *couvert*, used in restaurants throughout Europe, can mean a place setting or a cover charge (sometimes hidden), an ambiguity that Fitzgerald must have been aware of.

### 347.36 Mazuma Americana

A fanciful name, like several others in "Macaroni." *Mazuma* is slang for paper money, from the Yiddish *mezuma/mezumen*, meaning cash. Fitzgerald uses the word in "'Not in the Guidebook,'" a 1925 short story included in the Cambridge edition of *All the Sad Young Men* (2007), p. 244.

### 354.16–17 Tommy Gibbons... Mike's young brother

Tommy Gibbons, a native of St. Paul, Fitzgerald's home town, was a successful heavyweight boxer in the 1910s and 1920s. His older brother Mike Gibbons was a prominent middleweight during the same period.

### 355.5–9 John Alexander Borgia... the Emperor Tiberius

Fitzgerald would have expected his readers to recognize the House of Borgia, a powerful ecclesiastical and political family in Renaissance Italy. The Borgias were accused of many crimes, including bribery and murder.

Tiberius, mentioned in the sentence that follows, served as Roman Emperor from AD 14 to 37. He withdrew permanently to Capri in AD 26 and ruled in absentia for the remainder of his life. Tiberius was rumored to be pursuing a life of sexual licentiousness during his years on the island.

### "What Kind of Husbands Do 'Jimmies' Make?"

367.11–12 Teapot Dome... wounded-veteran graft

Scandals during and after the administration of Warren G. Harding. The Teapot Dome and the Veterans Bureau scandals involved bribery and the selling of government property for a fraction of its proper value.

367.23 a boy in my class at Princeton

This is Charles W. Donahoe, nicknamed "Sap," Fitzgerald's classmate at both the Newman School and at Princeton. Fitzgerald mentions Donahoe in "Pasting It Together" (without naming him) as a man of exemplary morals, a man who "represented my sense of the 'good life.'"

### "Our Young Rich Boys"

371.4 Madame Glyn

Fitzgerald means Elinor Glyn, a British author of romantic novels that were risqué for the time. Glyn was known for popularizing the "It" concept—a not-so-veiled reference to sex appeal. Her work, both as a novelist and a scriptwriter, had influence on the careers of the movie stars Gloria Swanson and Clara Bow. "Dancing with the Darkies" earlier in the same sentence has not been identified.

372.1–6 Ted Coy... Ben Lyon... Michael Arlen... Nick Carter... Young Wild West... Henty books

Ted Coy was a Yale football hero; Ben Lyon was a 1920s movie star; Michael Arlen was the author of *The Green Hat* (1924); Nick Carter was a private eye in a popular dime novel series; Young Wild West (mentioned in this volume in "The Cruise of the Rolling Junk") was a dime novel series;

the Henty books, by G. A. Henty, were juvenile fiction based on stirring events in military history.

### 374.5 chorus girls in the Follies

Chorines in Florenz Ziegfeld's *Follies* were rumored to be of pliable morality. Rich boys pursued them with gifts and mash notes. Several Ziegfeld girls went on to success in Hollywood or on stage, including Anna Held, Gilda Gray, Lilyan Tashman, and Paulette Goddard.

### 374.23 our local Savonarolas

The name of Girolamo Savonarola, a fifteenth-century Italian Dominican friar and preacher, is synonymous with fierce opposition to sin, vanity, and secular culture. Savonarola was excommunicated by the pope in 1497 and burned at the stake in 1498.

### 374.26–27 the program . . . female Ben Turpin

By "the program," Fitzgerald means the dance cards on which young men were expected to sign up for dances with young women. It was considered proper to fill in the dance cards of plain girls; a "female Ben Turpin" (after the cross-eyed vaudeville and burlesque actor) would have been particularly unattractive.

### 376.1–2 the good old lancers and the shimmee

The Lancers, a variation on the quadrille, was a nineteenth-century dance popular at formal balls in the South. The Shimmy (usually spelled "shimmee" by Fitzgerald) was a semi-scandalous dance of the 1920s; it was popularized by Gilda Gray in the Ziegfeld *Follies* and performed by Mae West in her cabaret act.

# ILLUSTRATIONS

12.

"There was no reserved ~~sign~~ card on it", I protested "We were shown here and our order was taken – "

"Don't argue", said my wife quietly. "Let's go. It's the rate of exchange." "I can put ~~in~~ up a table for you ~~on the other side of the room~~ just inside the pantry door," ~~said~~ ~~nuzz~~ The head waiter.

~~"Can't you put one in for the Dumbells too.~~

~~He looked at the two young men, who shook their heads.~~ We got up and stood facing them all for a moment, trying to think of some crushing remark to make. But nothing occurred to us, so, scornfully rejecting the substitute table, we swept (I believe that's the word) out the door into the cool December afternoon.

"I don't like this place," I said, as a Facisti Colonel tried to brush us from the sidewalk ~~as a sign~~ in token of his ~~appreciation of~~ spontaneous admiration for my wife, "I don't like these people, or our hotel or this ~~filthy~~ city. Let's go away."

"We can't."

~~"Why~~ "And why not?"

"Because we're ~~just~~ keeping ~~within~~ our schedule. ~~And~~ If we moved before spring we'd get behind."

"I think we ought to get out."

"But it seems ~~seems~~ so silly ~~thing to do! Just as~~ just as we begin to save something we get bored and move on."

~~"Anybody can save if they live badly enough – but~~ "But what are we spending ~~Heaven knows eleven hundred a month~~ would buy more than

1. Page 12, surviving typescript of "The High Cost of Macaroni," with Fitzgerald's revisions. F. Scott Fitzgerald Papers, Princeton University Libraries.

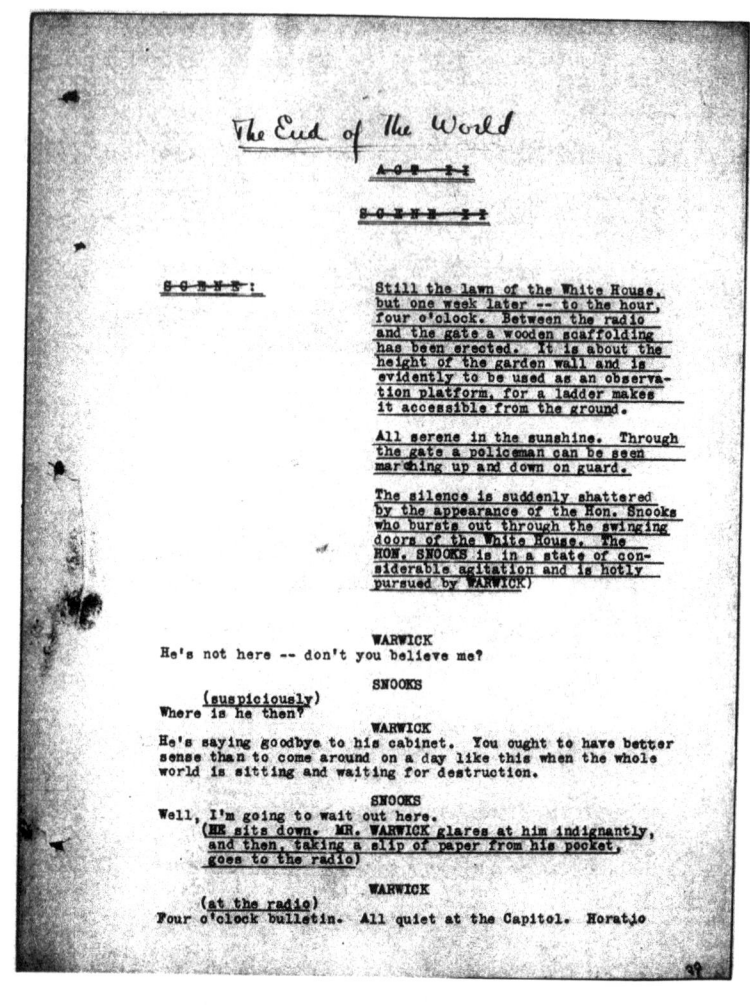

The End of the World

ACT 2

SCENE 2

SCENE: Still the lawn of the White House, but one week later -- to the hour, four o'clock. Between the radio and the gate a wooden scaffolding has been erected. It is about the height of the garden wall and is evidently to be used as an observation platform, for a ladder makes it accessible from the ground.

All serene in the sunshine. Through the gate a policeman can be seen marching up and down on guard.

The silence is suddenly shattered by the appearance of the Hon. Snooks who bursts out through the swinging doors of the White House. The HON. SNOOKS is in a state of considerable agitation and is hotly pursued by WARWICK)

WARWICK
He's not here -- don't you believe me?

SNOOKS
(suspiciously)
Where is he then?

WARWICK
He's saying goodbye to his cabinet. You ought to have better sense than to come around on a day like this when the whole world is sitting and waiting for destruction.

SNOOKS
Well, I'm going to wait out here.
(HE sits down. MR. WARWICK glares at him indignantly, and then, taking a slip of paper from his pocket, goes to the radio)

WARWICK
(at the radio)
Four o'clock bulletin. All quiet at the Capitol. Horatio

2. "The End of the World," addenda for a planned second production of *The Vegetable*. F. Scott Fitzgerald Papers, Princeton University Libraries.

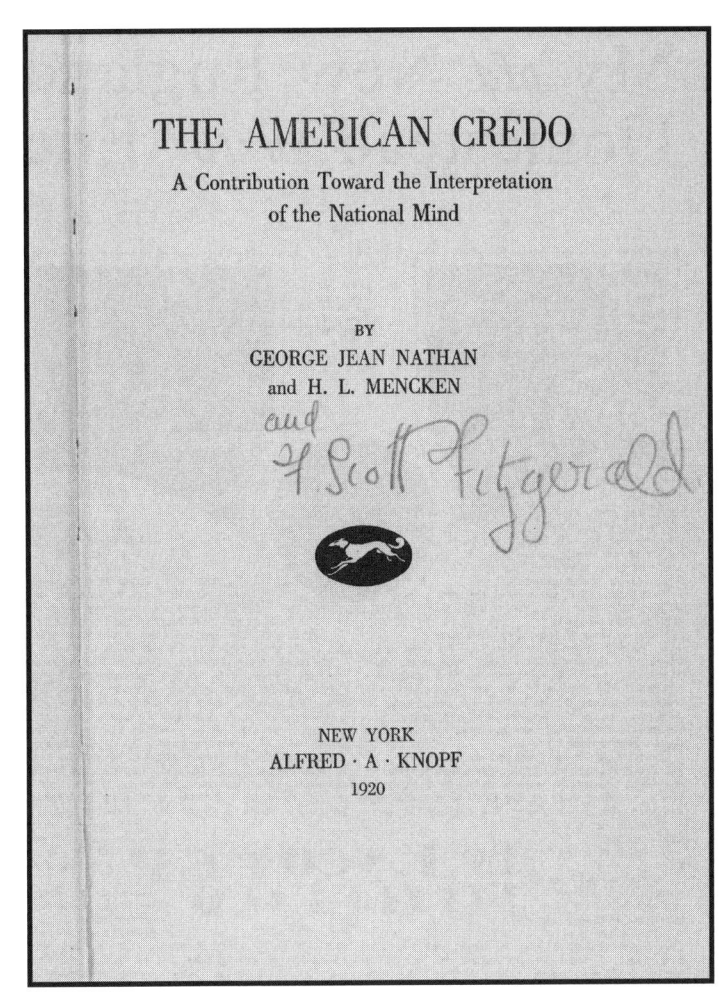

# THE AMERICAN CREDO

A Contribution Toward the Interpretation
of the National Mind

BY
GEORGE JEAN NATHAN
and H. L. MENCKEN
*and
F. Scott Fitzgerald*

NEW YORK
ALFRED · A · KNOPF
1920

3. Title page, Fitzgerald's copy of *The American Credo*. F. Scott Fitzgerald Papers, Princeton University Libraries.

# My *old* New England Homestead *on the* Erie

*Illustrations by Russell Patterson*

¶ "Jack, or whatever your name is," she said. "I must have it."

## By F. SCOTT FITZGERALD

IT was some ten years ago that, as I trundled my wife along on one of our annual jaunts into the country, her eyes fell eagerly upon it—the house of our dreams.

"Jack!" she cried, gazing over the side of the wheelbarrow, "Jack, or whatever your name is, I must have it!"

I went inside and picked it up for a song. At first sight it would seem that I got the worst of my bargain, for the lovely old Colonial lines of the place had been almost obliterated by successive generations of vandals—the shingles of the roof were covered with cross-word puzzles, the fine old windows were defaced by bars (my treasure was now the local jail), and the pre-Braddock bathroom had been padlocked by some rustic board of health these fifty years.

The price agreed upon included our wheelbarrow, several strings of bright beads, half a dozen confederate bonds and about seventy-five cents in cash. As I handed it over a foreboding seized me, and I said to the owner, who was none other than a shrewd New England Yankee:

"How a b o u t the old hand-made nails?"

He failed to u n d e r stand.

Glancing around I perceived a fine Chippendale toothpick-holder on t h e table—and in it were the old hand-made n a i l s. They had been used to cheat the dentist these two hundred years! I could scarcely restrain my incredulous laughter. My wife couldn't either. Neither of us could scarcely restrain our incredulous laughter.

"Bye the bye," he said (interpolating some rustic expression as "Oh, shucks", "Do you want it delivered?"

"No," I said firmly, "I want it left where it is. We will move in tomorrow."

And move in we did. Never will I forget those first eight years—such a sound of hammers and nails and chisels and corkscrews was never heard in that quiet neighborhood before. I have since been told that the noise caused some nasty talk in the boiler factory half a mile away.

We began at the beginning. First, we had the whole modernized inside taken out and replaced with a quaint interior that we picked up at an auction in Atlantic City. When that was done we removed the outer walls and built them up again out of old bricks. We kept, of course, the old shape; we were offered something nice for that but we refused it. The next step was to lift up the house on four automobile jacks of wrought iron, dig out the overlay of modern soil, and replace it with some more lovable dirt that we had stumbled upon in one of our rambles through the older and more putrid parts of Virginia. Winter was almost upon us. With desperate haste we g o u g e d out the steam heat—the last pipe was thrown from the window on the day the first snow fell.

There was our house. What to put in it—that was the question.

We had the hand-made nails but, as my wife humorously remarked, they were no good to sit on. Besides that we had an old Haig and Haig bottle bought from a professional man—he had a set which he hated to break, but I prevailed upon him; a sewing machine run by acetylene (ah, but they built well in those days!); and a left-handed diaval set.

18

4. Magazine text, "My Old New England Homestead on the Erie," *College Humor*, August 1925. F. Scott Fitzgerald Papers, Princeton University Libraries.